AF632704

A PEEP AT
INDOLOGY

A PEEP AT
INDOLOGY

S. G. Moghe

D.K. Printworld (P) Ltd.
NEW DELHI-110015

Cataloging in Publication Data — DK

Moghe, S.G. (Shantaram Ganesh), 1935 -
A peep at Indology.
Includes bibliographical references (p.).
Includes index.

1. Indology. I. Title.

ISBN 81-246-0032-5

First Published in India in 1994

© *Author*

No reproduction or translation of this book or part thereof in any form, except brief quotations, should be made without the written permission of the Author and Publishers.

Published in India by :
D.K. Printworld (P) Ltd.
Regd. office : H-12, Bali Nagar
NEW DELHI - 110015
Phone: (011); 546 6019 *Fax:* (011) 546-5927

Printed at : D.K. Fine Art Press (P) Ltd. Delhi-110052

Dedicated to

Govt. Arts & Science College Aurangabad
And
Marathwada University, Aurangabad
which have the largest share in my
all-round progress in life

Preface

I am very much attracted by the different aspects of Indology connected with *Veda, Rāmāyaṇa, Mahābhārata,* Classical Sanskrit literature and Dramaturgy.

In this collection of 12 writings, the two articles on the *Veda* reveal the style of the Vedic poets incidentally throwing light on the stylistic peculiarites of the classical Sanskrit literature and the evaluation of the contribution of Prof. Velankar to Vedic Indology.

Dharma-Śastra is my favourite subject and hence the connection of *Dharma-Śastra* with the *Rāmāyaṇa* and the *Mahābhārata* proved very fascinating to me and I contributed chapters on the concepts of a witness and a deposit, throwing important light on these aspects particularly untouched by Dr. P.V. Kane.

The study of a constellation *Rohiṇī* in the *Rāmāyaṇa* particularly in connection with the later Sanskrit literature proved to be very interesting.

The two chapters on the classical Sanskrit literature evaluate the commentaries of Hemādri, Raṅganātha, throwing shed of light on the aspects both conceptual and literary and particularly untouched by Dr. Kane, Gajendragadkar and others.

A chapter on Bahurūpamiśra is based on the Sanskrit commentary *Abhijñāna Śākuntala Carcā* by anonymous commentator and Bahurūpamiśra's commentary on the *Daśarūpaka* is also equally important from the point of view of textual criticism.

In view of the wide range of these writings, I am tempted to title the book as *A Peep at Indology*. For bringing out this tempting collection, the entire credit is to be given to D.K. Printworld (P) Ltd., New Delhi. The publishers also deserve credit for taking keen interest in this work and also giving excellent get up and printing.

23-5-1994
Aurangabad

S.G. Moghe

Contents

Acknowledgements

Out of the bunch of 12 writings, selected here, the two viz., 'Contribution of Prof. H.D. Velankar to Vedic Indology' and 'Style of the Vedic Poets' have appeared in the book *Prof. Velankar and Vedic Indology*. The two chapters on the *Rāmāyaṇa* — 'The influence of the *Rāmāyaṇa* on the *Abhijñāna Śākuntalam*', and Sadhu Ram's comments on the same and my rejoinder to Sadhu Ram — have been published in the *Journal of the Ganganatha Jha Kendriya Sanskrit Vidyapitha,* Allahabad, in Vols. 31 (1975) and 34 (1978) respectively. 'This constellation *Rohiṇī* in the *Rāmāyaṇa* and later poets' is published in the *Bhāratīya Vidyā,* Vol. XXX. The chapter '*Dharma-Śastra* aspects of the *Rāmāyaṇa* was sent to the Asiatic Society, Bombay, for the Seminar on the *Rāmāyaṇa* organized in February 1993. 'The concept of a witness in the *Mahābhārata* and *Dharma-Śāstra* literature' and 'Hemādri's *Darpaṇa* on the *Raghuvaṁśam*' have been accepted for publication by the *Oriental Journal,* Tirupati. Another chapter '*Dharma-Śāstra* concept of Nyāsa and Sanskrit literature' is accepted by the *Journal of the Oriental Institute,* Tirupati. "Evaluation of the Commentary 'Marmāvabodhinī' on the *Harṣacaritam*" is accepted for publication by the *Journal of the Ganganatha Jha Kendriya Sanskrit Vidyapitha,* Allahabad. Another chapter 'Raghavabhaṭṭa's Novel Interpretation of the *Śākuntalam*' is accepted for publication by the *Journal of the Marathwada University*. The article on 'Bahurūpamiśra is accepted for publication by the Oriental Institute and Manuscripts Library, Kerala.

To the editors of all these journals, I express my gratefulness for permitting me to indude these articles in this book.

S.G. Moghe

1

Style of the Vedic Poets

AFTER reading the reviews on the works of my revered Gurujī Professor H.D. Velankar, at the hands of the competent scholars, I am almost tempted to write this chapter. The simple reason at the back of this chapter is to reveal or bring to light some stylistic peculiarities of the Vedic poets in the light of the writings of Velankar. It must be mentioned in this very context, that due credit is not given to Velankar, for the aspects revealed by him, by the reviewers whose reviews[1] appear to be patently superficial or mainly based on reading only the preface[2] of the life-time work of the author. Alternatively, it is also observed that some of the reviewers pinpoint only a particular point of their choice, pass some remarks and endorse some views. This appears to be the tendency of most of the reviewers, if not all. It should be noted here that the reviewers do not show the patience of an angel to go through the entire book of the author and then pinpoint favourable and unfavourable marks about the author. It is due to this tendency that a gross injustice is likely to be caused to the author whose work remains unimportant or the important points of his writings are not properly highlighted. In addition to this, I have also minutely observed the tendency of some reputed indologists[3] to show the disagreement with the particular author particularly on his death and that, also without minutely examining the view of the author. Needless to say that this kind of tendency is likely to create some unfavourable atmosphere in the circle of that scholar who is seen to have occupied a predominant position in the particular university. This tendency also tends to belittle the author who also cannot come back (on his death) to give his rejoinder to the peculiar comments passed on his work.

Incidentally, however, it must be stated here that those scholars who have focused their attention on the general and critical approach to any work, naturally neglect the linguistic approach which is adopted by another scholar. Hence it is evident that for the proper understanding of any work, there should be the judicious assimilation of various approaches which certainly becomes a case of impossibility in the case of a single person. In fact, both the methods or approaches are complementary to each other.

Incidentally, in this chapter, I have tried to note the peculiarities of the Vedic poets in the style of the poets of classical Sanskrit literature, either in the body of the chapter or in the foot-notes. While dealing with the particular aspect of the style of the Vedic poets, I have also recorded the progress made by the later scholars and whenever possible a casual reference is made to the reviews on some such progress by drawing attention to the reviews published in the Journals.

I also take this opportunity to express my limitations in this branch of learning. I do not claim that I have utilised the complete writings of Velankar for this purpose. But the readers, I hope, will certainly agree with me, only after reading this complete chapter, that I have not missed any important point which deserves to be highlighted. Whatever books and papers could become available to me by the strenuous effort, will be found utilised in the best possible manner for the purpose of this chapter which is indeed, a tribute to my teacher.

Now I proceed further with the topic, proper to highlight the stylistic features of the Vedic poets who were the 'Conscious Artists'.

(1) It is the peculiar feature of the style of the Vedic poets that they make use of the adjectives for the substantives in the course of their poetic competitions. This could be illustrated by referring to the *Ṛg-Veda,* I.25.12, II.23.7, VII.63.7, VII.68.9, VIII.30.3. The adjective *parāvataḥ* in the *Ṛg-Veda,* VIII.30.3 qualifies the region, which is not mentioned in the *mantra* as such.

(2) The Vedic poets have profitably used the Vedic word *Purā* in connection with the form of the present tense, only to convey the sense of the past. For the elucidation of this point, attention may be drawn to the *Ṛg-Veda,* VI.65.4d, VII.56.23, VII.88.5 and

X. 117.2. In the *Ṛg-Veda,* X.117.2, it is suggested that though he has enjoyed (his food-donor's food), for a long time, now when (in need) he does not get a sympathiser. Here the word *Purā*[5] is connected with the form *vindate* and the above sense is suggested.

(3) Personification may be treated as another stylistic feature of the Vedic poets. Here a reference could be made to the *Ṛg-Veda,* VI.55.1 and X.155.5. In the former case, the word *vimuc*[6] in the *Pūṣan* hymn, is quite likely a personified deliverance from danger or dangers. In the latter case, however, faith is personified[7] as a deity. Anthropomorphism is another such term used in this context. Prof. Velankar has elsewhere remarked[8] that there is the least evidence of the *vala* being anthropomorphised. Incidentally, it may be remarked that Dandekar has shown some cases[9] of such anthropomorphism in the Vedic Mythological Tracts.

(4) It is a peculiar feature of the writings of Vedic poets that they have employed some words[10] not in the primary sense but only in the secondary sense. Thus the word *Madhu* meaning 'Sweet' is found utilised in the secondary sense of 'Milk of a cow in the *Ṛg-Veda,* X.68.8. And another case of *Barhis* may be cited. The word *barhis* meaning grass, is used in the sense of a sacrifice in the *Ṛg-Veda,* II.3.8. The word *Īriṇa* is also conveying the sense of 'unfruitful source' in the secondary sense and not in the primary sense of 'a small ditch on a desert land' as hinted at by the learned Professor.

(5) It is a remarkable feature of the style of Vedic poets that they employ some words[11] as ending in both a vowel or/and also a consonant. For the clarification of this point, attention may be drawn to the use of the word *cakṣuḥ* in the *Ṛg-Veda,* X.90.13 and *cakṣuṣ* at *Ṛg-Veda* ,VII.97.2. Similarly the word *Vanu* at *Ṛg-Veda,* IV. 30.5 and *Vanuṣ* at *Ṛg-Veda,* IV.50.11, VII.219, VII.25.3, and VII.38.5. This word *Vanuṣ* is used in the sense of an 'enemy'. Here, however, I resist the temptation of adding many more illustrations of this type.

(6) At times, however, we notice that the Vedic poets have developed the tendency of forming a word by connecting two words together. Velankar calls this as 'double formation'.[12] He illustrates this point by the example of *patsutaḥ* in the *Ṛg-Veda,* I.32.8. This word is formed by joining the two words *patsu* +

pattaḥ. This word simply means 'at the feet'. We have also the example of *Vājinīvatī* at *Ṛg-Veda,* VII.75.5. This is also a case of double formation. Here we have the combination of the words *Vājinī* + *Vājavatī*. This expression *Vājinīvatī* has the sense of 'One who has wonderful gifts'. This word is used with reference to the goddess 'Uṣas', at two places of the *Ṛg-Veda,* I.48.16 and VII.75.5. But in the *Ṛg-Veda,* V.80.3, however, we have the expression *Viśvavārā,* in the same sense.

(7) It is also the speciality of the Vedic poets that they sometimes, refer to themselves[13] in a general manner or in a third person or with a patent adjective applicable to the composer of the hymn only. In the *Ṛg-Veda,* VII.61.2, Vasiṣṭha describes himself as a *dīrghaśruta vipraḥ,* i.e., a far-famed priest. Velankar also draws attention to the *Ṛg-Veda,* I.49.2, in which the expression *suśravasaṁ janaṁ* is used. At times, however, we get the expression *supeśasaṁ* used by the poet to refer to himself in a general manner.

(8) Repetition of one and the same word may also be treated as another characteristic feature of the Vedic poets. Velankar remarks that such a repetition[14] of word simply indicates a variety or type. He adds that the use of the expression *Sanitā dhanaṁ dhanam* at *Ṛg-Veda,* II.23.13, is used in the sense of 'a winner of every kind of wealth'. And the repetition of the expression' *vāmam-vāmam'* at *Ṛg-Veda,* IV.30.24 is one more case in point. In the *Ṛg-Veda,* we find the reiteration of one and the same word or even preposition seems purposeful and significant. In the *Ṛg-Veda,* I.115.2d, we have the line *Vitanvate prati bhadrāya bhadraṁ* which reminds one of the line[15] of Bhavabhūti in the *Mālatī-Mādhavaṁ*. In the *Ṛg-Veda,* the idea at the back of the reiteration is that one blessing should lead to another blessing. I prefer to note below in the references the progress on the point of repetition or reiteration of a word with some detailed observations.

(9) Condensation or compression of a word may also be treated as a distinguishing feature of the writing of the Vedic poets. It may be noted here that they have shortened some of the forms of the past Passive participles in the course of their writings. This naturally helps to achieve word economy in the poetry. Here the case of the form *anutta* may be cited. This form is utilised[16] in the *Ṛg-Veda,* VII.34.11. This form is derived from the root *nud* in

the sense of 'to resist, assault or assign'. Velankar further adds the usage of this expression as *Anuttam kṣatram* and *anuttam manyum* at *Ṛg-Veda,* VII.31.12 with reference to Indra. The idea of 'resistless rulership or resistless anger' is conveyed by means of the form *Anutta.* Velankar also cares to give other illustrations of this type of shortening of the words or roots as *bhagatti Maghatti* and *Vasutti* employed at the *Ṛg-Veda,* IX.65.17, VIII.24 and VIII.61.7 respectively. It may be noted here in passing that the idea of shortening the form of a root in the *Ṛg-Veda* is found utilised in the Classical Sanskrit for shortening the proper name of a person particularly in the *Harṣacaritam* of Bāṇabhaṭṭa, as pointed out by the commentator[17] Raṅganātha and particularly unnoticed by MM. Dr. Kane, Gajendragadkar and others on this particular count.

(10) Handling the nick-name or the pen-name of a person also appears to be the style of the Vedic poets. The students of the hymns devoted to Aśvins, know very well that Pedu is helped by the Aśvins. However, his pen-name[18] or nick-name *Aghāśva* is used owing to his bad luck in respect of a horse. He was, however, favoured with a white horse that proved to be the killer of the enemies. Velankar has clarified this point at two places.[19]

(11) The employment of the derivative forms otherwise known as *Taddhita* forms in the Pāṇinian grammar, appears to be the habit with the Vedic poets. Here a reference could be made to the following illustrations. *Purohiti* — priestly work at *Ṛg-Veda,* VI.61.7, VII.83.4, and VII.60.12, *Naryaṁ vasu* at VI.53.2; *Samarya* at IX.1.7; *Nādyah* — son of rivers at II.35.1, and X.111.2, *Gārṣṭeya* at X.111.2. It may be noted here in passing that Indra is known as *Gārṣṭeya,* i.e., son of Gṛṣṭi, Similarly the use[20] of the form *jāhnavī* at III.58.6b, and I.116.19 (in the sense of offspring of Jahnu or wife) These two senses are suggested by Sāyaṇa and Geldner. The use of the expression *Paidvo vājī* at I.116.6 in the sense of 'a horse belonging to Paidu'. It should be noted here in passing that Pāṇini has made a very exhaustive use of this technique of derivative nouns in his *Aṣṭādhyāyī,* by introducing various terminations, senses, with exceptions and counter-exceptions. It is due to this that it is well said that *Taddhimūḍhāḥ pāṇinīyāḥ,* i.e., the students of Pāṇini are best confused by the chapter on *Taddhita.*

(12) The language of the Vedic poets is purely decocative. They have made the best use of the principles of figures of speech later on defined, explained, and illustrated by the writers on *Alaṁkāra-Śāstra*. Velankar has located the *Alaṁkāras* in the Vedic poetry such as *Anuprāsa, Atiśayokti, Rūpaka, Samuccaya, Śleṣa, Śṛnkhalā*. *Upamā* as is clear[21] from the general index of the *Maṇḍala,* VII p. 279. It is rather surprising that the mind born son of Velankar, i.e., S.A.Upadhyaya has not cared to give the index of the *Alaṁkāras,* particularly in the Ṛkssktaśatī However, casually it may be pointed out that Veḷankar has located the Alaṁkāras[22] known as *Vibhāvanā* and *Atiśayoktt* in the famous *Akṣa-Sūkta* of the *Ṛg-Veda,* X.34.9. Incidentally, it may be noted here that by the expression *Jāriṇī* in the *Akṣa-Sūkta,* we have the precursor of the *Abhisārikā* type of heroine in the later Sanskrit literature and explained in the *Rasārṇava Sudhākara.*[23] Incidentally, it may be mentioned here that Velankar has seen the early beginnings of poetics in the hymns of the *Ṛg-Veda*. It is the noteworthy feature of the writings of Velankar that he has never used the material of his student[24] for Doctorate degree in his own published work.

(13) Another peculiarity of the Vedic poets is that they have used some words only in the plural number. The word[25] *Kṛṣṭīḥ* is employed by the Vedic poets at *Ṛg-Veda,* I.160.5, III.59.1, IV.30.2 and V.1.6. This word *Kṛṣṭīḥ* is used here in the sense of 'People'. One will have the pleasure in noticing this tendency[26] in the writing of the classical Sanskrit literature.

(14) Velankar has not failed to note the use of the preposition on the part of the Vedic poets, together with a verb or even independently, for showing the concept[27] of depth and nearness. The employment of the preposition *Api* at *Ṛg-Veda,* III.1.21, III.59.4, X.14.6 and X.131.7 tends only to signify 'depth'. Velankar has also demonstrated[28] that the the preposition *Vi* is associated with the roots *Ṛ, Vṛ* or *Ruj,* the object being something like दुर: or *dṛḍhā*. But in some cases, that preposition *Vi* seems to have been used quite independently in the sense of 'in spite of 'or 'not caring for'. Dr. S.S.Bhave has added an interesting point here. He states[29] that when *vat* is added to a preposition, it gives the sense of an intended action. Kuntaka,[30] the author of *Vakroktijīvitam,* deserves the credit for throwing more light on the employment of the

preposition.

(15) At times, however, it is pointed out by Velankar that the language of the Vedic poets has become symbolic. Here attention[31] of the serious readers may be drawn to the *Ṛg-Veda,* VIII.95.6 in which the expression *Ṛtasya dvārau* occurs. Velankar adds here that *Ṛta* is a symbol for sacrifice. It may be noted, in passing, that this type of symbolism is further continued by some scholars[32] at full length. Incidentally, however, it may be noted that in the Classical Sanskrit literature, we have the abundant cases of symbolic language and the symbols also are employed for purposes not only one.

(16) It is the stylistic peculiarity of the Vedic poets to change the gender of a word particularly by the attraction of some words in the *mantras.* For the clarification of this point, attention may be drawn to the *Ṛg-Veda,* I.48.14, VII.22.9, and VIII.8.6. In the *Ṛg-Veda,* I.48.14, as pointed[33] out by Velankar, *yam* was actually intended in place of *ye* as *sa* in *C* shows but actually by the attraction of the important word *ṛṣayaḥ,* it is changed to *ye.* I leave the other places mentioned above to the readers to appreciate.

(17) As indicated by Velankar, the Vedic poets also are fond of some expressions or phrases in English language. Thus in the *Ṛg-Veda,* we have the phrase *vasnam car* — in the sense of 'to haggle about the price of a thing, as employed in the *Ṛg-Veda,* X.34.3. We also meet with the phrases *śiva-asa* at *Ṛg-Veda,* X.34.2 in the sense of 'to be favourable to' or another phrase *mitram kṛ* or *dha* or *mṛdike asa*[34] at *Ṛg-Veda,* VIII.48.12. It may be noted in passing that in the *Ṛg-Veda,* we have the opportunity to note several such phrases but the cases cited above and particularly suggested by Velankar, are enough to prove my case.

(18) There is also a peculiar tendency of the Vedic poets to use one and the same word[35] in different genders and also with different senses. For example, the word *Janus* at *Ṛg-Veda,* I.58.2, in the neuter gender, conveys the sense of birth. When, however, the word is utilised in the masculine gender, it signifies 'a creature'. Similarly the word *artha* is found in the different senses and also in the different genders. This tendency is easily noticeable in the Classical Sanskrit[36] literature and even in the Sanskrit

lexicons.

(19) The Vedic poets have enriched their language by using different expressions to convey one and the same sense. Possibly they appear to have believed in the principle that repetition of one and the same word again and again indicates the poverty of expression. This is the principle[37] found in the *Kāvyālāṁkāra-Sūtra* of Vāmana. To convey the sense of a hymn, the Vedic poets have used the expressions like *sumati, dhī, dhīti, brahman, manā, mantra, manmana, venā, sukīrti, mati, manīṣā, brahmakṛti* etc. This point can be slightly elaborated by pointing out that the concept or idea of death is also conveyed by the Vedic poets by the expressions such as long darkness, or long and long sleep etc. We get such expressions[38] particularly with reference to the Paṇis in the *Ṛg-Veda,* I.32.10, II.27.14, IV.51.3, X.108.4 etc. As a matter of fact, the Vedic poets have composed hymns in a competitive spirit and in their competition, we get the origins of the later Sanskrit poetics. The different expressions and adjectives used by the Vedic poets to depict the personality of Uṣas proved to be inspiring to the modern scholars[39] like Dr. H.R. Divekar.

(20) It is also a noticeable feature of the style of the Vedic poets that they at times, employ one word[40] as a common noun and the same also serves the purpose of a proper noun. It is due to this peculiar style that the readers are likely to be confused. Velankar has brought this point home to the readers that the word *Rebha* appears as a common noun in the sense of a 'singer' in the *Ṛg-Veda,* VII.63.3 and VII. 76.7. He also adds that the same word is also found, used as a proper noun at *Ṛg-Veda,* I.116.24 and I.118.6. Here it may be noted that the word *Rebha* is derived from the root *Ribha* to praise or glorify.

(21) The language of the Vedic poets has at times, become purely allusive. The *Ṛg-Veda,* IV. 30 can be cited as an illustrative of this type. Elsewhere, in the *Ṛg-Veda* also we can notice this tendency. The expression *agohyasya ātithye* used in the *Ṛg-Veda,* IV.33.7 is simply allusive. Similarly, the *Ṛg-Veda,* I.116.13 is making an allusion to the story of *Vadhrimatī* and *puraṁdhi.* This tendency[41] of mythological allusions have almost become a common feature of the known Sanskrit poets like Kālidāsa, Bhāsa, Bhavabhūti and others.

(22) Writing one and the same word in two different ways, without having any change in the meaning of the word, is also a noteworthy feature of the style of the Vedic poets. Thus, the word *pratna* is also written as *pratana* in the sense of 'ancient' in the *Ṛg-Veda,* III.9.8, III.42.9 and IV.50.1. We have one more illustration of this type as *matha* or *mantha* at III.29.6. At the end of the Second *Maṇḍala*[42] of the *Ṛg-Veda,* II.42.1 we find the use of the expressions such as *śakunaṁ, śakuni* and *śakunti.* It may be observed that this kind of tendency is noticed not only in some of the Sanskrit lexicons[43] but also in the writing of the gifted poet like Kālidāsa particularly in his *Raghuvaṁśam* and *Meghadūtam* as noted by Hemādri.

(23) The language of the Vedic poets has also become metaphorical when the occasion so demands. This tendency becomes neatly observed in the Seventh *Maṇḍala* of the *Ṛg-Veda*. One has to resort to the metaphorical sense only when the literal meaning becomes totally inapplicable in a particular context. Thus, for example, the use of the expression *tamas* at *Ṛg-Veda,* VII.73.1, conveys the metaphorical sense[44] of 'ignorance or despondence' etc. as suggested by Velankar and not its usual sense of 'darkness'. One may add one more illustration here. The word *āpaḥ* does not convey the sense of 'water' in the *Ṛg-Veda,* VII.56.24 and naturally it is to be taken in the metaphorical sense of 'danger'. It may be remarked here that Velankar has shown these senses in his notes on these particular places.

(24) It is significant to note that in the style of the Vedic poets we have to notice some conventions.[45] It is but proper that they have assumed white colour for fame. This point can be properly elucidated by drawing attention to the *Ṛg-Veda,* VII.24.5d which simply means 'put in us bright fame as you put the (bright) day in the heaven. Here it is worthy of note the expression *dyāṁśromatam.* In passing, it may be casually remarked here one gets some idea of the conventions of poetry later on properly developed in the *Alaṁkāra-Śāstra.*[46] Incidentally, however, it may be pointed out that the later-writers on *Alaṁkāra-Śāstra* employ the expression *Kavisamaya* for the conventions of poets and poetry and in the classical Sanskrit literature. We very often meet with such conventions with the proper examples.

(25) The promiscuous[47] use of the words may be treated as one more important aspect of the style of the Vedic poets. In such a use, we find that though the word is used in a particular case, it actually conveys the sense of another case. In Pāṇini's language, this technique is popularly known as *Vyatyayo bahulam.* It may be noted here that in the *Ṛg-Veda,* II.20.1 and II.33.6, we get the examples of this type. In the *Ṛg-Veda,* II.33.6, however, we have the example of the locative case in place of the ablative case. Velankar has cited such examples in the course of his notes. It may be noted here that the great Śaṅkarācārya has also used this principle[48] in explaining and interpreting the words in the *Sūtras* of *Bādarāyaṇa*. Incidentally, however, it may be pointed out that the learned Professor Velankar has used the technique of *Vyatyayo bahulaṁ* to advocate[49] his theory of Word economy and *Ṛg-Vedic* interpretation. In passing, it may be noted here that even in the Classical Sanskrit literature, we notice this tendency in the writings[49] of the reputed poets like Kālidāsa and others.

(26) It appears that the Vedic poets seem to have developed some concepts for the abstract things or an abstract noun. Thus, the concept of friendship can be formed by the exchange of seven words with each other by walking seven steps with another person. This seems to be the concept easily noticeable[50] in the Classical Sanskrit literature. For this concept, attention may be drawn to the *Ṛg-Veda,* II.19.7, in which we have the expression *asyama tat saptam asusanaḥ*. The line here simply means' May we enjoy that friendship of you, while strengthening us ' (through a desire for fame.). Velankar also draws attention to the *Atharva-Veda,* 5.11.10 in which the expression *saptapadaḥ sakhā,* occurs. A clear reference to this concept also occurs in the *Ṛg-Veda,* X.8.4cd. Here, however, in a passage[51] from the Second *Maṇḍala,* there is no reference to the marriage ceremony in which husband and wife become friends by walking seven foot-steps which is treated as a rite in the marriage ceremony particularly in the *Dharma-Śastra* literature. A slight change in the rite, however, is noticed in the *Rāmāyaṇa,*[52] particularly on the point of friendship.

(27) To use present active participles to convey the sense of the present tense, also seems to be the style of the Vedic poets. We are fortunate in getting an example of this type in the *Ṛg-Veda,* II.11.4.

Here in this passage, the present active participle forms — *dadhānaḥ* and *vardhayantaḥ* denote the sense of the present tense, as suggested[53] by Professor Velankar. We can collect other examples of this type from the *Ṛg-Veda*. But the example cited here is sufficient to prove the stylistic feature of the Vedic poets.

(28) Professor Velankar has significantly pointed out that in the style of the Vedic poets, we find the peculiarity. They employ some words as conveying both the agent noun and action. One may draw the attention to this peculiarity[54] of the Vedic poets by citing the *Ṛg-Veda,* V.26.4 in which the expression *Havyadātiḥ* is used. Prof. Velankar suggests that this expression conveys both the senses of 'giver of offerings and also the act of giving offerings. Incidentally, it may be pointed out that the editor of the *Ṛksūktaśatī* seems to have forgotten, perhaps through oversight, to consider this expression *havyadātiḥ* in the select glossary p.185 and 326, as is clear from the important[55] foot-note.

(29) To use one and the same word, in two different senses, as per the context, but without having any change in the gender and number, seems to be the speciality of the writings of Vedic poets. It must be mentioned here that this is not a case of pun also. This point could be expounded[56] by a concrete example. In the *Ṛg-Veda,* when we come across the expression *sabhā,* it conveys the sense of a 'learned assembly'. This sense becomes available to the readers of the *Ṛg-Veda,* I.19.20, II.24.13 and VIII.4.9. But when, however, the word *sabhā* occurs in the context of the *Ṛg-Veda,* X.34.6, it has the sense of a 'gambling hall', which is more famous also in the *Mahābhārata, Smṛti* works and also in the *Kauṭilīya Arthaśāstra.* The word *vidaṭha* however, is used in the *Ṛg-Veda,* in the sense of 'sacrificial assembly' at several places such as I.85.1, I.143.7, II.12.15, II.23.19, II.33.15, II.35.15, V.63.2, VIII.48.14 etc. In this very context, it is equally important to note the sense[57] of *Rāj* in two distinct senses. It is to be used in the *Parasmaipada.* It simply means 'to rule over or shine'. Velankar guardedly remarks that the sense of *'Rāj* — to shine' is accepted when there are clear indications such as locative form or an adjective signifying brilliance connected with it, and very rightly concludes that even this is more or less subjective. One may remark here that this note is indeed, illuminating on the style of the Vedic poets.

(30) The language of the Vedic poets often touches the sacrificial system. Hence we find references to the priests, their duties, offerings, sacrificial ditch (Vedi) sacrificial similes, sacrifices and also the deities connected with the sacrificial activities. Here a reference could be made to the Āprīl hymns in the *Ṛg-Veda*, indicating the deities of the sacrifice. At times, however, we find references to the patrons and the *Dāna-stuti* hymns become more important in this context. Velankar has touched all these points at different places[59] in his notes on the Agni hymns. Dr. K.R. Potdar has dealt with the problem of the sacrifice in the *Ṛg-Veda* at great length and the sacrificial language also has become inspiring to the authors of the *Brāhmaṇa* literature and Upaniṣadic language, the aspect which is incidentally touched[60] in the foot-note.

In conclusion, the language of the Vedic poets reveals different peculiarities of the writings — such as symbolic, allusive, decorative, poetic, metaphorical, personalising, derivative, repetitive, condensable, conceptual, idiometic, conventional, sacrificial, anthropomorphic, and full of the variations of double formation of words, use of adjectives for substantives, rich in vocabulary, and exhibiting various variations in the poetic devices, — the most of which have largely influenced the later Sanskrit literature particularly *Brāhmaṇa* literature, Upaniṣadic literature, classical literature and even the Sanskrit lexicons. As all these aspects are revealed by the writings of Professor Velankar, I take this opportunity of paying tribute to him by borrowing his own views and examples.

References

1. *Ṛg-Veda Maṇḍala* II reviewed by Dr. Ram Gopal, In *Vishveshvarananda Indological Journal,* Vol.5 (2) p. 214.
2. *Ṛg-Veda Maṇḍala* VII reviewed by Dr. V.S. Agrawal, in *Bhāratī.* 6(2) 118-20. K.V. Sarma, *VIJ.*14, pp. 319-25.
3. R.N. Dandekar's *Exercises in Indology,* pp.102n, 128n, and also pp. 118, 115 etc. where he refers to him as some scholars. In the former case, i.e., *ṚV.,* VII.33.9, Dr. Dandekar is bold in figurative interpretation and suggesting some such words as 'and yet' to connect 9ab with 9ed together, without at the same time, quoting any textual authority for such interpretation. In the latter case, Prof. Velankar is interpreting *ṚV.* in the light of the *ṚV;* while Dr. Dandekar is interpreting the same from the cultural point of view. Hence the conclusions

of both the scholars are different. It may be added here, 'one is more impressed by Dr. Dandekar's glamour of the knowledge of foreign scholars rather than by his command over the peculiarities of the Vedic language and usage of the Vedic words', which incidentally, may be considered as the strong point of the writing of Prof. Velankar.

4. The technique of using only the adjective and not substantives is noted by Prof. Velankar in the *Ṛksūktaśatī,* p.236. It may be noted here that this tendency is also seen in the classical Sanskrit, particularly when Kālidāsa uses the expression *gāṇḍīvadhanvā* in the *Pūrva-Megh* for Arjuna in the st. No.48 (S.K.De's second edition, 1970) and the same device in the *Raghuvaṁśam,* III.9 as noted by Hemādri.

5. This principle is explained in the *Ṛksūktaśatī,* p.289. Here, incidentally, it may be added that this principle is used in a reverse manner to suggest near future following the rule of Pāṇini, III.3.4 to interpret the famous line from the *Uttara-Megha — Āloke te nipatati purā* etc. St. 82.

6. For the symbolic use of *Vimuc* see *Ṛksūktaśatī,* p.199.

7. In the *ṚV.,* I.151.5, *Śraddhā* is personified. Oldenberg thinks that the abstract thing is personified in the *Ṛg-Veda* as noted by R.N. Dandekar in *Exercises in Indology,* p.208. In the *Meghadūtam,* Kālidāsa has rivers as personified heroines.

8. *Ṛksūktaśatī,* p.286.

9. R.N. Dandekar, *Vedic Mythological Tracts,* pp. 45, 92, 105, 107, 110n, etc. for personification.

10. For the words employed in a secondary sense, see *Ṛg-Veda Maṇḍala* II. p.121, *Maṇḍala* III P.153, and *Maṇḍala* VII., p.284. Incidentally, it may be added that in the Sanskrit literature, the word *Vidhi* is used in a secondary sense and not in the primary sense in which it is generally found used in the canons of *Pūrva-Mīmāṁsā.* Kālidāsa has made this kind of use of a word in a secondary sense, particularly in his entire literature.

11. In the classical Sanskrit we find the tendency of using one and the same word as ending in both the consonant and a vowel. For example, the word *jarā* and *jaras — jaṭāyu* and *jaṭāyus* in the *Śabda-bheda-prakāśa,* p.4. Incidentally, it may be added that the word *apsarā* is also written as *Apsaras.* Kālidāsa has employed the word *anapsarā* in the *Vikramorvaśīyam* as *anapsarā iva pratibhāsi,* p.6.

12. *Ṛksūktaśatī,* p.103.

13. *Ibid,* p.109.

14. *Ṛg-Veda Maṇḍala* VI, General Index, p. 283.

15. One may quote the line *bhadraṁ bhadraṁ vitara bhagavan bhūyase maṅgalāya/ Mālatī-Mādhavam.* I. It may be added that Dr. T.G.Mainkar has discussed some aspects of poetic *Ṛg-Vedic* repetitions, pp.1-116 (Poona University publication,1966). The writer of this note has shown about thirty purposes at the back of Motivations in an article 'motivations of *Punarvacana*'

contributed to the *Journal of the Asiatic Society*, Bombay, 1974-76, pp, 127-35.

16. H.D. Velankar, *Ṛg-Veda Maṇḍala* VII, p. 90. It may be noted here that in the Glossary to the *Ṛg-Veda Maṇḍala* VII, pp 237-38 the expression used for *anutta* is unopposed. While in the actual translation on pp. 76 and 90, it is translated as resistless. There should have been the uniformity of expression and not of the meaning only in the translation and glossary which is missing here, in spite of the meticulous care taken by Prof. S.A. Upadhyaya. One must also admit that both the expressions 'unopposed and resistless' have one and the same meaning.

17. As opposed to this in the *Harṣacaritam*, we notice the tendency of shortening the proper name of a person as shown by the commentator 'Raṅganātha', p.323 and particularly un-noticed by Dr. P.V. kane, Gajendragadkar, p.168 and others. Here रामदत्त is shortered as रामिज on the ground of compassion.

18. H.D.Velankar, *Ṛg-Veda-Maṇḍala* VII, p.164 and *Ṛksūktaśatī*, p. 116.

19. Also see the *Ṛg-Veda*, I.116.6, I.119.9 in the *Ṛksūktaśatī* and *ṚV.*, VII.71.5b

20. *Ṛksūktaśatī*, p.118 notes the view of Geldner who compares the form *Mānavi* with *Jahnāvī* and treats it as the wife of Jāhnu. Also see *admasadya* at *ṚV* VIII.43.19 and VIII.44.29a in the sense of a 'duty of a priest who supervises the preparation of the sacrificial offerings and works under the chief priest Adhvaryu. Incidentally, it may be noted that Prof. Velankar has not added any special note on such derivative forms. In fact, he has made a very meagre use of Pāṇini for example at *ṚV.*, II. 23.12 P.63. etc.

21. *Ṛg-Veda Maṇḍala* II, Index I (Linguistics) p.119 and *Ṛg-Veda Maṇḍala* III, Index I, p.151.

22. For *ṚV*, X.34.9, see *Ṛksūktaśatī*, p.266.

23. For *abhisārikā* — See *Rasārṇa-Sudhākara*, pp.57-60.

24. The Ph.D. thesis of Miss. I.N. Dike on the topic 'The early beginning of poetics in the *Ṛg-Veda*' is deposited in the library of the University of Bombay — in the year 1959. It may be noted in passing that Dr. T.G. Mainkar has also dealt with this topic perhaps on a small scale in his book *Ṛg-Vedic foundations of Classical Poetics*, Ajanta Books International, Delhi.

25. Also see *Ṛksūktaśatī*, p.321.

26. This tendency is noticed in the classical Sanskrit literature particularly in the use of the expressions such as *dārāḥ, sikatā, samāḥ, varṣāḥ* etc. For details see *Amaramaṇḍana* of Kṛṣṇasūri, ed. by V. Raghavan, Deccan College, Pune. The writers of this note has already noted this tendency in his Sanskrit work *Śānta-Ārāmaḥ*, p. 67.

27. *Ṛg-Veda Maṇḍala* III, p.142 and *Ṛksūktaśatī*, p.160 of H.D. Velankar.

28. *Ṛg-Veda-Maṇḍala* VII, p.55. It is rather surprising that Prof. S.A. Upadhyaya has not made an entry for *vi* in the above sense in the select glossary, p.266, when in particular, this is a peculiar feature.

29. Dr. S.S. Bhave, *Soma* hymns of the *Ṛg-Veda*, IX.6.4, p.32.

30. Also see : Kuntaka's *Vakroktijīvitam* under II. 31 and 33 (Dr. K. Krishnamoorthy's edition, Dharwar, 1977).

31. H.D.Velankar, *Ṛg-Veda-Maṇḍala* VII, p.208.

32. In passing, it may be noted that Dr. S.A.Dange has made a more detailed study of the Pastoral Symbolism from the *Ṛg-Veda* (Poona University, Publication), 1970 and *Sexual Symbolism from the Vedic literature,* Ajanta Books International, Delhi, 1985, although it is true that all his theories to solve the riddles of the *ṚV* have not appealed to the mind of the scholars. Interested readers may see the review in the *A.B.O.R.I,* Vol. LXIV, 1983, pp. 294-97 on the *Sexual Symbolism from the Vedic Literature* at the hands of Dr. P.D.Navathe. Besides, some scholars like Dr. P.L.Bhargava are not in favour of the research of Dr. Dange. Dr. T.G.Mainkar held (in the private capacity) that Dr. Dange's research is a clear case of Pornography. The writer of this note feels that the research work of Dr. Dange is, indeed, a patch work.' However, we have to admit the fact that he has persued this topic as a life-time dedicated work. In the classical Sanskrit literature, one finds the use of the symbols of flowers, bee, river etc. for different purposes particularly at the hands of Kālidāsa. Jagannatha, has, however used the symbols to reveal the nature of the persons and in passing to throw light on the life he has led, particularly in the *Anyoktivilāsa* of the *Bhāmīnivilāsa.*

33. *Ṛksūktaśatī,* p.108.

34. *Mṛlike asya sumatau syāṁ/Ṛg-Veda,* VII. 48.12d.

35. Mark the use of the expression *artha*(M) and *arthani*(N) in the *Ṛg-Veda.*

    Also see: *Ṛksūktaśatī,* p.213. It is noteworthy that the word *nakṣatram* means the sun, when it is used in the neuter gender and singular number as at *ṚV,* X.156-4ab and VII.81.2 and VII.86.1. But when the word *nakṣatram* is used in the Neuter Gender but in the Plural number at I.50.2 and X.68.11, it means the stars.

36. Even in the classical Sanskrit literature, we mark this tendency. The word *karaka* is found used in both the masculine and feminine genders. This is already indicated by me in the *Śānta-Ārāmaḥ,* p. 63. Also see the use of the word *Madhu-Amaramaṇḍana,* p.43.

37. *Naikam padaṁ dviḥ prayojyam.* Vāmana's *Kāvyālaṁkāra-Sūtra.*

38. We find the use of the expressions *Dīrgha tamisrā* at II.27.14, *Dīrgham tamaḥ* at IV.41.3cd, and the expression *tamaso vimadhye, Ṛksūktaśatī,* p 177.

39. Select articles of Dr. H.R. Divekar (in Marathi), article on *Uṣecā vilāsa āṇī vikāsa,* pp. 133-38. (Divekar literary publication committee, Pune 2, 1975).

40. See *Ṛg-Veda Maṇḍala* VII., p.147. *Ṛksūktaśatī,* p. 119, for a proper name at I.116.24. Also see notes on I.117.4, X.39.9ab.

    Attention may be drawn to the expression *Rebha* in the sense of a bard, in the *ṚV.,* I.127.10. Velankar adds here one more reference to *ṚV.,* VI.11.3cd, Cf H.D.Velankar, Hymns to Agni in *Maṇḍala* I. In *Journal of the University of Bombay,* Vols. 32 and 33, part 2, Sept. 1963, p.11.

41. *Ṛksūktaśatī,* pp.166-71. The tendency of mythological allusions is quite obvious in the classical Sanskrit literature and particularly in the writings of every Sanskrit poet like Kālidāsa, Bhavabhūti etc.

42. Cf. *ṚV.*, II.42.1 and 3 and glossary to *Maṇḍala* II, p.115. Also Cf: VI.28.7, I.23.9 and I.23.10.

43. The word Mathurā is also written as Madhurā — see Hemādri on the *Raghuvaṁśam,* 15.28 and also the *Śānta-Ārāmaḥ,* p.63.

44. H.D. Velankar, *Ṛg-Veda-Maṇḍala* VII, pp.133 and 165. The meaning of VII.73.1 is further supported by Prof. Velankar by quoting *ṚV.*, V.31.9d in favour.

45. Cf. *Ṛg-Veda-Maṇḍala* VII., p.66. It may be noted that this poetic convention is known in the later Sanskrit literature and particularly in the *Alaṁkāra-Śāstra* as *Kavisamaya.* It may be noted that ignominy is having black colour.

46. Also see Dr. V.M.Kulkarni's monumental work, *'Studies in Sanskrit Sahitya Sastra,* Sanskrit rhetoricians on poetic conventions,' pp.19-27, publ. by B.L. Institute of Indology, Patan, 1982.

47. It may be noted here that later on Prof. Velankar has utilised this principle of promiscuous use to advocate his famous theory of 'Word economy and *Ṛg-Veda* Interpretation, In *ABORI,* 1964, pp.1-16. It may be added that for the use of genitive in place of dative see *Ṛg-Veda,* III.16.3. p.42.

48. Śaṅkarācārya has employed this principle of *Vedānta Sūtra,* I.1.1 to explain *Brāhmaṇaḥ jijñāsā.*

49. This tendency is noticed by Mallinātha on the *Raghuvāṁśam,* V.9.

50. Cf. *Mahābhārata —*

Kālidāsa also believes that friendship can be formed by the exchange of seven words — Read : *Yataḥ satāṁ sannatagātri saṅgataṁ manīṣibhiḥ sāptapadīnaṁ ucyate*/Kumārasaṁbhavan.

51. Cf. *ṚV-Maṇḍala* II, p. 55.

52. In the *Rāmāyaṇā,* IV.5. however, Rāma and Sugrīva circumambulate the fire to form the friendship. It should, however, be noted that in the *ṚV,* II.19.7, the friendship is formed to strength oneself for fame.

53. Cf. *ṚV-Maṇḍala* II, p.28.

54. *Ṛksūktaśatī,* p.185.

55. Possibly when *dāti* is separated from another word like *vīryam,* i.e., when it is not a compound, it is treated as a subjunctive form at two places VII.15.12 and VII.42.4. Here it is not used in both the senses of action and agent. Besides, in the *Ṛksūktaśatī,* Select Glossary, p.326, there is no entry for *dāti* in both the senses. In addition to this, under *havya* on p.351, there is no mention of *havyadāti,* when in particular, this is the peculiarity the Vedic language.

56. *Ṛksūktaśatī,* p.196.

57. H.D. Velankar, Hymns to *Agni* in *Maṇḍala* I, In *J.U.B.* Vols. 32-33, part 2, Sept. 1963, p. 33.

58. K.R.Potdar, *Sacrifice in the Ṛg-Veda,* Bhāratīya Vidyā Bhavan, 1953.

59. A few references may be found in the notes on the *Agni* hymns in the First *Maṇḍala* of the *ṚV.* particularly published in the *Journal of the University of Bombay* and also the Agni hymns in the *Maṇḍalas* II, III, VII and *Ṛksūktaśatī.*

60. Dr. T.G. Mainkar has shown the similarities in the sacrificial language of the *Brāhmaṇas* and the *Upaniṣads* particularly in the course of his lectures in the *Kaushika Lecture Series,* Poona. 1970 — *Yajñīya Saṁhitā āṇi Upaniṣads,* pp.46-59. A mention may be made of the work *'Sacrifice in the Brāhmaṇas,'* a Ph.D. thesis of Dr. G.U.Thite, Published by the Poona University, 1975.

2

The Concept of a Witness in the *Mahābhārata* and *Dharma-Śāstra* Literature

In the *History of Dharma-Śāstra,* Vol. III, Dr. Kane has dealt with the concept of a witness very exhaustively. But it is found that some of the references from the *Mahābhārata* have escaped his eagle eye, though he has consulted the source of the *Rāmāyaṇa* and the *Mahābhārata* for the purpose of *Dharma-Śāstra*. Hence an attempt is made in this chapter to compare in brief the matter that is available in the *Mahābhārata* with that of the *Dharma-Śāstra* material.

Dr. Kane has clarified the concept of a witness on the basis of the *Viṣṇu-Dharma-Sūtra,* VIII.13 and Medhātithi on the *Manu-Smṛti,* VIII.74. The quotations that he has given in the *History of Dharma-Śāstra,* Vol. III, p.331 come near to the thought expressed in the *Mahābhārata,* II.61.76. In the *Mahābhārata,* II.61.76, it is pointed[1] out that he is called a witness who has directly seen (the incident) and directly heard (the conversation or speech between the concerned persons) and kept it mind and who speaks the truth. It is further said that such a witness is never dissociated from *Dharma* and *Artha,* the two important goals of human life.

It would be interesting to note that in the *Dharma-Śāstra* literature, the concept of a witness is connected with a merit or a demerit. In the *Gautama-Dharma-Sūtra,* 13.7-8, the concept of a witness is associated with *puṇya* and *pāpa*. The *Gautama-Dharma-Sūtra* advocates that if a witness does not speak the truth, he will simply incur the sin. The *Gautama-Dharma-Sūtra* goes one step further and points out the benefit in the form of heaven for speaking the truth and hell[2] for telling lies — in the case of a witness. It is worth while to note that in the *Mahābhārata,* the concept of a witness is not connected with heaven and earth.

Herein lies the novelty of the *Dharma-Śāstra* literature.

On the concept of a witness, the *Mahābhārata,* II.61.70 has contributed a very interesting thought. Whenever any sin[3] takes place, and is not censured, the person who is the senior-most and who is particularly present on the spot, incurs half the sin. One who is the direct performer of a sin incurs one-fourth of the sin. One-fourth of the sin is, however, incurred by the members of the Assembly who did not censure the censurable deed. In this way, the thought expressed in the *Mahābhārata* is really noteworthy particularly on the point of the distribution of the quantity of a sin. From this discussion, it goes without saying that the senior-most person and the members who do not censure the censurable deed are given more blame than the performer of a sin in the *Mahābhārata*.

It would be equally important to note the position when the sin is directly censured in the presence of a performer of a deed. The *Mahābhārata* expresses a very important view in this respect. It is further held[4] in the *Mahābhārata,* II.61.71 that the senior-most persons become free from the sin, when they directly blame or condemn the censurable deed. Here in the matter of blaming a censurable act, even the other members of the Assembly stand included. In such a case, the sin is wholly transferred to a doer of a censurable act. In other words, the performer alone is held responsible for the act.

In this very context, it would be pertinent to bring to the notice of the readers that the *Mahābhārata* has considered the position of the witnesses speaking untruth from an altogether different angle. It is pointed out, for example, in the *Mahābhārata,* II.61.74 that the persons speaking untruth destroy the effect of *Iṣṭāpūrta*[5] of seven generations on both the sides (of father and mother) and they further experience the sorrows of other ladies. This citation from the *Mahābhārata* appears to connect the concept of a witness speaking untruth with the results or effects of the charitable deeds one has performed during the life. A dispassionate reader will have to admit here whole-heartedly that the *Mahābhārata* points out the dire consequences of speaking untruth, as compared with the concept of going into a hell of a witness.

Here it would be worthy of note to point out that the *Mahābhārata* has contributed a novel view on the point of some persons who should not be accepted as witnesses. Here this view is based on the profession which the persons follow. The *Mahābhārata,* V.35.37 specifically points[6] out that a palmist, a merchant who was formerly a thief, a medical practitioner who was formerly a painter, an enemy, a friend and an actor should be treated as unacceptable as witnesses in the Court matters. Here it is evident that the list (if admitted) shows that it is connected with the professions and the relations of a person in the society. This viewpoint of the *Mahābhārata* has no parallel in the entire *Dharma-Śāstra* literature. A curious reader of *Dharma-Śāstra* comes across the lists (perhaps exhaustive) in respect of unacceptability of a person for a particular purpose in respect of the *Śrāddha* aspect of the *Dharma-Śāstra.* But on the point of witnesses, the *Dharma-Śāstra* has nothing to contribute on the point of witnesses from the point of view of professions and public relations of a person with the society.

Here attention may be drawn to a peculiar view referred to in the commentary Keśava Vaijayantī on the *Viṣṇu-Smṛti,* VIII.13. This quotation given by Nandapaṇḍita is not identified by the editor from the *Mahābhārata.* Killing anybody is treated as a sin. The quotation[7] relied upon by Nandapaṇḍita simply indicates that by killing a person (perhaps most dangerous) on the earth, if many people become happy, then in his killing there is no sin. Naturally, the performer of such an act become free from a sin. From this it follows that even a witness to such a killing is not sure to incur any sin. This thought of the *Mahābhārata* is really important and should not be neglected by the serious readers of *Dharma-Śāstra.*

The above discussion would lead one to the conclusion that the *Mahābhārata* has contributed thoughts on the concept of a witness in respect of speaking the truth, untruth, censuring the deeds, not censuring the deeds, quantity of transferring the sin to the performers of the act and witnesses, and unacceptability of a witness on the grounds of professions the social relations of a person. The *Dharma-Śāstra,* however, connects the concept of a witness with the fruits of heaven and hell, and thereby shows its speciality as compared with the thought in the *Mahābhārata* which concentrates on the direct dire consequences in respect of *Iṣṭāpūrta*.

References

1. समक्षदर्शनात् साक्ष्यं श्रवणाच्चेति धारणात् ।
   तस्मातं सत्यं ब्रुवन् साक्षी धर्मार्थाभ्यां न हीयते ॥
   महाभारत, II. 61.75 (Cr. edition, Poona) Also see. P.V. Kane*, History of Dharma Śāstra,* Vol. III., p. 330.
2. The *वामन-पुराण*, 12.40b points out महारौरव नरक for a कूटसाक्षी । (*वामन-पुराण*, Kashiraj Trust, Varanasi, edition.)
3. अर्धं हरति वै श्रेष्ठः पादो भवति कर्तृषु
   पादश्चैव सभासत्सु ये न निन्दन्ति निन्दितम् ॥
   महाभारत, II, 61.70.
4. अनेना भवति श्रेष्ठा मुच्यन्ते च सभासदः ।
   एनो गच्छति कर्तारं निन्दार्हो यत्र निन्द्यते ॥
   महाभारत, II, 61.71.
5. For a discussion on *Iṣṭāpūrta* vide P.V. Kane, *History of Dharma-Śāstra,* Vol. II/I, p.157 and Vol. II/II pp. 843-44. However, a reference to *Iṣṭāpūrta* in relation to a witness has escaped the notice of Dr. Kane.
6. सामुद्रिकं वणिजं चोरपूर्वं
   शलाकपूर्णं च चिकित्सकं च ।
   अरिं च मित्रं च कुशीलवं च
   नैतान् साक्ष्येष्वधिकुर्वीत सप्त ॥
   महाभारत, V. 35. 37. - Also see for this aspect याज्ञवल्क्यस्मृति. II.70-71
   Also see : P. V. Kane, *History of Dharma-Śāstra,* Vol. III., pp. 334-35.
7. बहवः सुखमेधन्ते हते यस्मिन् वसुन्धरे ।
   तास्मिन् हते न दोषोऽस्ति पातकं नोपपातकम् ॥ This *महाभारत* citation is quoted in केशव-वैजयन्ती on *विष्णुस्मृति*, VIII. 13 (Adyar Library, edition, Madras, 1964.)

3

Dharma-Śāstra Aspects of the *Rāmāyaṇa*

RIGHT at the very outset, it may be remarked that the present chapter is divided into three parts. In the first part, I have made references to the *Dharma-Śāstra*[1] material from the *Rāmāyaṇa*, Dr. P.V. Kane has mainly relied upon his voluminous *History of Dharma-Śāstra*. In the second part of this chapter, I have made the ample use of the material from the *Dharma-Śāstra* authors quoting the portion from the *Rāmāyaṇa* to substantiate the *Dharma-Śāstra* points and particularly those which have escaped the notice of the learned Dr. P.V. Kane. In the third part of this chapter, however, I have dealt with such aspects of *Dharma-Śāstra* which have escaped the notices of the writers on *Dharma-Śāstra* and also MM. Dr. Kane. It may be remarked here only incidentally that I have tried to compare at some places the material from the *Rāmāyaṇa* with that of the *Mahābhārata*. Here an attempt is also made to see how far the views expressed in the *Rāmāyaṇa* received acceptance at the hands of the writers on *Dharma-Śāstra* and modifications introduced by them deserve special mention. In passing, I have also utilised the material from the classical Sanskrit literature, only to show how the evolution has taken place in respect of the views that are expressly only incidentally in the *Rāmāyaṇa*.

Before I proceed further, I may add that Dr. Kane in the course of his discussion in the *History of Dharma-Śāstra*, makes a reference[2] to the two learned papers of Dr. Bhabatosh Bhattacharya of Calcutta, dealing with the citations from the *Rāmāyaṇa* in the *Dharma-Śāstra* digest works. From the remarks of Dr. Kane, it is evident that Dr. Bhattacharya was more concerned with the point whether the citations from the *Rāmāyaṇa* becoming available in the *Dharma-Śāstra* digests, can be traced back to the original *Rāmāyaṇa* or not. He has stated that some of the citations can be identified but many other citations could not be identified. I must, however, state that Dr. Bhattacharya was less concerned with the thought development of the *Dharma-Śāstra* aspects, though I do not have the fortune of going through his learned papers.

Incidentally, however, it may be mentioned here that for the purposes of the *Rāmāyaṇa* and the *Mahābhārata,* I have made the best use of the critical editions of these works.

As far as the aspects of the *Rāmāyaṇa* referred to by Dr. Kane are concerned, I give here the brief summary of his discussion for the readers only to appreciate the second and third parts of the chapter. Dr. Kane points out that there should be no education on *pratipad* day; the marriage of Rāma and Sītā took place on the Uttarā-Phālgunī constellation; *Abhaya-dāna* is treated as the highest ideal for good warfare; the food for the *Śrāddha*-ceremony is decided; the importance of *Gayā* is stressed for the performance of the *Śrāddha* and its glorious fruits also are pointed; the position of women, the importance of self-immolation, the marriageable age, golden image of a wife for the *Aśvamedha* sacrifice are noted; He has made a a reference to the caste of *Guha,* the important point that a Kṣatriya cannot perform a sacrifice; He has shown the reference to the three wives to annoint the horse at the time of the *Aśvamedha* sacrifice; He has pointed out the duties of a king and a punishment to the king Nṛga on account of neglecting the dispute between two brāhmaṇa brothers in respect of a curse and his falling into the hell; the king's right to collect one-sixth part of the corn by way of a *bali* and one-fourth share in the merit of the sages; divine origin of kingship, condemnation of a murder of messenger, the principle of 'Might is right' in the absence of proper ruling of a king; He has also discussed the education of Rāma and the point of preservation of the dead body of Daśaratha in the tub of oil etc.

From this brief survey of the discussion in the *History of Dharma-Śāstra,* it is quite evident that Dr. Kane has discussed the *Vyavahāra, Ācāra, Śrāddha* aspects and the position of women and the holy places in the *Rāmāyaṇa* etc. One will have to admit that taking into consideration the profound scholarship of Dr. Kane in the vast field of *Dharma-Śāstra,* he has not failed to do justice to the *Rāmāyaṇa* in the volumes of *History of Dharma-Śāstra.*

Coming to the Second part of this chapter, I briefly mention here that the writers on *Dharma-Śāstra* have made the proper use of the material from the *Rāmāyaṇa* to explain the various *Dharma-Śāstra* aspects. I mention here only those aspects which have escaped the eagle eye of Dr. Kane.

(1) The peculiar aspect of the *Ācāra* portion of the *Dharma-Śāstra* deserves mention here. In a matter of selecting a lady as a wife, there is a lot of discussion[3] in the *Dharma-Śāstra*. But the writers on *Dharma-Śāstra* make a mention of a particular behaviour of women in general that they do not have hatred or love towards any person. They may cling to any person of their choice irrespective of any consideration. This passage from the *Rāmāyaṇa* is relied upon by Caṇḍeśvara in the *Vivāda-Ratnākara*, Lakṣmīdhara in his *Kṛtyakalpataru Vyavahāra Kāṇḍa*[4] p.607 and the commentary of Bālaṁbhaṭṭi on the *Ācāra* portion of the *Mitākṣarā* on the *Yājñvalkya-Smṛti* p.219.

(2) So far as the *Vyavahāra* aspect of *Dharma-Śāstra* is concerned, we have an important piece of information from the commentary of Bālaṁbhaṭṭi on the *Mitākṣarā* on the *Yājñavalkya-Smṛti*, II.135. Here actually the topic under discussion is the line of heirs competent enough to succeed to the property of a dead person. Here Bālaṁbhaṭṭi relied upon a passage from the *Rāmāyaṇa* and pointed out that the kings abandon[5] their own sons (in the matter of succession to the property) if they are not beneficial to the interest of a kingdom and take (actually) adopt even the sons of other persons provided they are powerful and more competent to shoulder the responsibility of the kingdom. Here he makes a reference to the story of Sagara who prohibits[6] his eldest son (particularly in the matter of succession) to the throne.

(3) There is an interesting quotation from the *Rāmāyana* in two digest works. Pṛthivandra in his *Vyavahāra Prakāśa*[7], p.62 and Lakṣmīdhara in his *Kṛtyakalpataru- Vyavahāra Kāṇḍa* give an identical quotation from the *Rāmāyaṇa* to the effect that if a king fails to attend to the duties in respect of the work of the citizens, then he is cooked in the terrible hell.

(4) So far as the *Śrāddha* aspect of *Dharma-Śāstra* is concerned, Devaṇṇabhaṭṭa in his *Smṛticandrikā-Śrāddha-Kāṇḍa*, p.

416 notes a stanza[8] from the *Rāmāyaṇa* to the effect that 'if nothing is available for the *Śrāddha*-ceremony, then even oil may be given. There is another interesting point[9] that if for a *Śrāddha*-ceremony the seeds of sesamum do not become available, then one may offer the libations of water to the dead ancestors even without sesamum. This stanza is quoted in the *Smṛticandrikā-Śrāddha-Kāṇḍa,* p.193. If, however, proper food cannot be provided to the brāhmaṇas at the *Śrāddha*-ceremony, then one may offer[10] the food which one takes daily to the brāhmaṇas. This view is mentioned in the *Smṛticandrikā-Śrāddha-Kāṇḍa,* p.46 and Bālaṁbhaṭṭi on the *Ācāra* portion of the *Mitākṣarā* on the *Yājñavalkya-Smṛti,* p.525. Dr. Kane, however, draws our attention to the commentary of Medhātithi on the *Manu-Smṛti,* V.7 in which the same stanza is found quoted. It may be observed here that Dr. Kane has not considered these sources of the *Dharma-Śāstra* authors; yet his study of the commentary of Medhātithi on the *Manu-Smṛti* has stood him in good stead.

(5) On the point of *Abhaya-Dāna,* Dr. Kane has forgotten a very important reference from the commentary of Aparārka on the *Yājñavalkya-Smṛti,* though he has quoted the views of Aparārka profusely in the course of his discussion in the volumes of *History of Dharma-Śāstra*. Aparārka in his commentary on the *Yājñavalkya-Smṛti,* p.385 refers to the view[11] of the *Rāmāyaṇa* that if a person has come for protection and leaves the house of a person without being protected, then while going he also takes away all his merit. This important view of the *Rāmāyaṇa* noted by Aparārka has escaped the notice of Dr. Kane.

(6) We have one important view[12] from the *Rāmāyaṇa* particularly relied upon by Lakṣmīdhara in his *Kṛtyakalpataru-Śuddhi-Kāṇḍa,* p.92. Here the meaning of the *Rāmāyaṇa* verse is that after the death of one's relative, one should stop sorrow and also stop shedding tears. If, however, one continues to shed tears after the death of a relative, then the dead relative may curse him. Here there is a reference[13] to the story of Bhuridyumna that he went to heaven by his good deeds; but he fell down from the heaven by the continuous tears of his relatives. This is possibly narrated to Rāma to keep control over the sorrow for the death of his revered father Daśaratha; otherwise he may fall down from the heaven.

(7) Here is a case of twisting of the spirit of the stanza from the *Rāmāyaṇa* on the part of the writers on *Dharma-Śāstra*. The stanza[14] under discussion is available to us from the *Rāmāyaṇa*, VI.11.55, particularly dealing with the reaction of Hanumān on the arrival of Bibhīṣaṇa to the side of Rāma. This stanza simply means that though an attempt is made by a person to curb his internal mind, any how it comes out (even against the will of a person). It is worth noting here that this stanza is found quoted by Śūlapāṇi[15] in his commentary on the *Yājñavalkya-Smṛti*, I.13-15 and Lakṣmīdhara in his *Kṛtyakalpataru-Vyavahāra-Kāṇḍa*[16], p.78. Lakṣmīdhara quotes this stanza to recognise the sign of a wicked person. Śūlpāṇi, however, has quoted this stanza to show as to how one should read the mind of a person. Here the topic under discussion is *pratyākalitam*.

Now I come to the third part of this chapter. Here I would like to discuss only those cases which have escaped the notices of the *Dharma-Śāstra* authors and also Dr. Kane.

(1) As regards the caste-system in the *Rāmāyaṇa*, Dr. Kane's position is already discussed by me in the first part of this chapter. Here it seems that two important references from the *Rāmāyaṇa* have escaped the notice of the above authorities. In the *Rāmāyaṇa*, II.57.37 we have a reference to the case of Śrāvaṇa who is killed by Daśaratha in the course of his hunting expedition. We come to know that Śrāvaṇa is an off-spring of a *Vaiśya* father and *Śūdra* mother, thereby giving rise to the caste known as *Karaṇa*. One may add here that both Mallinātha and Hemādri on the *Raghuvaṁśaṁ*, IX.76 also help us in this respect. (ii) In the *Rāmāyaṇa*, II.76.30, we have a reference to the caste known as *Vṛṣala*. (iii) One more important reference to a caste occurs in the *Rāmāyaṇa*, III. 54.18, where Sītā refers to Rāvaṇa as a *Cāṇḍāla*. All these three references are important from the *Dharma-Śāstra* point of view.

(2) As regards the *Dāna* aspect of *Dharma-Śāstra*, we have a reference to the *Prītidāna* to Sītā by the wife of Atri in the *Rāmāyaṇa*, II.114.11. Here Anusūyā out of love to Sītā gives the garment, ornaments and garlands of flowers. (ii) *Abhaya-Dāna* is already referred to by me in the second part of this chapter. Here it may be noted that Nīlakaṇṭha in his *Dāna-Mayūkha* quotes a stanza from the *Rāmāyaṇa* to stress the importance of *Abhaya-*

Dāna. (iii) As regards the varieties of *Dāna*, we have a very important view in the *Rāmāyaṇa*, I.12.28 that the donation made with the feeling of contempt is treated as the worst type of *Dāna*. Here attention may be drawn to Dr. Kane's important reference[17] to the *Mitākṣarā* on the *Yājñavalkya-Smṛti*, I.203 showing the varieties of donation. In the *Rāmāyaṇa*, it is expressed[18] that the a donation made with contemptuous feeling kills a donor. This important view of the *Rāmāyaṇa* has not attracted the mind of Dr. Kane.

(3) As regards the *Saṁskāra* aspect of the *Dharma-Śāstra*, we find that the marriage of Rāma and Sītā took place on the Uttārā Phālgunī constellation. This has a reference to the *Rāmāyaṇa*, I.17.22a and I.72.17. It is rather surprising that in the vast *Dharma-Śāstra* literature and even in Astrology, this constellation is not recommended. This is further evident from the present author's discussion[19] in the *Studies in the Dharma-Śāstra*. (ii) As regards the *saṁskāra* known as *Nāmakaraṇa*, it is only mentioned that this *Saṁskāra* was performed after eleven days from the birth of a child. But it may be noted here that no specification in respect of the constellations for this *Saṁskāra* has any place in the *Rāmāyaṇa*. It should be borne in mind that the later writers[20] on *Dharma-Śāstra* and astrology have gone to the extent of prescribing auspicious constellation for this sacrament. This will have to be regarded as a development made by the *Dharma-Śāstra* authors over the *Rāmāyaṇa* position. (iii) Marriage is regarded as an important sacrament. We get a good deal of discussion in the *Dharma-Śāstra* and *Gṛhyasūtra* literature in respect of selecting a girl as a wife for the marriage. In the *Rāmāyaṇa*, IV.23.8, Tārā the wife of Vālin, expresses the view[21] (only after the murder of Vālin by Rāma) that one should not give one's daughters in marriage to a person who is brave. In Dr. Kane's *History of Dharma-Śāstra*, we do not have any important discussion on this point. Here the readers may be referred to Hemādri's commentary *Darpaṇa* on the *Raghuvaṁśam*, VI.23. Here Hemādri refers to the viewpoint[22] of the *Smṛtikāra* known as *Vṛddha-Parāśara* who specifically holds the view that people should not give their daughters in marriage to the illiterate, staying far away, pauper, brave and those who have concentrated their mind on the path of salvation.

One is tempted to express the view that the feelings of Tārā are more adequately expressed in this stanza of *Vṛddha-Parāśara*. Perhaps the view in this respect has become more wider. While reading, it may be remarked that Mallinātha, however, is of no use to the readers, on this important point of *Dharma-Śāstra*.

(4) The position of a widow has also become a topic of discussion in the *Dharma-Śāstra* literature. Tārā, the wife of Vālin, has expressed her sorrowful feelings by stating categorically[23] that a lady devoid of husband, though having a (good) son and good wealth, to her credit, is called as a widow by the wise. Here the viewpoint of the *Kapila Smṛti* deserves special mention. This *Smṛtikāra* holds that if a lady is having a son, then she should not be called a widow. This peculiar view[24] of Kapila, has however, not become the centre of attraction of the scholars like Dr. Kane and others. Incidentally, it may be remarked here that the *Dharma-Śāstra* is essentially evolutionary and this important thought development over the *Rāmāyaṇa* should be noted as very significant in the evolutionary history of thoughts pertaining to *Dharma-Śāstra*.

(5) As regards the *Prāyaścitta* (expiation) aspect of *Dharma-Śāstra*, we have the identical views of the *Rāmāyaṇa* and the *Mahābhārata*. In the *Rāmāyaṇa*, IV.33.12, it is held that for an ungrateful person, there is no expiation as such. Attention may be drawn to the important view[25] of Yudhiṣṭhira in the *Mahābhārata*. He treats *Agni* as ungrateful for having burnt the three persons — Dhṛtarāṣṭra, Gāndhārī and Kuntī — after having personally received help from Arjuna in the matter of burning the Khāṇḍava forest. This incident refers to the *Mahābhārata*, 15.46.11 and 12.

(6) As regards the *Vyavahāra* aspect of *Dharma-Śāstra*, we have to deal with the problem of a murder of a woman. MM. Dr. Kane has touched this point slightly in his *History of Dharma-Śāstra*. Here the question of the murder of Tāḍakā otherwise known as Tāṭikā deserves some consideration. It is further evident from the *Rāmāyaṇa*, I.24.15-16 that Viśvāmitra provoked Rāma to murder Tāṭakā. He also supported his view by referring to two cases — the murder of the wife of the sage Bhṛgu by Viṣṇu and the murder of Mantharā the daughter of Virocana by Indra. We also get another case of Paraśurāma's killing his own mother

Reṇukā at the instance of his father Jamadagni. A clear reference to this occurs in the *Rāmāyaṇa,* II.18.27-29. For killing Tāṭakā, Viśvāmitra states the grounds[26] that she does not follow any *Dharma* and obstructs the regular function of the sacrificial activities. In the *Rāmāyaṇa,* Rāma tries to defend his case against Viśvāmitra. If, however, we consider the case in the light of the *Raghuvaṁśam,* XI.17 and Bhavabhūti's *Uttara-Rāma-Caritam,* the position changes considerably. In commenting on the *Raghuvaṁśam,* XI.17, both Mallinātha and Hemādri treat Tāṭakā as a rash woman and hold that there is nothing wrong if anyone kills such a rash person. They also quote verses from the *Manu-Smṛti* in their favour. In this very context, it would be proper to throw light on the viewpoints expressed in the *Mahābhārata.* In the *Mahābhārata,* V.80.18, Draupadī categorically refers to the viewpoint[27] of the knowers of *Dharma* that one incurs sin for not killing a person who deserves to be killed. She also adds that just as there is a sin in killing a person who does not deserve to be killed, in the similar manner there is a sin in not killing a person worthy of being killed. There is one more view[28] ascribed to Bṛhaspati in the *Mahābhārata,* VI.103.95 that even a senior-most rash person deserves to be killed. If, however, one considers the thoughts expressed above in respect of *Dharma-Śāstra,* particularly in relation to the murder of a woman, there is nothing wrong in the killing of Tāṭakā on the part of Rāma. In his notes (p.391) on the *Uttara-Rāma-Caritam,* Dr. G.K. Bhat treats this blunder on the part of Rāma as a case of humanisation of his character. Kṣemendra in his *Aucityavicāra-Carcā* has considered this problem from the point of view of propriety. The modern scholars and even the commentators of the *Uttara-Rāma-Caritam* like Ghanaśyāma have not considered the *Dharma-Śāstra* aspect of this case. Here it may be added that the *Manu-Smṛti,* IX.232 and *Viṣṇu-Dharma-Sūtra,* V.9-11 lay down the punishment of murder for women who are the killers of men, infants and brāhmaṇas. If, however, one is prepared to consider this case from the point of view of the science of interpretation otherwise known as *Pūrva-Mīmāṁsā,* it is possible to point out that the text of the *Manu-Smṛti* is of a general nature and the text of the *Rāmāyaṇa* will have to be treated as a case of *Viśeṣa-Śāstra* or a particular statement. Thus, by making the principle of the *Sāmānya-viśeṣa-nyāya* applicable to the present case, one can justify the behaviour of Rāma with reference to Tāṭakā.

(7) The concept of *Nyāsa* (deposit) is also a subject-matter of *Dharma-Śāstra*. In the *Rāmāyaṇa,* I.65.13, the bow of Śiva is treated as a deposit. The bow of Viṣṇu also has become the subject of *nyāsa* in the *Rāmāyaṇa,* I.74.21. It is further interesting to note that even a sword has become the subject of a deposit. It should be noted in this context that the non-sentinent things have become the subject of a deposit and this has naturally no place in the *Dharma-Śāstra* literature. Bharata treats the kingdom of Rāma as a deposit with him in the *Rāmāyaṇa,* II.107.14. It is further to be noted that Sugrīva takes care to return the kingdom of Vālin, which he preserved as a deposit as is evident from the *Rāmāyaṇa,* IV.10.4. Here one will have to admit that the concept of a deposit has become wider in the *Rāmāyaṇa*. The *Dharma-Śāstra* authors have, however, compressed the scope of this term as is evident from the discussion pertaining to this term in the commentaries of Viśvarūpa and Vijñāneśvara on the *Yājñavalkya-Smṛti,* II.66-67 and further discussion in the *History of Dharma-Śāstra* by Dr. Kane. In the *Rāmāyaṇa,* III. 43.16, Rāma hands over Sītā as a deposit in the hands of Lakṣmaṇa particularly when the former goes in persuit of Mārīca in the form of a golden deer. Treating a sentinent object (particularly woman) as a deposit in the hands of a trustworthy person is, indeed, a novel contribution of the *Rāmāyaṇa* to the *Dharma-Śāstra*. Needless to say that this has largely influenced Bhāsa in his *Svapnavāsavadattam*. Kālidāsa has, however, made a distinct advance over this concept by treating Śakuntalā — an unmarried daughter — as a deposit in the hands of a father. This short survey reveals that this concept has undergone evolution. Incidentally, it may be noted here that in the *Mahābhārata,* Dhṛtarāṣṭra hands over the people and his kingdom to Yudhiṣṭhira as a matter of deposit.

(8) The concept of *Bhṛṇahā* — (1) killer of an embryo plays very very important part in the *Dharma-Śāstra* literature. MM. Dr. Kane has discussed this topic at good length in the *History of Dharma-Śāstra* and even Dr. P.K. Gode and others have given the meanings of this word in the Sanskrit Dictionary originally prepared by V.S. Apte and revised by these scholars. But whatever

meanings are not assigned to this term by these scholars, alone are given in the present discussion. (i) Bharata holds that the behaviour of Kaikeyī is responsible for the death of Daśaratha and goes to the extent of treating this behaviour as a case of or amounting to *Bhṛṇahatyā*. This is evident from the *Rāmāyaṇa,* II.68.4. Possibly Bharata treats the death of a principal person in the family as the destruction of the family and goes to the extent of treating it as a case of *Bhṛṇahatyā*. (ii) In the *Rāmāyaṇa*, before fighting with Vālin, Dundubhi expresses an important thought[29] on this point. This thought simply means that one who kills an intoxicated person, afflicted person, a person overcome by passions, and one who has slept, is treated as indulging in *Bhṛṇahā*. (iii) In the *Mahābhārata,* I.78.33, this concept[30] of *Bhṛṇahā* is connected with the sexual life. Here it simply means that one who does not approach a woman desirous of sexual intercourse, is treated as *Bhṛṇahā*. (iv) In the *Mahābhārata,* it is further held that one who does not approach a married wife after the period of menstruation is treated as a *Bhṛṇahā*. (v) In the *Dharma-Śāstra* literature, it is Nīlakaṇṭha who in his *Prāyaścitta Mayūkha,* p.82 quotes the view[31] of *pracetas* to the effect that one who kills a pregnant woman, a pregnant cow, child and an aged man is treated as *Bhṛṇahā*. This explanation from the pen of *Pracetas* has escaped the notice of many scholars. It would be evident from this explanation that the concept of a *Bhṛṇahā* is made wider by the *Smṛtikāra* as compared with the explanation available from the *Rāmāyaṇa* and the *Mahābhārata*. (vi) Śabara goes to the extent of holding that killing a child in the womb is as good as killing a prospective sacrificer. All this survey leads one to the conclusion that this concept has undergone evolution.

The above discussion reveals that the *Rāmāyaṇa* betrays important aspects of *Dharma-Śāstra* and in the later *Dharma-Śāstra* literature some modifications have taken place and sometimes the concepts become wider or even narrower as per the outlook developed by the *Smṛtikāras*, commentators and even the *Mahābhārata*. In passing, one will have to admit that the above discussion would prove to be very interesting and illuminating on the *Dharma-Śāstra* aspects of the *Rāmāyaṇa*.

References

1. P.V. Kane, *History of Dharma-Śāstra,* Vol.I, pp.399-402; Vol.II, pp. 87, 109, 395, 445, 510n, 511, 513, 551n, 558n, 562, 578, 594, 627, 641, 720, 733, 1145n, 1238; Vol. III, 2, 6, 24, 29, 37, 42, 46, 47n, 49, 53n, 62, 71, 72, 95-96, 105-106, 108, 129, 171, 177, 180, 190, 195, 203, 209n, 243, 846; Vol. IV, 214, 223, 233, 237, 416, 534, 597, 647n, 653n, 688, 707, 710; Vol. V, p. 1629.
2. *Ibid.,* Vol.I, pp. 388-89.
3. S.G. Moghe, *Studies in the Dharma-Śāstra,* pp. 4, 5 and 14; Also see P.V. Kane's *History of Dharma*-Śtāstra, Vol.II.
4. नैवाङ्गनानां दयितो नापि द्वेष्योऽस्ति कश्चन । सर्वमेवावलम्बन्ते लता गहनजा इव ॥ कृत्यकल्पतरु *व्यवहारकाण्ड,* p. 607.
5. औरसानपि पुत्रान् हि त्यजन्त्यहितकारिण: । समर्थान् संप्रतिगृह्णान्ति परानपि नराधिपा:॥ बालंभट्टी *व्यवहाराध्याय,* p. 240.
6. तवैव वंशे सगरो ज्येष्ठपुत्रमुपारुधत् ।
   असमञ्ज इति ख्यातं तथाऽयं गन्तुमर्हति ॥
   Ibid, p. 240.
7. पौरकार्यं हि यो राजा न करोति सभास्थित: । व्यक्तं स नरके घोरे पच्यते नात्र संशय: ॥ पृथ्वीचन्द्र *व्यवहार प्रकाश,* p. 62.
8. *स्मृतिचांद्रिका-श्राद्धकाण्ड,* p. 416 (Gharpure's edition).
9. देवण्णभट्ट's Comments on this stanza deserve mention. तिलालाभेऽपि तद्विहीन तर्पणाभिप्रायम् । *Ibid.,* p. 193.
10. इङ्गुदैर्बदरैबिल्वै: रामस्तर्पयते पितॄन् ।
    यदन्न: पुरुषो लोके तदन्नास्तस्य देवता: ॥
    Ibid, p. 181.
11. विनष्ट: पश्यतो यस्य रक्षितु: शरणागत: । आदाय सुकृतं तस्मात् सर्वं गच्छत्यरक्षित: ॥ *अपरार्क,* p. 385.
12. अतिशोकानले दग्ध: पिता ते स्वर्गत: प्रभु: ।
    शपेन् त्वां मन्युनाविष्ट: तस्मादुत्तिष्ठ राघव ॥
    कृत्यकल्पतरु-शुद्धिकाण्ड, p. 92.
13. *Ibid.,* p. 93.
14. आकारश्छाद्यमानोऽपि न शक्यो विनिगूहितुम् ।
    बलाद्धि विवृणोत्येव भावमन्तर्गतं नृणाम् ॥
    रामायण, VI. 11.55.
15. आकारश्छाद्यमानोऽपि निग्रहीतुं न शक्यते ।
    बलाद्धि विवृणोत्येव भावमन्तर्गतं नृणाम् ॥
    शूलपाणि's *दीपकलिका* on *याज्ञवल्क्यस्मृति,* I. 13-15, p. 38. Here the first line presents different readings.
16. *कृत्यकल्पतरु-व्यवहारकाण्ड,* p.78 agrees with the readings in the *रामायण,* पृथ्वीचन्द्र, *व्यवहारप्रकाश,* p.62, however, reads शक्तो for शक्यो of the *रामायण.*

17. P.V. Kane, *History of Dharma-Śastra,* Vol. II/I, p. 113.

18. अवज्ञया न दातव्यं कस्यचित् लीलयाऽपि वा ।
अवज्ञया कृतं हन्यात् दातारं नात्र संशयः ॥
रामायण, I. 12.28.

19. S.G. Moghe, *Studies in the Dharma-Śāstra* pp. 179-80.

20. *Ibid.*, pp. 179-80.

21. शूराय न प्रदातव्या कन्या खलु विपश्चिता ।
शूरभार्यां हतां पश्य सद्यो मां विधवा कृताम् ॥
रामायण, IV. 23.8.

22. दूरस्थानामविद्यानां मोक्षधर्मानुयायिनाम् ।
शूराणां निर्धनानां च न देया कन्यका बुधैः ॥ *वृद्धपराशर* quoted by हेमाद्रि on *रघुवंश*, VI. 23.

23. पतिहीना तु या नारी कामं भवतु पुत्रिणी ।
धनधान्यैः सुपूर्णापि विधवेत्युच्यते बुधैः ॥
रामायण, IV. 23.12.

24. जीवपुत्रा या नारी विधवेति न चोच्यते ।
पतिपुत्रविहीना या विधवेति उच्यते बुधैः ॥
कपिलस्मृति, St. 593. (*स्मृतिसदंर्भ*, Vol. V.).

25. Cf. *Mahābhārata,* 15.46.11-12.

26. राज्यभारनियुक्तानामेष धर्मः सनातनः ।
अधर्म्यां जहि काकुत्स्थ धर्मो ह्यस्या न विद्यते ॥
रामायण, I. 24.16.

27. यथावध्ये भवेद्दोषो वध्यमाने जनार्दन ।
स वध्यस्यावधे दृष्ट इति धर्मविदो विदुः ॥
महाभारत, V. 80.18.

28. ज्यायांसमपि चेच्छक्र गुणैरपि समन्वितम् ।
आततायिनमामन्त्र्य हन्याद्घातकमागतम् ॥
महाभारत, VI. 103.95.

29. यो हि मत्तं प्रमत्तं वा सुप्तं वा रहितं भृशम् ।
हन्यात् स भ्रूणहा लोके त्वाद्विधं मदमोहितम् ॥
रामायण, IV.II.34.

30. अभिकामां स्त्रियं यस्तु गम्यां रहसि याचितः ।
नोपैति स च धर्मेषु भ्रूणहेत्युच्यते बुधैः ॥
महाभारत, I.78.33.

31. स्त्री-गर्भिणी, गो-गार्भिणी, बाल-वृद्धवधे भ्रूणहा भवति । *प्रायश्चित्तमयूख*, p.82 (Gujarati Printing Press edition, Bombay).

P.S: Here the *उत्तररामचरितम्* ed. by G.K. Bhat, Popular Publishing House, Surat, 1965 is used for राम's humanisation.

4

Dharma-Śāstra Concept of *Nyāsa* and Sanskrit Literature

MM. Dr. P.V. Kane has discussed the topic of *Nyāsa* in his *History of Dharma-Śāstra,* Vol. III, pp. 454-60. He has dealt with the topic at full length. Incidentally, it may be noted in this very context that Dr. Kane has also made incidental references to the *Rāmāyaṇa, Mahābhārata* and classical Sanskrit literature in the course of his discussion in his voluminous work. But in the context of *Nyāsa,* however, it is noticed that some of the important sources have escaped his eagle eye and hence it is necessary to do some justice to this topic in the light of the evidences furnished by the *Rāmāyaṇa, Mahābhārata* and classical Sanskrit literature. Here it may be mentioned that I am going to restrict the discussion pertaining to Bhāsa, Kālidāsa, Daṇḍin and Śūdraka. My main aim, however, is to bring to light the important aspect that the concept of *Nyāsa* has undergone several changes and the theory of evolution becomes fittingly applicable to this very concept.

Before proceeding with the discussion from the point of above sources, it would be necessary to clarify the position of *Dharma-Śāstra* views on this concept. MM. Dr. P.V. Kane has shown that there are three terms in the Sanskrit Dictionary — *Nikṣepa, Upanidhi* and *Nyāsa* — which are used synonymously and more correctly understood by the author of the Amarakośa, as noted earlier. It must be stated here that the *Manu-Smṛti,* VIII. 149=Vasiṣṭha *Dharma Sūtra,* 16-18=*Kauṭilīya Arthaśāstra,* III.12 treat *Nikṣepa* and *Upanidhi* as distinct. There is however, a sharp difference of opinion between Viśvarūpa and Vijñāneśvara on the *Yājñāvalkya-Smṛti,* II.67, on the point of counting. Nikṣepa[1] is a deposit entrusted to a man after counting the articles in his presence. Here the view of Viśvarūpa[2] is that when the article is to be deposited with another person, its nature should be properly described. Vijñāneśvara, however, in his Mitākṣarā[3] on the *Yājñavalkya-Smṛti,* II.67 takes *nyāsa* as an article handed over to some member in the house for delivering the same to the head of the house and particularly in his absence. Here it must be stated that in the explanation of Vijñāneśvara, there is no reference to the counting or measuring of the article, which is perhaps the strongest point in the elucidation of Viśvarūpa.

In this very context, it would be pertinent to refer to the view of Mitramiśra, the author of the *Vyavahāra Prakāśa.* He categorically states[4] that when the article is properly measured or unmeasured in the very presence of a person to whom it is to be handed over by a person and then handed over to him as a deposit through his son, then it is treated as *nikṣepa.* His explanation of *Nyāsa* is virtually the same as is recorded earlier as that of Vijñāneśvara. He further adds that *Upanidhi* means[5] handing over a sealed object, without counting the same, to the depositee. From this discussion, it is quite evident that Mitramiśra completely agrees with Vijñāneśvara on the point of *Nyāsa,* though in explaining the other terms he seems to differ from the author of the Amarakośa.

MM. Dr. P.V. Kane has also further added that the deposit is to be handed over in the presence of a witness and it is also to be returned to the depositor in the presence of a witness and if not returned, he will have to pay the price or perform an ordeal to prove his innocence in the event of the theft of a deposit. All these points and even others are passed over here for the simple reason that the background given above is sufficient for an enlightened reader to appreciate the points which I am going to put forth before the readers for the proper understanding of the theory of evolution.

It would be interesting to know the approach of the *Rāmāyaṇa* to this concept. In the *Rāmāyaṇa,* I.65.13, the bow of Śiva is treated as a deposit. The bow of Viṣṇu[6] is also regarded as a deposit in the *Rāmāyaṇa,* I.74.21. Even a sword[7] is accepted as a *nyāsa* in the *Rāmāyaṇa,* III.8.15. These three examples clearly go to prove that in respect of the things mentioned the question of counting or measuring does not, at all, arise. One may say here that the nature of the above-mentioned things, though not specifically clarified, is so evident that it hardly needs any specification. From these examples, it is further evident that gold or silver need not be treated as the only objects or articles for deposit. What these examples convey is that a thing which is the most important from the point of view of a particular person can become the object of a *nyāsa* or deposit.

It may be further pointed out that Bharata accepts the responsibility of the king from Rāma as a case of *nyāsa* at the *Rāmāyaṇa,* II.107.14. Bharata also agrees to return the kingdom to Rāma on his coming from the forest and particularly after the expiry of the stipulated 14 years. One may add here that even Sugrīva accepts the responsibility of the kingdom of Vālin, as and by way of deposit and returns[8] the same to him particularly on his return. If one bears in mind that even a kingdom can become an object of *Nyāsa,* then one may be fair in drawing the legitimate conclusion that in the *Rāmāyaṇa,* the concept of a deposit is employed in a wider sense. One may also be tempted to state that the writers on *Dharma-Śāstra* in particular, have compressed this wider concept particularly in dealing with the *Vyavahāra* aspect of the *Dharma-Śāstra.* Incidentally, it may also be added here that in handing over the above deposits, no regular formalities appear to have been undergone and particularly those which are noticeable in the vast *Dharma-Śāstra* literature.

One would be surprised to note that even Sītā has become the subject of a deposit at the hands of Rāma particularly in the *Rāmāyaṇa,* III.43.16[9]. Before hotly persuing the demon Mārīca in the form of a golden dear, in the *Rāmāyaṇa,* Rāma hands over Sītā to Lakṣmaṇa as and by way of a deposit. From this glaring example, it is further evident that not only insentinent object but even the sentinent object has become the subject of a deposit in the *Rāmāyaṇa.* It must be mentioned that the writers on *Dharma-Śāstra* have not, at all, consulted or cared to read the *Rāmāyaṇa* and the *Mahābhārata* from the point of view of the concept of a deposit.

It would be interesting to draw the attention of the readers to the evidence from the *Āśramavāsika Parvan* of the *Mahābhārata.* When, however, Dhṛtarāṣṭra decides to go to the forest, he hands over all the people of the kingdom, as a deposit at the hands of Yudhiṣṭhira in the *Mahābhārata,* 15.14.13[10]. He also categorically states that (all of) you have become a deposit at the hands of this warrior Yudhiṣṭhira. From this piece of textual evidence, it goes without saying that, in handing over the citizens as a deposit at the hands of Yudhiṣṭhira, the concept of *nyāsa* has become more wide and perhaps more comprehensive. It is also surprising that in the *Mahābhārata,* 15.12.17, Dhṛtarāṣṭra gives an important piece of advice to Yudhiṣṭhira that after having acquired a kingdom, one should establish tranquillity in the kingdom and may deposit it with the rich[11]. This information becomes available to the readers in the speech of Dhṛtarāṣṭra. Here the expression used is *nikṣipet* which is also understood in the *Mahābhārata* in the sense of a deposit. Hence there is some point when in the Amarakośa the words *nikṣepa, upanidhi* and *nyāsa* are used synonymously.

If, however, one consults Bhāsa's play the *Svapnavāsavadattam,* then one would realise that the minister Yaugandharāyaṇa hands over Vāsavadattā to the princess Padmāvatī as and by way of a deposit. In this very context, it would be pertinent to note the remark of the chamberlain that it is very difficult to protect or guard a deposit[12]. It may be noted here that Vāsavadattā is handed over to Padmāvatī, for a political purpose. Besides, it was expected that Padmāvatī would stand as a surety or guarantee for the character of Vāsavadattā. It may be only casually observed that treating Vāsavadattā as a deposit (particularly a married lady as a deposit) is the direct influence of the *Rāmāyaṇa* on the writing of Bhāsa.

The use of ornaments as a deposit also occurs in the *Cārudattam* of Bhāsa[13]. In the first Act, it is Vasantasenā, the Gaṇikā, who hands over the ornaments to Cārudatta, particularly when she was afraid of the rascals such as Śakāra, Viṭa and others. Here while handing over the ornaments to Cārudatta, the conditions of *Dharma-Śāstra* are not fulfilled. From the fourth Act of the *Cārudattam,* it becomes quite clear that she deposited the ornaments with Cārudatta, out of good confidence or trust in his virtues[14]. This is particularly clear from the remark of the Vidūṣaka in the fourth Act. Incidentally it would be worthy of note to point out the remarks of the Vidūṣaka that the Gaṇikā did not show any formality in accepting the pearl necklace which was handed over to her, on the loss of the ornaments of the Gaṇikā. In fact, the *Cārudattam* partially fulfils the conditions of the *Dharma-Śāstra* in respect of a deposit that if a deposit is lost, one must make good the loss, though the primary condition of weighing or measuring the ornaments is not adequately fulfilled in the body of the drama. From this discussion, it is quite clear that the ornament is deposited out of truth or confidence in the good qualities of another person.

If, however, we turn to the drama *Śākuntalam* of Kālidāsa, we would come to know that Kālidāsa, has indeed, made a distinct advance in the concept of *nyāsa*. Here the attention of the readers may be drawn to the last stanza of the fourth Act of the *Śākuntalam,* in which Kaṇva treats *Śakuntalā* — an unmarried daughter as a deposit of a husband with a father. Treating an unmarried daughter as a deposit[15] is indeed an advancement over both the *Rāmāyaṇa* and the *Svapnavāsavadattam* of Bhāsa.

Here incidentally, it may be pointed out that in the fourth Act of the *Śākuntalam*[16], Śakuntalā goes to the extent of handing over a creeper as a deposit at the hands of her two friends — Anasūyā and Priyaṁvadā. Here one may be tempted to advance the view that in the Kālidāsian plays, nature is a living organism and the handing over a creeper as a deposit is also to be treated as a case of distinct advance in the concept of the *Nyāsa*.

In the *Mṛcchakaṭikam* of Śūdraka, however, the first thing that one notices is that both the expressions *nyāsa* and *nikṣipyante* are used synonymously and without observing any conditions of the *Dharma-Śāstra* as such. While handing over the ornaments as a deposit to the depositee, Vasantasenā passes a significant remark that deposits are entrusted or deposited with the persons and not with the houses[17]. From this important observation of Vasantasenā, it goes without saying her supreme confidence in his virtues and particularly the virtues of Cārudatta who has become pauper at that time. Here also the question of handing over a deposit to the son of the head of the family is out of consideration. In the present case, however, she has directly handed over her ornaments to Cārudatta without weighing or measuring the same. This again is a good proof that the conditions of *Dharma-Śāstra* are thrown overboard in the classical Sanskrit literature.

In the *Daśakumāracaritam* of Daṇḍin, however, the concept of *nyāsa* appears to have been used rather differently. Here the son of Kāmapāla, otherwise known as Mūlārṇava is given as a deposit by the *Yakṣa kanyā Tārāvalī* to the queen Vasumatī just to shampoo the feet of the king Rājavāhana. It is rather surprising that this Mūlārṇava is shown as so brave that he is capable of fighting with thousands of warriors combined together. Incidentally, it may be remarked[18] that the purpose at the back of a deposit is to shampoo the feet of a king, a purpose which is definitely unknown to *Dharma-Śāstra* literature and even to other works on classical Sanskrit literature.

From the foregoing discussion, the following legitimate conclusion may be drawn just to show how the evolution has taken place in the concept of *Nyāsa*.

(1) In the *Amarakośa* and the *Mṛcchakaṭikam*, the terms — *Nyāsa* and *Nikṣepa* — are used synonymously.

(2) In the *Dharma-Śāstra* literature, there is a difference of opinion between Viśvarūpa and Vijñaneśvara and Mitramiśra is in agreement with Vijñāneśvara.

(3) In the *Rāmāyaṇa*, the concept of *Nyāsa* is used in a wider sense of kingdom as a deposit.

(4) In the *Mahābhārata*, however, instead of laying down the limitations of the kingdom, the citizen of the kingdom have become the subject of a deposit. This is also a more wider use of the concept.

(5) We notice the influence of the idea of a married lady as a deposit in the *Rāmāyaṇa* over the writing of Bhāsa.

(6) Kālidāsa has made a distinct advance in this concept by treating even unmarried lady as a deposit of a husband with the father of a daughter.

(7) The writers of the classical Sanskrit literature have gone to the extent of treating both sentinent and non-sentinent objects as the subject of a deposit.

(8) The purposes for which the concept of *Nyāsa* is utilised seem to be different. The purposes such as confidence in the virtue

of a person, shampooing the feet of a person, love for a person or even for a political purpose.

(9) The Classical Sanskrit and the *Rāmāyaṇa* and the *Mahābhārata* evidences go to prove that the rules of *Dharma-Śāstra* are not at all followed. Hence here we find only the liberal use of the term, though some of the conditions are seen to have been observed in respect of returning the deposit to the concerned persons.

(10) Strictly speaking, whatever are the conditions laid down in the *Dharma-Śāstra* literature for a *Nyāsa*, are not, at all, followed in the usual practice of the people as revealed by the works of reputed poets.

References

1. ग्राहकस्य समक्षं गणयित्वा स्थापितं निक्षेप: ।
   मित्रमिश्र's *व्यवहारप्रकाश*, p. 280.
2. न्यासो निर्दिष्टस्वरूपं द्रव्यं यद्रक्षणार्थं समर्पितम् । विश्वरूप on *याज्ञवल्क्यस्मृति*, II.66.
3. न्यासो नाम गृहस्वामिनेऽदर्शयित्वा तत्परोक्षमेव गृहजनहस्ते प्रक्षेपो गृहस्वामिने समर्पणीयमिति । मिताक्षरा on *याज्ञवल्क्यस्मृति*, II. 67
4. गृहस्वामिनोऽसमक्षं गणितमगणितं वा तास्मिन्नागते एतद् दातव्यमित्युक्त्वान्यस्य तत्पुत्रादे: हस्ते दत्त: न्यास: । मित्रामिश्र's *व्यवहारप्रकाश*, p. 280.
5. मुद्राङ्कितं समक्षमगणितं स्थापितमुपानिधि: इति ।
   Ibid., p. 280.
6. इदं च वैष्णवं राम धनु: परपुरंजयम् ।
   त्तच्चीके भार्गवे प्रादाद्विष्णु: स न्यासमुक्तमम्
   रामायण, I. 74.21.
7. तास्मिंस्तदाश्रमे निहित खड्ग उत्तम: ।
   स न्यासविधिना दत्त: पुण्ये पतीस तिष्ठत:॥
   रामायण, III. 8.15.
8. न्यासभूतमिदं राज्यं तव निर्यातयाम्यहम् ।
   रामायण, IV. 10.4.
9. न्यासभूतासि वैदेहि न्यस्ता मयि महात्मना।
   रामेण त्वां वरारोहे न त्वां त्यक्तुमिहोत्सहे॥
   रामायण, III. 43.16.
10. एष न्यासो मया दत्त: सर्वेषां वो युधिष्ठिर ।
    भवन्तोऽस्य च वीरस्य न्यासभूता मया कृता ॥
    महाभारत, 15.14.13.
11. लब्धं प्रशमयेद्राजा निक्षिपेत् धनिनो नरान् ।
    ज्ञात्वा स्वविषयं तं च सामादिभिरुपक्रमेत् ॥
    महाभारत, 15.12.17 (B.O.R.I, Pune)

12. दु:ख न्यासस्य रक्षणम् । स्वप्नवासवदत्तम्, I. 10
भासनाटकचक्रम्, p. 5.
13. *चारुदत्तम्,* Act I before St. 29
भासनाटकचक्रम् p. 212.
14. तत्रभवतश्चारुदत्तस्य गुणप्रत्यायननिमित्तं खलु त्वयालंकारस्तस्मिन् निक्षिप्त: । स तेन द्यूते हारित: ।
चारुदत्तम्, Act IV. before verse 6, *भासनाटकचक्रम्,* p. 244.
15. प्रत्यर्पितन्यास इवान्तरात्मा ।
शाकुन्तलम्, IV. 22.
16. हला, एषा द्वयोरुभयोर्हस्ते निक्षेप: ।
शाकुन्तलम् Act IV after st. 13.
17. पुरुषेषु न्यासा: निक्षित्प्यन्ते न पुनर्गेहेषु ।
मृच्छकटिक, Act I.
18. यस्तस्य सुतो यक्षकन्यया देवस्य राजवाहनस्य पादशुश्रूषार्थं देव्या वसुमत्या हस्तन्यास: कृत: सोऽहमस्मि।
दशकुमारचरितम्, p. 177.

5

Influence of the *Rāmāyaṇa* on the *Abhijñāna Śākuntalam*

A NEW LIGHT

In this Chapter, an attempt is being made to point out with conclusive evidence the influence of the *Rāmāyaṇa* on the *Śākuntalam*[1] of Kālidāsa. Dr. H.B. Jain has already pointed out in his article some aspects of the influence of the *Rāmāyaṇa* on the *Śākuntalam*. In this chapter, I have, therefore, tried to deal with those new points that are not touched or handled by the learned doctor in his article, with a view to throwing new light on this topic.

In the first Act, when the charioteer was just explaining to his master the cause as to why the deer and advanced to a long distance he came to a level ground. This passage[2] shows that the knowledge of the evenness and unevenness of the ground is absolutely necessary for a charioteer running the chariot. This knowledge is possible in the case of our dramatist in view of his having read the *Rāmāyaṇa, Yuddhakāṇḍa*[3] 104.19, where the essential knowledge of the position of a ground and other factors is incidentally conveyed to a charioteer who is required to go to the battle-field. Kālidāsa has, it appears, fruitfully employed the principle of this knowledge in the *Śākuntalam*.

The idea that the performers of the religious duties become possessed of a guardian due to the visit of an officer of the King or a King to the penance-grove hinted at in the first Act of the *Śākuntalam*, in the words of Anasūyā "*sanāthā idānīṁ dharma-cāriṇaḥ*" also has its trace in the *Rāmāyaṇa, Araṇyakāṇḍa*, 7.8, when in particular, Rāmā visits the penance-grove of the sage known as Sutīkṣṇa. The following line[4] uttered by the sages deserves to be specially noted. This idea must have been at the back of the mind of our gifted poet.

The idea of respecting or worshipping the king with fruits and nuts by the sages, referred to in the second Act of the *Śākuntalam,* when the two hermit boys approach the king Duṣyanta with fruits (*iti phalāni upāharataḥ*) for help. This has its trace in the *Rāmāyaṇa, Araṇyakāṇda,*[5] 12.31, where the sage Agastya worships Rāma by offering him fruits and roots. Possibly Kālidāsa has adopted the mode by which the king is to be respected or worshipped by the sages. In this connection, the only possible difference that can be pointed out by a careful reader is that in the second Act of the *Śākuntalam,* the two hermit boys approach the King for help and here in the *Araṇyakāṇḍa,* Rāma visits the hermitage of Agastya; otherwise the mode of worship adopted in both works is also the same.

The conception that the king rightfully protecting the subjects gets the merit of the sages, put in the mouth of the king Duṣyanta[6] also can be traced to the *Rāmāyaṇa, Araṇyakāṇḍa,*[7] 6.14, when the sage Śarabhaṅga went to heaven, the other sages approached Rāma for help and uttered this stanza. In this respect, it is possible to say that Kālidāsa has differed from the *Rāmāyaṇa* in respect of the share of the merit, the king gets from the sages, and followed the *Mahābhārata.* Here incidentally it deserves to be noticed that Kālidāsa has not made a reference to the fact that the king shares the demerits of the subjects too. The idea of the king sharing the demerits of the subjects is very well brought out by Karṇa in the *Karṇa-parvan* of the *Mahābhārata* while making the down-right condemnation of the people from the Vāhīka country. The stanza[8] put in the mouth of Karṇa may be noted in this context.

The episode of Triśaṅku incidentally referred to by the remark of the Vidūṣaka in the words *"Triśaṅku ivāntarāle tiṣṭha"* in the second Act of the *Śākuntalam,* also can be traced back to the *Rāmāyaṇa, Bālakāṇḍa,*[9] *Adhyāya* 60, when Viśvāmitra decides to send Triśaṅku to the heaven in the bodily form and gods too, do not allow him to come up and hence the poor chap was required to stay in the midway. It is equally possible to say here that Kālidāsa might have at the back of his mind the present story from the *Harivaṁśa,* 1.12.23 of the *Mahābhārata.*

The idea of the Viśākhā constellation appearing beautiful in the company of the moon, referred to in the third Act of the *Śākuntalam* by the king Duṣyanta[10] also can be traced back to the *Rāmāyaṇa, Yuddhakāṇḍa,* 76.15. The following lines[11] in this context deserve to be quoted. In this respect, it can be incidentally noted that Kālidāsa has used the expression *śaśāṅka lekhā* and Vālmiki has used the expression *Pūrṇa-candra*. But here one will have to admit that the use of this idea on the part of Kālidāsa is really ingeneous and poetic as compared to the one in the *Rāmāyaṇa* in view of the context in which it is used.

In the fifth Act of the *Śākuntalam,* when both Duṣyanta and Śakuntalā argue out their cases by making cogent argument, Śakuntalā makes a downright condemnation of Duṣyanta[12] thereby indicating that he resembles a dangerous well, the opening of which is covered with grass and which consequently looks like ordinary ground. The above simile in the case of our poet is possible in view of his knowledge of the *Rāmāyaṇa Kiṣkindhākāṇḍa, Adhyāya* 17. Here the incident is like this. When Rāma discharges an arrow at Vālī at the instance of Sugrīva, Vālī starts making downright condemnation of Rāma, by comparing him to a well covered with grass. In this connection, the lines[13] actually put in the mouth of Vālī by the poet Vālmīki deserve to be noted. This significant simile of Vālmīki, must be at the back of the mind of our poet. The only possible distinction that can be pointed out by a discernible reader is that in the *Rāmāyaṇa,* Vālī finds fault with Rāma by using this simile; while in the fifth Act of the *Śākuntalam,* it is Śakuntalā who tries to find fault with the king Duṣyanta. The simile in this context is apt in bringing the point home. Here one has to keep at the back of one's mind that both Vālī and Śakuntalā are the parties who are hurt by the opponents. One was physically and perhaps mortally wounded; while the other one, i.e., Śakuntalā was mentally wounded. How ingeneous is the use of this simile on the part of our dramatist Kālidāsa!

Again the idea of Śāraṅgrava in the fifth Act of the *Śākuntalam,* that the position[14] of a married woman becomes pitiable and ridiculous in the absence of her association with her husband also has its trace in the *Rāmāyaṇa*[15], *Ayodhyākāṇḍa,* when Sītā successfully pleads her case for persuading Rāma to take her to the forest. In this context, the expression *kulasyādhayaḥ* used by Kaṇva in his pithy advice to his worthy daughter Śakuntalā in the fourth Act, must be borne in mind by a careful student of the Kālidāsian litrature. One may note here that the expression *kulapānsani* of *Rāmāyana* must be at the back of the mind of Kālidāsa in using the expression *kulasyādhayaḥ* in the *Śākuntalam*.

Duṣyanta's significant remark "*anirvarṇanīyam para-kalatraṁ*" in the fifth Act of the *Śākuntalam*, looking at Śakuntalā or *dāratyāgī bhavāmyāho parastrīsparśapāṅsulaḥ*, V 29, is indeed a considerable advancement upon the particular portion of the *Rāmāyaṇa*. In the *Rāmāyaṇa, Araṇyakāṇḍa*, Mārīca while trying to advice Rāvaṇa, very rightly points out that *paradārābhimarśana*, i.e., molestation of the wife of other tends to produce a great sin and will end in the complete annihilation of the family of the demons. And hence Rāvaṇa should swerve from molesting the wife of other person. In this respect the lines[16] from the mouth of Mārīca will serve as an instance in point. Kālidāsa has really made an advancement in the moral standard upon Vālmīki by making the two comments in the *Śākuntalam*. Kālidāsa's hero is not ready to cast an (amorous) glance at the wives of others. Far from it is the talk of the molestation of the wives of others.

A reference to the *rohita* fish in *Praveśaka* of the sixth Act of the *Śākuntalam*, is also very significant. We do not get any definite information about this *rohita* fish elsewhere. But a reference to this fish occurs in the *Rāmāyaṇa, Araṇyakāṇḍa*[17]. While going to the *Ṛṣyamūka* mountain, Rāma points out that in the *puṣkariṇī* Pampā on the way, there are different kinds of fishes. And in the list of these fishes, there is a reference to the *rohita* fish. This incident of the *Araṇyakāṇḍa* might be at the back of the mind of our poet Kālidāsa in making a reference to the *rohita*, particularly in the sixth Act of the *Śākuntalam*.

A reference to Mātali in the heart of the sixth Act, again is very significant. Here Mātali, at the command of Indra, approaches Duṣyanta requesting him to mount on the car of Indra for going to the heaven in order to defeat the group of demons called Durjaya at the head of the battle. In the *Rāmāyaṇa* also in order to bring about the destruction of Rāvaṇa for releasing the gods from the clutches of Rāvaṇa, Indra sends Mātali with a chariot on the *terra firma* just to help Rāma against the battle with Rāvaṇa. This is referred to in the *Rāmāyaṇa, Yuddhakāṇḍa*. In this respect, the verses[18] from the *Yuddhakāṇḍa* deserve to be noticed. In the *Rāmāyaṇa,* Indra was mainly concerned with the welfare of the gods and for that purpose sends Mātali with a chariot. Here in the sixth Act of the *Śākuntalam,* Indra wanted to help the gods in destroying the demons and so takes the help of Duṣyanta and for that purpose he sends Mātali with a chariot. Is this not a close similarity between the *Rāmāyaṇa* and the *Śākuntalam*?

In the *Praveśaka* of the sixth Act of the *Śākuntalam,* the policemen[19] tell the fisherman that he will be an offering to a vulture or he will see the mouth of a dog. Here it is evident that Kālidāsa is possibly referring to the severe punishment imposed upon the thieves caught red-handed. Though it is true that in the *Rāmāyaṇa,* such a punishment is not imposed upon any one, yet in the *Rāmāyaṇa*'s *Yuddhakāṇḍa,* there is a reference to the offering of the body of a person dead in a battle to the vultures, jackals and others, probably for eating purpose. In this respect, the following stanza[20] from the *Rāmāyaṇa*'s *Yuddhakāṇḍa* deserves special attention. The only possible difference between the two statements is that in the *Rāmāyaṇa*'s *Yuddhakāṇḍa,* Indrajit utters this stanza with special reference to Lakṣmaṇa; while in the *Śākuntalam,* the second policeman address the fisherman with this remark. Any way, the expression "*gṛdhrāśca nipatantu tvām*" of the *Rāmāyaṇa* is in agreement with the expression *gṛdhrabalirbhaviṣyasi* of the *Śākuntalam.*

Some of the popular poetic conventions or the superstitions used by Kālidāsa such as the throbbing of the arm, eye and the idea that the tears of sorrow are hot are also practically referred to in the *Rāmāyaṇa*'s *Araṇyakāṇḍa* and the *Ayodhyākāṇḍa.* Needless to say that much stress can be given on this point. The throbbing of the arm of Duṣyanta in the first Act when he visits the hermitage of Kaṇva and also the throbbing of right eye of Śakuntalā when she visits the court of the king Duṣyanta, referred to by Kālidāsa can be traced back to the *Rāmāyaṇa's Araṇyakāṇḍa*[21] when both Rāma and Lakṣmaṇa came back to the hermitage after killing the deer, the left eye of Rāma began to throb. Moreover, the idea that the tears of sorrow are hot, as referred to in the *Śākuntalam*, III.12, also can be traced back to the *Rāmāyaṇa's Ayodhyākāṇḍa*, when Sītā requests Rāma to take her to the forest, her tears, at that time, were described by Vālmīki to be hot. In this respect, the following stanza[22] deserves special attention.

Some of the descriptions of the heroine given by Kālidāsa in his *Śākuntalam* resemble those given in the *Rāmāyaṇa*. In this connection, the attention of a careful reader can be invited to the description of Śakuntalā in the first Act, verse 21, which runs thus *komala-viṭapānukāriṇau bāhū*. The latter part of this stanza stands in comparison with the description of Sītā made by Rāma. In this respect, it will not be out of place if the following line[23] is quoted. Again the description of Śakuntalā separated from her husband in the seventh Act of the *Śākuntalam*,[24] can be favourably compared with the description[25] of Sītā separated from Rāma, as it occurs in the *Sundarakāṇḍa*. The line quoted in the foot-note is sufficient to serve the purpose. The epithets *dhṛtaikaveṇiḥ* and *vasane paridhūsare vasānā* of Śakuntalā resemble those of Sītā such as *eka-veṇīdharā vivarṇāṅgī*. Possibly this description of Sītā in the *Sundarakāṇḍa* is at the back of the mind of our poet Kālidāsa.

In conclusion, the above discussion clearly indicates the immense influence of the *Rāmāyaṇa* on the *Śākuntalam* of Kālidāsa. However, this does not detract Kālidāsa from his merits and poetic ability and dramatic techniques. At times, however, Kālidāsa has made an advancement in thought over the *Rāmāyaṇa*. And sometimes, he has made the apt and judicious use of the ideas, similes, thoughts and superstitions scattered in the *Rāmāyaṇa*, in his *magnum opus* with a telling effect. On the whole, one will be tempted to say that though Vālmīki has exercised supreme influence on the works of Kālidāsa and the *Śākuntalam* in particular, yet he (Kālidāsa) is not a servile or blind imitator or follower of the work of Vālmīki.

Prof. Sadhu Ram's Comments

1. Shri Moghe says that "knowledge of the evenness and unevenness of the ground is absolutely necessary to a charioteer running the chariot", and sees the influence of *Rām.* "*sthala-nimnāni*

bhūmeś ca samāni viṣamāṇi ca." on *Śāk.* "*udghātinī bhūmir iti.*" One may ask — Is such a knowledge not necessary for the modern motorist ? Has he to be influenced by *Rām.* for it ? It is the genius of Kālidāsa that he has used (or coined) *udghātinī* 'throwing up or jolting' with reference to a moving vehicle. Had Vālmīki also used this word in *Rām.*, then alone influence could be suspected.

2. Moghe sees the influence of *āśramo'yaṃ.... sanātha iva sāmprataṃ (Rām.) on sanāthā idānīṃ dharmacāriṇaḥ (Śāk.).* This kind of courtesy is ingrained in the mind of every Bhāratīya by our Vedic culture. We always greet a respectable guest or even a common visitor with words : *Āiye baiṭhiye, yeh to āpa kā hī ghara hai or Āpa to isa ghara ke mālika hain* ? This does not mean influence of *Rām.*

3. Similarly, 'worshipping the king with fruits and nuts by sages, or hermit boys (*Śāk.*) does not require the influence of *phalair mūlaiś ca pūjayitvā Rāghavaṃ (Rām.)* on Kālidāsa to say: *iti phalāny upaharataḥ.* All people entertain guests with something available for refreshment.

4. The sharing of merits and demerits of the subjects by the king for his protection or oppression is also commonly met with in Sanskrit literature.

5. The story of Triśaṅku, and the comparison of an undecided person or one in suspense is also common in Indian literature.

6. "The position of a married woman becomes pitiable and ridiculous in the absence of her association with her husband", as said by Moghe is nothing but our custom that a married woman should remain with the family of her husband and not live perpetually or for a long time in her parental house, otherwise she is suspected and defamed.

7. Reference to *Rohit* fish (*Śāk.*) is found not only in *Rām.* but also in many other books and treatises, e.g., *Manusmṛti, Mahābhārata,* etc.

8. *Rām.* did not influence Kālidāsa to describe the incident of Mātali approaching Duṣyanta for help to defeat the group of demons (*Śāk.*). In almost all cases of atrocities committed by demons, the oppressed are advised by Brahmā, Nārada or other

holy persons to approach some god or goddess for help.

9. It is puerile to find the influence of the words of Indrajit *gṛdhrāś ca nipatantu tvām (Rām.)* with reference to Lakṣmaṇa on the words of policeman *(gṛdhra-balir bhaviṣyasi (Śāk.)* to the fisherman. Vultures, jackals, etc. always flock over corpses of war and carcasses. Nobody offers them to eat. The learned writer has not understood the meaning of *bali* here. It does not mean 'offering', but means 'feed or food or meat'.

10. Superstitions and omens are widely prevalent among both the urban and rural folks. The throbbing of the limbs, eyes, etc., and the encounter of a cat, Brāhmaṇa in the morning, sneezing, etc., do not require the influence of *Rām.* on the person who observes them.

Rajoinder to Prof. Sadhu Ram's Comments

I. (i) It seems that Shri Sadhu Ram is giving a modern touch to this problem by citing the example of a modern motorist. It should be remembered here that the merits of Kālidāsa's work are to be determined by the standard of the time in which he flourished. The example of a modern motorist, though convincing, misses the point at issue. (ii) One will have to appreciate that there is a sharp difference in the skill of a charioteer and a motorist. One cannot be compared with the other on this count. (iii) It is true that Vālmīki has not used the expression *'udghātinī bhūmir iti'* in his *Rāmāyaṇa, Yuddhakāṇḍa,* 105.19-20. But the entire description in the *Rāmāyaṇa* gives the varieties of ground. Here the expressions *sama, viṣama,* etc. in the *Rāmāyaṇa, Yuddhakāṇḍa* 105.19-20 come very near to the expression *udghātinī bhūmir* and also the expression *samadeśa* in the text of Kālidāsa. (iv) It should also be noted that the influence of the *Rāmāyaṇa* on the *Śākuntalam* can be traced in respect of the concept of a particular thing as well as similarity of language and expression. Here the present description in the *Śākuntalam* satisfies both the requirements and hence there is no point in denying the influence of the former over the latter.

II. Here again Shri Sadhu Ram is going off the point. His argument is based on the general understanding of our Vedic culture. It must be emphasised here that in a specific study particularly based on two specific texts, one should make specific references to the particular texts. Shri Sadhu Ram has ignored this basic principle. Besides, the title of my paper is too clear to need any further elucidation. (ii) The example cited by Shri Sadhu Ram is not a happy one. It has the classical modernity in it. (iii) It may also be pointed out here that we do not receive every guest with the remark that this house belongs to you or you are the master of this house. (iv) Moreover, culture varies from region to region and person to person and it has the basis of a status at the back of it. (v) It may be respectfully pointed out that Kālidāsa makes a sharp distinction on the point of courtesy shown by the hermit girls to the King Duṣyanta in the *Śākuntalam,* Act I and the courtesy shown by Raghu in receiving Kautsa in the *Raghuvaṃśam,* Canto V. In this very context, it is worthy of mention that Kālidāsa has used the expression *Viṣṭara* which is representative of the tradition of *Gṛhyasūtra* literature. This difference in culture deserves to be noted. It is a matter of hard fact that Shri Sadhu Ram has ignored this sharp distinction that can generally be noticed by a close study of the works. Hence I do not think it proper to agree with Sadhu Ram on the point of courtesy.

III. Shri Sadhu Ram's argument that all people entertain guests with something available for refreshment also does not prove his conviction. He is applying the general principle of entertaining guest to the particular cases of King Rāma and Duṣyanta. This, itself, does not appear sound. (ii) He has forgotten the important point that we do not entertain all guests with refreshment. (iii) The mode of entertaining guests also is different in different regions and in different centuries. To clarify this point further, one may quote at random the passage from the *Aitareya Brāhmaṇa* which runs thus हविरातिथ्यं निरूप्यते सोमे राजन्यागते । (I.15). In the fourth Act of the *Uttara-Rāma-Caritam* of Bhavabhūti, Saudhātaki remarks 'येन परापतितेनैव सा वराकी कपिला कल्याणी मडमडायिता । The remark of Dāṇḍāyana is further clear on this point. He states that the writers of *Dharma-Sūtra* works prescribe that the religious house-holders should offer a calf, a bull or a goat in honour of a guest who happens to be a Vedic Brāhmaṇa. (iv) In the absence of any material, even the agreeable speech is regarded as a mode of entertaining a guest by the *Manu-Smṛti,* III.101 and in the remark of Duṣyanta भवतीनां सूनृतया

गिरा कृतमातिथ्यम् we have the influence of the *Manu-Smṛti*. (v) Over and above, the worship of guest forms a subject of the *Gṛhyasūtra* literature, *Smṛtis* and *Dharma-Śāstra* works. It may be noted here that Kālidāsa very minutely represents the shades of curture that is imbibed by us from Vedic literature, *Rāmāyaṇa* and the *Mahābhārata*. In view of these arguments, it is hard to agree with Shri Sadhu Ram who remains contented with the general approach to the subject.

IV. Shri Sadhu Ram's argument that the concept of sharing merits and demerits of the subjects by the king is commonly met with in the Sanskrit literature is also founded on the general understanding and not on the particular understanding of the specific texts on which my writing is based. Here again it may be respectfully pointed out that I am not highlighting this point in the light of the Sanskrit literature in general as assumed by Shri Sadhu Ram. It may be repeated here that the title of my article is explicit on the scope of the matter that is under discussion. Here in this chapter I could have multiplied the instances but I thought it quite proper to substantiate my point with one good case. My line of argument is clear on this point and hence I agree to disagree with Shri Sadhu Ram on this count.

V. Again Shri Sadhu Ram's argument in respect of the case of Triśaṅku is of a general character and it need not be dealt with by me specifically. This point is actually as good as answered by me in discussion on paras II, III and IV. I, therefore, do not think it fit to subscribe to the line of argument adopted by Sadhu Ram on this point of Triśaṃku. (ii) Shri Sadhu Ram has also ignored that, I have also pointed out the possibility of the other source of the *Mahābhārata*. From this, it is evident that I am not at all insisting on my source to prove my case. A dispassionate research worker should never insist on the particular source only.

VI. There is no substance in the argument of Shri Sadhu Ram that it is our custom that the position of a married woman becomes pitiable in the absence of her association with her husband. Now-a-days, the position is quite otherwise. Neither a husband nor a wife would care a row of pins for the opinion of others about them. They only think that their names will stink in the nostrils of good people. Besides, the position of a husband will become lowered in the eyes of public, if he is abandoned by his wife. (ii) It should be remembered here that Kālidāsa has before him the ideal of Sītā as a model for the description of Śakuntalā in the *Śākuntalam*. This situation can perhaps be properly grasped if one carefully notes the expression *'balavadapiśikṣitānā* in the *Śākuntalam*, Act. I.2. and also the line from the *Raghuvaṁśam*, Canto I.2 which runs as 'अथवा कृतवाग्द्वारे वंशेऽस्मिन् पूर्वसूरिभिः।' In the absence of this ground, the very text of Kālidāsa would become superfluous.

VII. Again it is not a good argument of Shri Sadhu Ram that a reference to Rohita occurs in the *Mahābhārata* and the *Manu-Smṛti* and hence the source of the *Rāmāyaṇa* relied upon by me cannot be accepted. Here it may be stated that we cannot verify the exact source of our gifted poet Kālidāsa. (ii) In my article I have observed that no definite information about this *Rohita* fish is available elsewhere. I have never stated that we do not get a reference to this fish. I hope one will understand a difference in the two expressions 'reference and information'.

VIII. It must be pointed out here that the argument of Shri Sadhu Ram in respect of the incident of Mātali is also of a general character. This need not be answered by me. The same is already treated as replied by my observations in the Paras II, III, IV and V. I would like to be free from the fault of repetition.

IX. It is worth emphasising here that Shri Sadhu Ram is side-tracking the main point of argument discussed by me by calling my source as puerile. I have also shown that the kind of punishment referred to in the *Śākuntalam*, has no place in the *Rāmāyaṇa*. Besides, a reference to vultures, jackals and others flocking over corpses of war is not a basis for the *Śākuntalam*. Only important point to be noted here is that Kālidāsa has made a clever use of the idea of *Rāmāyaṇa* so as to serve his dramatic purpose by possible reference to a punishment likely to be imposed upon a fisherman who is caught with the lost property, i.e., a ring. (ii) it is correct to say that corpses are not offered to vultures, jackals. In the *Mahābhārata* (*Strī Parvan*, Chapters 26 and 27) we find a reference to the dead bodies of the warriors on the sides of Kurus and Pāṇḍavas and these are ceremonially disposed of by

Dharmaraja and others only at the end of the *Mahābhārata* War. It is also true that dead bodies are never offered to such vultures and others as is the custom prevalent among the Parsee people. But in the *Rāmāyaṇa,* what Indrajit means to say is that Rāma and others may not find time to dispose of the dead body of Lakṣmaṇa ceremonially and in that case it is likely to be devoured by vultures and others. Kālidāsa has made the clever use of this incident to create a military humour by compelling a police man to pass the interesting remark with reference to a fisherman. (iii) It is a matter of profound regret that Shri Sadhu Ram has not cared to refer to the standard English editions of the *Śākuntalam* to see how the word *bali* is translated there. I refer Shri Sadhu Ram to the 6th edition of the *Śākuntalam* by Prof. A.B. Gajendragadkar, p. 129 and Prof. Saradaranjan Ray's 16th edition of the *Śākuntalam,* p. 542. These two scholars have rendered the word *bali* as offering. (iii) George Bühler in his English Translation of the *Manu-Smṛti,* III. 74 translates the word *bali* as offering. (iv) The word *bali* also occurs in the context of Vaiśvadeva rite and there the food or the rice is to be sprinkled over with *ghee* or with curd or milk but not with oil or salt.[26] (v) The word *bali* also occurs in the *Jaiminīya Brāhmaṇa.* 'सुपर्ण एष एव ते बलिर्भविष्यत्येतदन्नम' (II.438) and is translated as 'a share' by Prof. G.V. Devasthali in his edition of the *Inter Arts Sanskrit Selections,* 1954-56 of the University of Bombay. (vi) Besides, the word *bali* is also explained by the commentators like Medhātithi, Kullūka and others on the *Manu-Smṛti,* III. 70, 74 and 104. (vii) The word *bali* is properly explained in the *Āhnika-Kāṇḍa* of the *Smṛticandrikā* of Devaṇṇabhaṭṭa (p. 577, Mysore edition, 1914). The above references clearly indicate that the word *bali* cannot be translated as 'feed or food or meat' as assumed by Sadhu Ram. In conclusion I am constrained here to say that Sadhu Ram has not understood the idiom of the English language in translating the word *bali* and his rendering of the word as 'feed or food or meat' is not only not acceptable but it does not bring out the sense of the *Dharma-Śāstra* literature pointed out above and also the sense of 'a share' taken by Prof. Devasthali.

X. Shri Sadhu Ram has not answered to my specific observation of the supersitition that the tears of sorrow are hot and for this superstition in *Śākuntalam,* Kālidāsa owes to the *Rāmāyaṇa.* As regards other superstitions, I have not shown any comparison between Kālidāsa and Vasaṇta-Rājaśakuna (earlier than 1150 A.D. according to Dr. Kane) to show the points of resemblance. Shri Sadhu Ram is interested in making general observations and not specific. Moreover, I have not dealt with the aspect of superstitions at full length. I have quoted a specific case from the *Rāmāyaṇa* to which he has no answer to give.

In conclusion, the present author is constrained to hold reasonably that the arguments advanced by Shri Sadhu Ram or the comments made by him are superficial, general, and based on the common sense understanding of Vedic culture. His comments have no bearing on the study of the two specific texts relied upon by me. On the meaning of the term *bali*, further Shri Sadhu Ram is completely unsatisfactory.

References

1. "अभिज्ञानशाकुन्तल पर वाल्मीकि-रामायण का प्रभाव", published in the *Vikram*, Kālidāsa Special Number X. 1957. vide pp. 63-68.
2. "आयुष्मन्! उद्घातिनी भूमिरिति मया रश्मिसंयमनात् रथस्य मन्दीकृतो वेगः। तेन मृग एष विप्रकृष्यन्तरः संवृत्तः। संप्रति समदेशवर्तिनस्ते न दुरासदो भविष्यति।
3. स्थलनिम्नानि भूमेश्च समानि विषमाणि च।
   युद्धकालश्च विज्ञेयः परस्यान्तरदर्शनम्॥
   युद्धकाण्ड 105.19॥
   उपयानापयाने च स्थानं प्रत्यपसर्पणम्।
   सर्वमेतद्रथस्थेन ज्ञेयं रथकुटुम्बिना॥
   युद्धकाण्ड, 105.20॥
4. स्वागतं ते रघुश्रेष्ठ राम सत्यभृतां वर।
   आश्रमोऽयं त्वया क्रान्तः सनाथ इव सांप्रतम्॥
   अरण्यकाण्ड, 78॥
5. एवमुक्त्वा फलैर्मूलैः पुष्पैश्चान्यैश्च राघवम्।
   पूजयित्वा यथाकामं ततोऽगस्त्यस्तमब्रवीत्॥
   अरण्यकाण्ड, 12.31॥
6. यदुत्तिष्ठति वर्णेभ्यो नृपाणां क्षयि तद्धनम्।
   तपःषड्भागमक्षय्यं ददत्यारण्यका हि नः॥
   Act 2, v. 13.
7. यत्करोति परं धर्मं मुनिर्मूलफलाशनः।
   तत्र राज्ञश्चतुर्भागः प्रजा धर्मेण रक्षतः॥
   अरण्यकाण्ड, 6.14॥

8. ईदृशा ब्राह्मणेनोक्ता वाह्लीका मोघचारिण: ।
येषां षड्भागहर्ता त्वमुभयो: शुभपापयो: ॥

महाभारत, कर्णपर्व, 30.27 ॥

9. स्वर्गलोकं गतं दृष्ट्वा त्रिशंकुं पाकशासन: ।
सह सर्वैः सुरगणैरिदं वचनमब्रवीत् ॥

रामायण, बालकाण्ड, 60.16 ॥

10. किमत्र चित्रं यदि विशाखे शशाङ्कलेखामनुवर्तते ।

11. तयोर्मध्ये कपिश्रेष्ठ: शोणिताक्षप्रजंथयो: ।
विशाखयोर्मध्यगत: पूर्णचन्द्र इवाबभौ ।

रामायण, युद्धकाण्ड, 76.15 ॥

12. "क: इदानीमन्यो धर्मकच्चुकप्रवेशिनस्तृणच्छन्नकूपोपमस्य तवानुकृतिं प्रतिपत्स्यते ।"

शाकुन्तलम् Act V.

13. सत्वां विनिहितात्मानं धर्मध्वजमधार्मिकम् ।
जाने पापसमाचारं तृणै: कूपमिवावृतम् ॥

रामायण, किष्किधाकाण्ड, 17.22 ॥

14. सतीमपि ज्ञातिकुलैकसंश्रयां जनोऽन्यथा भर्तृमतीं विशङ्कते ।
अत: समीपे परिणेतुरिष्यते प्रियाप्रियाऽवा प्रमदा स्वबन्धुभि: ।

शाकुन्तलम् 5.17 ॥

15. न त्वहं मनसाप्यन्यं दृष्टास्मि त्वदृतेऽनघ ।
त्वया राघव गच्छेयं यथान्या कुलपांसनी ॥

रामायण, अयोध्याकाण्ड, 30.7 ॥

16. परदाराभिमर्शात्तु नान्यत्पापतरं महत् ।

अरण्यकाण्ड, 38.30 as also

निवार्यमाण: सुहृदा मया भृशं प्रसह्य सीतां यदि धर्मयिष्यसि ।
गमिष्यसि क्षीणवल: सबान्धवो यमक्षयं रामशरास्तजीवित: ॥

अरण्यकाण्ड, 38.33॥

17. रोहितांश्चक्रतुण्डांश्च नलमीनांश्च राघव । पम्पायामिषुभिर्मत्स्यांस्तत्र राम वरान् हतान् ॥

रामायण, अरण्यकाण्ड, 73.14 ॥

18. रथेन मम भूयिष्ठं शीघ्रं याहि रघूत्तमम् ।
आहूय भूतलं यात: कुरु देवहितं महत् ॥
इत्युक्तो देवराजेन मातलिर्देवसारथि: ।
प्रणम्य शिरसा देवं ततो वचनमब्रवीत् ॥

रामायण, युद्धकाण्ड, 103.7-8 ॥

19. गुध्रबलिर्भविष्यसि, शुनो मुखं वा द्रक्ष्यसि ।

शाकुन्तलम्, Act VI.

20. अद्य गोमायुसङ्घाश्च श्येनसङ्घाश्च लक्ष्मण ।
गृध्राश्च निपतन्तु त्वां गतासुं निहितं मया ॥

रामायण, युद्धकाण्ड, 88.23 ॥

21. मृशमाव्रजमानस्य तस्याधो वामलोचनम् ।
प्रास्फुरच्चास्खलद्रामो वेपथुश्चास्यजायते ॥

रामायण, अरण्यकाण्ड, 61.1 ॥

22. एवमुक्ता तु सा चिन्तां मैथिली समुपागता ।
स्नापयन्तीव गामुष्णैरश्रुभिर्नयनच्युतैः ॥
रामायण, अयोध्याकाण्ड, 29.23 ॥

23. नूनं विक्षिप्यमाणौ तौ बाहू पल्लवकोमलौ ।
रामायण, अरण्यकाण्ड, 61.33a ॥

24. वसने परिधूसरे वसाना
नियमक्षाममुखी घृतैकवेणिः ।
अतिनिष्करुणस्य शुद्धशीला
मम दीर्घं विरहव्रतं बिभर्ति ॥
शाकुन्तलम् Act VII.21 ॥

25. एकवेणीधरा दीना भर्तृचिन्तापरायणा ।
भूमिशय्या विवर्णाङ्गी पद्मिनीव हिमागमे ॥
रामायण, सुन्दरकाण्ड, 58.60 ॥

26. P.V. Kane, *History of Dharma-Śāstra,* Vol. II (2), p. 744.

6

The Constellation Rohiṇī in the *Rāmāyaṇa* and the Later Poets

ROHIṆI is the name of the fourth lunar mansion (containing five stars) figured by a cart. She is one of the twenty-seven daughters of Dakṣa and is regarded as the favourite consort of the moon. The constellation is called Rohiṇī because of the red appearance of the principal star. In this chapter , therefore, an attempt is being made to point out the information furnished by the *Rāmāyaṇa* about the constellation Rohiṇī in association with the other planets — the Moon, the Mars, the Comet, the Mercury, the descending node and the fiery phenomenon in the sky otherwise known as Ulkā. In addition to this, the information supplied by the later poets — both Sanskrit and Prākṛt poets — is brought to the notice of the readers. In this respect, it can be added that I have tried to restrict myself to the works of Kālidāsa and Bāṇa among the Sanskrit poets and Rāma Pāṇivāda, the author of the well-known Prākṛt poem *Uṣāniruddham*. After making the proper comparison of the information furnished by the *Rāmāyaṇa* and the later poets, an attempt is made to show the originality and indebtedness of each other in respect of the information utilised by these poets. The following is an attempt in this direction.

The association of the moon with the constellation Rohiṇī is generally described in the Sanskrit literature as a good example of the happy union of married couples. This idea is fruitfully employed by Vālmīki in the *Rāmāyaṇa* in connection with the couple of Rāma and Sītā. It is generally considered that the wife should be always in the company of the husband and must follow the foot-steps of him every now and then. The idea of Sītā following Rāma is well-brought out by Vālmīki with the shining example of the constellation Rohiṇī following the moon. This idea[1] is twice repeated in the *Rāmāyaṇa*— in the *Araṇyakāṇḍa* and also in the *Ayodhyākāṇḍa.*

Sometimes, however, the association of the constellation Rohiṇī with the planet Mars is also hinted at in the *Rāmāyaṇa.* This association is never considered as a happy one. On the contrary due to this association, the position of the constellation Rohiṇī becomes more miserable particularly in the company of the Planet Mars. This is evident from the portion[2] of the *Sundarakāṇḍa* of the *Rāmāyaṇa,* in which it is described that the position of Sītā became more pitiable and miserable in the company of Rāvaṇa as is the case of the constellation Rohiṇī in the company of the planet Mars. Such a type of combination possibly indicates the malignant aspect even astrologically. Here also one is tempted to say that the poet is more influenced by the object of comparison. Anyhow, it seems that in order to convey the miserable condition of Sītā, Vālmīki, the Ādi Kavi, has resorted to this astrological simile.

At times, however, it appears that the association of the constellation Rohiṇī with some cruel planets is not considered as a very happy thing. While describing the pitiable condition of Sītā particularly in the midst of the demonesses, Vālmīki has introduced the beautiful simile[3] of the constellation Rohiṇī surrounded by some planets. Here also it seems that Vālmīki is more carried away by the idea of the cruel attitude of the demonesses towards Sītā. It is significant to note that the expression '*sagrahām iva Rohiṇīm*' is explained by the commentators as 'surrounded by the cruel planets! They do not take proper care to point out the particular cruel or wicked planet possibly in the mind of Vālmīki. They remain satisfied with the expression *krūragrahāviṣṭām.* Perhaps this might have given a clue or hint to the poet Vālmīki for showing unhappy results.

It is further clear that the association of the constellation Rohiṇī with the planet Comet (*dhūmaketu*) is not considered as a happy sign. It is interesting to note that Vālmīki has described Sītā attempting to escape from the clutches of Rāvaṇa by introducing the simile[4] of the constellation Rohiṇī troubled by the Comet. In this context, it is interesting to note comments[5] of Govindarāja. It is also surprising to note that the word *dhūmaketu* is explained by the above commentators as *ketu.* Actually and even astrologically it is believed that the planets — *Ketu* and *Dhūmaketu* — are treated as different. It is here further interesting to remember that the commentary of Tilaka on the *Rāmāyaṇa,* describes *ketu* as having smokey colour.

Besides, it deserves to be noted that the simile of the association of the constellation Rohiṇī with the Moon is given by Vālmīki to show the happy married couple. This is evident from the description[6] in the *Sundarakāṇḍa* of the *Rāmāyaṇa.* Here the above simile is introduced in the case of the married couple of Arundhatī and Vasiṣṭha. It appears that for the happy union of the married couple, this has become the standard comparison. It deserves to be noted in this context, that the list of ideal married couples is given from the stanzas 10 to 14 of the Sarga 24 of the *Sundarakāṇḍa* of the *Rāmāyaṇa,* to show that Sītā wants to be in the company of Rāma.

In addition to this, in the *Sundarakāṇḍa* of the *Rāmāyaṇa,* the constellation Rohiṇī is further described as the best of all the constellations and endowed with all the good qualities. This is evident from the description[7] of the heavenly women put in the mouth of Hanumān.

Further it is clear that the position of the constellation Rohiṇī overpowered by some other planet having the red colour, i.e., the Mars becomes pitiable. The poet Vālmīki brings out the pitiable and miserable condition of Sītā being harassed by Rāvaṇa, with the help of his telling illustration.[8] Here also it seems that the poet Vālmīki is more influenced by the object of comparison.

Over and above, the overpowering of the constellation Rohiṇī by the planet Mercury (*Budha*) also foretells the miserable condition. This simile is used by the poet Vālmīki to show the miserable condition of Sītā when she was caught hold of by Rāvaṇa. This is evident from the description[9] of the *Aranyakāṇḍa* of the *Rāmāyaṇa.* The same idea is again repeated in the *Yuddhakāṇḍa*[10] of the *Rāmāyaṇa.* Is it possible to hold on the basis of this line from the *Yuddhakāṇḍa* of the *Rāmāyaṇa* that the constellation Rohiṇī is the mother of the planet Mercury ?

At times, however, we fail to understand the name of the planet, in whose association the position of the constellation

Rohiṇī becomes more pitiable. This is evident from the description[11] that occurs in the *Araṇyakāṇda*. Perhaps at this place, the association of the constellation Rohiṇī with the planet *Ketu* (descending node) is hinted at.

Again it is interesting to note that the attack by the great Ulkā on the constellation Rohiṇī is described. This also perhaps shows some undesirable effects. While describing the idea that Sītā was attacked by the angry Śūrpaṇakhā, the simile of the great Ulkā overpowering the constellation Rohiṇī, is introduced by the poet. This is clear from the description[12] of the *Araṇyakāṇḍa*.

Now coming to the works of Kālidāsa, it seems that in the third Act of the drama *Vikramorvaśīyam* the queen Auśīnarī wishes to have the company of the king Purūravā, in order to put an end to the vow of Priyānuprasādana Vrata, in the presence of the conjunction of the moon with the constellation Rohiṇī in the sky. So, in this drama, it is only once that a reference[13] to the constellation Rohiṇī occurs.

When in the seventh Act of the *Śākuntalam*, the union of the hero Duṣyanta with the heroine Śakuntalā takes place, after the long standing separation of about 7 years, Kālidāsa had introduced the simile of the conjunction of the moon with the constellation Rohiṇī, after the period of the eclipse is over. Here it appears that for the happy union of the married couple, Kālidāsa has employed the idea[14] of the union of the Moon and the constellation Rohiṇī.

Coming to the works of Bāṇa, it can be cleverly pointed out that in the *Harṣacaritam*, Rohiṇī is mentioned as the special favourite wife of the moon out of the 27 constellations. In other context, Bāṇa describes the constellation Rohiṇī as. उत्कोटिकेयूरपत्र-भङ्गपुत्रिका प्रतिबिम्बगर्भकोमलं मुखं चन्द्रमसमिव हृदयस्थितरोहिणीकमुद्वहन्तम्. In the *Kādambarī,* Bāṇa further describes[15] the constellation Rohiṇī as if marked with the Alaktaka dye applied to the feet by Rohiṇī who was angry with the Moon in some love-quarrel. He again refers[16] to this idea in the *Pūrva-Bhāga* of the *Kādambarī*. It appears that Bāṇa is relying upon some mythological account that in an angry mood, the constellation Rohiṇī kicked the moon, her husband. It seems that this may be treated as a general code of behaviour of the women when in love-quarrels, they kick their husbands with their foot.

In another context, Bāṇa makes a reference[17] to the curse by Dakṣa to the moon for showing special favour to Rohiṇī, among the 27 constellations. In this respect, it is possible to say that Bāṇa must be relying on some mythological account.

If we read the Prākṛt poem *Uṣāniruddham* by the poet Rāma-Pāṇivāda, we will come to know that he also refers[18] to the moon as the lord of the constellation Rohiṇī. It may be noted here that in this poem, a reference to the constellation Rohiṇī occurs only once.

Conclusion

From the above information, it becomes evident that the concept of the happy union of the married couple is best illustrated with the simile of the conjunction of the moon and the constellation Rohiṇī, by Vālmīki, Kālidāsa, Bāṇa and Rāma-Pāṇivāda. The other aspects of the association of the constellation Rohiṇī with the other planets like the Mars, the Mercury, the Comet, the descending node and the Ulkā are referred to only in the *Rāmāyaṇa* by Vālmīki. Here also one is tempted to say that the poet is more influenced by the object of comparison rather than by the standard of comparison. It is also further interesting to remember that the association of the constellation Rohiṇī with the other planets is not at all referred to by Kālidāsa, Bāṇa and Rāma-Pāṇivāda. Actually Kālidāsa could have used the simile of the conjunction of the constellation Rohiṇī with the other cruel planets in respect of Urvaśī being taken away by the demon Keśin. But it appears that such a type of simile is not at all used by Kālidāsa. Again Bāṇa also deserves due credit for showing the anger of the constellation Rohiṇī, to the moon by kicking him by means of her foot marked with the *alaktaka* dye. Even Vālmīki has not made a reference to this idea. Bāṇa's idea of the father-in-law Dakṣa cursing the moon for giving special favour to the constellation Rohiṇī, particularly in the *Kādambarī* is a good idea, not at all referred to by Vālmīki, Kālidāsa, and Rāma-Pāṇivāda. Any way, the information supplied by the poets — Vālmīki, Kālidāsa and Bāṇa is interesting and the conclusion shows the indebtedness of the later poets to

Vālmīki and the originality of Bāṇa in some respects, though he has not touched upon the other aspects of Vālmīki in connection with the association of the constellation Rohiṇī with the other planets. Vālmīki, being the Ādi Kavi, deserves proper credit for more imaginative power than the later poets. The above descriptions of the constellation Rohiṇī in the works mentioned above have influenced the poetic conventions of the later Sanskrit and Prākṛt poets in respect of the idea of ideal happy married couples.

References

1. सीताप्यनुगता रामं शशिनं रोहिणी यथा ।

   बालकाण्ड, I. 28.

   Also Read: *अयोध्याकाण्ड*, 16.41.

2. पीडितां दु:खसंतप्तां परिक्षीणां तपस्विनीम् ।
   ग्रहेणाङ्गारकेणेव पीडितामिव रोहिणीम् ॥

   सुन्दरकाण्ड, 15.22.

3. अशोकवनिकामध्ये शोकसागरमाप्लुताम् ।
   ताभि: परिवृतां तत्र सग्रहामिव रोहिणीम् ॥

   सुन्दरकाण्ड, 17.24.

4. चेष्टमानामथाविष्टां पन्नगेन्द्रवधूमिव ।
   धूम्यमानां ग्रहेणेव रोहिणीं धूमकेतुना ॥

   सुन्दरकाण्ड, 19.9.

5. यद्वा ग्रहेण ग्राहकेण आच्छादकेनेति धूमकेतुविशिष्यते ।

   रामायण, p. 1809.

6. यथा शची महाभागा शक्रं समुपतिष्ठति ।
   अरुन्धती वासिष्ठं च रोहिणी शशिनं यथा ॥

   सुन्दरकाण्ड, 24.10.

7. रोहिणी ज्योतिषां ज्येष्ठा श्रेष्ठसर्वगुणाधिका ।

   सुन्दरकाण्ड, 33.7.

8. अत्र सा मृगशावाक्षी रावणेनोपरुध्यते ।
   अभिभूता ग्रहेणेव लोहिताङ्गेन रोहिणी ॥

   युद्धकाण्ड, 24.7.

9. जग्राह रावण: सीतां वुध: रवे रोहिणीमिव ।

   अरण्यकाण्ड, 49.16.

10. प्राजापत्यं च नक्षत्रं रोहिणीं शशिन: प्रियाम् ।
    समाक्रम्य बुधस्तस्थौ प्रजानामहितावह: ॥

    युद्धकाण्ड, 102.33.

11. रोहिणीं शशिना हीनां ग्रहवत् भृशदारूण: ।

    अरण्यकाण्ड, 46.6.

12. अभ्यगच्छत् सुसंक्रुद्धा महोल्का रोहिणीमिव ।

अरण्यकाण्ड, 18.17.

13. कञ्चुकी-तंत्र संनिहितेन देवेन प्रतिपालयितुमिच्छामि यावच्चन्द्ररोहिणीयोग इति ।

विक्रमोर्वशीयम् Act III.

14. उपरागान्ते शशिनः समुपगता रोहिणी योगम् ।

शाकुन्तलम्, Act VII, 226.

15. रतिकलहकुपितरोहिणीचरणालक्तकर सलाच्छिछतमिच्छि....।

कादम्बरी Para-166 (Kane's editions).

16. रोहिणीचरणताडनलग्नमलक्तकरसमिवोदयरागं दधानः ।

कादम्बरी पूर्वभाग Para 203 (Kane's editions).

17. दर्शयन्निवचिरकाललग्नं दक्षशापात् अनलदाहचिह्नम् ।

कादम्बरी, Para 181.

18. ......जो रोहिणीवल्लहो ।

उषानिरुद्धम्, IV.73.

7

Contribution of Prof. H.D. Velankar to Vedic Indology

PROFESSOR Hari Damodar Velankar has devoted more than four decades for the study of the *Ṛg-Veda* and has contributed a lot to the study of the *Ṛg-Veda*. Actually I do not consider myself to be a competent person to determine the nature and merit of his contribution to this branch of learning. In fact, there are many competent scholars to undertake this task; but their old age and some developed ideologies may not permit them to undertake this task in a dispassionate manner. Hence I am almost prompted to pay my humble tribute to my Professor H.D. Velankar (who is more popularly known among the students as *Gurujī*) particularly on the occasion of his centenary. In doing this work, I must admit my own limitations in the branch of Vedic Studies. However, I am almost tempted to undertake this work, remembering the line of Kālidāsa *'tad guṇaiḥ karṇamāgatya cāpalāye pracoditaḥ'* and also because I have also made good reading of some Vedic books and research papers and reviews in the course of the last twenty-five years and more. In paying my respectful tribute to my revered *Gurujī*, I have the pleasure in expressing the same feelings which he has already expressed with reference to the German scholar, Oldenberg, particularly in his Preface to the *Ṛg-Veda Maṇḍala*, second, p. ix. 'In all cases of such a difference, from the earlier authors, I have fully placed my grounds before the reader and made my own suggestions for improvement with the reverent attitude of a pupil who would urge his point before the master with all humility but forcefully and fearlessly.' I must state here that I could do no better than highlighting the different aspects of his Vedic research and interpretation.

1. Prof. Velankar's significant contribution to the Vedic interpretation lies in his well-known theory of word-economy and *Ṛg-Vedic* interpretation. He has ably shown in this chapter the salient features of his theory in the chapter contributed to the *Journal of the Bhandarkar Oriental Research Institute* of Poona in the year 1964. It may be noted here that even in his notes[1] on the *Maṇḍalas,* II, III, VII and even the *Ṛksuktasatī,* as he has stressed this point in season and out of season. As he had drunk deep in the fountain of the *Ṛg-Veda,* he could advance this theory with the niceties of the Vedic language. His main intention here is to show that the *Ṛgvedic* poets were conscious artists and had handled this technique intentionally and with a definite poetic purpose. He further firmly holds that this theory may yield correct meanings of some of the *Ṛgvedic* passages that seem to baffle all attempts at interpretation.

2. His introduction of the three varieties of similes, is, indeed novel and unknown even to the domain of *Alaṁkāra-Śāstra.* He has introduced — decorative, illustrative and emotional — similes in the course of his lectures and notes. Here, it may be noted that he has also made a specialised study of the Similes in the *Atharva-Veda.* He has also given exhaustive treatment to the similes[2] in the *Vāmadeva Maṇḍala,* i.e., fourth *Maṇḍala* of the *Ṛg-Veda.* He has given good treatment to the nature of the decorative[3] simile in the *Ṛg-Veda,* V. 80 particularly in his well-known book in the Marathi language *Path of devotion in the Ṛg-Veda.* He has also thoroughly discussed the emotional[4] similes in the *Ṛg-Veda,* by classifying the similes under the different heads of (i) Mother and child, (ii) mother cow and calf, (iii) father and son, (iv) husband and wife, (v) Lover and maiden, and (vi) friend and friend. It may be incidentally noted here that in explaining the similes of the *Ṛg-Veda,* Velankar has given full concentration on the idiom and usage the Vedic language and has also shown his disagreement with the grand-masters like Sāyaṇa, Oldenberg, Geldner, L. Renoue and others, with good reasons. Here he has also noted the stylistic peculiarities of the Vedic poets by introducing proper comparison of the Vedic passages. A dispassionate reader of his articles will be surely tempted to describe Prof. Velankar as a 'simile specialist'.

3. Prof. Velankar has very ably advocated his famous theory that the real devotion in the *Ṛg-Veda* will have to be traced to the hymns dedicated to Indra. In this respect, attention of the serious readers is drawn to his introduction[5] to the *Ṛg-Veda Maṇḍala* VII, and his course of three lectures[6] on the path of devotion in the *Ṛg-Veda*. In his lectures, in particular, he has thoroughly discussed this problem covering 90 printed pages and at the end given the Index of the passages[7] (collected from all the ten *Maṇḍalas*) and particularly relied upon by him for this theory. Incidentally, he has shown that the real *Bhakti* cannot be traced back to the *Varuṇa-Sūktas* in which Varuṇa is always shown as angry, with the devotee for the reasons unknown to the devotee. There is hardly any hymn in the *Ṛg-Veda* in which Varuṇa is not shown as angry. He further firmly believes that the *Bhakti* in the *Varuṇa-Sūktas* is of a lower type. Here we find the example of the master-servant relationship. In the *Varuṇa-Sūktas,* god is always shown as very great and a devotee very small. Naturally, in this *Bhakti,* we have the Western touch. He further points out that in the *Indra-Sūktas,* the devotees try to go near to Indra, by establishing relation with him, appealing to him emotionally, and by arguing with him. He further adds that whatever spirit is maintained by the *Indra-Sūktas,* the same is really retained by the Indian saints like Tukārāma,[8] on the Indian soil. He has further quoted passages[9] from the *Ṛg-Veda* to indicate the angry nature of Varuṇa. Incidentally, it may be mentioned here that as usual Dr. R.N. Dandekar has upheld the viewpoint[10] of the Western scholars and tried to trace the *bhakti* doctrines in the *Varuṇa Sūktas.* It must be noted here that Dr. Dandekar has not cared to refer to the viewpoint of Prof. Velankar particularly on the doctrine of *Bhakti*. Besides, he has no convincing reply to give to the points of Prof. Velankar, noted above by the writer of this note. A dispassionate but independent reader will not resist the temptation of passing the remark that Dr. Dandekar's writing appears to be 'simply one sided', particularly on this count, though one has to admit that his writing has the merit of rich command of the bibliographical material particularly in his Vedic Mythological Tracts which has, indeed, given the correct idea of the horizons of Vedic mythology to the writer of this note. If, however, one considers the passages relied upon by both these veterans — both qualitatively and

quantitatively — then one will be definitely inclined to agree with the viewpoint of Prof. Velankar, brushing aside the viewpoint of Dr. Dandekar. One is also constrained to remark in the present context, that Dr. Dandekar's attitude seems to be *ardhasatyena toṣaṇam* (satisfaction by knowing half the truth), which he is trying to avoid (perhaps) outwardly only.

4. The question often arises whether the *Ṛgvedic* hymns bear testimony to the idol worship or idolatry and *Liṅga*-worship and mother cult. Prof. Velankar categorically holds[11] that in the *Ṛg-Veda* when the words such as — *adeva, ugradeva, ardhadeva, sudeva, Vāmadeva* and *Sahadeva* — occur, they do not have any reference to the physical worship of an image or symbol. He holds against Macdonell (*Vedic Mythology,* p.155) who tries his best to establish *Liṅga*-Worship in the *Ṛg-Veda*. Here in passing, it may be noted that even in the 'path of devotion in the *Ṛg-Veda*', Prof. Velankar has clarified his position[12] on this count. He also adds that if such a cult of *Liṅga*-worship had existed in the days of the *Ṛg-Veda,* its traces could have been noticed in the later Vedic literature and particularly in the *Atharva-Veda*. Here incidentally, it should be noted that Dr. Dandekar has discussed this topic of mother cult in his *Exercises in Indology,* pp 14, 50 and *Vedic Mythological Tracts,* pp.260-66, and 269-71 and tried to prove the existence of mother cult. The expression *Tryaṁbaka* also helps him to draw this conclusion and further in support of his conclusion tenders other evidences and quotes the viewpoint of Johansson in his favour. Here again it should be remembered by a careful reader that Dr. Dandekar has not led any evidence from the *Atharva-Veda* to prove the mother-cult, which is perhaps, the significant point of the argument of Prof. Velankar. Incidentally, it may be noted that Dr. Dandekar has not referred to the view of Prof. Velankar on this important aspect. Hence, a cautious reader will be tempted to remark that Dr. Dandekar's writing appears to be simply one-sided. In this very context, it should be remembered that Dr. Dandekar himself has shown the attitude of the scholars towards the Vedic document, in his very competent but lengthy survey of the works of Western scholars on the Vedic Religion and Mythology. Here in this article and even elsewhere (this article appears in a book form)[13] he has indicated that Hillebrandt tries

to interpret the *Ṛg-Veda* from the *Ṛg-Veda* itself (p.200), Oldenberg in his interpretation of the *Ṛg-Veda* has covered the Vast vedic literature (p.205), Pischel and Geldner treat the *Ṛg-Veda* as an Indian document and try to understand it in the light of later Indian literature (p.217), Brunnhofer sees the phonetic similarities of the Vedic persons and names with those in *Ancient Iran* (p.189) etc. It should be noted here that Prof. Velankar belongs to the fold of those scholars who try to interpret the *Ṛg-Veda* with the help of the *Ṛg-Veda* as far as possible as it is the work of the Classes and also with the help of *Atharva-Veda* which is the work of the masses and the later Indian literature. Here Dr. Dandekar is trying to interpret the *Ṛg-Veda* with the help of Ancient Indian Culture and the relation of the Vedic civilization with the help of the Mohanjodaro civilization and hence in the conclusion of both the scholars, there seems to be a vast difference. It should be also noted in this context, that Dr. Dandekar has not contradicted Prof. Velankar, by entering into the fold which is accepted by Prof. Velankar. Hence, the writer of this note feels very rightly that a serious scholar should take into consideration, all the possible sources, without hiding any important source, and then draw the legitimate conclusion. As this is not the case with the writing of Dr. Dandekar, particularly on this count, I would like to express the desire that this topic should be considered by the scholars (who are competent in handling all the possible sources) and then draw the legitimate conclusions which should be acceptable or worthy of consideration of all the scholars. If, however, one is almost inclined to interpret the *Ṛg-Veda* in the light of the Vedic literature only as the fold of some scholars indicated above, then the readers will be surely inclined to agree with Prof. Velankar's viewpoint.

5. It must be emphasised in this very context, the contribution of Prof. Velankar with reference to some hymns (these are actually two — on which Prof. Velankar has written introductory notes) particularly in comparison with the viewpoint of Western scholars. On the *Ṛg-Veda,* VII. 103, he has clarified his position in a better manner in his note in the *Ṛksūktasátī* (p 230) as compared with his note in the *Ṛg-Veda Maṇḍala* VII, p.202. The *Ṛg-Veda* VII.103 is a famous *Maṇḍūka Sūkta,* which is treated by the Western scholars like Max-Müller, Muir, and Geldner, as a parody

against the Viśvāmitras. Velankar does not subscribe to this view and then cares to state the grounds[14] for his view. It should be only casually remembered here that Prof. Velankar never brushes aside the views of other scholars with the tone of an authority. He, in fact, gives a faithful presentation of the view of other scholars, and then he states as to why he does not agree with them. He always adopts the view of a dispassionate researcher and never dubs the views of others as unauthoritative, as is the case with the writing of Prof. Dandekar, who always takes pleasure in dismissing[15] the views of others simply with the tone of an authority.

Prof. Velankar has given a very lengthy note on the *Ṛg-Veda,* VII.55 in his *Ṛksūktaśati,* p. 122-24. He treats this hymn as a sleep-charm. Many Western scholars like Pischel, Lanmann, Bloomfield, Macdonell and Oldenberg hazard a supposition that this hymn is a lover's charm. Prof. Velankar very mildly suggests that this is not correct.[16] He further points out that the original sleep-charm of the *Ṛg-Veda* is converted into a love-charm by the author of the *Atharva-Veda.* He also points out the changes made by the *Atharvanic* author in the original hymn and very rightly concludes that this hymn is comparatively a late hymn.

6. Though Prof. Velankar has accepted the aids of the predecessors like Sāyaṇa, Oldenberg and Geldner, in translating and adding notes to the *Ṛg-Vedic* hymns, it must be stated here that he is not a servile imitator[17] of these scholars. At times, has also suggested different interpretations which have not so far, attracted the mind of the scholars. Hence it would be necessary to know the standpoint of Prof. Velankar in interpreting the *Ṛg-Vedic* hymns. It must be mentioned here that Prof. Velankar never takes any pleasure in summarily dismissing the views of these accredited masters of the *Ṛg-Veda.* Whenever, he wants to suggest an interpretation different from the one already suggested by these grand-masters, Velankar adopts the policy of a sound and matured scholar, who never insists that he alone has understood the whole of the truth. Hence, whenever, he is inclined to disagree with the predecessors, he generally passes the remarks 'very likely', unlikely, not-convincing, not satisfactory, probable, doubtful, and surely'. All these remarks further display his reverential attitude towards the masters. This kind of attitude in passing the

remarks deserves to be emulated by the scholars who have to view the matter in the right perspective. In the light of this background, I would like to reveal the different approaches of Prof. Velankar, particularly on his points of arguments.

Sāyaṇācārya and Prof. Velankar

(1) He completely disagrees with Sāyaṇācārya in interpreting the *Ṛg-Veda,* VIII.91 which is the famous *Apālā-Sūkta*. Here Sāyaṇācārya quotes a passage from the *Śāṭyāyana Brāhmaṇa,* to reveal the voluptuous nature of Indra. Prof. Velankar makes bold to disagree[18] with this authority on the ground of the complete spirit of the *Ṛg-Veda* and particularly of the *Apālā-Sūkta*. He categorically points out that in the entire *Ṛg-Veda,* we do not have a piece of evidence to show the voluptuous nature of Indra. Hence, it is not possible to accept the interpretation suggested by Sāyaṇācārya on the basis of the *Śāṭyāyana Brāhmaṇa*. It may be noted here that in the *Atharva-Veda,* one gets the faint traces of the voluptuous nature of Indra as indicated by Dr. Dandekar in his *Vedic Mythological Tracts*[19]. In passing, it may be remarked that the writers on *Purāṇas* are mainly responsible for spreading the voluptuous nature of Indra, through some concocted stories. Here the textual authority is rejected on the ground of the spirit of the *Bhakti* doctrine revealed in the entire *Ṛg-Veda*.

(2) Prof. Velankar further rightly holds that in interpreting the *Ṛg-Veda,* some ideas should be attested by the Vedic evidence. In interpreting the *Ṛg-Veda,* II.42.2 and particularly the expression *pitryām pradiśām* as referring to the southern direction (preferred by Sāyaṇācārya), Prof. Velankar significantly points[20] out that the assignment of quarters to the deities is surely post-*Ṛg-Vedic* and hence he very guardedly remarks that the interpretation offered by Sāyaṇācārya is too modern to be convincing.

(3) Prof. Velankar takes into account the practices revealed by the *Ṛg-Vedic* hymns to interpret the particular expressions in the particular hymns. In interpreting the expression known as *uttāna-hastāḥ* in the *Ṛg-Veda,* III.14.5, Prof. Velankar holds the opposite view of Sāyaṇācārya. Here he significantly points[21] out that the upward stretching of the hands must be understood as a part of salutation. In this practice, the bent head is placed upon the raised

hands folded together. He supports this practice by quoting the *Ṛg-Veda,* VI.16.46 and X.79.2 in his favour and remarks that Sāyaṇa's explanation on the *Ṛg-Veda* ,V.16.46 is probably correct. In the present context, however, his explanation that the hands are raised only to accept the oblations, cannot be favoured. It may be noted, in passing, that here the explanation is shown to be unsatisfactory on the ground of the practices prevalent in the Vedic society and particularly revealed by the Vedic hymns.

(4) Similarly in interpreting the expression *vadhūḥ* in the context of the *Ṛg-Veda,* VII.18.22, Sāyaṇācārya treats it as a reference to a maid-servant. In this respect, he is followed by Geldner. Here Prof. Velankar significantly points out that the expression *Vadhūḥ* in this context, really conveys the sense of a *mare* and supports this meaning by drawing attention to the usage of this expression in the *Ṛg-Veda,* VIII.68.17 and I.56.1 and I.140.6, in which the word *vadhū* occurs in the context of the horses. Here Prof. Velankar guardedly remarks that the word *vadhū* very likely[22] means *a mare.* It should be noted, in passing, that Prof. Velankar suggests that alternative explanation which becomes acceptable and tries his best to support it by Vedic usage and does not write with the tone of an authority.

(5) When, however, the question arises as to how the expression *'rava'* occurring in the *Ṛg-Veda,* III.31.6 is to be interpreted, Prof. Velankar first refers to the explanation of Sāyaṇācarya as indicating the sense of 'the lowing of the eagerly waiting cows'. He points[23] out that the word *Rava* is never used in the case of the cows. He further adds that the word *Rava* is more likely a war-cry of Bṛhaspati and Angiras family. For this interpretation, however, he draws our attention to the *Ṛg-Veda,* V.45.2b and IV.1.16cd. He also adds that in the case of the cows the root *vāś* is used and the root *ru* or *rava* is never used. One will appreciate here Velankar's command of the usage of the Vedic words and expressions.

(6) When, however, Sāyaṇācārya holds, in interpreting the expression *kakuhaḥ* at *Ṛg-Veda,* III.54.14, as a nominative plural of *Kakuha,* Prof. Velankar simply observes that this is less likely[24] and takes it as nominative singular. Here is a case of difference of

opinion between the two scholars on the ground of grammatical point.

(7) When, however, Prof. Velankar notices that in interpreting a particular expression, Sāyaṇācārya has neglected the importance of an accent which is very important in the *Ṛg-Vedic* interpretation, Prof. Velankar rightly observes that this becomes unacceptable. In interpreting the expression *āvṛtam* in the *Ṛg-Veda*, II.36.6, Sāyaṇa's explanation as *ṛtvigbhi veṣṭitam* has properly neglected[25] the importance of the accent. Prof. Velankar takes *āvṛtam* as accusative infinitive like *avṛte*, the dative infinitive at the *Ṛg-Veda*, III.42.3.

(8) Prof. Velankar has also paid proper attention to the sacrificial matter in interpreting the *Ṛg-Vedic* hymns. Thus, in interpreting the *Ṛg-Veda*, III.28.3, Prof. Velankar points out that even Sāyaṇācārya is not aware of a sacrifice in which a stale cake is offered as an oblation. Hence it is but proper on the part of the Prof. Velankar to show that the name and nature of this kind of peculiar sacrifice is a case of *terra incognita* even for Sāyaṇācārya. Generally, Sāyaṇācārya is bent upon offering a sacrificial interpretation of the *Ṛg-Vedic mantras*. Hence Prof. Velankar's remark[26] on this point is most appropriate. I only wish that some modern scholars should consider this point and throw light on the name and nature of a sacrifice in which, in particular, a stale cake is offered as an oblation.

From this, it is quite evident that Prof. Velankar shows his disagreement with Sāyaṇa on the grounds of accent, usage of the Vedic words, practices preserved by the Vedic hymns, grammatical point, idea warranted by the Vedic evidence and proper consideration of the textual authority in the light of the background of Vedic hymns.

Western Scholars and Prof. Velankar

It would be interesting to note the approach of Prof. Velankar with reference to the views of the Western scholars like Oldenberg, Geldner and Renou, in particular.

(1) In interpreting the hymns of the *Ṛg-Veda*, there is one method of studying the hymn as a whole, interpreting the words

in relation to the context and assuming that the author of the hymn has a connected idea and unity of purpose. In interpreting the last hymn of the Tenth *Maṇḍala* of the *Ṛg-Veda,* Oldenberg considers the first stanza as unconnected with the hymn and hence an interpolation. Prof. Velankar has shown his difference of opinion with the viewpoint of Oldenberg. He points out that in the opening stanza of this hymn contains an appeal to *Agni,* and the reference to the pouring of a common offering occurs in the verse No.3. This is sufficient to establish unmistakably the unity of the first stanza with the hymn as a whole. Here is an appeal made by a priest to his friends and comrades and not a song of appeal for unity among the people at large. He, therefore, very rightly concludes[27] that Oldenberg's arguments are obviously inconclusive on the point of interpolation.

(2) Prof. Velankar is at variance with Oldenberg in interpreting the word *Sūda* in the VII.36.3. Oldenberg takes it in the sense of 'pool' and he is followed by Geldner in this respect. Prof. Velankar simply adds[28] that the reason of the context does not recommend the sense so suggested by these scholars. He holds that *Sūda* is from *Svad*— that is sweetner here and hence the rain cloud whose water is used for preparing the *Soma* drink.

(3) There is also a difference of opinion in interpreting the expression *duṇāśa* occurring in the *Ṛg-Veda,* VII.32.7. Both Oldenberg and Geldner take this word as referring to enemy. Prof. Velankar, here, attracts the mind of the readers to the usage[29] of this word in the *Ṛg-Veda,* such as *Dūṇāśam kṣatram* at *Ṛg-Veda* VII.18.25, *duṇāśa dakṣinā* at VI.27.8 and *dūṇāśaḥ rayiḥ* at *Ṛg-Veda,* IX. 63.11 and concludes that this expression in the *Ṛg-Veda,* VII.32.7 refers to Indra as 'unassailable or inimitable'. He further adds here that the root *naś* means to reach. It may be noted here that on the basis of the usage of the Vedic words, Prof. Velankar has shown his disagreement with Oldenberg.

(4) Prof. Velankar seems to have given meticulous attention to the meanings of the words in the *Ṛg-Veda.* The question arises as to how the word *kṣapāvān* in the *Ṛg-Veda,* VII.10.5 is to be interpreted. Oldenberg takes the sense of 'the lord of the earth'. Prof. Velankar takes it in the sense of 'the lord of the night', and remarks[30] that the *Ṛg-Veda* does not attest this meaning 'the lord

of the earth' to a word.

(5) When, however, there is a difference of opinion among the Western scholars on the meaning of a particular root-form and sense, Prof. Velankar agrees with Grassmann as against the schoolars like Oldenberg and Geldner. The form *vivekṣi* occurs in the *Ṛg-Veda,* VII.3.4. Oldenberg and Geldner take the form *vivekṣi* as form a root *viś* to attack. Prof. Velankar cites[31] the authority of Grassmann and takes it as from a root *vic* to separate and/or distinguish and thus shows his disagreement with these scholars.

(6) At times, however, Prof. Velankar refers to the *Pada-Pāṭha* to show that the interpretation adopted by Oldenberg, if accepted, goes against the *Pada-Pāṭha.* For this purpose, he draws attention to the *Ṛg-Veda,* II.24.2 and points out that according to Oldenberg the four verbs in this stanza are to be connected with the four relative clauses and hence the accent plays very important part here. Prof. Velankar simply shows[32] that this technique goes against the *Pada-Pāṭha.*

(7) Sometimes, however, Prof. Velankar refers to the explanation of Oldenberg and offers an alternative explanation. This is the point to be noted with reference to the *Ṛg-Veda,* II.17.8. Here Velankar takes[33] *Āpāṁsi* as a sacrificial work and states that Indra may be said to have secured sacrifical work for the priest from the patron. Oldenberg, however, takes it as Indra's own exploits which he may be said to have bestowed upon his worshipper, when he performed them for him. One will note here that Prof. Velankar's explanation is an alternative explanation on this count.

(8) Prof. Velankar has pointed out a defect in the interpretation of Oldenberg from the point of an accent. In interpreting the *Ṛg-Veda,* II.19.4, Oldenberg suggests an emendation to consider *dāśat* as an accented participle in place of *dāśat.* If, however, this is accepted, then it would involve the change[34] of the accent of *hanti* to a *nighāta,* according to Prof. Velankar. He further adds that there would be no ground for its present accent.

(9) The question arises whether the preposition is to be connected with a word or a verb in the *mantra,* we have a typical position in the *Ṛg-Veda,* II.4.7. Here the point is whether the preposition *abhi* is to be construed with or connected with *urvīm*

or the verbal form *vi-asthāt.* Oldenberg connects *abhi* with *urvīm*. Prof. Velankar here connects it with *vi-asthāt* and points out the Vedic usage in his support by referring to the *Ṛg-Veda,* I.74.8, VII.34.5 and X.65.15. It is significant to note his remark[35] 'I think it rather goes with *vi-asthāt,* deserves to be noted and it is indicative of his innate modesty before the master.

From the above discussion, it is evident that Prof. Velankar departs from Oldenberg on the grounds of Vedic usage, *Pada-Pāṭha,* difficulties in accent, attestation of a particular meaning for the particular expression, contextual position, and the unity of the hymn.

Geldner and Prof. Velankar

(1) When, however, there is a conflict between Sāyaṇācārya and Geldner, on the meaning of a particular word, Prof. Velankar appears to side[36] with Sāyaṇācārya. The question arises as regards the meaning of the expression *Bhāga* in the *Ṛg-Veda,* I.72-5. Geldner takes it as a share allotted to us by Gods. But Sāyaṇācārya takes it as *devasaṁpradākaṁ bhāgam* — their share alloted to Gods by us. Here Prof. Velankar follows Sāyaṇācārya and further states the reason for his view. He adds that 'd' supplies a reason for what is said in 'C'.

(2) Prof. Velankar also boldly controverts Geldner in interpreting the *ṚV.,* I.127-10. Here Geldner takes the word *apidhi* in the sense of 'obstructions or covers'. Prof. Velankar suggests[37] that like *paridhi* (*ṚV,* 10.95.15), *apidhi* has the sense of encompassing sticks which are dear to him (*Agni*).

(3) Prof. Velankar departs from Geldner in interpreting the expression *paśutṛpam,* in the *ṚV,* VII.86.5. Geldner takes[38] it as 'stealing away the animals on the basis of *Tṛp=Tṛf* (*Avestā*) to steal. Prof. Velankar points out that if this interpretation is accepted, then the word *Paśu* would be unmeaning[39] and hence he hesitates to accept this mode of interpretation. Besides, if the expression *paśutṛpam* is taken in the sense of 'satisfying the animal then the reason why the thief is to be released becomes evident. He further points out that the *Manu-Smṛti,* XI.196 makes a reference to the custom of releasing a thief, provided, the sheaf of hay is accepted

by a cow. Prof. Velankar thus tries to interpret *ṚV* in the light of the later Indian literature. Here it may be noted that as usual Dr. Dandekar upholds[40] the viewpoint of Geldner and tries to remark that the interpretation offered by Prof. Velankar is obviously untenable. Here it should be again noted that Dr. Dandekar writes with the tone of an authority, as is keeping with his nature and leaves the points of Prof. Velankar, unanswered. He has no reply to the peculiarity of the simile in the present context for which Prof. Velankar has also relied upon the *ṚV,* II.28.6c and VIII.67.14,18. Besides, he has no reply to the unmeaning of the word *paśu,* if the interpretation of Geldner is favoured. Here also, it is evident that Dr. Dandekar's writing is one-sided and he ignores the points of Prof. Velankar, conveniently. One is also tempted to observe that Dr. Dandekar has not developed his intellectual faculty to appreciate the peculiarities of the similes in the *Ṛg-Veda,* which is indeed, the strong point of the writing of Prof. Velankar. Hence it would not be wrong if it is casually remarked that Dr. Dandekar's view does not deserve approbation at the hands of the scholars.

(4) As regards the role of *Agni* in sending down rains, there appears to be no unanimity of thought between Geldner and Prof. Velankar. On the *ṚV,* I.69.8, Prof. Velankar refers to Geldner who relies on the *ṚV,* I.140.2 for the regeneration of the plants and herbs by *Agni* with the help of Maruts through the rains, after he had burnt them as his fuel. Prof. Velankar very significantly observes[41] that *Agni's* role or part in sending down rains is not very well attested in the *Ṛg-Veda.*

(5) In interpreting the expression *Viśve* in the *ṚV.,* I.168.4, Sāyaṇa and Geldner are on one side and Prof. Velankar is on the other side. Both Sāyaṇācārya and Geldner take *Viśve* in the above place as referring to the ancient sacrificers. Prof. Velankar vigilantly observes[42] that a sacrificer attaining *devatva* or going to heaven, is surely post-*Ṛg-Vedic.* He also states the logic at the back of it. He points out that the *Ṛbhus* are said to have attained godhood not by sacrifice but by their skill and hard-work and draws our attention to the *Ṛg-Veda,* I.208 and III.60.2. Hence their explanation becomes unacceptable in the present context.

(6) The propriety of the expression *asme* in the *Ṛg-Veda,* I.72.2 is understood by Prof. Velankar as referring[43], to *asmabhyaṁ*

or *asmāsu* with reference to *Agni* who is now with us but not as *asmākaṁ* as hinted at by Geldner.

(7) In explaining the significance of the expression *tatāpa* Prof. Velankar seems to be in complete disagreement with Sāyaṇācārya and Geldner. Both Sāyaṇācārya and Geldner take *tatāpa* as referring to the pains of a gambler at the sight of the excellent condition of the wives of others. Prof. Velankar here adds that the Vedic usage[44] of the root *tap* to pain, refers to the pains on account of one's own loss and not at the sight of the prosperity of other. Here the usage of the Vedic root is a strong point of argumentation of Prof. Velankar. We also get another example of this type in understanding the expression *abhicakṣe* in the *ṚV*, X.34.5, for which I refer the readers to the discussion[45] in the *Ṛksūktaśatī*.

(8) There is also a difference of opinion between Geldner and Prof. Velankar to interpret the expression *Asura* in the *ṚV*, III.29.14. Geldner takes that this expression refers to *Vṛtra*. Prof. Velankar relies[46] on the context and points out that the two words *mātā* and *asura* here refer respectively to the *adhara* (lower) and *uttara* (upper) *araṇis* (sacrificial sticks).

(9) Prof. Velankar seems to disagree with Geldner particularly when he neglects the accent in interpreting the *ṚV*, III.49.2. Here Geldner connects the lines 'c' and 'd' together and neglects the *nighāta* accent of *amināt* in 'd' Prof. Velankar simply points out that the lines 'c' and 'd' cannot construed together, for the simple reason[47] that this amounts to simply neglecting the accent known as *nighāta*. He further adds that Sāyaṇa's attempt in this respect, seems to be unnecessary.

From the above discussion, it is quite evident that Prof. Velankar shows his disagreement with Geldner on the grounds of the usage of the Vedic words and verbs, accent, the attestation of a particular idea with reference to a particular god, by stressing the point of interpetation that *ṚV* is to be interpreted in the light of later Indian literature and *Avestā* is not a safe guide in this respect, and also sides with Sāyaṇa against Geldner on the interpretation of the word *Bhāga*.

Renou and Prof. Velankar

It may be noted here that Prof. Velankar has expressed the sense of gratitude to Louis Renou for the kind sympathy and encouragement given to his work, particularly in his Preface p.v to the *Ṛg-Veda Maṇḍala* VII. Though he has made some use of the work of Renou, Prof. Velankar has some occasions to differ from him.

(1) When the question arises as regards the interpretation of the form *johūtraḥ* in the *ṚV,* II.10.1, Renou tries to interpret it in the passive sense. Prof. Velankar simply points out that this form is used in the active sense and supports his interpretation by quoting *ṚV,* I.118.9 and II.20.3 and also the view of Wackernagel. It must be noted here that Prof. Velankar translates[48] this as 'frequent invoker of gods' and not as 'fit to be invoked' following Sāyaṇa, Geldner and Renou.

(2) In interpreting the expression *arakṣasā manasā* in the *ṚV,* II.10.5, the question arises whether this expression is to be construed with *Agni* or devotee, both Geldner and Renou construe it with *Agni.* Prof. Velankar connects[49] it with a devotee and refers the readers to the *Ṛg-Vedic* usage of this expression at VII.85.1a (*arakṣasaṁ manīṣām*) and V.87.9 (*arakṣaḥ havam*) and connects it with a devotee. Prof. Velankar translates the above expression as 'with a mind which has no association with a devil'.

(3) We have a problem in the *ṚV,* II.4.7 as to how the form *asvādayat* is to be interpreted. Renou follows Geldner and translates it as '*Agni* prepared it as it were for his meal'. Velankar disagrees[50] with this mode of Renou and translates *'Agni,* has, as it were, sweetened the earth (while burning the dry grass over it) and has stated the reason in the note on this stanza, for which I refer the readers to the *ṚV. Maṇḍala* II.'

(4) When, however, it is noticed by Prof. Velankar that Renou has neglected the word *na* altogether, he simply notes this in his note on the *ṚV,* II.4.5 and elucidates[51] this point to the readers.

(5) In the *ṚV,* III.17.5, there is a reference to *Agni's* predecessor. Velankar here suggests that the first of the three brothers mentioned in the *ṚV,* I.164.1, and who sat down in the capacity of inviting priest and invitee god, is actually referred to in the present case. He further checks[52] Renou's reference to the *ṚV,* VIII.11.10

and simply observes that this does not seem to be appropriate. From this, it is quite evident that Prof. Velankar takes pretty care to check the references given by the foreign scholars to support their mode of interpretation.

(6) Prof. Velankar has also shown that Renou's translation and construction of *ṚV*, III.22.4 and joining 'd' with *Agnayaḥ* are unsatisfactory. Renou translates this portion as 'who frees men from diseases and are equivalent of great sacrificial foods'. Velankar, however, translates the line as '*Agni* is requested to accept our sacrifice and the great sacrificial foods which are free from disease (for being given to us), Velankar states[53] the reason that the acceptance of the foods is not for ourselves but for being used as a gift.

(7) In passing, Velankar has followed Renou at some places of the *ṚV*, III.27.2, III.54.2 etc. It should also be noted here that though Prof. Velankar nas occasions to differ from the foreign scholars on the points of Vedic interpretation, he has also, at times, quoted passages from the *ṚV* in defence[54] or support of the interpretation of these scholars, which I reserve to point out only in the foot-note.

Reactions on the Works of Prof. Velankar

It would be worth our while to consider some possible reactions on the work of Prof. Velankar, particularly in this context.

(1) If it is said that Prof. Velankar's translation and notes do not reveal impressive command over the bibliographic material which incidentally is the strong point of the writings[55] of Jan-Gonda (as noted by Dr. Dandekar), the simple reason for this is that Velankar himself has admitted his limitations in respect of the first hand knowledge of German and French works and also the non-availability of these books in India.

(2) Sometimes, it is said that Velankar has not considered historical evidence in interpreting the words *dāsa, dasyu, ahi*, etc. that occur in the body of the text of the *Ṛg-Veda* and particularly in the context of the Indra hymns. It may be pointed out that he has tried to retain these words as they are. It must be stated here that Prof. Velankar appears to hold the view that the *Ṛg-Veda*

being an Indian document, is to be interpreted only in the light of later Sanskrit works. On account of this approach, naturally we also cannot expect any light from the historical side, for the importance[56] of such words, a reference may be made to Dr. Dandekar's *Vedic Mythological Tracts.*

(3) It appears that Prof. Velankar has ignored the anthropological and sociological approaches to the Vedic interpretation. It must be stated here that other scholars like Jan Gonda[57] and others have considered this approach and hence it is also not necessary to make the duplication of the work. It must be stated that Velankar has laid limitation on his work by his own approach to the subject. Hence there is no point in blaming him in any manner as such.

(4) It seems that Velankar has not given proper consideration to the Vedic interpretation from the point of view of the comparative mythology and comparative linguistics. Here it should be noted that Prof. Velankar's approach is simply linguistic and more correctly textual. Possibly, he has not treated comparative linguistics as a safe guide in interpreting the *ṚV* as is clear from his elucidation[58] of the expression *paśutṛpam* in the *ṚV,* VII.86.5.

(5) It is also urged that Prof. Velankar has not given more attention on the sexual and pastoral symbolism and sexual interpretation of the *ṚV.* One may say that this topic seems to have been persued by the scholars[59] of repute as a life-time work. Here it may be casually remarked that Velankar has touched this aspect and has not persued this topic to the fullest extent.

(6) At times, it is evident that Velankar's notes do not give us more correct idea about the cultural life of the Vedic *āryans.* It may be noted here that some scholars have done this work. Here a reference could be made to the work of some scholars who have perhaps done more justice to this aspect. Incidentally, it may be noted that in the introduction[60] to the *Ṛg-Veda Maṇḍala* VII Prof. Velankar has discussed some cultural points of *Bhakti* doctrine in the *Ṛg-Veda* with reference to Varuṇa, Vasiṣṭha and *Bhakti.* He has also elsewhere discussed at some length the relation of the Viśvāmitras with Vasiṣṭha and Vasiṣṭha and Jamadagnis in the introduction to the seventh *Maṇḍala* of the *ṚV.* Incidentally, it

may be added here that this shortcoming (perhaps in the eyes of other scholars) is removed by Prof. S.A. Upadhyaya, who has written a note on the cultural[61] life as revealed in the third *Maṇḍala* of the *ṚV.* It must be noted here in passing that Dr. Dandekar deserves credit for concentrating on this aspect, personally by writing some articles[62] and also guiding his student Dr. V.G. Rahurkar, for the thesis[63] in the University of Poona. Incidentally, it may be noted that Dr. Rahurkar has made ample use of the material of Dr. Dandekar scattered in several articles.

(7) At times, however, it is likely to be urged that Prof. Velankar has not made use of Pāṇini as an aid to the *Ṛg-Vedic* interpretation. It must be stated that P. Thieme and Dr. S.S.Bhave held the conviction that Pāṇini is almost an unfailing guide in the interpretation of the *ṚV.* Prof. Velankar appears to have made the use of Pāṇini relied upon by Sāyaṇa, as the occasion so demanded. Incidentally, it may be remarked that Prof. Velankar has made abundant use of the Vedic Grammars of Macdonell and other Western scholars. It may be stated that Dr. G.V.Devasthali, the grateful pupil of Prof. Velankar, has realised the importance of Pāṇini in the *Ṛg-Vedic* interpretation as is clear from the articles[64] contributed by him to the *Annals of the Bhandarkar Oriental Research Institute,* Pune, though in the beginning he appeared to be slightly against[65] the utility of Pāṇini for the Vedic interpretation. In passing, it may be added that the writer of this note has also made some attempt[66] to interpret the *ṚV,* II.41.11 with the help of grammatical authorities. In passing, it may be stated here that when the word *suvīryam* occurs in the *ṚV,* VII.97.4, Prof. Velankar takes it as a *Tat-puruṣa* compound. Dr. S.S. Bhave, however, would interpret it as a *Bahuvrīhi* compound on the basis of Pāṇini's *Aṣṭādhyāyī,* VI. 2.120 which runs as *Vīravīryau ca.* On account of this approach, however, there is to be seen a difference in interpretation. In passing, the viewpoint of Dr. M.A. Mehendale, in interpreting the expression *vicakrame* in the *Viṣṇu-Sūkta* of the *ṚV,* I.154.1 deserves a mention[67] on this point.

(8) It would be interesting to note that Prof. Velankar has correctly appreciated the importance of Yāska's *Nirukta* in the *Ṛg-Vedic* interpretation. One would be happy to note that he has also guided a thesis[68] for Ph.D. on Yāska's *Nirukta* and *Ṛg-Vedic*

interpretation. This thesis is deposited in the library of the University of Bombay. It may be added that Mrs. S.S. Pradhana has contributed a few articles to the *Annals of the Bhandarkar Oriental Research Institute,* on the difficulties in the corrupt text of Yāska. Incidentally, it is worth noting the viewpoint[69] of Dr. Dandekar that the etymology of a word with reference to a deity, must represent the essential characteristic of a deity. He has pointed out that the etymological derivations suggested by Sāyaṇa, with reference to the word *Rudra* are linguistically unsound and hence unacceptable. Dr. Dandekar however, derives the word *Rudra* from the root *rud* (which is lost in this sense) to be red, basing his etymology on the lost practice among the people.

(9) At times, it may appear that Prof. Velankar has not considered the importance of the *Upabṛmhaṇa,* i.e., the *Mahābhārata* and *Purāṇas,* as a good source of Vedic interpretation. This source is handled[70] by Dr. T.G. Mainkar with references to the two Vedic hymns X.95 and X.102. *Ṛg-Veda,* X.102 is treated by Prof. Velankar as a race theory. While Dr. Mainkar has considered this as a war-theory on the basis of the *Paurāṇic* evidence. Dr. S.G.Kantawalla has also offered *Paurāṇic* interpretation of the *Saramā-Paṇi-Saṁvāda* (*ṚV,* X. 108) and *Purūravā-Urvaśī* dialogue of the *Ṛg-Veda* elsewhere. Incidentally, it may be remembered in this very context, that Prof. Velankar has not ignored the importance of this source. He has guided a thesis[71] for Ph.D. Degree of the University of Bombay, on the topic 'Indra in the post-Vedic literature, and the causes of his deterioration in the *Purāṇas.* Prof. G.H. Godbole has written this thesis under the guidance of Prof. Velankar. From this, it is quite evident that Prof. Velankar has handled this source through his pupil, perhaps on a grand-scale as compared with the meagre attempts on the part of the scholars mentioned above.

(10) It may be pointed out that Prof. Velankar has also considered the philosophical interpretation of some of the hymns of the *ṚV.* It may be noted here that he has translated and explained cosmological hymns of the *ṚV.* Incidentally, it may be added here that he has also discussed in one article[72] 'The Vedic Origin of the story of Naciketas' on the *ṚV,* X.135, in a volume presented to Louis Renou. It should be noted that this volume is

published after the sad demise of the learned Professor Velankar. Incidentally, it should be noted here that Prof. Velankar has not given any expression to the sectarian interpretation of the *ṚV* as is offered by Madhva, Vallabha and others. Dr. S.G. Kantawalla has discussed the sectarian interpretation[73] of the *ṚV*, I.154.6 in the Professor Baladev Upadhyaya felicitation volume issued by the Ganganatha Jha Research Institute *alias* Ganganath Jha Kendriya Sanskrit Vidyapitha, Allahabad. One may add here that A.S. Tiwari has contributed an article (perhaps more lengthy) on the Sectarian interpretation of the *ṚV*. to the *Journal of the Ganganatha Jha Kendriya Sanskrit Vidyapitha*, Vol.45, 1984, pp. 95-112. Prof. R.B. Athavale has also offered philosophical[74] interpretation of some of the *Mantras* of *ṚV*. with the help of the stanzas from the *Śataślokī* of Śaṅkarācārya. Incidentally, it may be mentioned here that the sectarian interpretation of the *ṚV*, I.154.6, given by Vallabhācārya may be supported by quoting the line of the *Kṛṣṇāṣṭakam*[75] of Śaṅkarācārya. Here it should be noted that Aravinda's mystic interpretation of some of the *mantras* has not become the subject of the attraction of the scholars. It may be noted, in passing, that Dr. M.D. Paradkar has made a reference to this mystic interpretation[76] with reference to the goddess Sarasvatī, particularly in his recently published book in Marathi known as *stabaka*.

(11) It may be respectfully submitted that the modern scholars have not considered the aid of the *Pūrva-Mīmāṁsā* works for interpreting some of the words of the *ṚV*. Here a reference could be made to the expressions such as *Kīkaṭa*, *Naicāśākha*, and *pramaganda* occurring in the *ṚV*, III.53.14. These words also occur in the commentary of Kumārilabhaṭṭa on the *Pūrva-Mīmāṁsā Sūtra*, I.2.50. It may be noted here that Kumārila understands these words differently[77] as compared with the meanings assigned to these words by Prof. Velankar. Incidentally, it may be mentioned that Prof. S.A. Upadhyaya in his Introduction to the *ṚV Maṇḍala* III, has referred to some explanations even by quoting the book *The Seers of the Ṛg-Veda* by Dr. V.G. Rahurkar. But the treatment given here is far from being satisfactory. The writer of this note[78] prefers to note these points of the *Mīmāṁsakas* in the foot-note with a detailed note on the same. It should, however, be

mentioned that Sāyaṇācārya has made some use of the doctrines of the *Pūrva-Mīmāṁsā* in interpreting some of the *mantras* of the *ṚV.* The writer of this note has already emphasised the importance of the science of *Pūrva-Mīmāṁsā* for Vedic interpretation elsewhere. But the scholars seem to have ignored the importance of this important branch of learning.

(12) The tendency of the *prākṛtism* is also noticed by Prof. Velankar in the context of the *ṚV.* when in particular *na* becomes *ṇa*. Dr. G.V. Devasthali has contributed a paper on the *Prākṛtism* in the *ṚV.* and Dr. M.A. Mehendale has noticed the *prākṛt* tendency[79] in the famous *Maṇḍūka-Sūkta* of the *ṚV.* particularly in a paper contributed to Dr. S.K. Belvalkar felicitation Volume.

(13) At times, however, some scholars have offered the explanations quite different from the explanations of the *Ṛg-Vedic* words given by Prof. Velankar. Dr. Ram Gopal has discussed the significance of the expression[80] *svar-dṛś* in the Dr. R.N. Dandekar felicitation volume, by taking the word in the sense of 'one who shows heaven.' Dr. P. Thieme has also discussed at full length the expression[81] *duroṇa* in the *Ṛg-Veda,* particularly in the above volume and has thus suggested other meanings of the word. I resist the temptation of adding illustrations of this Kind.

Conclusion

In conclusion, in paying my respectful tribute to my revered *Gurujī* the late Prof. H.D. Velankar, on the occasion of his centenary, I must add that he has contributed a lot to the Vedic interpretation by his rich command over the accent, usage of the Vedic words and verbs, contextual explanation, attestation of a particular idea by the evidence from the *Veda,* spirit of the Vedic hymns to decide the validity of the textual authority, contradicting the renowned scholars on the ground of the unity of purpose of a hymn, grammatical point, manner and practices preserved in the Vedic hymns, showing difficulties in the interpretations of others from the angle of accent, and *Pada-Pāṭha,* utilising the source of the later Indian Sanskrit literature and displaying the difficulties in the use of *Avestā* for Vedic interpretation, hinting at symbolic interpretations, properly utilising some sources for the pupils for the Ph.D. Degree and showing disagreement with the grand-masters of the Vedic scholars with the reverent attitude of a pupil but fearlessly and forcefully. On this occasion, I have only prayer to the Vedic scholars of the world that some scholars should come forward and enrich the Vedic interpretation by making the judicious assimilation of all the sources that are incidentally referred to in the body of this chapter and also the sources which have escaped my eye, for the benefit of the future scholars.

References

1. For word economy, See *ṚV. Maṇḍala* II. 1.1, 2.2, 4.9, 6.3, 14.2, 19.2, 24.15, 28.5, 29.1, etc.

   Maṇḍala III. I.1.2; 6.4,5; 8.5, 9.6, 10.5, 14.2, 15.4 etc. *Maṇḍala* VII, 25.5, 19.10, 48-1, 75.2, 81.4, 85.4 etc.
2. *Journal of the Asiatic Society of Bombay,* Vol.18, pp. 1-43.
3. See *Path of Devotion* (in Marāthī), p.46. It may be noted that this point of decorative simile has no place in the *Ṛksūktaśatī,* p.192. It may also be noted here that Miss. K.N. Velankar has written a Ph.D. thesis on 'Decorative Simile in the *Ṛg-Veda,* under the guidance of Prof. Velankar. This thesis is deposited in the Library of the University of Bombay, 1966.
4. *Bhāratīya Vidyā,* Vol. 25 Nos. 3 & 4, 1965, pp. 1.43.
5. H.D. Velankar, *ṚV-Maṇḍala* VII, introduction pp. i-iv.
6. H.D. Velankar, *Path of Devotion,* pp. 91-94.
7. *Ibid.,* pp. 85-90.
8. *Ibid.,* pp. 89-90 for the *abhaṅgas* of Tukārāma quoted by Velankar.
9. *Ibid.,* pp 86-87 quotes passages from the *ṚV.* I.24.9, I.24.11, I.25.1, I.25.19, II.28.5, V.28.7, VII.86.3, VII.88.6 and VII.89.5 to show the angry nature of *Varuṇa.*
10. R.N. Dandekar, *Exercises in Indology,* pp. 113-21 for the article on *Varuṇa, Vasiṣṭha* and *Bhakti.* (Ajanta Publications, Delhi, 1981).
11. H.D. Velankar, *Ṛg-Veda-Maṇḍala* VII, introduction, pp. x-xi.
12. *Path of Devotion in the Ṛg-Veda,* p. 76. It may be noted that when Arbaman holds that Vedic Indians were familiar with the temples and idol worship (quoted in *Vedic Mythological Tracts,* p.245n), Dr. Dandekar discards this view and surprisingly agrees with Prof. Velankar, though he has not referred to the viewpoint of Prof. Velankar.
13. R.N. Dandekar *Exercises in Indology,* pp. 169-245 for a lengthy but competent survey of the works of Western scholars at the hands of a competent scholar.
14. H.D. Velankar, *Ṛksūktaśatī,* p. 230. For the views of scholars like Jan Gonda, also see: V.G.Rahurkar's *The Seers of the Ṛg-Veda,* pp.134-36 (Poona University publication, 1964).

15. Many illustrations of this type can be cited even by writing an independent paper. For examples, Dr. G.K. Bhat's view on the *Saṁvāda-Sūktas* stands summarily dismissed at the hands of Dr. Dandekar. Cf. *Exercises in Indology*. p. 128. Dr. Dandekar has also dismissed the views of Dr. Kane and Dr. V.M. Apte on the point of the controversy on *Vrata* in *MM. Dr. P.V. Kane Commemoration Monograph*, p.11 (published by the University of Bombay, 1974). This is his nature, in the opinion of this writer.
16. See: *Ṛksūktaśatī*, p. 208. In his notes on *Ṛg-Veda Maṇḍala* VII, 1.55 (p.124), Prof. Velankar has referred to the *Kauśika Gṛhyasūtra*, the purpose of which is to hypnotise an unwilling women for an easy approach and consequently changes are made by the *Ātharvaṇic* poet to turn it into a love-charm. It seems that in the *Ṛksūktaśatī*, pp. 207-08, an important reference to the *Kauśika Gṛhyasūtra* appears to have been omitted by Prof. S.A. Upadhyaya.
17. For the critical examination of the views of Western scholars, consult P.75-82.
18. *Path of devotion in the Ṛg-Veda*, p. 60 rejects the viewpoint of *Sāyaṇācārya* based on the *Śāṭyāyana Brāhmaṇa*.
19. R.N. Dandekar, *Vedic Mythological Tracts*, p.163. Dandekar adds here that Indra seems to be expert in female lore and as such assumes male and female forms as per his wish.
20. H.D. Velankar, *Ṛg-Veda*, *Maṇḍala* II, p.115.
21. H.D. Velankar, *Ṛg-Veda-Maṇḍala* III, p.39.
22. *Ṛg-Veda Maṇḍala*. VII, p.52.
23. *Ṛg-Veda Maṇḍala* III, p.71.
24. *Ibid.*, p. 127.
25. *Ṛg-Veda Maṇḍala* II, p. 103.
26. *Ṛg-Veda Maṇḍala* III, p.59.
27. *Ṛg-Veda-Maṇḍala* II, Introduction, pp. ix-x.
28. *Ṛg-Veda Maṇḍala* VII, p.96.
29. *Ṛg-Veda Maṇḍala* VII, p. 78.
30. *Ibid.*, p. 34.
31. *Ibid.*, p.15. Here he supports this by *ṚV*, X. 124.5c.
32. *Ṛg-Veda Maṇḍala* II, p. 65.
33. Here, however, Prof. Velankar has suggested an alternative explanation and has not criticized Oldenberg. Also see *ṚV. Maṇḍala* II. p.51. It may be noted here that in the Glossary to *ṚV. Maṇḍala* VII, the word is shown as having the sense of a work, p.238. The same is the case with the Glossary of *Ṛksūktaśatī*, p.314. But the above meaning and *ṚV.* II.17.8 have no place there.
34. *Ṛg-Veda Maṇḍala* II, p.54.
35. *Ibid.*, p.17. This is, indeed, in keeping with the spirit of pupil's humility before the master.
36. H.D.Velankar, *Ṛg-Veda Maṇḍala* I, Agni hymns on I.72.5 particularly in the

Journal of the University of Bombay, Vol.31, part 2, 1962, p. 17.

37. Mark his remark *'Apidhi* are surely not obstructions.' H.D. Velankar,' Hymns to Agni in *Maṇḍala* I, In *J.U.B.,* Vol.33, part 2, 1963, p.11.

38. *Ṛg-Veda Maṇḍala* VII, p.189 and Also *Ṛksūktaśatī,* p.224. It may be noted here that Geldner is contradicting his own accepted position. He had held that the *Ṛg-Veda* is to be interpreted in the light of the Indian works. Here he is trying to interpret the root *tṛp* with the help of *Avestā.* This position becomes appreciable from R.N. Dandekar's, *Exercises in Indology,* p.217, clarifying the standpoint of the Western scholars with reference to the interpretation of the *Ṛg-Veda.* If, however, the position of Geldner as represented by Dandekar is correct, then the charge of self-contradiction can be levelled at the doors of Geldner. If this stand is changed on account of the criticism of Oldenberg, then we have to admit that he has shifted the emphasis.

39. It must be noted here that Prof. Velankar is trying to interpret *ṚV.* with the help of the later Indian literature and particularly the *Dharma-Śāstra* text, *Manu-Smṛti,* XI.196.

40. Dr. Dandekar, *Exercises in Indology,* writes in his article on *' Varuṇa, Vasiṣṭha* and *Bhakti,* pp. 113-21 and treats Prof. Velankar's view as untenable. It should be noted here that Dr. Dandekar has no reply to the point that the word *paśutṛpam* would be insignificant if the sense of *tṛp* to steal is accepted. Besides, Dandekar has not, it seems, developed the faculty of appreciating the peculiarities of the Vedic language and usage and the similes in the present context. Hence his discussion seems only one-sided. In addition to this, he has no reply to the *Ṛg-Vedic* passages relied upon by Prof. Velankar, for suggesting that the release of somebody is a topic under discussion. Dandekar is interpreting the expression *' paśutṛpam* with the help of *Avestā,* as is the case with Geldner. Moreover, he feels that in a passage relied upon by Prof. Velankar, there is a reference to a cow and not *paśu.* It must be mentioned here that cow is also a *paśu* or an animal, though perhaps a specific animal in the present context. This argument of Dr. Dandekar is simply lame and does not stand to reason. Hence, the writer of this note feels that it would be wrong to accept the viewpoint of Dandekar on this point which is, in fact, not at all debatable. It is the general tendency of Dandekar to agree with the Western scholars and disagree with Indian scholars in particular. Further, it is unfair on the part of Dandekar, to write very roughly on the view of others. He has not learnt of disagreement with other scholars, by maintaining also their dignity in the matter. All his remarks most simply show his tone of an authority, which is, not at all, creditable to him.

41. Hymns to Agni in *Maṇḍala* I. On I.169.8, *JUB,* Vol. 131, part 2, 1962, p. 9.

42. *Ibid.,* p.7. In the *Mahābhārata,* XII.9 d 10SV, however, we have a reference that Rantideva went to heaven by performing sacrifices. C.R. Deshpande has pointed out this in his article 'studies in the recensions and versions of the *Mahābhārata'* an article contributed to *'Homage to Dr. Mainkar'* pp.18-30.

43. *Ibid.,* p. 15.

44. *Ṛksūktaśatī,* p. 267.
45. Also see *Ṛksūktaśatī,* p. 114 for another example of *dṛśaye no asthāt* / in *ṚV.* V. 80.5.
46. *Ṛg-Veda Maṇḍala* III, p.67.
47. *Ṛg-Veda Maṇḍala* III, p.110.
48. *Ṛg-Veda Maṇḍala* II, p.25.
49. Here Velankar simply remarks that 'there is no point in saying with Geldner and Renou that Agni's mind is *arakṣaś, Ṛg-Veda-Maṇḍala* II, p. 26.
50. *Ṛg-Veda Maṇḍala* II, p.17.
51. *Ibid.,* p.16.
52. *Ṛg-Veda Maṇḍala* III, p.44.
53. *Ibid.,* p. 51.
54. For the defence or support of the views of Renou or Sāyaṇa, or Geldner. Cf. H.D.Velankar, *Maṇḍala* II, p.111, *Maṇḍala* III. pp. 40,137, *Maṇḍala.* VII. pp. 111, 137, 182.
55. R.N. Dandekar, *Exercises in Indology,* pp. 144, 191, 191n, 242.
56. R.N. Dandekar, *Vedic Mythological Tracts,* pp. 170, 170n, 172.
57. R.N. Dandekar, *Exercises in Indology,* p. 242 particularly for anthropological approach of Jan Gonda to *Ṛg-Veda,* VII, 103.
58. See fee-note 39.
59. S.A.Dange, *Pastoral Symbolism from the Ṛg-Veda.* Also Sexual symbolism from the Vedic literature and his other articles in the Marathi book *Aśvatthācī pāne.*
60. H.D. Velankar, *Ṛg-Veda Maṇḍala* VII, Introduction, pp. i-x and xix to xxxi.
61. S.A. Upadhyaya's Introduction to *Ṛg-Veda Maṇḍala* III, pp. v-x.
62. R.N. Dandekar, *Exercises in Indology,* pp. 68-93, 98-111, 113, 132 etc.
63. V.G.Rahurkar, *The Seers of the Ṛg-Veda.*
64. G.V. Devasthali papers on *Vyākaraṇa* in the *A.B.O.R.I.*

    Vol. No. LXII, 1981, pp. 193-212.

    Vol. No. LXIV, 1983, pp. 137-48.

    Vol. No. LXI, 1980, pp. 205-09.

    Vol. No. LXIII, 1982, pp. 233-38.
65. Pāṇini as an aid to *Ṛg-Vedic* interpretation, pp.20-26 for the article of G.V. Devasthali, In *H.D. Velankar Commemoration Volume,* 1965.
66. Grammatical interpretation of *Ṛg-Veda,* II.41.11, by S.G. Moghe, In *J.G.J.K.S.V.,* Allahabad, Vol. Nos. 38-39, 1982-83 pp. 13-16.
67. M.A. Mehendale's article, In *A.B.O.R.I.,* Vol.63, pp. 225-26. Here Dr. Mehendale has shown that the author of the Kāśikā has unnecessarily restricted the sense of *vicakrame,* i.e., placing foot-steps with reference to animals.
68. Mrs. S.S. Pradhana has written a thesis on '*Yāska's Nirukta* and *Ṛg-Vedic*

interpretation' under the guidance of Prof. Velankar. This thesis is deposited in the Library of the University of Bombay, 1965.

Also see her article in the *A.B.O.R.I.,* LXIII, 1982, pp. 157-70.

69. R.N. Dandekar, *Vedic Mythological Tracts,* p. 254.

70. Dr. T.G. Mainkar, *The Upabṛnhaṇa and Ṛg-Veda Interpretation,* pp. 18-39 (published by L.D. Institute of Indology, Ahamedabad).

71. G.H. Godbole has written a Ph.D. thesis on 'Indra in the Post-*Ṛg-vedic* period: an examination of the sources of Indra's degradation as it appears in the *Purāṇas*' under the guidance of Prof. Velankar. This thesis is deposited in the Library of the University of Bombay in the year 1954.

72. Also see - Prof. Velankor and Vedic Interpretation-pp. 269-280.

73. *J.G.J.K.S.V.* Allahabad, Vol.37, 1981 pp. 69-76.

74. *Journal of the Asiatic Society of Bombay,* Vols. 49, 50, 51 of 1974, 1975 and 1976, pp. 15-22.

75. The line *'satāṁ dhātā svaccho nigama-gaṇa-gīto vrajapatiḥ* of the st.8, *Śrikṛṣṇāṣṭakam* of Śaṅkārācarya lends support to the sectarian interpretation of *Viṣṇu-Sūkta,* I 154.6 particularly offered by Vallabhācārya.

76. M.D. Paradkar *Stabaka* (in Marāthī - A collection of his articles) pp. 41-42.

77. S.G Moghe, Studies in the *Pūrva-Mīmāṁsā,* p. 36 has already noted the point that the modern scholars have ignored the importance of *Pūrva-Mīmāṁsā* and the *Bhāṣya* of Kumārila on I.2.50.

78. Kumārila on the *Pūrva-Mīmāṁsā*, I.2.50 takes the word *Naicāśākha* as 'wealth of eunuch' and Pramaganda as 'one who earns money or livelihood by low means. In the *Mīmāṁsā-Kośa,* Vol.IV, p. 2397, the word *Naicāśākha* is taken in the sense of ' a city'. While in the *Mīmāṁsā, Kośa,* Vol. III p. 1461, the word *Kīkaṭa* is explained as the persons who do not believe in sacrifice and are treated as atheist. They are also taken as very miserly people. It may be noted that modern scholars have not paid proper attention to the *Mīmāṁsā* source for the interpretation of the Vedic words.

79. M.A. Mehendale's article ' Vedic Akhkhala = Pali Akkula, In *Dr. S.K. Belvalkar Felicitation Volume,* pp, 12-15. It may be noted here that Prof. Velankar takes the expression *Akhkhalikṛtya* as onomatopoetic (See *Ṛksūktaśatī,* p. 231). Dr. Mehendale takes it in the sense of a 'bleat', i.e., cry of a sheep. Here he has noted the *prākṛt* tendency of the Vedic poets.

80. Dr. Ram Gopal's article on 'The *Ṛg-vedic* compound *Svar-dṛś,* In *Dr. R.N. Dandekar Felicitation Volume,* pp, 337-42. He takes the word in the sense of 'one who shows heaven. 'Prof. Velankar takes the compound to mean' one who looks like or on the sun. in the *Ṛg-Veda Maṇḍala* VII.

81. Dr. Paul Thieme's article on *Duroṇa,* In *Dr. R.N. Dandekar Felicitation Volume,* pp. 435-44. He gives a lengthy treatment to this topic and suggests different meanings as per the context. Prof. Velankar takes it in the sense of a 'home'.

8

Hemādri's *Darpaṇa* on the *Raghuvaṁśam*

It may be remarked at the very outset that the extracts from the commentaries of Vallabha, Hemādri, Dinakara and others on the *Raghuvaṁśam* are published by the Nirnaya Sagar Press, Bombay in the year 1948. Here the concentration is on the commentary of Mallinātha. But in the year 1973, the commentary *Darpaṇa* of Hemādri on the *Raghuvaṁśam* is edited by the learned scholar Revaprasad Dvivedi for the Kashiprasad Jayasval Research Institute, Patna. The review on this work has also appeared in the *Annals of the Bhandarkar Oriental Research Institute*, Pune.

Incidentally it may be added here that P.K. Gode has also already proved that Hemādri, the author of the *Vratakhaṇḍa*, *Dāna Khaṇḍa* etc., is totally different from Hemādri, the commentator of the *Raghuvaṁśam*. This Hemādri has flourished in Karnataka in the fifteenth century A.D. In this chapter, therefore, an attempt is made to evaluate the commentary of Hemādri, particularly in comparison with that of Mallinātha. Incidentally, references to the other commentators of the *Raghuvaṁśam* are also made as the occasion demands.

1. The important feature of the commentary *Darpaṇa* is that it gives us the etymological explanations of some words like *Rājadhānī* on the *Raghuvaṁśam*, XVI.22, *Agastya* on XV.53, *Aga* means[1] a mountain Vindhya who is ordered by Agastya. Hence he came to be known as Agastya. Similarly *Rājadhānī* means a place[2] where a king stays. It may be noted in passing that Mallinātha passes over this point of etymology in silence particularly on the above-mentioned places. Hence the utility of *Darpaṇa* can hardly be denied.

2. Hemādri impresses us as a good student of Sanskrit Dictionaries. Incidentally, it may be mentioned here that sound

knowledge of Sanskrit dictionaries is also a strong point of the writings of Mallinātha. But here one is tempted to advance the view that on this point Hemādri has certainly outdone Mallinātha. The word *samā* occurs in the plural number in the *Raghuvaṁśam,* VIII. 25. In his comments on this place, Hemādri adds[3] that the word *Samā* is also found used in the singular number. He also takes care to support his view[4] by quoting *pratāpamārtaṇḍa* in his favour. If, however, one consults this important place of the commentary of Mallinātha, one will be disappointed by Mallinātha's silence on this point. Hemādri appears to have mastered the dictionary known as *Śabdabhedaprakāśa.* It is surprising that Mallinātha does not appear to have made the best use of this commentary in elucidating the examples from the *Raghuvaṁśam.* Here the point can be best clarified by the word Hanumān[5] on the *Raghuvaṁśam,* XIII.64, *Jyeṣṭha* on XII.25, *Mathurā* on VI.48. Here Darpaṇakāra points that these words are also written differently, and takes resort to *Śabdabhedaprakāśa.* Mallinātha disappoints his interested readers without a word of comment on these words. Hence the importance of this *Kośa* utilised by Hemādri seems to be supreme in understanding the peculiarities of Kālidāsa. It is further interesting to note that Hemādri also notes the limitations of the Sanskrit Dictionary. One can clarify this point by his *Darpaṇa* on the *Raghuvaṁśam,* II.31. Here he refers[6] to the *kośa* of *Halāyudha* for the three types of elephants. But our commentator Hemādri notes[7] four types of elephants and without additional comments displays the limitations of the *Kośakāra Halāyudha.* If, however, one takes the pains of consulting Mallinātha on this crucial point, one will have to note that Mallinātha is not making a comment of this type which is absolutely essential for the knowledge of the subject.

3. His difference of opinion with Mallinātha is also a noteworthy point of the study of *Darpaṇa.* Here the attention may be drawn to the two expression *Somārkavaṁśye* in the *Raghuvaṁśam,* VI.8 and *Sūryavaṁśyā* in VII.71. Mallinātha explains these words by taking the termination *ya* to show the birth in that family. Hemādri differs from Mallinātha and points out that *Sūryavaṁśyā* means good or best in the family of *Sūrya.* Here he quotes[8] the authority of Vāmana, the author of the

Kāvyālaṁkāra-Sūtra. Though the commentator Mallinātha has also consulted the work of Vāmana on his *Kāvyālaṁkāra Sūtra*, yet he does not appear to have made the best or the judicious use of the work of Vāmana for interpreting the words in the *Raghuvaṁśam*. Here a dispassionate reader is bound to give due credit to Hemādri[9] for making the clever use of the authority of the *Alaṁkāra Śāstra* for interpreting the text of *Kālidāsa*.

4. For understanding a difference between the two words, however, the commentary *Darpaṇa* excels the *Sanjīvinī* of Mallinātha. Here a question arises as regards a difference between the two words — *Viraha* and *Viyoga*. *Kālidāsa* has used the word *viraha* in the *Raghuvaṁśam*, VIII.57. Hemādri first quotes *Rasakāra* to show the synonymous nature of the words *viraha*, *viyoga* and *vipralambha*. But he makes a choice of the Sanskrit dictionary known as *Śabdārṇava* to point out[10] that when the separation (*viyoga*) from a dead beloved becomes life-long unbearing as causing pain, then this *viyoga* is known as *viraha*. On consulting the commentary of Mallinātha on this point, it becomes quite evident that Mallinātha has not enlightened his interested readers.

5. It will be interesting to see the contribution of Hemādri from the point of view of *Dharma-Śāstra*. Here attention may be drawn to the *Raghuvaṁśam*, VI.23. In his comments on this stanza, Hemādri quotes a stanza from the text of *Vṛddha Parāśara* to indicate the persons who should not be be given the daughters in marriage. In this respect, the stanza simply means[11] that those persons who are always away (from home), who are not educated, who have concentrated their mind on getting emancipation, who are brave and who are pauper, should not be given the daughters. In this very context, it is important to obsreve that this view of *Vṛddha-parāśara* has escaped the notice of MM. Dr. Kane particularly in his *History of Dharma-Śāstra*, when in particular, he discussed the qualifications of the persons to whom the daughters may be given in marriage. He has not at all discussed the aspect of the persons disqualified for marriage. Here again it may be said, while reading that Mallinātha has nothing to do or add on this place. (ii) When, however, Mallinātha resolves the conflict in respect of the purity of a Kṣatriya (qualified) on the *Raghuvaṁśam*, VIII.73, by quoting the text of *Parāśara*[12], it may be added that

Hemādri also agrees with Mallinātha but quotes the *Viṣṇu Smṛti*[13] in support. In this respect, it may be significantly added that the present author has discussed the novel interpretation of Mallinātha of the *Manu-Smṛti,* V.83 with reference to the *Raghuvaṁśam,* VIII.73. This has also appeared in his *Studies in the Dharma-Śāstra,* pp. 47-50. One is surprised to note the identical, thoughts of Mallinātha, Mādhavācārya (otherwise known as Parāśara-Mādhava) and Hemādri on the point of the qualified Kṣatriya getting purified on the tenth day, after the death of his wife. (iii) When, however, the question of the murder of Tāṭakā otherwise known as Trāṭikā arises in the *Raghuvaṁśam,* XI.17, Mallinātha quotes the text of the *Manu-Smṛti,* VIII.350 pointing out that there is nothing wrong if a rash person is killed by anybody. Here in this context, it should be noted that Hemādri quotes the same line from the *Manu-Smṛti,* but without disclosing the source of the line or the source is unidentified by the editor of the *Darpaṇa* on the *Raghuvaṁśam.* Incidentally, Hemādri also quotes[14] the viewpoint of the law-giver known as Kātyāyana that men-killing women deserve to be killed. Here, one is tempted to express the view that on the murder of Tāṭakā, there is not only the identical view of the two *smṛtikāras* — Manu and Kātyāyana — but also between the two commentators — Mallinātha and Hemādri. But Hemādri's choice of the quotation of *Kātyāyana* is more appropriate. In passing, it may be remarked that in Vālmīki's *Rāmāyaṇa,* Viśvāmitra has expressed the view that she (Tāḍakā) does not follow any rules and is bent upon destroying the institution of sacrifice. (iv) On the *Raghuvaṁśam,* X.57, the question arises as regards the caste of Sumitrā, the mother of Lakṣmaṇa. Mallinātha passes over this point in silence. But it is Hemādri who remarks that she is *saṅkarajā,* i.e., born as a result of the mixture or combination of two castes. It is further interesting to remember that Hemādri quotes[15] the commentator of Jayamaṅgalā on the *Bhaṭṭi-Kāvya,* I.13. (v) In explaining the significance of the expression *sahadharmacāriṇī* in the *Raghuvaṁśam,* XIX.55, it is Hemādri who clarifies the concept of *Pativratā,* i.e., a chaste woman by quoting the text[16] of *Vṛddha-Hārīta* in favour and further the comments of Vijñāneśvara on the *Yājñavalkya-Smṛti.* Mallinātha, as usual, has not touched this place.

6. As regards the novel interpretations of Hemādri, a few references will not be out of place. Here in explaining the expression *ātmā*[17] as a king on the *Raghuvaṁśam,* V.34, Hemādri does not quote any authority but significantly observes that by the word *ātmā* the king is expected to be expressed. On the *Raghuvaṁśam,* XVII.30, we find Hemādri interpreting the word *mahat* as a kingdom. He supports this by quoting[18] Māgha's *Śiśupāla-Vadham,* XIV.13. One will be surprised to note that Mallinātha is not of any use to the readers at these two places. Besides, when the expression *Daṇḍakāraṇya* occurs in the *Raghuvaṁśam,* XII.9, Hemādri adds[19] that Daṇḍakā was the proper name of the daughter of the sage Bhārgava. If one consults the extracts of the other commentaries on these places, then one will be fully convinced of the novel (novel because they are newly offered by Hemādri) interpretations of Hemādri for which no praise is too high.

7. A dispassionate reader is also impressed by Hemādri's knowledge of *Nāṭyaśāstra* and *Alaṁkāra-Śāstra* particularly in the interpretation of the text of the *Raghuvaṁśam.* Hemādri treats Sītā as a *Dhīrā* type of heroine on the *Raghuvaṁśam,* XIV.61 on the famous line *mām lokavādaśravaṇāt ahāsīḥ śrutasya kiṁ tat sadruśaṁ kulasya.* Here he quotes[20] the text of *Vāgbhaṭa* in favour. This text of *Vāgbhaṭa* simply means that that is to be treated as a type of *Dhīrā* type of *nāyikā* who addresses her guilty lover out of anger in a round-about manner or zigzag way. Mallinātha has nothing to do any addition on this important place. In explaining the *gāṁbhīryaṁ* in the personality of Rāma particularly on the *Raghuvaṁśam,* XII.8, Hemādri quotes[21] the text of Bharata's *Nāṭyaśāstra* which simply means that that this is known as seriousness when the feelings of anger, joy, fear, etc. are not observed in the case of a person, on account of his personal power. Mallinātha simply explains this stanza without bringing out the real significance of the adjectives. (ii) In locating the *Khaṇḍitā nāyikā* on the *Raghuvaṁśam,* V.68, however, a good reader notices respectable amount of resemblance between the two commentators.

8. Another important feature of the commentary of Hemādri is that he has a good grasp of the theory of *Rasa* propounded by

Bharata and properly explained by the later writers on the *Alaṁkāra-Śāstra*. Here attention may be drawn to the *Darpaṇa* on the *Raghuvaṁśam*, XI.20. Here the readers are impressed by a very exhaustive note of Hemādri on the *Rasa*, quoting the works such *Śṛngāratilaka*, *Kāvyaprakāśa*, and Kṣemendra's *Aucityavicāracarcā*. Here it may be noted that this portion of the commentary covers two pages 296-97. This very detailed note on *Rasa*, has, however, no parallel in the *Sanjīvinī* of Mallinātha. It is rather significant to add that Hemādri discusses here the relative relation of the *Rasas* — principal and subordinate position of the *Rasa*. Here he adds that in the delineation of the *Bībhatsa rasa*, the depicting of the *Śṛngāra rasa* as a subordinate does not contribute to any demerit as such. It is rather surprising that though Bharata has accepted eight sentiments, yet there are nine *rasas* in the *drama* in the opinion of Halāyudha. This view of Halāyudha and particularly of the author of the Sanskrit dictionary desrves special notice as it is cleverly noted by Hemādri.

9. Hemādri has created a good impression on the mind of his careful readers by defending Kālidāsa on certain expressions such as *vānta* in the *Raghuvaṁśam*, VII.6 and *vṛṣasyantīṁ* in XII.34, by quoting Daṇḍin[22] as an authority on the *Alaṁkāra-Śāstra* — to make our gifted poet Kālidāsa free from the fault of obscenity. Here he significantly remarks that if one gives up the primary meaning of a word and resorts to the secondary meaning of a word, then it will not become a case of vulgar use of the expression. As usual, Mallinātha has not considered the above expressions from the eyes of the *Alaṁkāra-Śāstra* and hence nothing is to be expected from Mallinātha on such an important aspect of obscenity. On the expression *vṛṣasyantīṁ* in XII.34, Hemādri refers[23] to the viewpoint of Haradatta, the author of *padamañjarī*, that the use of the expressions — *aśva, vṛṣa*, etc. with reference to women and men is not proper. Here in this case, Hemādri has shown improper use of the expression on the part of Kālidāsa, by quoting the grammatical authority. Mallinātha does not care to refer to Haradatta, an important writer on Grammar, on such an important place. Herein lies the importance of the commentary *Darpaṇa* — perhaps superiority of *Darpaṇa* over *Sanjīvinī*.

10. Another important aspect of the commentary of Hemādri

is that in his *Darpaṇa* he has employed some *Mīmāṁsā*, technical terms and popular maxims. He has employed, for example, *Punarvacana* on the *Raghuvaṁśam*, IX.6, *Samuccya* at VI.37 and IX.7, *Atideśa* on IX.86, *Anuvāda* on IX.55. When, however, the expression *tilaka-talakaḥ* is used by Kālidāsa in the *Raghuvaṁśam*, IX.55, Hemādri observes[24] that when one and the same word is repeated with two different meanings, then it does not contribute to any demerit as such. Hemādri finds support to his view in Mahimabhaṭṭa's *Vyaktiviveka*. On this count also, Mallinātha does not impress his readers.

In conclusion, one will have to admit that Hemādri has indeed, occupied a very significant position in explaining the *Raghuvaṁśam* from the points of *Rasa*, *Dharma-Śāstra*, *Alaṁkāra-Śāstra*, *Nāṭyaśāstra*, *Vyākaraṇa*, Sanskrit dictionaries, novel interpretations, etymology, better explanation by exhibiting distinguishing capacity as compared with the popular but erudite commentator Mallinātha. One is, hence, tempted to observe that in some respects, Hemādri has shown his palm of superiority over Mallinātha. However, the utility of both the commentators is complementary to each and other and their relative importance can hardly be gainsaid by any appreciative student of the subject.

References

1. अगं अद्रिं विन्ध्यारव्यं स्त्यायति शब्दापयति अगस्त्य: ।

   दर्पण, p. 429.
2. राजा धीयते स्थीयिते अस्यामिति ल्युट् ।

   Ibid., p. 429.
3. समाशब्दो बहुवचनान्त एकवचनान्तो वा ।

   Ibid., p. 192.
4. शरत् स्त्रियां समा च स्त्री भूम्येकत्वे च दृश्यते ।

   Ibid., p. 192.
5. हनुमान् हनूमानपि शब्दभेदप्रकाशे ।

   Ibid., p. 377.
6. हलायुधस्तु - भद्रो मन्दो मृगन्श्चेति विज्ञेयास्त्रिविधा गजा: ।

   Ibid., p. 12.
7. भद्रो मन्दो मृगश्चैव संकीर्णश्चेति जातय:, चतस्र: करिणां तासां भद्रन्तर्मद एव य: ।

   Ibid., p. 11.
8. *दर्पण*, p. 126 quotes वामन's *काव्यालंकार सूत्रवृत्ति*, V. 2:51.
9. *Ibid.*, p. 203.

10. मृतप्रियाणामत्यन्तं यावज्जीवार्तिदायिनम् ।
वियोगं विरहं प्राहुः दुःसहं पूर्वसूरयः ॥
Ibid.,p203 quotes *शब्दार्णवः* ।

11. दूरस्थानामाविद्यानां मोक्षधर्मानुयायिनाम् ।
शूराणां निर्धनानां च न देयाः कन्यका बुधैः ॥
Ibid., p. 132.

12. क्षत्रियस्तु दशाहेन स्वधर्मनिरतः शुचिः ।
मल्लिनाथ on *रघुवंश*, p. 211.

13. 'विद्वान् क्षत्रियश्चेद् दशाहम्' इति विष्णुस्मृतिः ।
दर्पण, p. 209.

14. पुरुषध्न्यः स्त्रियों व्रध्याः इति कात्यायनः ।
Ibid., p. 295.

15. सुमित्रा संकरजेति भट्टिकाव्ये (१.१३) जयमंगलाकारः ।
Ibid., p. 277.

16. *दर्पण*, p. 539 quotes *वृद्धहारीत* 8.198 and comments of विज्ञानेश्वर on *याज्ञवल्क्यस्मृति.*

17. आत्मपदेन राजा विवक्षितः अन्तरात्मा वा ।
दर्पण, p. 103.

18. 'महद् राज्ये विशाले च' इति विश्वः ।
Ibid., p. 483.

19. दण्डका नाम भार्गवकन्या, तयोपलक्षितं वनम् ।
Ibid., p. 325.

20. 'सा धीरा वक्ति वक्रोक्त्या प्रियं कोपात् कृतागसम्' ।
हेमाद्रि's दर्पण, p. 403 quotes this line of वाग्भट ।

21. यत्र प्रभावादाकारात् क्रोधहर्षभयादयः ।
भावस्था नोपलक्ष्यन्ते तद् गाम्भीर्यमुदाहृतम् ॥
भरतनाट्यशास्त्र, 22.38 is quoted in *दर्पण*, p. 325.

22. मुख्यार्थं परित्यज्य गौणेऽर्थे वर्तमानो वान्तशब्दो न ग्राम्यः ।
दर्पण, p. 159.

23. *दर्पण*, p. 333 quotes हरदत्त's *पदमञ्जरी* on पाणिनि's *अष्टाध्यायी*, VII. 1.51.

24. तिलकशब्दस्य द्विः उपादाने भिन्नार्थतया न दोषः ।
दर्पण, p. 240.

9

Evaluation of the Commentary *Marmāvabodhinī* on the *Harṣacaritam*

BĀṆBHAṬṬA'S *Harṣacaritam* has become the centre of attraction of the scholars of the different disciplines of Indology. The foreign scholars like E.B. Cowell and F.W. Thomos have given us the English rendering of this historically important work. The Nirnaya Sagar Press, Bombay has published the commentary of Śaṅkara on the *Harṣacaritam*. Dr. P.V. Kane has written exhaustive notes on the same to expound this otherwise difficult text. Numerous papers touching different aspects of the *Harṣacaritam* have also appeared in the course of the last seventy-five years and more.

It may be noted here that the University of Kerala deserves the credit of bringing out the edition of the *Harṣacaritam* with the commentary of Raṅganātha, in the year 1959. This edition also contains some introduction pointing out that the present author Raṅganātha appears to be different from Raṅganātha, the commentator of the *Vikramorvaśīyam* of Kālidāsa. Moreover, the present Raṅganātha belongs to the part of Kerala as is evident from the important point that in the course of his Sanskrit he gives us the Malayalam equivalents of the Sanskrit words. The name of the commentary *Marmāvabodhinī* is also significant and is very exhaustive and significant on many interesting points. So far, no attempt is made by any scholar to critically evaluate this important commentary. Hence in the present chapter, the present author has decided to do some justice to this work particularly in comparison with the scholarly notes by P.V. Kane, published in the year 1918. It is further evident that Dr. P.V. Kane did not find time to consult this commentary after its publication, for the simple reason that he was busily engaged with his *magnum opus History of Dharma-Śāstra*. Incidentally, however, I may refer to the notes written by

A.B. Gajendragadkar and the translation of Cowell and Thomas, as the occasion so demands.

1. The significant aspect of this commentary is that the commentator gives us the definitions of some words like *Dhīra* (p.53), Ahaṁkāra[1] (p.82), *dākṣiṇya*[2] (p.41), *Audārya*[3] (p.46), *Lāvaṇya* (pp.33 and 233) etc. Here it may be noted that Raṅganātha quotes from the *Kośa of Divākara* on all these important places of the *Harṣacaritam.* It may be incidentally pointed that Dr. Kane never makes up his mind to give the definitions of these words and treats them as comparatively simple. Hence the importance of this commentary is certainly supreme in giving proper understanding of the basic concepts when they are used by Bāṇabhaṭṭa in the course of his writing.

2. At times, however, Raṅganātha clarifies the concept in such a nice manner that one does not meet with that kind of beautiful explanation in Dr. Kane's notes. To clarify this point, one may draw attention of the readers to the expression *sugṛhītanāmā* that occurs in the *Harṣacaritam.* Dr. Kane in his notes on the *Harṣacaritam* Part I, p.61 simply translates this expression as 'one whose name is auspicious'. There is nothing wrong in the translation. But the inner meaning of this expression is not at all brought out by the translation. The commentator Raṅganātha, however, in his commentary on page 40 gives us a quotation[4] which simply means that servants take the auspicious name of a person (really master) by heart and not by speech. That is why it is auspicious. One is bound to be impressed by this explanation. Incidentally, it may be noted here that the source of this quotation is not given by Raṅganātha nor is it identified by the editor of the commentary. This explanation will bring out the unhappy nature of the explanation of Dr. Kane. One may draw attention to one more case. The expression *Kukkuṭa-vrata* occurs in the commentary on the *Harṣacaritam* (p.58). Here in explaining this expression our commentator Raṅganātha, however, gives us two quotations to clarify the idea. The first quotation[5] means 'One who observes a vow to hide only the sin, is known as observing the *kukkuṭa vrata.* This appears to have been quoted from the *smṛti* work the source of which is not known or it is quoted by him by the force of memory. He also gives us another quotation[6] which means that

one who enjoys the chaste woman of other persons rather forcibly is said to be observing the vow of a cock. If, however, one compares these two quotations with the explanations given by Dr. Kane in his notes on the *Harṣacaritam,* pp.84-85, one would be struck by the originality of the explanation of Raṅganātha. Dr. Kane takes it as 'devouring the cocks ' or 'one whose conduct was not ferocious'. One is here inclined to agree with the explanation of Raṅganātha which is refreshingly original and deserves to be appreciated by the serious students of the *Harṣacaritam.* This discussion also helps us to infer reasonably that the commentary *Marmāvabodhinī* is really touching the vital parts of the work as and as such it is more significant.

3. It is a significant aspect of this commentary that at times, one comes across the resemblance between the notes of Dr. Kane and also the commentary *Marmāvabodhinī.* One could clarify this point by drawing attention to the expression *Asidhārāvratam* that occurs in the *Harṣacaritam* (p.102). Here Raṅganātha points out by a quotation[7] meaning that when a man shares bed with a woman, without experiencing any passion or emotion, then he is said to be observing the vow of an edge of a sword. This is very difficult for a couple to follow. He supports this idea by quoting the *Raghuvaṁśam* in support. Dr. Kane in his Notes (Vol. I, p.139) gives a different quotation and refers to Mallinātha on the *Raghuvaṁśam,* 13.67. One is indeed surprised by the identical thoughts of these two scholars on this important point. There are other points[8] of resemblance between the two, which I note below in the foot-note.

4. At times, however, the unsatisfactory nature of the commentary of Raṅganātha is revealed only by a close student of *Dharma-Śāstra* and *Pūrva-Mīmāṁsā.* Here a reference could be made to the expression *Upasaṅgrahaṇam* (p.57) and *Āmikṣā* (p.69). Here it may be added that Raṅganātha explains[9] the term *Upasaṅgrahaṇam* as 'salutation by embracing or touching the feet of another person'. One may infer only on the face of it that that there is nothing wrong in the explanation. Actually the meaning is acceptable. But to a student of *Dharma-Śāstra,* this sense will not appeal. Actually in the *Dharma-Śāstra,* this word means 'touching the right foot of a person by a right hand and left foot by a left hand.

Here attention may be drawn to Dr. Kane's discussion[10] in the *History of Dharma-Śāstra* for a more correct explanation of this term. Here it may be incidentally mentioned that Kane's translation of this expression as 'who made a respectful salutation' (Notes, p.57) is satisfactory for a general reader. It must be mentioned in this context that Dr. Kane concentrated his mind on *Dharma-Śāstra* after writing his notes on the *Harṣacaritam* : otherwise he would have definitely given references from the *Dharma-Śāstra* texts. One should also note that by the use of this expression Bāṇabhaṭṭa has indeed revealed his knowledge of *Dharma-Śāstra*. The same is the case with the expression *Āmikṣā* on page 69 by Raṅganātha. Here he relies on the dictionary[11] of *Amara*. Kane also notes the similar explanation in his notes on p.94. For a better explanation however, I draw the attention of the readers to the explanation[12] from the pen of Gaṅgānātha Jhā in his *Mīmāṁsā-Maṇḍana* and the *Mīmāṁsā-Kośa*. Any way, the unsatisfactory nature of the commentary can hardly be ignored by a serious student of *Dharma-Śāstra*.

5. One is also further impressed by the complementary character of the commentary of Raṅganātha. Whatever matter is not available in the notes of Kane, becomes available to the readers from the commentary *Marmāvabodhinī*. Here a reference could be made to the expression *Śrīparvata*. Kane treats this as a historical place and explains it with the help of the *Mahābhārata, Vanaparva*, 85.19-20. Here it should be noted that Raṅganātha on p.12 points out the significance[13] that there is a lustre on this mountain which has the power to protect the people from all troubles and it is responsible for the prosperity of the people. If one reads this information dispassionately, one would be convinced regarding the complementary character of this commentary. (ii) Whenever the expression *Siddhiyātrā* occurs in the *Harṣacaritam*, Kane simply explains it as 'auspicious for expedition'. This explanation is simply giving the rendering of the expression. For a clear-cut explanation of this term, one will have to consult the *ṭīkā* of our commentator on p.319. He quotes a stanza[14] here which simply means that is known as a successful expedition, when undertaking the same, the king brings for himself a great success. This explanation is certainly more illuminating even from the point of

view of a casual reader of the *Harṣacaritam.* (iii) Similar is the case with the expression *Mahāratna* when it occurs in the *Harṣacaritam.* Kane quotes an authority to show six great jewels. But Raṅganātha quotes a stanza[15] which shows that there are seven jewels and this list of Raṅganātha is also slightly different the one that is given by Kane. Hence one can hardly ignore the complementary character of the commentary of Raṅganātha. The utility of Raṅganātha, therefore, for understanding the *Harṣacaritam,* is very supreme particularly on this interesting point.

6. Sometimes, however, the commentary *Marmāvabodhinī* helps us to remove doubts in the important details of a particular thing. Here a reference could be made to the expression *Prajāpatayaḥ* in the *Harṣacaritam.* Kane in his Notes on the *Harṣacaritam,* Vol. I, pp.18-19 depends upon the *Manu Smṛti,* I.62 and points out only ten *prajāpatis.* He further adds that in the list of the *prajāpatis,* we do not find the names of Manu, Dakṣa and Cākṣuṣa. In this very context, the commentary p.13 has an important part to play. Here our comentator relies on the *Mahābhārata* and quotes verses[16] from the *Mahābhārata* to indicate the list of 21 *Prajāpatis.* Here also it is evident that the names of Manu and Dakṣa are found in the list of the *Mahābhārata,* though there is not the mention of the name of Cākṣuṣa. From this quotation of the *Mahābhārata,* it is further evident that the doubt in the mind of the careful readers in respect of Manu and Dakṣa as *prajāpatis* is removed. It would be further interesting to see how far the verses relied upon by Raṅganātha are accepted in the critical edition of the *Mahābhārata.* But this is the topic which I reserve for some other occasion.

7. At some places, however, a different reading also can be regarded as furnishing the readers with additional information on the particular point of the *Harṣacaritam.* Here a reference can be made to the expression *galad-grantha-daṇḍakodgārinī.* In Kane's *Harṣacaritam,* p.41, Kane connects this expression with the art of reproducing the portion of the *Veda* by the students by dropping some of the lines. In Short, Kane has connected this expression with the *Ācāra* aspect of the *Dharma-Śāstra* dealing with the modes of repetition of the Vedic *Mantras.* In this very context, it would be pertinent to draw the attention to the commentary[17] of

Raṅganātha on page 135. Here Raṅganātha prefers the reading as *Gara-grantha-daṇḍakodgāriṇī* and suggests that Garagrantha appears to be some contemporary writer of Bāṇa whose writing was full of long compounds. He was specially known for writing obscene things. It is further curious to note that Raṅganātha explains the word *Daṇḍaka* as the group of words forming good compounds, on the basis of the dictionary of Halāyudha. If this explanation is accepted then one is seen as imitating the style of Garagrantha. Any way, one has to admit that the different reading preferred by Raṅganātha has helped him to offer an altogether different explanation and the piece of information with reference to Garagrantha is also very important, as the contemporary of Bāṇa. (ii) Here attention may be drawn to the stanza No.15, (st, 14 of Kane's edition.). Here we find a reference to Setu. Kane takes it as referring[18] to *prākṛt* poem called *Setubandha* or *Rāvaṇa Vadha.* (Notes, p.11) Pravarasena is regarded as the author of *Setubandha.* But Raṅganātha on p.9 takes *Setubandha* as a poem written by Nala. If such different readings are collected from the edition of the Raṅganātha, one will be able to supply new information to the readers which is not at all available with the help of the scholarly edition of Kane.

8. Brevity is another technique supposed to have been adopted by Bāṇa in the course of his writings in the *Harṣacaritam.* Here a reference could be made to the name 'Rāmadatta' that occurs in the edition of Raṅganātha on p.323. This name is shortened by Bāṇa as ' Rāmila'. It is further interesting to note that our commentator has taken care[19] to quote the *Aṣṭādhyāyī* of Pāṇini, V.3.79 which has helped Bāṇa for this short form. It is further surprising that neither Thomas and Cowell nor Kane and Gajendragadkar have noticed this tendency in the writing of Bāṇa at this place. Here the name is shortened on the ground of compassion. Hence Raṅganātha deservas credit for throwing light on the peculiar technique of Bāṇa in respect of Brevity which is regarded as the special device of the Vedic poets and even Kālidāsa, as shown by the present author in an article ' Is *Lāghava* possible in the Kāvya?', contributed to the *Journal of the Ganganatha Jha Kendriya Sanskrit Vidyapitha,* Vol. XL, 1987, pp. 157-67. It must be stated here that Raṅganātha touches those places of the

Harṣacaritam on which the other scholars are silent. I resist the temptation of collecting more examples of this type of brevity.

9. It would be interesting to note the limitation of this commentator. In fact, he has not at all considered the historical evidence in interpreting the text of the *Harṣacaritam*. Kane, on the other hands, takes into consideration the historical side for this purpose. He also consults the source of land-grants which has no place in the comments of Raṅganātha. Raṅganātha appears to have been trained in a traditional manner and is seen fully satisfied by the knowledge of Pāṇini's *Aṣṭādhyāyī*, Sanskrit dictionaries and the art of testing the usage with the help of the Sanskrit literature that is available to him. It may be stated here that the modern scholars take a very wide view in the matter and consult all possible sources of *Dharma-Śāstra, Alaṁkāra-Śāstra, Purāṇas, Smṛtis,* digest authors, commentators of the *smṛtis,* etc. Hence one is tempted to say that the study of both — the traditional and modern scholars is indeed complementary to each other. The modern readers are also likely to be impressed by Raṅganātha's equipment of the list of authorities he has quoted in season and out of season, to which a reference can be made from the last six pages of the edition of *Marmāvabodhinī*.

10. At times, however, one notices the difference of opinion among the traditional scholars and the modern scholars. This point can be expounded by referring to a case of the expression *Vyuthānabuddhiḥ* in the commentary *Marmāvabodhinī,* p.178. Kane in his Notes on Vol. II, p. 11 takes it as a cessation of the state of *yogic* trance. Gajendragadkar in his Notes on p.31 explains the term *yoga*. Raṅganātha on p. 178 explains[20] it as the independent behaviour backed up by intellect. He explains *vyutthānam* with the help of the Sanskrit dictionary *Vaijayantī*. He also refers to the view of some who take[21] it as referring to the 'obstructive intellect'. Others, however, take[22] it as *Udrekabuddhiḥ*. Any way, one notices here the different explanations of the expression. There are some such expressions which I prefer to indicate in the foot-note.

From the foregoing observation, one would be right in holding that the commentary *Marmāvabodhinī* will prove to be very useful to the modern scholars from the point different aspects referred to above.

References

1. अहं तु शक्तः कार्येऽस्मिन् नामी शक्ताश्च जन्तवः ।
   इत्थमस्पृष्टर्थकार्यार्थ – गुणदोषा त्वहङ्कृतिः ।

   मर्मविबोधिनी, p. 82.

2. दाक्षिण्यं नाम तत्प्राहुः स्वानुकूल्यं प्रवृत्तिषु ।
   प्राणानप्याददानस्य स्थातुं शक्तिर्न यद् भवेत् ॥

   Ibid., p. 41.

3. दानमभ्यवपत्तिश्च तथा च प्रतिभाषणम् ।
   स्वजने वा परे वापि तदौदार्यं प्रकीर्तितम् ॥

   Ibid., p. 46.

4. भृत्यैर्नामास्य पूज्यत्वाद् हृदयेन सुगृह्यते ।
   न तु वाचोच्यते तस्मात् सुगृहीताभिधानता ।

   Ibid., p. 40.

5. यः कारणं पुरस्कृत्य व्रतचर्यां निषेवते ।
   पापं व्रतेन प्रच्छाद्य कौक्कुटं नाम तद्व्रतम् ॥

   Ibid., p. 58.

6. बलात्कारेण या भुक्तिः साध्वीनां परयोषिताम् ।
   तां कौक्कुटव्रतमिति कथयन्ति मनीषिणः ॥

   Ibid., p. 58.

7. पुरुषस्यैकशय्यायामेकान्ते यत् स्त्रिया सह ।
   निर्विकारमवस्थानमसिधाराव्रतं तु तत् ॥

   Ibid., p. 102.

8. (i) ईतयः – Kane. p. 190 = *मर्मविबोधिनी*, p. 142.
   (ii) मञ्च - Kane p. 211 = *Ibid.*, p. 360.

9. उपसंग्रहणं पादग्रहणेनाभिवादनम् ।

   मर्मविबोधिनी, p. 37.

10. P.V. Kane, *History of Dharma-Śāstra*, Vol. II/I pp. 334, 335n.

11. आमिक्षा सा श्रुतोष्णे या क्षीरे स्याद् दधियोगतः ।

    मर्मविबोधिनी, p.69.

12. तप्ते दुग्धे दधिप्रक्षेपे दुग्धं विकृतं भवति। कश्चिदंशो घनीभूय पृथग्भवति अवशिष्टश्च जलरूपेणावतिष्ठते ।
    यच्च घनीभूतं तदाभिक्षेति ।

    मीमांसामण्डन, p. 162.

13. श्रीपर्वते हि जगतामभ्युदयसूचकमूर्ध्वं ज्वलदग्निरूपं ज्योतिर्लिङ्गाख्यं ज्योतिस्तेजः प्रकाशते ।

    मर्मविबोधिनी, p. 12.

14. यस्यां तु यात्रासमये समारूढे नराधिपः ।
    प्राप्नोति महतीं सिद्धिं सिद्धियात्रेति सा स्मृता ॥

    मर्मविबोधिनी, p. 319.

15. अश्वो गजः स्त्री पुरुषः खड्गश्च गृहतन्त्रकम् ।
    मन्त्री चैतानि रत्नानि कथ्यन्ते चक्रवर्तिनाम् ॥

    Ibid, p.187.

16. ब्रह्मा स्थाणुर्मनुर्दक्षो भृगुर्धर्मस्तपो दमः ।
मरीचिरङ्गिराश्चात्रिः पुलस्त्यः पुलहः क्रतुः ॥
वसिष्ठः परमेष्ठी च विवस्वान् सोम एव च ।
कर्दमश्चापि यः प्रोक्तः कृतो विकृतिरेव च ॥

मर्मावबोधिनी, p.13.

17. गरग्रन्थों नाम बाणभट्टकालजातः कश्चिदश्लील ग्रन्थप्रणेता कविरित्युपदेशः ।
दण्डकं समासाढ्यपदमाला । 'समासप्रायमाख्यातं पदजातं तु दण्डकम्' हलायुधः ।

मर्मावबोधिनी, p. 135.

18. सेतुना प्राकृतकाव्यविशेषेण, नलकृतसेतुबन्धेन च । *Ibid.*, p. 9.

19. रामिल रामदत्त । रामिलः रामदत्तशब्दाद् घनि लचौ च
(पा. 5.3.79) इत्यनुकम्पायामिलच् ।

मर्मावबोधिनी, p. 323.

20. स्वतन्त्रवृत्तियुक्ता बुद्धिः । 'स्वतन्त्रवृत्तिः व्युत्थानम् इति वैजयन्ती' ।

Ibid., p. 178.

21. प्रतिरोधबुद्धिरिति केचित् ।

Ibid., p. 178.

22. उद्रेकबुद्धिरित्यन्ये ।

Ibid., p. 178.

10

Rāghavabhaṭṭa's Novel Interpretation of the *Śākuntalam,* IV.17.d.

THE advice given by Kaṇva to his adopted daughter Śakuntalā and particularly put by Kālidāsa in the mouth of Kaṇva has become immortal in the Sanskrit literature. Here the question can be raised as regards the exact interpretation of the line *vāmāḥ kulasya adhayayaḥ*. Modern scholars like Prof. A.B. Gajendragadkar, Prof. S. Ray and others it as 'others (i.e., who do not follow the advice) become bane to the family.' In their opinion, therefore, the married ladies who do not follow the above advice, simply spoil the good name of the family.

If, however, one concentrates one's mind on the mode of interpretation adopted by the Sanskrit commentators, like Rāghavabhaṭṭa, one would be impressed by an altogether different interpretation. In this very context, it should be noted that the Sanskrit commentators give more emphasis on the Sanskrit dictionaries which are very rarely found utilised by the modern scholars. The writer of this note is happy to mention only simply incidentally that he has stressed the importance of the Sanskrit dictionaries in the matter of interpretation of the Sanskrit texts elsewhere.[1]

In the present case, Rāghavabhaṭṭa takes the word *vāmāḥ* as referring to married ladies and quotes[2] the dictionary of *Amara* in support. He further takes pretty care to give an altogether different meaning of the word *ādhayaḥ*. He quotes the *Viśva Kośa*[3] to show the different meanings of the word *Ādhih*. This word is found used in the sense of 'mental torture, prison, calamity, foundation, etc. If, however, one reads the commentary of Rāghavabhaṭṭa one would come to know that Rāghavabhaṭṭa prefers the sense of 'foundation'. This meaning, however, is not, at all, favoured by the modern scholars.

In the light of the above discussion, it is quite evident that Rāghavabhaṭṭa would interpret the line as 'Married ladies are the foundations of the family'. Any good student of Sanskrit literature would be bound to be impressed by the novel interpretation of Rāghavabhaṭṭa who incidentally sees the glorification of the position of the married ladies in the family of their husband. Needless to say that the modern scholars detect here a warning to a married lady that in case she does not follow the important piece of advice of Kaṇva, she would be bane to the family, indicating thereby that her behaviour would decide the fame or bad name of the family.

Incidentally, it may be remarked here that whether one agrees with the interpretation of Rāghavabhaṭṭa or not, one has to note his novel interpretation purely based on the knowledge of the Sanskrit dictionaries, and thereby high-lighting the importance of the Sanskrit dictionaries in the interpretation of the Sanskrit texts.

References

1. S.G. Moghe, *शान्त-आरामः*, pp. 68-75.

2. 'वामौ वल्गुप्रतीपौ वा इत्यमरः' ।

   अर्थद्योतानिका on शाकुन्तलम्, p. 144.

3. कुलस्याधयः कुलाधिष्ठानानि । वामा वक्राणित्यर्थः । आधिर्माडायां प्रत्याशायां च बन्धने । व्यसने चाप्यधिष्ठाने' इति विश्वः ।

   Ibid., p. 144.

Here the Nirnaya Sagar Press, Bombay edition of 1947 is used for *अर्थद्योतनिका of राघवभट्ट on शाकुन्तलम्.*

11

A Note on Bahurūpamiśra

DR. A.N. Pandey has brought out the edition of the *Daśarūpaka* of Dhanañjaya with the commentary Dīpikā by Bahurūpamiśra on behalf of the Bharatiya Vidya Prakashana, Varanasi, in the year 1979. In his Introduction to this edition, Dr. Pandey has placed Bahurūpamiśra in the fourteenth century A.D. and has based his edition on the two transcripts of the manuscripts deposited in the Govt. Manuscript Library, Madras and Oriental Research Institute and Manuscripts Library, University of Kerala, Trivandrum.

In writing this chapter, I draw the attention of the readers to the edition of the *Abhijñāna-Śākuntala-Carcā* edited by Dr. K. Raghavan Pillai and published by the University of Kerala as No. 195 in the year 1961. The commentator of this commentary is some anonymous writer who is placed in the fifteenth century A.D. If this is correct, then the following interesting piece of information may be added to the matter already collected by the learned Professor.

It may be noted here that this anonymous commentator quotes Bahurūpamiśra as Bahurūpakamiśra at two places.[1] From this, it becomes quite evident even to a casual reader of dramaturgy that the name of the commentator of Dīpikā on *Daśarūpaka* is presented differently. It is further evident that Bahurūpamiśra treated the first stanza of the drama *Anargha-Rāghava* as a case of Nāndī. The anonymous commentator further refers to the view of Bahurūpamiśra that there is no fault even if three or four *aṅgas* of *sandhi* are dropped by a dramatist.

The influence of Bahurūpamiśra is further noticed on the writing of the anonymous commentator particularly when the latter detects[2] the *sandhyāṅga* known as *vilobhana* in the celebrated stanza from the *Śākuntalam*. The only possible difference that can perhaps be pointed is the difference in the language.

Bahurūpamiśra[3] has used the expression *Duṣyanta* in place of *nāyaka* employed by the anonymous commentator of the *Śākuntalam*. Here it should be noted that the anonymous commentator has not directly referred to the name of Bahurūpamiśra but this can be known only by the comparison of both the passages in the texts of both the authors.

Another glaring example of the influence is also noticed when one compares a passage[4] from the *Abhijñāna-Śākuntala-Carcā*, p.70 with the original passage[5] available on page 38 of the edition of Dr. Pandey. It would be proper on our part to quote both the passages in the foot-notes. By comparison, it becomes quite clear that the anonymous commentator notes the reading *vilope* for *lope* and *abhāvenāpi* for *abhāve*. It should be significantly noted that these readings noted by the anonymous commentator have no place in the edition of Dr. Pandey, though it is true that the difference in readings does not contribute to the difference in the meaning.

The very fact that this anonymous commentator is placed in the fifteenth century A.D. further lends support to the viewpoint of Dr. Pandey that Bahurūpamiśra *alias* Bahurūpakamiśra is to be probably placed in the fourteenth century A.D. One may incidentally refer to the view of Dr. V. Raghavan that Bahurūpamiśra must be later than 1250 A.D.

From the foregoing discussion, it would be fair to conclude that the commentary of the anonymous commentator on the *Abhijñāna-Śākuntala* — renders help to us in the matter of textual criticism, shows the influence of the writing of Bahurūpamiśra on the writings of the anonymous commentator and further lends support to the date of Bahurūpamiśra fixed by the learned professor and conjectured by Dr. V. Raghavan. The piece of information has escaped the notices of Dr. Raghavan and Dr. Pandey.

References

1. तथाहि बहुरूपकादिभिरनर्धराधवादिषु प्रथमश्लोकाः नान्दीत्वेन कथिताः ।

अभिज्ञान-शाकुन्तल-चर्चा, p.2

and अत्र बहरूपकमिश्राः....... एवं त्रिचतुराङ्गविलोपेऽपि न दोषः ।

Ibid., p. 70.

2. राजा उपपद्यते – 'मानुषीषु' इत्यादि शकुन्तलागुणाख्यानान्नायकानुरागोपबृंहणाद्विलोभनाख्यामिदमङ्गम् ।

अभिज्ञान-शाकुन्तल-चर्चा, p. 59.

3. इति शकुन्तलागुणाख्यानाद् दुष्यन्तरागोपबृंहणामिति ।

दीपिका on *दशरूपक*, p.15.

4. एवं त्रिचतुराङ्गविलोपेऽपि न दोषः । प्रयोजनाधीनत्वादङ्गानाम् । प्रयोजनस्य त्रिचतुराभावेनापि सिद्धत्वादिति ।

अभिज्ञान-शाकुन्तल-चर्चा, p.70.

5. एवं त्रिचतुराङ्गलोपेऽपि न दोषः प्रयोजनाधीनत्वादङ्गानाम् । त्रिचतुराभावेऽपि सिद्धत्वात् ।

दीपिका on *दशरूपक*, p.38

Also cf. *अभिज्ञान-शाकुन्तल-चर्चा*, p. 69 and दीपिका on *दशरूपक*, p. 38 for a passage quoted from भोज's *श्रृंगारप्रकाश*, XII, p. 505 (identified by Dr. Pandey in his Notes on p. 151.).

12

Is *Lāghava* Possible in *Kāvya?*

LĀGHAVA means brevity of expression, consisting in shortness of a syllable even in poetry. Here particularly on the basis of *Darpaṇa* of Hemādri, a commentary on Kālidāsa's *Raghuvaṃśa,* some techniques of *Lāghava* in poetry have been brought to light by the author.

The concept of *Lāghava,* i.e., brevity seems to be very popular with the grammarians.[1] We have the well-known *paribhāṣā* which states that grammarians rejoice over the saving of half a mora (in formulating a grammatical *sūtra*) as much as over the birth of a son. Very recently Ojihara has shown in a series of articles that the *Vārttikas* of Kātyāyana are not clipped like the *sūtras* of Pāṇini and they are not subject to the same principle of brevity expressed by the metarule about the saving of half a mora, as noted by Frits Stall.[2]

I. One will be willing to admit whole heartedly that in the daily life or popular practice[3], people have more regard for *gaurava* which is quite opposite of *lāghava.* People do not try to express their ideas by resorting to few words. They take great pleasure in elaborating the idea to the audience or to the readers. One may expound this point by drawing the attention of the serious readers to the commentary of Hemādri on the *Raghuvaṁśaṁ,* V. 32 and IX. 36. Here he specifically points out the viewpoint[4] of the author of *Pāṇinīyamatadarpaṇa,* who shows that people have less regard for the brevity in the daily popular practices. He also shows on IX.36[5] that when actually a thing is applicable to the part of anything, people make it applicable to the whole of it. When however, a part of the village is burnt, we always notice people talking about the entire village being burnt. This again is the tendency of the people.

II. Hemādri in his *Darpaṇa* on the *Raghuvaṁśam*[1], III.35 and XV.88 has correctly shown how the *lāghava* is achieved by the great poet Kālīdāsa. Instead of using the expression Godāvarī, Kālidāsa[6] has used the expression *Godā.* Here the use of the short forms helps one to achieve *lāghava.* Instead of saying Godāvarī, the great poet has used the expression 'Godā' at the above place. One may notice that even the Mīmāṁsakas are very acute in using the principle of the maxim *Nāma nyāya* for the purpose of achieving brevity. When one says *Bhāmā,* it refers to *Satyabhāmā.* A careful student of the *Vedānta* would remember here that even the great Śaṅkarācārya has used the principle of the *nāma nyāya* in his[7] commentary on the *Brahma-sūtra* of Bādarāyaṇa and even Devaṇṇabhaṭṭa in his *Smṛticandrikā*[8] has made the best and judicious use of this principle for the interpretational purpose.

III. One would be curious to know that the use of the alternative form of the pronouns helps us to achieve the said brevity. Even though it is true that Hemādri has shown this kind of device, yet it must be pointed out in the present context that Dinakaramiśra[10] in his commentary on the *Raghuvaṁśam,* XV. 69 running as *geye ko nu vinetā vām* etc. has shown that here *vām* stands for *yuvāṁ,* and has referred to the view of the commentator Daksiṇārvartanātha, and the example of *Bhāmā* for *Satyabhāmā* which is already quoted above. Possibly the use of the alternative forms of pronouns helps the good poets to achieve brevity as observed by the commentators of the poetry.

IV. The device of the *Vyatyayo bahulam* used by Pāṇini can also be fruitfully utilised for this purpose. Here it must be remarked that a word standing in one case also stands for another case. Thus, when one says that a word in the accusative case also stands for dative case or some other case, it becomes a case of *Vyatyayo bahulam* of Pāṇini. But here it should be noted that Hemādri has made the best use of the work of Vāmana's *Kāvyālaṁkāra-Sūtra* to suggest this device. Here according to this device, though the word stands in a particular case, it actually stands for another case. It is not expected to serve the double purpose of both the cases. For the elucidation of this interesting point, it would be better to draw the attention of the readers to the commentary of Hemādri on the *Raghuvaṁśam,* VIII. 46 and

XIV. 40 where *te* and *me* stand for *tvayā* and *mayā* as shown[10] by Vāmana in his *Kāvyālaṁkāra-Sūtra*. Thus, though Kālidāsa has used the expression *himasekavipattiratra me nalinī pūrvanidarśanaṁ gatā* the word *'me'* convey as the sense of *mayā* which aims at achieving the brevity. One would observe here that the principle of *vyatyayo bahulam* indicating that one word stands for another case is interesting and for a fuller and perhaps more appropriate discussion on this aspect, one may refer to the present author's paper[11] published elsewhere.

V. One may refer here to the another device by which the brevity could be achieved. If the adjective is very prominent, then the person to whom it refers need not be mentioned, since the intended meaning could be easily conveyed by the device so used by the poets. For the clarification of this device, one could draw the attention of the readers to Hemādri's *Darpaṇa*[12] on the *Raghuvaṁśam,* III.9 and V.32. In the *Raghuvaṁśam,* III. 9 the expression *sāgarāṁbarām* refers to the 'earth'. Similarly the use of this device is also noticed by the commentator Pūrṇasarasvatī[13] on the *Meghadūtam*. If the adjective is very well-known and it refers to a particular person only, then this device stands to the advantage of the great poets.

VI. Sometimes, however, even by dropping a particular word governing a particular case, the principle of brevity could be achieved. Here it seems that good poets dispense with such words whose absence is not likely to affect the proper sense which is expected to be conveyed by a particular stanza. One may throw light on this device by showing the relevance of the commentary[14] *Darpaṇa* on the *Raghuvaṁśam,* XV.75. Here in this stanza, though the word *saha,* i.e., together, is totally absent, yet it conveys the sense of *saha* which the great poet Kālidāsa wants to convey. Thus, the absence of some word or the dropping of some word, in a stanza, helps good poets to achieve brevity which is the peculiar characteristic of the grammarians as such.

VII. Another important device for aiming at brevity can be pointed here. The use of possessive terminations (*matup pratyayas* in Pāṇini's Grammar) also helps us to convey the intended sense. Kālidāsa's use of the word *Hanūmat* in the *Raghuvaṁśam,* XIII.64 is a case in point. Here Hemādri has made significant[15] observations that the word *hanu* refers here to only a part of the face and the addition of the *matup* termination aims at censure. One may add here one more case. It would be equally interesting to note that Mallinātha in his commentary[16] on the *Raghuvaṁśam,* I.91 points out that the termination *ini* in *putrin* is indicative of praise or glorification. Hence, one may say that the proper use of the termination of Pāṇini's Grammar helps a competent poet to achieve the intended principle of brevity. One may find out some such terminations which convey also such ideas at the back of the mind of the poet or even the commentator.

VIII. The adequate use of derivative forms otherwise known as *Taddhita* forms, in Pāṇini's Grammar can also be regarded as a good device at the hands of good poets. Thus, the use of the forms such as *Kāruṇika* in the *Raghuvaṁśam,* X.70 and *maithileyau* in XV. 62 point in the same direction. Instead of saying 'two sons of Maithilī', Kālidāsa has used the expression[17] *maithileyau* which helps him to drop one word. It would be equally possible for a good reader to collect many such examples from the *mahākāvyas* of great poets. Hence here only the device is explained by casual references to only two illustrations.

IX. The proper use of compounds on the part of the poets can also be regarded as an effective remedy by which the brevity could be achieved. Thus, one may note here the use of the compound known as *Śākapārthivādī* or *madhyamapadalopa,* as the device, which would be more useful for dropping of some words for the purpose of brevity. For the clarification of this device, one may read with advantage the significant[18] observations of Hemādri on the word *Bimbādharā* in the *Raghuvaṁśam,* XIII.16.

X. The employment of some important maxims also could be treated as an important device at the hands of a prospective poet to achieve brevity. Hemādri has employed the principle[19] of *Vṛddhakumārīvara-nyāya* to explain the significance of the *Raghuvaṁśam*[20], IX. 91. Here the curse from the parents of Śrāvaṇa comes as blessings to the king Daśaratha. This idea is explained by Hemādri by the above maxim which is also fruitfully used by Patañjali in his *Mahābhāṣya* and Kumārilabhaṭṭa in his *Tantravārttika* as noted by the learned editor Revaprasad Dvivedi, for which he deserves handsome compliments. Here one may say that this brevity is conceptual rather than verbal. Here by the use of few words, a great poet can express the ocean of meaning. Thus, one may say without any fear of contradiction that the adequate use of the principles of maxims can also be regarded as a good device any good poet can utilise for the purpose of brevity.

XI. Here it would be proper to note some devices which aim at unnecessary multiplication of presumption which is otherwise known as *Gaurava*. The words which are repetitive in poetry may preferably be dropped by a good poet. Hemādri has shown in his *Darpaṇa*[21] on the *Raghuvaṁśam,* VI. 64 that when the intended sense of 'southern direction' could be easily conveyed by the word *dakṣiṇa* in the stanza under discussion, the use of the expression *diśaḥ* appears superfluous. Hemādri also demonstrates[22] on the *Raghuvaṁśam* V.8 that when the purpose is already served by the expression *nivāpa,* the use of the expression *pitṛṇām* becomes redundant. Hence for aiming at brevity, it is necessary for a good poet to achieve brevity by dropping some words which are repetitive.

XII. Hemādri has significantly shown that when it is possible for a good poet to convey the intended sense by the use of a single word, one complete or even half a line should not be composed. If, however, this kind of device is not used, then the unnecessary description adds to *gaurava* and not to *lāghava*. This point could be clarified by reading with good advantage the commentary[23] *Darpaṇa* of Hemādri on the *Raghuvaṁśam,* II. 75. Here the whole sense of first line could have been conveyed by the use of the expression 'moon'. But Kālidāsa has employed one complete line for it. Here one may notice that Hemādri has quoted Vāmana's *Kāvyālaṁkāra Sūtra,* III.2.2 to show '*padārthe vākyavacana*'. From this point, it is evident that a good poet is expected to economise the words to convey the intended good sense of any *kāvya* or any verse. Here it appears that Kālidāsa has incurred the fault of *Gaurava*.

XIII. Here one is constrained to observe that sometimes the use of the expressions like *sthala, phala, bhitti,* etc. when used in poetry, no doubt convey the sense[24] of glorification. But such words aim at unnecessary multiplication of presumption and will have to be treated as cases of *gaurava* and not of *lāghava*.

One could like to clarify this point by the example of the word *gaṇḍabhitti* used by Kālidāsa in his *Raghuvaṁśam*, V.43. Hemādri here observed that the word *bhitti* is for the purpose of glorification and quotes the work *Gaṇaratnamahodadhi* in support. When the sense of a word could be conveyed by the simple word, such words only aim at glorification and add to *gaurava.*

XIV. One is also happy to note that the devices which are brought to light above are free from the faults[25] of *Vākyabheda, Parisaṁkhyā* (Exclusion), the principle of *dehalīdīpaka nyāya* which occurs in construing one word twice, imagining more meanings than one, etc. already pointed out by the present author against the interpretational theory of word economy and *Ṛgveda* interpretation so ably advocated by the learned Professor H.D. Velankar.

From the foregoing discussion, the following legitimate conclusion may be drawn.

(1) Word economy is a device special to the grammarians.

(2) In daily popular practices, it is *gaurava* that is favoured and not *lāghava.*

(3) However, the devices of short forms, alternative forms, compounds, derivative words, use of significant adjectives, *Taddhita* terminations, popular maxims etc. help a good poet to achieve brevity — both verbal and conceptual.

(4) One may avoid the fault of *gaurava,* i.e., unnecessary multiplication of presumption by avoiding repetitive words, unnecessary adjectives, the construction of a sentence for a word, etc.

(5) By the above devices, *lāghava* can be achieved in poetry in the eyes of grammarians.

(6) On the point of *lāghava* by the use of maxim, there is complete agreement between *the commentators* of the Kāvya portion, Patañjali and the Mīmāṁsakas.

(7) The above devices also are free from the faults which are generally levelled against the method of interpretation by the well-known Mīmāṁsakas.

References

1. शब्दिकास्तु–ह्रस्वसंज्ञकवर्णवृत्तिधर्मविशेष इत्याहु: ।

   न्यायकोश p. 704.
2. *Science of Ritual,* p. 30.
3. काशिकावृत्तौ च 'समुच्चये सामान्यवचनस्य' इत्यत्र लौकिके शब्दव्यवहारे लाघवं नाद्रियते ।

   दर्पण on *रघुवंश'* V. 32, p. 102.
4. पाणिनीयमतदर्पणे - अक्ष्यादिशब्देन विनापि देहे स्यादेव काणादिगुण: प्रतीत:, तथापि लोको गुरुलाघवं प्रत्यानादराच्छब्दमपि प्रयुङ्क्ते इति ।

   Ibid., p. 102.
5. लोकेऽपि समुदायस्य व्यपदेशो हि दृश्यते, ग्रामो दग्ध: पटी प्लुष्टेत्येकदेश–क्रियास्वपि इति पाणिनीयमतदर्पणे ।

   Ibid., p. 233.
6. गोदा गोदावरीनद्याम्–इति शब्दभेदप्रकाशे ।

   Ibid., p. 367.
7. *शांकरभाष्य* on *ब्रह्मसूत्र* III. 3.39.
8. *स्मृतिचंद्रिका–श्राद्धकाण्ड* p.415.
9. *रघुवंश* p.392. Also See *दर्पण*, p. 434.
10. ते–मे शब्दौ द्रष्टव्यौ त्वयामयेत्यस्मिन्नर्थे इति वामन: ।

    दर्पण, p. 199.
11. A Note on Prof H.D. Velankar's "Word Economy and Ṛgveda interpretation", *A.B.O.R.I.* P. 253.
12. वामन:–विशेषणप्रयोगादेव विशेष्यप्रतिपत्तौ जातायां विशेषणमात्रस्यैव प्रयोग: ।

    दर्पण, p. 39.
13. Also See पूर्णसरस्वती's विद्युल्लता Commentary on गाण्डीवधन्वा in *मेघदूत*, p.74.
14. सहशब्देन विना सहशब्देन (सहार्थतृतीया) प्रयोग: 'वृद्धो यूना' इति निर्देशात् ।

    दर्पण, p. 436.
15. हनुर्वदनैकदेश: कुत्सितो यस्येति निन्दायां मतुप् ।

    दर्पण, p. 377.
16. प्रशंसायामिनिप्रत्यय: । मल्लिनाथ on *रघुवंश*, I.91.
17. मैथिलेयौ कुशलवौ जगतुर्गुरुचोदितौ ।

    रघुवंश, XV. 62.
18. बिम्बाकारोऽधर: विम्बाधर: । शाकपार्थिवत्वात् समास: ।

    दर्पण, p. 361.
19. वृद्धकुमारी (वर) न्यायेन पुत्रोत्पत्ति: सुतशोकेनाक्षिप्ता ।

    Ibid., p. 257.
20. *रघुवंश*, IX. 91.
21. दक्षिणाशब्देन सिद्धे दिक्शब्दो लाघवानादरात् ।

    दर्पण, p. 148.
22. निवापशब्देन पितृज्ञानात् पितृशब्दोक्ति: प्रशंसार्था पुष्पमालावत् ।

    Ibid., p. 94.
23. पदार्थे वाक्यरचना । अत्र चन्द्रपदवाच्येऽर्थे नयनेत्याद्युक्तम् ।

    Ibid., p. 35.
24. भित्तिशब्द: प्रशंसार्थ: । *Ibid.,* p. 107.
25. *Ibid.,* pp. 251-57.

Bibliography

Journals

Journal of the Asiatic Society, Bombay, Vol.18, and 51/52/53 of 1974/75/75.

Annals of the Bhandarkar Oriental Research Institute Pune, Vols LXXI,1980; LXII, 1981; LXIII, 1982; LXIVI, 1983.

Journal of the University of Bombay, Vols. 31, 32 and 33 of 1961, 1962 and 1963.

Bharatiya Vidya, Vol.25, 1965.

Journal of the Ganganatha Jha Kendriya Sanskrit Vidyapitha, Allahabad, Vol.37, 1981 and Vols. 38-39, 1982-83.

Unpublished Materials

The early beginning of poetics in the *Ṛg-Veda* by I.N.Dike (Ph. D. dissertation) deposited in the University of Bombay, 1959.

Indra in the post-Ṛgvedic period: An examination of the sources of Indra's deterioration as it appears in the *Purāṇas* by G.H. Godbole (Ph. D. dissertation) deposited in the University of Bombay, 1954.

Yāska's *Nirukta* and *Ṛg-Vedic* Interpretation by Mrs. S.S. Pradhan, (Ph. D. dissertation) deposited in the University of Bombay, 1965.

The seers of the *Ṛg-Veda* by V.G. Rahurkar, Poona University Thesis published by Poona University, 1970.

Sacrifice in the *Brāhmaṇas,* by G.U. Thike, published by Poona University, 1975.

The theory of the *Sandhis* and *Sandhyāṅgas* by T.G.Mainkar, published by Ajanta Publications, Delhi.

Books

Amaramaṇḍana ed. by V. Raghavan, Deccan College Post Graduate Research Institute, Pune.

Āpastaṁba Dharma-Sūtra ed. by George Bühler, Bombay Sanskrit and Prakrt Series, 1932.

Bhoja's *Śṛṅgāraprakāśa,* published by Mysore.

Exercises in Indology by R.N. Dandekar, Ajanta Publications, Delhi 1979.

Aparārka on the Yājñavalkya-Smṛti, Ānandāśhram Sanskrit Series, Poona, 1902-1903.

Dashakumaracaritam published by Panashikar with two Sanskrit commentaries, Nirnaya Sagara Press, Bombay.

Daśarūpaka with Dīpikā of Bahurūpamiśra by A.N. Pandey,Bhāratīya Vidyā Prakashan, Varanasi, 1979.

Abhijñāna-Śākuntala-Carcā by Anonymous commentator, Kerala University Publication, 1961.

Rāghavabhaṭṭa's Arthadyotanikā on the Śākuntalam published by Nirnaya Sagar Press, Bombay, 1947.

Gautama Dharma-Sūtra with the commentary of Maskari published by Mysore University, 1917.

Bālaṁbhaṭṭī on the Vyavahāra Adhyāya of the Mitākṣarā on the Yājñavalkya-Smṛti by J.R. Gharpure, Hindu law Text Series, Bombay, 1917.

Hemādri's Darpaṇa commentary on the Raghuvaṁśam published by Kashiprasad Jayasval Institute, Patna, 1973.

Raghuvaṁśam with the commentary of Mallinātha and extracts from the commentaries of others, publ. by Nirnaya Sagar Press, Bombay, 1947.

Uttara-Rāma-Caritam of Bhavabhūti with the commentary of Ghanashyama, P.V.Kane, Motilal Banarsidass, Delhi.

Uttara-Rāma-Caritam of Bhavabhūti with Eng. Tr. and Notes by G.K. Bhat, Surat Publishing House, 1965.

Harṣacaritam of Bāṇabhaṭṭa with Notes by P.V. Kane, 1918, Motilal Banarsidass, Delhi.

Harṣacharitam of Bāṇabhaṭṭa with the commentary *Marmāvabodhinī* of Raṅganātha, pub. by Kerala University, 1959.

History of Dharma-Śastra by P.V.Kane, pub. by B.O.R.I., Pune.

A critical edition of the Mahābhārata, pub. by B.O.R.I., Pune.

A Critical edition of the Rāmāyaṇa, pub. by Baroda Oriental Institute.

Studies in the Dharma-Śastra by S.G.Moghe, Ajanta Publications, Delhi, 1991.

Studies in the Pūrva-Mīmāṁsā by S.G.Moghe, Ajanta Publications, Delhi, 1984.

Kṛtyakalpataru of Lakṣmīdhara-Śuddhi-Kāṇḍa and Vyavahāra, published by Oriental Institute, Baroda.

Vyavahāra Prakāśa of Pṛthvicandra, pub. by Bharatiya Vidya Bhavan, Bombay.

Devaṇṇabhaṭṭa's Smṛticandrika, by J.R. Gharpure, Hindu Law Text Series, Bombay.

Śulapāṇi's Dipakalika on the Yājñavalkya-Smṛti by J.R.Gharpure, Hindu Law Text Series, Bombay.

Smṛtisandarbha published by Mansukhalal Mor, Calcutta, 1952-53.

Mitramiśra's Vyavahāra Prakāśa, Chowkhamba Sanskrit Series, Varanasi, 1929.

Viśvarūpa's commentary on the Yājñavalkya-Smṛti published by University of Kerala.

The Cārudattam of Bhāsa, Bhāsa Nāṭaka-Cakram by C.R. Deodhar, Motilal Banarsidass, Delhi.

The Daśarūpaka, ed. by Panasikar, Nirnaya Sagar Press edition, Bombay, 1947.

The Vikramorvaśīyam of Kālidāsa with three commentaries, pub. by Sanskrit Academy, Osmania University, 1966.

Viśvanātha's Sāhitya Darpaṇa, Nirnaya Sagar Press edition, Bombay, 1910.

The Commentary of Vīra-Rāghava on the Mahāvīracaritam of Bhavabhūti, pub. by Nirnaya Sagar Press Bombay, 1910.

The commentary Rasamañjarī of Pūrṇasarasvatī on the Mālatī-Mādhavam of Bhavabhūti, pub. by Kerala University, 1953.

Śākuntalam with the commentaries of Śaṅkara and Narahari, pub. by Mithila Institute, Darbhanga, 1957.

Kālidāsa — His Art and Thought by T.G.Mainkar, Deshmukh Prakashana, Pune.

The Theory of sandhis and Sandhyāṅgas, by T.G.Mainkar, Ajanta Publications, Delhi.

The Kāvyaprakāśā with the commentary of Someśvara, pub. by R.C.Parikh, Oriental Institute, Jodhpur, 1959.

The Kāvyaprakāśa with the commentary of Caṇḍidāsa, pub. by Shivaprasad Bhattacharya, Sarasvati Bhavan Series, Varanasi, 1965.

Kuntaka's Vakroktijīvitam by K. Krishnamoorthy, Karnataka University Publication, Dharwar, 1977.

H.D. Velankar Commemoration Volume, by S.N. Gajendragadkar, Bombay, 1965.

Ṛg-Veda Maṇḍala II by H.D. Velankar, Bombay University publication 1967.

Ṛg-Veda Maṇḍala III by H.D. Velankar, Bombay Uni. Pub. 1969.

Ṛg-Veda Maṇḍala VII by H.D.Velankar, Bharatiya Vidya Bhavan, Bombay, 1962.

Ṛksūktaśatī by H.D.Velankar, Bharatiya Vidya Bhavan, Bombay, 1973.

Path of Devotion, by H.D. Velankar, Kausika Lecture Series, Pune, 1952.

P.V. Kane Commemoration Monograph, University of Bombay, 1974.

Homage to Dr. T.G.Mainkar, C.R. Deshpande and Nalini Chapekar, Bombay, 1982.

Mīmāṁsā-Koṣa by Kevalananda Sarasvati pub. by Prajna Pathasala, Wai 1952-60.

Ṛ.N. Dandekar Commemoration Volume, by S.D. Joshi, Ajanta Books International, Delhi, 1984.

S.K.Belvalkar felicitation Volume.

Stabaka (In Marathi) A collection of papers by M.D. Paradkar.

Select articles of H.R.Divekar (In Marathi), Divekar Publication Committee, Pune, 1976.

Nīlakaṇṭha's Prāyaścitta Mayūkha, Gujarati Printing Press, Bombay, 1940.

Author/Title Index

Topical Index

AF632702

In the Path of Service

Takda, 1953 ~ Ashoka

Ashoka with Jyotirmoyee Devi

Krishnanagar, 1942~Ashoka

Calcutta, 1934~Ashoka on her graduation

Jabbalpur, 1978 - Ashoka with Shaibal

In the Path of Service
Memories of a Changing Century

Ashoka Gupta

Foreword by
Mahasweta Devi

Translated from the Bengali by
Sipra Bhattacharya
with Ranjana Dasgupta

Stree

IN THE PATH OF SERVICE:
MEMORIES OF A CHANGING CENTURY
was first published in February 2005 by STREE,
an imprint of Bhatkal and Sen,16 Southern Avenue, Kolkata 700 026

First reprint April 2008

© 2008 STREE

ISBN 81-85604-56-8

Price Rs. 450.00

All Rights Reserved. No part of this book may be reproduced
or utilized in any form or by any means without
prior written permission from the publisher.

Design by STREE, typesetting by Krishna Gopal Das,
74T Sultan Alam Road, Kolkata 700 033
and printed by Arunima Printing Works,
81 Simla Street, Kolkata 700 006

Published by Mandira Sen for STREE,
an imprint of Bhatkal and Sen,
16 Southern Avenue, Kolkata 700 026

To
the memory of my husband,
Shaibal Kumar Gupta,
who helped me find the path of service
and shared the journey with me.

Foreword

In the Path of Service: Memories of a Changing Century by Ashoka Gupta has inspired me and made 2005 a rewarding year. I have been fortunate in knowing Jyotirmoyee Devi, Ashokadi and her husband, Saibal Gupta, for a long time. They enveloped me with affection and encouragement, and the relationships I shared with them are something that I cherish. In the beginning, it took me a while to realize that Jyotirmoyee Devi was the mother of Ashoka Gupta and often came to visit her. I have always admired Jyotirmoyee Devi's writings and many years ago took my mother to meet her. The writer Anindita Devi was also very appreciative of Jyotirmoyee Devi's writings. Anindita Devi was my mother's maternal uncle's wife, her mamima. I decided to honour such writers in a great *Sangbardhana.* In 1972, six great women writers, amongst the pioneers, were felicitated in a grand ceremony at Rabindra Sadan, which was absolutely packed with an enthusiastic audience. The writers were Jyotirmoyee Devi, Giribala Devi, Punyalata Chakrabarty, Sailabala Ghoshjaya, Sita Devi and Shanta Devi. But I find that Ashokadi has not mentioned this event.

Ashoka Gupta is a remarkable workaholic. I was always astonished at how much she could do, at her organizational capacity. She could take care of the kitchen, collect and reach garments to Marichjhanpi, do many other tasks at the same time and never lose her cool. I started to read the book and soon realized that the story is known to me. Her book helps us to understand what a great role the women of an earlier generation played in their homes. Educated, truly learned in our scriptures and history, with a love for their motherland, they were the pioneers. These pioneers had a passion for learning. Jyotirmoyee Devi was truly extraordinary and made sure that her daughters faced no obstacles in their journey towards education. Right from childhood, her daughters learnt self-discipline and selfless service to society. And as their mother she remained a source of perpetual strength.

Ashokadi was married to a remarkable man, full of strength, clarity and a patriot as well. He was one of those civilians who were good officials, yet were patriotic and served their country well. Ashokadi is of the same calibre. She took good care of the joint family she had married into. Fully liberated, she worked with great energy and discipline during the crucial year of the 1942 Quit India movement, the Bengal Famine of 1943, relief work during the communal riots, building shelters and homes for the homeless women and children, running hospitals and centres for orphaned children. She and her husband were of Mahatma Gandhi's faith and till date she remains a true Gandhian: Service For All is her motto. She represents the great movement of women who worked to liberate themselves.

It is a glorious saga of a glorious era in our history. Of women marching forward to throw off their shackles, to ensure women's progress. It is an ongoing saga. I wish that there would be a Bangla edition and that it should be used as a textbook for studies on Indian women.

She has given us a tremendous example of service, which we, who have known her, must follow. Let us then follow her footsteps and make our lives worthwhile and carry on her work bit by bit so that her ideals can be found in our work too. She has taught us to give all that we have for others.

Kolkata, Jan 2005 — Mahasweta Devi

Contents

Preface

For sometime, many close relatives have been telling me to write my memoir. Mahasweta Devi, a younger friend of mine, would goad me whenever she got the chance, 'Ashokadi, write, write your memoir!' but I always felt hesitant, would anyone find it interesting? I have certainly seen momentous changes. My life spans nine decades and I have witnessed and participated in many events that have changed the lives of Indian women and made the society what it is today. At the same time I did not want to write a conventional memoir where I would be the main focus. I wanted to write about how I was drawn into social work and how I too was able to offer some contribution to making things better than I found them. If at all I were to write, I would want to write of how I was inspired by the example of Jyotirmoyee Devi, my mother, of how my husband, Shaibal Kumar Gupta, encouraged me in all my endeavours. Both of them have passed away, my mother in November 1988, my husband in June 1989, and I like to think that they would have appreciated this book too.

My husband would always tell me to write down whatever I had seen or experienced. My son, Partha, too, always urged me to write a book; perhaps because he was a historian he was keen to see that a record would be available. His wife, Narayani, a historian too, also encouraged me to write. But for a long time, I did not do anything, and then one day my eldest grandchild, Srirupa, the daughter of my eldest daughter, Shakuntala (Kunta), brought me her father's tape recorder and said that now I could get started.

It would have been hard for me to write by hand either in Bangla or in English, though there were some reports that I had written earlier—of my foreign trips—that were available and so it meant that it would not have been like starting from scratch. Srirupa's gift showed me that I could have what I wanted to say taped. The publisher suggested that I could record what I wanted to say in Bangla, and then this would be transcribed and translated into English. This is how the book came about. Sipra Bhattacharya and Ranjana Dasgupta sat with me, sometimes asking a question or asking for more details, which helped me to work out what I wanted to say. There were many sessions, many drafts, before the manuscript could be edited, then reviewed by me and put into production. My granddaughter, Nilanjana, Shakuntala's younger daughter, spent her summer vacation of 2004 in India, working on the final draft, putting it into shape so that the publishers could edit it. I am very grateful to Sipra, Ranjana and Nilanjana.

My daughter Kasturi helped me to read the proof and to select the photographs. If I did not acknowledge the help of my cousin Shyamal Sen, who deciphered the first paragraphs of the original tape, and the typist, Bedabati, who took down my dictation in shorthand, and my peon Sinheswar Ray, who kept track of all my loose papers I would be doing them an injustice. Mahasweta Devi readily agreed to write the Foreword. My niece Mandira, my cousin Deepali's daughter, of Stree Publishers, and her colleagues have been very supportive. I am thankful to all who have encouraged and helped me.

Kinship Terms and Place Names

Baba	father
Baromama	oldest among mother's brothers
Boudi	the wife of one's older brother (*bou*, wife; *di*, as suffix for older sister)
Dada/da as suffix	older brother
Dadamashai	maternal grandfather
Dadi	paternal grandmother
Didi/di as suffix	older sister
Didima	maternal grandmother
Ja	wife of one's husband's brother
Kakima	father's younger brother's wife
Mama	mother's brother
Mejda	second eldest brother
Mejdi	second eldest sister
Nonod	husband's sister
Sejomama	mother's third elder brother
Thakurda	paternal grandfather
Thakurma	paternal grandmother

When place names are referred to before independence, the author has used the version that was current then: Dacca, Krishnanagore, and so on. References to 'Calcutta' are scattered throughout the text and it was decided not to make the switch to the new usage, 'Kolkata'.

who was a member of the cabinet of the maharaja of Jaipur and a wealthy jagirdar. Moving from Patna after Baba's death to Jaipur, the home of my mother's family, thence to Delhi and finally to Calcutta, staying with relatives, I learnt at a young age to adjust myself to changing situations and circumstances. I came to recognize the importance of family bonds and cherish them. I became aware of the selfless way in which my mother's brothers took upon themselves the care of her large family, and perhaps this instilled in me the desire to fulfil family responsibilities to the utmost, a norm which has ever remained a guiding principle of my life. It was not as if anyone had tutored me on such duties, but having seen the people around me performing them silently and effortlessly, I too rook them in a matter-of-fact way. Indeed, shouldering family responsibilities became the training-ground for my later work in the field of social service.

I was perhaps fortunate in having the kind of family I did. Whether in Jaipur, or in Delhi or in Calcutta, they were educated and progressive. There was no question of not sending the girls to school, or of observing very strict rules of orthodoxy. My uncles were mostly professional men, financially well-off, and able to take on the responsibility of looking after six fatherless children easily. Moreover, though the family was mainly *prabashi,* it was imbued with Bengali cultural influences.[2] From an early age I was exposed to Rabindranath Tagore, Vivekananda, to Bankimchandra and Saratchandra, and their writings too must have enriched that subterranean pit of growing consciousness deep within me.

As a child, I spent long periods of time away from my mother. I was too young then to understand the contradictions of her situation–the very capable woman who managed an enormous family along with two sisters-in-law, young brides, aged about sixteen. Yet she chafed at her financial dependence on her father and brothers. While courageously raising her children, she was also preparing herself through close observation of the society around her and through rigorous study for her later career as a writer. The trials and tribulations of her life as a young widow made her specially sensitive to the condition of women, issues which she raised with unfailing courage and honesty in her stories, novels and essays. I was, of course, too young to understand this at the time; I now realize this on hindsight. And I can never underestimate her influence upon me. Her strength of character and personality has remained an inspiration to me all my life.

The first twenty years of my life were like the foundation of a building, a solid base upon which the edifice would be built later. This base would be strong enough to withstand the tremors of life's many surprises–many of them unpleasant–and strong enough too to take the weight of unplanned storeys added to the main structure as an afterthought.

Notes

1 Kshudiram Bose (1889-1908), a very young terrorist, inadvertendly killed two European women who were traveling in the carriage that he believed held his real victim, the oppressive Chief Presidency Magistrate, Kingsford. He was caught and hanged. He left behind an image of great courage and fearlessness.

2 *Prabashi* means 'settler', someone who lives away from his/her homeland.

One

Memories of Baba

I was only five and a half when my father, Kiron Chandra Sen, died. My memories of him are like scenes from a motion picture—brief vignettes that shine brightly like meteors but cannot provide the enduring light of day. My mother, Jyotirmoyee Devi, was later to become a famous writer, but while we were children, she was simply our mother. My siblings and I were very close age-wise. My elder sister, Amiya, my elder brother Arun and I had all been born between 1909 and 1912. Anubha was born within the next two years and in 1916 my younger brother, Amitava. My youngest sister, Anju, was born in 1918. She was only three months old when Baba passed away.

At that time, we lived in Bankipur, which was near Patna, and Baba was a lawyer in Bankipur Court. He could sing very well. When he returned from the kutchery, or judicial office, he would sit downstairs for a while, meeting his clients. Later in the evening, he would come up to the open terrace. It had already been sprinkled with water to cool it down, and mats had been spread out. A brass platter full of sweet-smelling jasmine wafted its fragrance all around. We would all sit surrounding Baba, the five older children, Ma with her embroidery, and Dadi, our paternal grandmother, with her paan basket. Baba would play the harmonium and sing, and all of us sang at the top of our voices with him. All, of course, except the three-month-old Anju. The songs were mostly by Rajanikanta Sen. We children were not particularly tuneful. But that evening-time ritual was very close to our hearts.

A similar secret ritual existed between our paternal grandfather, Hem Chandra Sen, whom we called Dadu, and us. Every night, his dinner would be served in a rather old-world, elaborate fashion. From the kitchen downstairs, Ma herself would bring his huge brass dinner plate, with fluffy luchis or fried puffed bread arranged alongside slices of fried brinjals, a variety of curries, sweets and khir, sweet thickened and flavoued milk, to his room. Dada and I lay quietly, pretending to be asleep while she served Dadu. When she had gone down again, we would race up to him and stand with our mouths wide open in expectation. He would feed us delicious bits of luchi di pped in the sweet khir. What a thrill this secret feast was for us!

Even though I was but a child, I had already developed a strong sense of com petition with my elder brother, Arun, whom I called Dada. I can remember sitting next to Ma while she sat at the sewing machine, trying to learn all the spellings of *Pratham Bhag*, a Bengali primer. Later that evening, she told Baba that I was bent on com pleting it, sim ply because Dada had already done so, and I was jealous! Anyway, led on by this sibling rivalry, I did indeed learn to read very fast, and Ma was delighted. She told my grandfather that soon I would be reading the *Ramayana* aloud to him!

I remember that a huge bed would be made up for us children, in which all of us, except our baby sister, slept together. The birth of my younger brother is also a vivid memory. On a particular night, Ma was confined to a small room at a corner of the terrace. The next morning, Dadi told us, 'Go and see, you have a brother.' So we went up and discovered a boy lying next to Ma. We were astonished. He seemed quite large to us–anyway, he was very fair skinned and quite big. How quietly he lay next to Ma! Yet, we had not been aware of any noise, any hullabaloo at the time of his birth.

There used to be a confectioner adjacent to our house, which sold big, hot jalebis, two for a paisa. On those occasions when we threw tantrums about our usual bread-and-milk breakfast, those delicious hot jalebis would be brought to tem pt us. Everyone said food was cheap there. We were a large family and my father's earnings were not very high. But we were never aware of any hardshi p. Fish was available at two annas a seer (a little less than a kg). A whole basketful of lichis could be had for only one or two rupees. When Baba went to the court at Danapur, he often brought a basket of mangoes for us and we enjoyed them tremendously. We always had a feeling of plenty, of comfort.

Ma was a wonderful cook. An uncle, my father's cousin, would call her 'madam'. He used to live with us. 'Well, Madam, what have you cooked today?' he would ask. I found it most amusing. Then on holidays, many people would come to the house. On those days, an enormous meal was cooked and everyone was fed heartily. Baba had acquired a bottle of Worcester sauce from somewhere. If Ma cooked mutton, Baba would go around pouring a little Worcester sauce on everybody's helping of meat, but for me, that spoilt the taste of the meat–spoilt my meal, in fact! Baba's maternal uncles lived in Patna. They too were extremely fond of Ma's cooking. I still remember Ma heaping aloo dum onto large brass platters, which she arranged beautifully and then sent these off to the uncles.

On the night Baba died, we had all been asleep. It was the month of Bhadra (mid- Aug to mid-Sept) in 1918. We woke up, perhaps on hearing the wailing, or maybe we were woken up. Then we went to his room. We found that Ma had collapsed on the floor next to the bed, and so had Dadi. Baba lay stretched out, covered with a sheet. He had been suffering from high fever for the last three days, having contracted influenza. He was thirty-seven.The place was thronged with people, all wailing and crying aloud, and there we were, in the middle of it all. Didi, my elder sister, was crying too. But the rest of us did not realize what had happened–had no conception of it. Then someone stepped forward and said that we children should not remain there. We were taken away to a neighbour's house. Dada probably remained at home as the funeral was about to take place and he would have to perform the last rites. We were fed and looked after in the neighbour's house. We only returned after Dada had come back from the cremation ground.

Soon after that Didima, Sarala Devi, our maternal grandmother, and Mama, Ma's brother and our maternal uncle–the eldest of her brothers, Dhitendra Nath Sen, later to succeed his father as the head of the household and as the jagirdar, arrived from Jaipur. The whole house was full of people. Both Ma and Dadi were absolutely dazed. So many events took place so fast. The *shradh* or rituals for the dead were performed, probably in the room in which Baba had died. People were fed one day. But we children ran around playing and jumping about, for we were not really touched by the grief which held the whole house in its grip. We had no understanding of what was happening.

That was the end of an early chapter of our lives. Within a fortnight, we all left Patna. My paternal grandparents–Thakurda and Dadi– went back to their ancestral home in Guptipara in the Hooghly district of Bengal taking my younger sister, Anubha, with them. Soon Thakurda would undertake a pilgrimage to Brindaban, convinced that he had to offer some penance to assuage the sorrow–and he felt that something wrong might have been done to bring about such a cruel blow–of losing his only son so early. We, the five remaining children, went with Ma to her parents' home in Jaipur. In those days, we had to change trains at Agra station to reach Jaipur. Agra was famous for its petha and dalmuth–crisp fried savouries. We bought some from Agra station itself. When we reached our maternal grandfather's house in Jaipur, my weeping mother was surrounded by mourning relatives. And there I was sitting by the window, eating dalmuth when such monumental changes were taking place in my life!

Two

From Patna to Jaipur to Delhi

Avinash Chandra Sen, my maternal grandfather, whom we called Dadamashai, now took charge of our lives. He was a cabinet minister of the native state of Jaipur and possessed an enormous jagir or estate. He had ten children and my mother, Jyotirmoyee Devi, was his second daughter. His five sons were younger than Ma. His eldest daughter, Abhamoyee, was widowed in 1929, and she too came with her five children to live in her parental home. Living in Dadamashai's care, we never faced any real financial deprivation, and he bore the expenses of our education and looked after all our needs. Later when we older children lived away from Jaipur for the sake of our education, we still thought of Jaipur as our home. My mother was very independent, and her financial dependence hurt her. Dadamashai had invested whatever money Baba had left in shares in her name, and from the interest she received from these she met her own pocket-expenses.

Surrounded by a vast family of aunts, uncles, older and younger cousins, we seemed to be lost in a totally different milieu. This was when Dada and I were sent to Delhi to study. Dada had been studying in a school in Patna, as did Didi, my elder sister. But when we came to Jaipur, their studies came to a halt as we were going through a very difficult, bewildering time. Gradually, Ma got a grip on herself. Suddenly, one day: in winter, November, to be precise, I heard that Dada was being sent to Delhi to continue his studies. Where would he study in Delhi? He would be living with Dadamashai's younger brother Aprakash Sen, whom we called Mejodadu. He was a doctor. By this time, I had turned six. I began to wonder, oughtn't I to go to school too? Though I did not express my secret wish to anybody, within two days I came to know that I too would be going to Delhi, and so off I went to Delhi with Dada. Didi continued her studies in Jaipur.

My formal education began in Delhi in 1919 when I was six years old. That was when I was admitted to Indraprastha School. In those days, Indraprastha School was like a missionary school and two of the senior-most teachers were Scottish ladies. It was situated behind Jama Masjid. My early memories are of a highly disciplined school. We would all stand in the courtyard and pray. The prayers were in Hindi. We would also sing some songs. After Assembly, we would go off to our respective classes: *Paheli* (first), *Dusri* (second), *Teesri* (third), and so on. This was a primary school. We sat on mats spread out on the floor. We carried wooden boards on which we rested our exercise books when we wrote. We would tie our books and other necessities in a three-cornered piece of cloth to make up a bundle. All the other girls had a board and that cloth. I was the only one who did not possess these very important articles, and I went home and actually fashioned them for myself.

I do not remember much about the lessons, but certain strange things remain embedded in my memory. The other girls would remark, 'Oh. You are Bengali! You must be a fish-eater!' Most people there were vegetarian and they did not eat meat and fish. So I would hastily say. 'No, no, I never eat fish! Truly, I've never seen a fish, let alone touched one.' I had to tell those fibs, otherwise they would not even sit next to me. Most of the girls were Jains, some were Hindus. There were a few Sikh girls as well. During the different festivals, their varied attire was quite fascinating. During the monsoon month of Sravan (mid-July to mid-Aug), they would wear flowers in their hair. In winter, they wore jackets or close-fitting angarkhas. I would wear a coat, or perhaps long pyjamas. I was usually dressed in boys' clothes, for I had not taken any frocks to Delhi. The other girls wore long flowing skirts and blouses. There were many ways in which I was different from them. My hair was cut short, they all wore their hair in long plaits.

I seem to have been quite active in the classroom. I remember that the teachers would call me to the front, and occasionally, I would have to lead the class during an oral lesson, or read out aloud while the others repeated the lesson after me. This was the usual system of studies in those days. I think I was awarded a prize when I was in Standard Two, but I do not know whether I was a good student at that time or not. In addition, Mejodadu had engaged a Bengali tutor who taught us Bengali at home.

While in school in Delhi, we were quite divorced from our mother tongue, but paradoxically the intellectual activity at home was focused on it. The famous literary journals, *Prabashi, Bharat Barsha* and *Bharati* came regularly to the house, as well as many other magazines such as *Manashi* and *Marmabani.* Politics was an integral part of life in those days and in 1919 the furore over the Jalianwala Bagh incident had not yet died down.[1] The killing of Shraddhanand had just taken place, the Khilafat movement was in progress.[2] Our house was just in front of the Parade Ground on Secretariat Road in Chandni Chowk. All the processions would pass before it, before our eager eyes. The Congress was in the forefront of the national movement.

I clearly remember the day when Shraddhanand was killed.[3] The shot had been fired, there was a great uproar—people fleeing in all directions. I remember all that. Also the day when Gandhiji appeared, flanked by those two leaders of the Khilafat movement, Moulana Shaukat Ali and Muhammad Ali. I was only seven years old, but already I could understand that terrible things were happening. So many things were being discussed by the elders at home. Sometimes my mother's aunts would come for a short visit. It was on one such occasion that people talked about using only Swadeshi cloth, handspun, khadi material. I noticed that from that day, Mejodadu's wife, nicknamed Helen, whom we called Mejodidima, gave up her lovely saris and began to wear only handloom saris. White handloom material was purchased and a red border was printed on it. When this sari was washed, the red of the border dyed the whole sari an uneven pink! Well, things were changing, and small as I was I noticed all this. No doubt, I was influenced by these incidents.

There were many pleasant interludes in the daily routine. Mejodadu and Mejodidima's two sons were called Nikhil and Anil. Nikhil was almost nine years older than Anil, who was two years younger than me. When I was seven, Anil was just five. I lived in Delhi for four years till 1922. We were the greatest of friends. Since he was so young, his parents usually took him wherever they went. In those days, it was the practice for doctors and other professional men to go for a ride in the evening. Fresh air was considered to be good for you. Mejodadu too would come home in the evenings, dress up, send for the horses and carriage from the stables and take a turn around Kashmiri Gate. When Mejodadu and Mejodidima went for their promenade, Anil and I would accompany them, sitting on the front-seat of the phaeton. That was the time when Mejodadu would quiz Anil and me on maths and spellings. Such things were easy for me and I would answer him promptly. Anil took longer, after all, he was a couple of years younger than me. It really gave Mejodadu pleasure to teach us during that hour of promenade. This was how most fathers managed to keep in touch with what their children were learning in spite of their busy schedules.

Mejodidma was very beautiful. She wore her sari in the fashion known as brahmika: the front end was draped over the left shoulder and hung quite low. There would be a few pleats at the front but many more at the back. The local ladies of Delhi wore their saris with the ends draped over the right shoulder and many pleats in front, as they do even now. At home, all the ladies of our family wore their saris very simply, in the common Bangla way. But I was more often than not dressed in a cotton vest and dhoti, tied male-fashion. When I came back from school, I'd quickly tie on a dhoti, wear a phiran or a loose cotton short kurta on top and go to eat lunch. School was from seven to eleven in the morning. Since my hair was cut short, I had no difficulty in getting ready for school. Mejodidima wanted to plait my hair. Every evening she would try tying it up. But when I went back to Jaipur during the holidays, my mother would exclaim, 'What have you done to your hair!' and promptly cut it short.

Ma's appearance too had undergone a gradual change by this time. Earlier, she used to wear a pair of gold bangles but she had taken them off now. She had given up wearing the thin-bordered dhotis in favour of plain, unadorned white saris. Her hair was cut short as was customary among Bengali widows. At this time, Didi, Amitava and Anju were with her in Jaipur. Dada and I were studying in Delhi. Anubha, our younger sister, was still with my paternal grandparents in Guptipara.

In Delhi, our fish-eating habits gave rise to many interesting experiences. On the one hand, it was considered to be taboo by the local people, so we could not do it openly, not even mention it by mistake. I even began to feel that it was a serious offence. But during monsoon, when the river Jamuna was in spate, we would go off to the river, below the fort. I would be wearing my dhoti and carrying a thin towel called gamchcha, and a creel. Anil would carry another one. We had a Bengali servant whom we called Gyanada. He was passionately fond of fish. We would catch those tiny fish, lots of them, and bring them home. Gyanada would fry them and when he sat down to eat his lunch, he would eat up all the rice and leave the fish for the last. He would finish the rice while just savouring the aroma of fried fish! On another occasion, someone had brought a tin of shrimps to the house. It was distinctly malodorous, and Mejodidima immediately ordered that it should be thrown away. But Gyanada begged and entreated and finally persuaded Mejodidima to have it cooked. What a terrible smell! While the whole house reeked, Gyanada was the only one who was quite happy!

During my schooldays in Delhi, our teachers taught us everything with such care and competence that we needed no more help at home. Reading, handwriting, arithmetic, even music, everything was seen to. In class I was the one to lead the others, so, my studies were never a problem. Dada was studying in the Anglo-Bengali School. A teacher of the school would come home to tutor him in the evenings. Occasionally, he set me a sum or two, but I always knew the answers. So when Mejodadu asked him about the progress of my studies, he always replied, 'What's the point of teaching her? She knows everything!'

When I was very small, there was some sort of competition with Dada. If he was moving ahead, why should I be left behind? He was a year-and-a-half older than me, and in Delhi, I was in a class below him. Later, that gap became much wider, mainly due to certain circumstances. By the time we reached the higher classes, Dada was three years ahead of me. Dada did his matriculation in 1927 and I did it in 1930.

Notes

1 On 13 Aug 1919 at Jalianwala Bagh, many Indians had gathered to protest against the repressive Rowlett Acts. Brigadier Dyer fired on this unarmed crowd that could not escape from this confined space. The massacre provoked a storm of protest.

2 The Khilafat movement was a protest by the entire Muslim world against the

dismemberment of the Ottoman empire by the Allies after World War I.

[3] A successful lawyer who gave up his practice and joined the the Arya Samaj after he met its founder, Swami Dayanand Saraswati. This Hindu reform movement wished to modernize Hindus and give them modern western education so that they would be no longer held back by moribund traditions and yet be still versed in the Vedas and other 'pure' traditions. Shraddhanand stood for Hindu-Muslim amity but was later assassinated by a Muslim fanatic.

Three

My Early Life in Jaipur

As small children, living apart from Ma and our younger siblings, our lives, Dada's and mine, had a sort of fractured quality. Mercifully, the love and care of our guardians saved us from any deep psychological distress we might otherwise have felt. When we lived in Delhi, Mejodadu kept a watchful eye on us while Mejodidima lavished her affection on us. Nikhil and Anil who were our mamas, our maternal uncles, were of our generation in age if not in relationship, and formed a close friendship with us. Every vacation, we would go back to Jaipur, which was our true home. Not only us, but also Ma's brothers and her sisters with their children, and many other members of a large extended family all assembled there for the holidays. We were a part of a big clamorous group of children and enjoyed ourselves to the hilt.

There were at least eight to ten of us who spent most of the time together, beginning with breakfast. The children who stayed in Jaipur, had their tutors coming to teach them their lessons in the morning. Though Dada and I were on holiday, we too would often sit down to study with that group. Or we might take a ramble through Dadamashai's enormous estate, picking fruit from the fruit trees, or picking the greens and vegetables that were grown especially for Dadamashai in the kitchen garden. There were many flowering trees and shrubs and we spent happy moments plucking blossoms. At noon, we would all go to bathe. After tea, teachers came to teach fine embroidery and other arts to the young girls and aunts. We all would pick up a few new stitches. But what we looked forward to the most was the session of music that took place in the evening. Classical music formed an important recreation in Jaipur and one of Dadamashai's cousins sang very well. The harmonium would be taken out and all of us would sing. Our own repertoire consisted mainly of Rabindrasangeet. Our day ended on a happy note. All of us youngsters slept together on beds made up on the terrace. So, with much talk, laughter and exchange of stories, we finally fell asleep.

Our life in Jaipur had certain peculiar features. The estate was surrounded by a high wall with cactus plants on a kutcha or mud structure and never did we go outside on our own. Once in a while, on the occasion of religious festivals or fairs, we might be taken to a temple or a fairground under the careful supervision of the mamas, but that was rare. Nor did outsiders come into the estate, apart from those who worked there or vendors who came to sell their wares. However, there was no opportunity for us to feel bored or even hemmed-in. The estate was so large, that exploring its various areas kept us occupied and fascinated. We would watch the team of water-carriers efficiently lifting water from the two enormous wells with the help of bullocks and supplying water to the huge house, the fields, gardens, orchards and tanks. Or in the evenings, the lamplighter, going from room to room trimming the wicks, polishing the lamps, filling the oil and lighting them caught our attention. He would greet us with, 'Jai Srijiki' as soon as he had lit the lamps.

One incident from those days that I look back on with amusement, was the time Dadamashai took me to the court of the maharaja of Jaipur. In Jaipur, purdah was very strict, and the only way I could witness the splendours of the royal court was by being dressed as a little boy. I remember being instructed to say that my name was

'Ashok Kumar Sen'. Fortunately, I was young enough to carry off the deception with aplomb!

Soon I came to realize that Ma had taken on part of the responsibility of running the enormous household. She would spend the mornings in the vegetarian kitchen (there was a separate kitchen where non-vegetarian food was cooked, and she as a widow was a strict vegetarian and would not enter it) or keep busy with other household work, which had been entrusted to her by her father. Baromama's young wife, Shantimoyee, aged sixteen, carried out household tasks under her supervision. So it was only after lunch that Ma had some time to herself. Often, I would spend some time with her then or just before going to bed. She began to read a lot, under the tutelage of her uncle, Mahendra Nath Sen of Natagar (the ancestral home of the Jai pur Sen family in 24-Parganas, Bengal). He was a librarian. Gradually, she began to write. Though most of her writing was done later, and published from Calcutta, she began to write around 1927, in Jai pur. That year around ten of her essays were published in the first four issues of the literary magazine, *Bijoli.* One story, 'Ladies' Club' was very good indeed. Sajani Kanta Das found it so interesting that he included it in his collection of Ma's stories entitled '*Raj-jotak*'.

When the vacations ended, I would return to Delhi. By going to Jai pur for my holidays I was able to keep in touch with Didi, Amitava and Anju. But Anubha, who was with our paternal grandparents in Gupti para, did not know us at all. In 1922, Ma brought Didi to Calcutta for her wedding. This was the first time since 1918 that all of us, the six brothers and sisters, were together.

Four

Calcutta: Duff School and My Intellectual Awakening

Didi's wedding in Asharh (mid-June to mid-July) 1922 was an important occasion for the whole family—the wedding of Avinash Chandra Sen's first grandchild, of Ma's eldest daughter. Didi was thirteen years old. Everyone was acutely aware of the misfortunes of my mother, so they were all the more determined that it should be a grand affair. The house was full of people. The family members from Baba's side came only a couple of days before the wedding. All the relatives were lavish with their gifts of ornaments for the bride. 'It's Jyoti's daughter's wedding,' they said, and wherever they might be, they sent a set of pearl or diamond or ruby ornaments, or just gold ornaments. Of course, gold was cheap then. So, Didi got plenty of jewellery. And books . . . beautifully bound volumes with gold lettering: Saratchandra's novels, and so much more. It was all to my benefit, for I sat and read them all. Aged just under ten, I had read all the novels Didi had been presented with!

After the wedding, Ma brought Dada and me to Calcutta. My sister Anubha, who had lived with my father's parents in Guptipara, also joined us, and the three of us were together after a long time. Dada joined Scottish Church Collegiate School and my sister and I were admitted to Duff School. One particular incident is still quite clear in my mind. On my first day in school, I was asked to do some sums, and my answers were wrong! How did that happen? Then we realized that I had muddled up the Hindi numbers with their Bangla counterparts, and got confused between the Hindi 7 and the Bangla 3. So, my lack of proficiency in Bangla cost me a year, and I was admitted to Standard One. But strangely enough, within a few days, my teachers had realized that my knowledge of arithmetic was good and they were sending me to Standard Two during the maths period. But during other periods, I remained in Standard One. Duff School really had an excellent system, and a great deal of personal attention was devoted to each student. There were about thirty-five of us, all told.

During this period, we were staying under the guardianship of our Sejomama, Abhayapada Sen, my mother's third brother. Although Dadamashai from Jaipur bore the cost of our education, Sejomama was the one who took care of us. He even gave Dada and me some pocket money at times. He dressed like a Marwari and left for the share market in the morning and returned late in the evening, often bringing black grapes and kachauris, a deep fried savoury with a spiced filling that I loved to eat. During the day, an old lady was in charge of us but there was no one to take care of us properly: to see what we ate, or whether we were comfortably and decently clothed or to guide our conduct. Though Dada was just a little older than me, he filled that role as best as he could. He would buy just those things I liked to eat, out of his pocket money, even though it was meagre. He was much more mature than me. Our father's early death had made him responsible beyond his years.

Dada read a great deal and I too had discovered the world of books by the time I was ten or eleven. I still remember the thrill that I got out of the beautiful picture printed on the first page of a torn book I had picked up at home. It seemed to open a new world for me. Then, Ma introduced me to Rabindranath's *Galpoguchcha.* Afterwards, I devoured Romesh Chandra Dutt's *Sansar O Samaj*, the biographies of great men and whatever other books I found in Sejomama's library. Children's magazines like *Mouchak*, *Shishusathi*, *Jadughar* and *Sandesh* were also our favourites. These magazines often held literary competitions for children, to encourage them to write. This was a popular pastime for all of us. I was never very successful. But I did manage to get a second prize once, and a first prize in the *Mouchak* competition. After that, I gave up entering these competitions. The other activity we used to enjoy, was writing for the handwritten *para* magazines that were circulated from house to house by enthusiastic amateur literateurs. In our locality, there was a hand-written newspaper called *Snehamayi*, circulated by one Prabhat Kiran Basu, who wrote in a neat copperplate. There were columns where the readers could express their views, and we did use them. To our dismay, Sri Basu disapproved of my handwriting! After his newspaper dropped out of circulation, two of us students began one of our own, called *Supti* (dormancy). When it came back to us after doing the round of the para, we read a comment, 'It would have been better had "Dormancy" remained dormant!'

Literary discussions were an integral feature of our house. All the popular journals like *Sabuj Patra, Prabashi, Bharatvarsha, Bichitra, Sanibarer Chithi, Sramik*–I was later to meet someone who was very involved with labour welfare and this journal, Santosh Kumari Gupta. Many other journals were subscribed to, and we could read them. My mother's room had the collected works of Vivekananda and Rabindranath. Poetry was read with interest and discussed. Almost automatically, we learnt to develop a taste for books and literature, which has remained a lifelong habit with me. As for schoolwork, an hour of studies in the morning and evening took care of that, and we had no need of tutors and extra lessons. Nor did our elders badger us to sit with schoolbooks. So, we were able to read as much as we wished.

During our schooldays, 1922-26, Anubha and I went to school by the school bus. If we walked, we never went unescorted; there would always be a male servant with us. Somehow, it was just not conceivable that we should walk alone to school. It was around 1925-26 that the realities of the political situation began to filter into my consciousness for the first time. The driver and the conductor of the school bus were Muslims. They were extremely good men, very gentle and courteous. They were particularly fond of Anubha. The conductor would pick her up in his arms and set her down on the ground. Now we heard talk of Hindu-Muslim riots for the first time. And we heard people discussing at home whether it was safe to allow us girls to be left under the supervision of Muslims. We were shocked. We had never before thought of the two men as being different from us because they belonged to a different community. We could not imagine that they could ever harm us, for they loved us so sincerely!

In 1921 the Prince of Wales and the Duke of Connaught came to Calcutta. There was a fever of excitement all over the city. Protests and strikes took place everywhere. We too wore our khadi saris and frocks as a mark of our patriotism. We used nothing made in foreign countries at home. This was the way in which the growing national consciousness found expression in homes such as ours.

Duff School played a major role in building up a certain consciousness in my mind: an attitude of service and compassion. When I went to the High School, that is, the senior classes, I was an enthusiastic participant in all the school activities. In fact, it is from Duff School that I learnt to involve myself in welfare activities. We would put up plays in order to raise funds. There was an institution called The Calcutta Orphanage on Balaram Ghosh Street. The children from that orphanage would be invited to the school and all of us would set to work, frying hot luchis and making a potato curry to feed them. During Christmas, students of different classes would go in batches to the hospitals, taking fruit for the patients. If there were floods, we would collect money for the victims—maybe just an anna or two. The desire and the enthusiasm to be of service, and the way to raise funds, I think I have learnt both these from Duff School.

Sometimes, Sejomama would take the whole affair of fund-raising as a joke. 'Mama, please give me an anna,' I'd ask. 'Why, are your missy-babas packing to go home?' he would tease me. 'No, this is for the flood-victims,' I'd say. 'Where's the flood—Kamachatka?' he'd ask. Wherever it was, I would cajole him and get my anna. We raised funds for earthquakes in Japan, which were quite frequent. Apart from feeding the children of the orphanage and taking fruit to the hospitals, there were many other things we did. Our teachers organized us into groups, assigned different duties to each group and then gave us a thorough orientation about how we should go about our tasks. We wore school badges with our names on them and went off on our appointed missions.

But my studies were not being neglected either. It was from Duff School that I sat for the Middle English School Scholarship Examination for the first time. I did not quite realize its importance and caused great tension to our headmistress and the senior teachers. On the day of the exam, there I was, walking to school at my usual pace, when suddenly Bordi, as we called Pramila Bose, our headmistress, appeared with a carriage. 'What's this? You're ambling along! Have you forgotten that you have an exam?' she scolded. 'But I am going for it!' I replied. She took me up in the carriage, and escorted me to my seat in the examination hall. She was an excellent headmistress.

I was awarded a scholarship in the Middle English School Scholarship examination. But the problem was that I was in the Sixth Standard and I was already fourteen years old. If I did not complete Standards Nine and Ten within two years, I would be quite old for the Matriculation exam. I wanted to try for a double promotion to another school, St. Margaret's. I would first have to appear for a test. I was good in arithmetic but I had never done any algebra or geometry. My mother's younger brother, Girija Nath Sen, who was a medical student, tutored me in a matter of ten days, drawing diagrams on the wall, explaining the sums and theorems and making me work them out. Everything became crystal-clear. Moreover, in those ten days, I developed a taste for maths that I never lost. Never again did I face any tension over maths. I sat for the test in St. Margaret's and was successful. They admitted me in Standard Nine. Of course, especially in geometry and algebra, I had to catch up with the class, but I did it, though it took some time. However, I always got the highest score in Bangla and maths right from the start.

Five

Ma and Dadi and My Matriculation

In 1924, Ma came to Calcutta when Didi was expecting her first child so that she could be with her. Hem Chandra Sen, our Thakurda, had died recently, and Dadi, our paternal grandmother, also left Guptipara for Calcutta to be with us. This situation was somewhat unusual. At first, Dadi was extremely distressed because it was really unusual for a woman in her position to seek shelter with her daughter-in-law's family. Boromama had written that it would be very difficult for her to stay with her own relatives in Guptipara alone and she should stay with us as our guest. After a while, she adjusted very well.

Now that Dadi was living with us, our meals became very interesting, very enjoyable, because she introduced many varieties of dishes to our rather lacklustre menu. In Jaipur we had got used to having a vegetable, a dal and something sweet for lunch everyday, while dinner would consist of mutton curry and roti finished off with a glass of milk. This sort of menu was not typical of the Bengalis of Calcutta or Bengal, it was too spartan, and definitely boring fare. But Dadi spiced up our meals by introducing dishes like mashed brinjals, steamed prawns, and fish curry. Now, we began to eat fish regularly, and that was something we all found quite delectable.

Didi gave birth to a bonny son in 1924 and returned to her parent's-in-law's household. Ma remained in Calcutta. I was twelve and would soon be attending high school, and Ma may have thought it was necessary for her to stay with me. The arrangements of the old house where we had lived for sometime changed. The property was divided up among my mamas and sold and a new house was built. A new chapter seemed to open for all of us. For me this was because I was starting a new level of education and whatever it would bring, and for Ma this was the moment when she began to write and build a career as a writer.

Now Ma came out of seclusion and began to go out. She would often visit a friend, Uma Devi, whom she called Bula, and in whose house she first met the poet Kanti Chandra Ghosh. They had carried out a correspondence earlier but never met. She would attend various literary and political gatherings, such as those organized by Subhas Chandra Bose and P. C. Ray, the scientist and nationalist. She made her way into a literary circle, and I always accompanied her everywhere. Among those with whom Ma started a friendship was Mrs. Margaret Urquhart, the wife of Dr. W. H. Urquhart, the Principal of Scottish Church College, and later, the Vice-Chancellor of Calcutta University. She had written a book, *The Women of Bengal*, a very valuable book for researchers. Mrs. Urquhart often came to Ma in the afternoons after lunch. She would ask Ma all sorts of questions about our customs and habits. I think she was collecting information for her book. There was a great deal of sweetness about her, which attracted me very much. Her book was excellent. It held up a picture of the position of women in the country, for exam ple, the fact that till a woman bore a child, a son, she was a nobody in the joint family. But her comments and criticism were made without much harshness or hostility. The book had photographs of Ma and Kamala Devi, Sir Ashutosh Mookherjee's widowed daughter, to portray the prevalent social customs widows had to follow. I remember Mrs. Urquhart arranged for Ma to be photographed at Bourne and Shepherd, the famous firm known for its quality photographic work in Chowringhee.

The teachers and the Princi pal of St. Margaret's were very fond of me, and I continued to fare well in my studies. In my last year in that school, I had another novel experience, that of staying in a hostel. During 1929-1930, Ma returned to Jai pur, and I would have been the only girl in an otherwise all-male establishment at home. I was always running errands for my uncles and cousins. Ma put me in a hostel, the St. Margaret School Hostel, so that I could study in peace. I enjoyed being with my new hostel mates and had a good time during those three months.

Most of the other girls in the hostel were Adivasi Christians from Ranchi. There was just another Hindu girl, Charu, who later married Mahendra Nath Dutta of Sahitya Sansad fame. Though she was a couple of years younger, she was taller than me, and she would help me to locate things in drawers too high for me to reach. There was also a Muslim girl called Anjuman Ara. She was from Jessore, but she wettled down very well. We all did everything together, eating our meals, our recreation times. The hostel was very inexpensive—we were charged just eleven rupees for food and were served non-vegetarian meals for both lunch and dinner!

On Sundays and Thursdays, we all had to go to church—Duff Church. We covered our heads while going to the church. We sang hymns, prayed and listened to the priest's sermon. I really enjoyed the service. At the end, someone would go around taking up collections, and we too gave whatever we could . . . an anna or perhaps a bigger coin. I felt I learnt a sort of discipline during the ceremony. This was a regular feature of my few months in a hostel.

By this time, I had already joined the Girl Guides though I never imagined then what a major role it was to play in my life in later years. During my Intermediate year, when I was in Bethune College, I went for a three-week training camp to Ooty. That was where we learnt many things: First Aid, Home Nursing, making clay ovens, wheel-chair use, camping in the open, all of which were of immense use to me later on. Our British trainers were particularly good at imparting such training. While at St. Margaret, there were many activities. In the Calcutta Museum grounds, various schools would organize Baby Shows and unlike the modern baby shows, these were health exhibitions. We would make charts, stage little skits on how to bring up healthy children, all these were things we did as Guides. The motto, 'help all the people at all times', became firmly fixed in my mind as a principle to be followed at all times. The attitude that one must be of service to society, to help wherever help was needed, to give aid to whoever asked for it unquestionably took root in those early years. In fact, right from Duff School, we had received such training from our principal, Pramila Bose, Mrs. Urquhart, from our teachers, Miss Hogg and Miss Knott. While I was at the Union Hostel, Duff School would send a thika gari, a horse-drawn cart, every Wednesday to collect me so that I could continue with my Girl Guide training. Moreover, hostel life imparted in me a basic discipline which allowed these ideas to take firm root. On top of which, Ma too, though without Girl Guide training, would take her suitcase and go off to nurse anybody who was ill or needed her help in the family, be it Almora or Agra or Delhi or Guptipara.

In spite of all these activities, my studies never suffered. We read the textbooks, never any notes. We were given homework. The emphasis of the teaching was on the subject, not on exams and question papers. Our teachers were very competent and we never had any tutors. I studied entirely on my own. I would get up at four in the morning. In winter, the sun rose almost at seven so I studied by candlelight. The superintending teacher also sat reading by candlelight. And it was the sound of the street hydrants–the washing of the streets that woke me! But my hard work paid off and that year, I stood first in the final examination with four Letters and Star marks.[1]

I appeared for my Matriculation from St. Margaret's. We had to go to Bethune College to write our exams, where seats for nearby schools were arranged. The school guard actually went with us, escorting us! I did well, securing four Letters in both mathematics papers, Bangla and Sanskrit.[2] In our student days, it was a matter of great pride to secure Letters. In fact I stood first among the girls in that examination and was awarded a scholarship of twenty rupees.

Dadamashai had died a few months after Didi's wedding, in 1923. His eldest son, Dhitendra Nath Sen, our Baromama, became the head of the family. According to the laws of the native states, he was the sole heir of that enormous estate in Jaipur. His younger brothers all took to professions. Baromama took the responsibility for educating the six of us, and from 1929 also the five children of my mother's older sister, Abhamoyee, who were all living in his household. Yet such was his generosity that we never felt embarrassed or neglected in any way. In fact, his younger brothers, my mamas, were practically in our age-group, and we formed a large, boisterous gang of young people and I often ruled the roost over them. I was specially bossy with the daughters of Boromama. The eldest, Chitra, and second eldest, Deepali, were always under my wing. Those wonderful holidays in Jaipur continued through these years: twenty of us converging from our different places of study, the days spent together, at night talking and chattering away on the terrace where all of us lay in our separate cots bathed in moonlight.

On the very day that my Matriculation results were declared, Boromama was leaving for England. As I touched his feet and bid him goodbye, I told him that I wanted to study further. 'Yes, of course,' he said, prepared as ever to bear the expenses of my education. Ma did tell me that I would face no problem as I was getting a scholarship. But she was wrong. I needed to pay eighteen rupees for my meals and and two rupees as laundry charges. So what would be left of the scholarshi p?

While I was a student, aged ten to sixteen, from 1922 to 1928, we lived in a very large house in Kartik Bose Lane. There were many wings, each one consisting of a central courtyard around which rose a line of rooms in two storeys. There was a small connecting door between each wing and the adjacent courtyard. One wing was the baithakkhana, the formal drawing rooms; another was the andarmahal or the living quarters; and the third the thakur dalan or the area reserved for worshi p and puja. We lived in a room on the first floor of one wing of the andarmahal. Ma had a small room, more like an office. The boys who were studying: my Dada, the younger mamas, had rooms further down the verandah. Sejomama's rooms were on the ground floor. The kitchen was also there. There was another andarmahal, where we used to stay when we first came to Calcutta. Later, as far as I can remember, it was rented out to tenants. The ground floor was let out but upstairs, there was a puja room, a small dining room, a guest room with a large verandah and next to it, a room reserved for Dadamashai's youngest brother, Dr. Hari Prasanna Sen. We all lived together, and had our meals altogether.

These years were very special because I really came close to Ma at a very crucial phase of growing-up. During my childhood, we had been parted from each other for long stretches of time, and during the holidays in Jai pur, she had been always overburdened with household responsibilities. Now, in Calcutta, I was able to take care of her a little: perform little chores for her. I would wash her clothes and put them out to dry. At night I would sli p into her bed and massage her feet, run my fingers over her forehead and the tired muscles of her neck. Who else was there to provide a little comfort to her, except me?

It was around this time that Didi had her first child. She came to us three or four months ahead of her confinement. Dadi stitched many kanthas or thin cotton quilts for the baby. All afternoon, she would sit and stitch those kanthas, some for the baby, some for Didi to use as a shawl. Each kantha was made up of innumerable pieces of cloth stitched together, then decorated with a wide variety of designs of flowers and other motifs. Dadi would trace out a flower and ask us to pick it out with tiny stitches. The kanthas were exquisite. That was the time I learnt stitching and embroidery.

Soon the time arrived for Didi's delivery. Sejomama said he would have a particular room cleared of furniture and prepared for the confinement on the twenty-fourth. Didi's newborn son was named Bikash. When the child was about two months old, an enormous load of gifts arrived from Didi's in-laws': a layette for the baby, complete with mattresses, sheets, quilts and even a mosquito-net that could be unfurled like an umbrella and placed on the sleeping child! And plenty of sweets for the whole family. Then when Didi returned to her husband's house with her three-month-old child, the compliment was returned from our side. All the things needed for her child were carefully selected, packed and sent with her, together with large quantities of sweets. Soon after that, her husband went abroad. Didi remained with her in-laws in Bandel.

Dadi used to visit the house of Barothakurma, her elder sister-in-law (the wife of her husband's older brother), on Sitaram Ghosh Street, with Anubha and me in tow. She would peep into the rooms of each member of the family and spend some moments with them. My sister Anubha was very lovely, so they all said, 'This daughter of Kironkaka [my father], is very beautiful. Look at her golden hair!' No one ever said I was pretty! We would pay our visits with Dadi, but Dada would sometimes go there on his own.

Gradually, I came close to that branch of my family. I came to know my cousins well. My Dadi's older sister-in-law had eight sons and three or four daughters. One of these ladies was a renowned author of those days, Phulkumari Gupta. Another lady belonging to that family was a labour leader, Santoshkumari Gupta. She had lived in Burma, and always spoke in English. She used to run a newspaper, called *Sramik*. I remember that my mother used to subscribe to it.

One of my father's cousins had married an Anglo-French lady. They had not quite adjusted to the family, which was fairly orthodox, and they lived separately on Theatre Road. The aunt wore a sari, was a member of Girl Guides and was actively involved in all kinds of social work. She would participate in those Baby Shows, Fetes and Exhibitions. I had seen her in these places, dressed in her blue uniform. She was very progressive and definitely made an impression on the wider family as well. So, even in that generation, there were these ladies who were more than housewives. They managed their homes, but also stepped out of the confining domestic sphere and did much meaningful work. I later came in close contact with Santoshkumari Gupta, whom I used to call Mashima. She worked with the jute mill labourers. After Partition, she ran a home for the needy refugees.

Perhaps, meeting these dedicated ladies had made more of an impression on me than I was aware of at the time. Here were women who had done much for society. Nor were they pursuing any selfish motives of their own; their aims were totally unselfish and oriented towards helping others. Perhaps I had unconsciously discovered my role models!

Dadi passed away while staying with us. That day, the whole house was flooded with relatives from my father's family. Dadi had been the wife of one of the senior-most elders of the family, the Sejokarta, or third eldest brother. A large number of handsome young men arrived carrying gamchas or very thin towels, ready to accompany her mortal remains on the last journey. Dadi's brothers-in law and sisters-in-law had sent their sons and grandsons for the funeral, and soon the courtyard was overflowing with them all. They dressed Dadi beautifully and bore her away with such clamour and enthusiasm that it was almost like a great celebration rather than a funeral. We were watching from our upstairs verandah. Dadi's enormous family punctiliously observed the rituals of the fifteen-day long period of mourning, but the young men were so obviously fond of their meat that it was a great strain for them to maintain a vegetarian diet for that long. The rituals of the fifteenth day, marking the end of the mourning period were held in the house of another grandmother, and this time too, everything was done with great flamboyance and fervour. Needless to say, the next day, enormous quantities of meat were cooked for the voracious crowd of young men. But through it all, we could comprehend how close-knit Dadi's family was, and how much they really loved her.

Borothakurma passed away shortly after that, but Dadi's youngest sister-in-law (the wife of her husband's youngest brother, Amulya Chandra Sen Gupta), another Thakurma, was alive when I got married. She was related to Ashapurna Devi. She was an erudite lady. Many women were emerging from the confines of domesticity at that time. Magazines for women, for children were being published. All sorts of issues were being debated. Women organized public meetings. Discussions were being held about the Hindu Code Bill, issues about the rights of women were being debated. This was 1926 or 1927. I was still in school. But a period of transition had definitely begun; a new age for women.

Notes

1 Marks of 75 percnt were considered to be star marks.

2 Those who received the highest possible marks, ie, 80 percent, were given 'Letters'.

Six

A Tragedy and I Join Bethune College

While our personal lives continued in a more or less smooth fashion, there was tremendous turmoil and change on the political front. These were the years of the advent of Mohandas Karamchand Gandhi into the nationalist movement and he transformed it from being limited to the educated who wished for more partici pation, and representation in government to a mass movement in the space of a few years. These momentous political events brought about changes in the lives of middle class women. Looking back, I feel that my mother, Jyotirmoyee Devi, was the best exam ple of the changing face of Indian women. She always took care that her daughters should be properly educated and never ever did she differentiate between my brother and me. As early as 1917, she had written an article on the trials faced by widows and denounced the social attitudes towards them. This was before her personal tragedy had taken place. After my father died, she was able to overcome all obstacles, to regain a sense of purpose in her own life, and find the strength to express her views in writing: portraying and speaking out about the realities of the joyless, aimless, wavering path of a woman's existence, her dependent role in society. She established an identity of her own as a writer, and gained great respect. Her writings were being published in the foremost magazines and periodicals, such as *Bharatbarsha, Prabashi* and *Uttara*.

We did not know that tragedy was waiting to strike us once again. We lost Didi in 1928. I was sixteen that year. Her husband had just returned to India from England where he had gone to train as a chartered accountant. He came to Bandel to take Didi and their three-year-old son to their new home. Many members of his family were afflicted by cholera and Didi who nursed the sick caught the disease and could not be saved. Didi was only nineteen when she died. This blow devastated Ma. She had thought that she had at last achieved a form of stability with her eldest daughter married and with a son, her eldest son having passed his Matriculation and her second daughter in Class Nine, when again Fate seemed to have taken it all away. We went back to Jai pur. With tremendous courage, Ma picked up the threads of her life once again. She sent Dada and me back to Calcutta so that our studies should not be interrupted.

I joined Bethune College[1] and was admitted to the Union Hostel, which was next to Scottish Church College. It was a cosmopolitan place, with students from many colleges: Bethune, Scottish Church, City, and Diocesan, all staying together. The warden was a Scotswoman. Everything was neat and tidy, well organized and disci plined. During the study hour, we all had to sit down with our books. We were not allowed to stroll about on the streets. Some girls would stand in the verandah in the evenings. But after some time, our warden forbade us to be out in the verandah after dark. It seems some persons had entered our hostel mistaking it for a house of ill repute!

Our meals were all set into a pattern. We would get tea, bread, milk and eggs for breakfast. Lunch consisted of dal and rice and fixed servings of vegetables and fish. When we returned after college, we had luchis or dalpuris, which were like luchis but made with a mixture of lentils and flour. On Sunday, there was stew and bread. I quite liked the food, and never complained like the other girls—especially the girls from East Bengal who were too finicky for my liking, always complaining that the cooking was horrible, and so on! They would all tease me, saying, 'Do you really like it?' Having lived in Delhi, Jaipur and Calcutta and exposed to different ways of cooking, I suppose I had got used to all kinds of food, and I really did not find anything wrong with the hostel food. So much so, that our Warden, Mrs. Singh, was very appreciative and she always held me up to the others as an example. 'Look at her,' she would say. 'She never complains!'

I shared a room with mainly Assamese and Khasi girls and one from Orissa. There were many girls with links with the revolutionaries, but they did not say or do anything openly. They kept very quiet about their activities. That is where I met Preetilata Wadeddar, Kamala Dasgupta and other revolutionaries and got to know them well.[2] In our school hostel at St. Margaret's, there was a system called the 'adopter' system. Each senior student had to adopt a junior one. That meant, supervising their studies, plaiting their hair, being watchful over their bedtimes, and so on. I feel that I received much more training in the hostel than I ever got at home. I learnt about wearing a nightdress. At home, we used to sleep in our saris. So when the girls asked me, 'Where is your *rat kameez* ?' I did not know what they were talking about. I then made some nightdresses for myself. We also learnt to adjust to different meal-timings. At home, we never ate rice at five in the evening, as we did in the hostel. Then at eight o'clock, we would have some bread-and-butter sprinkled with sugar after our study hour, just before going to sleep.

I used to walk to college. Scottish Church College was on the way. Since I had many friends there I often dropped in at the common room on my way to college. I had to cross Hedua to reach Bethune College. I was a science student, so I had to stay back late, till quarter-past five, for the practical classes everyday. Our professors were excellent, we never needed any outside help. I remember, Chintaharan Bhattacharya taught us Bengali, Santosh Kumar Chattopadhyay taught us chemistry. There was another professor called Ramapada Mazumdar who taught us English. Rajkumari Das was our Princi pal, and she also taught us English. A teacher, Stella Bose, wore her sari extremely high, almost knee-length, and black socks and shoes with it. The sari was worn in the Brahmika style, with pleats and the end draped over the left shoulder. We found her ways extremely amusing. Then, there was Sarojini Dutt, a widow, who always wore white. She was our botany teacher. She took us on many picnics. When we went to the Botanical Gardens to study trees she would take along so much food—cakes and dalmuth and oranges and sandesh—that we seemed to be spending more time eating and having fun, than learning about plants! She was a wonderful teacher as well. Later, in the fourth year, we had a male teacher, Sailen Kumar Nag.

In the junior classes, that is, the first and second years,we were not allowed to go out of the hostel on our own. If we had any shopping to do, three students would have to go together. I used to go to Pulinbihari's Akhara, near Rammohun Library, where I learnt how to fight with daggers and lathis or bamboo sticks. But we were not allowed to go alone, I had to wait till some older students were ready to accom pany me. Consequently, I was not in a position to go anywhere or do anything independently. Our warden in the Union Hostel was very strict. But one can understand her position. Those were the days of political unrest and student activity. No wonder she kept an eagle eye on us.

Between 1930 and 1932, the exploits of Surya Sen, Shanti-Suniti, Bina Das[2] and others like them were setting the hearts of young people on fire, leading them to radical politics. We read Sarat Chattopadhyay's *Pather Dabi* secretly and debated all sorts of political issues. I was getting to know some political activists among students. I used to go to the Scottish Church College common room quite often. That is where I saw Manikuntala Sen for the first time,[3] and where I met Suhasini, another girl with revolutionary conections, who would later marry my Dada, Arun. Imet Kamala Dasgupta[4] and others at the Rammohan Library. It was a place where these girls with political interests got together. Their method of work as to educate girls about political issues by giving them certain books to read.. I too borrowed those books once in a while. But since I was a junior and was not allowed to go about alone, it was not possible for me to join their activities.

Political unrest continued to gain momentum, following the Salt Satyagraha and the Dandi March. There were pickets at the gates of Bethune College led by Ila Sen and others. They said all the girls should give up going to college (Bethune was a government college), stay at home and work for the motherland. But no one had any clear idea of what 'working for the motherland' meant. Was it just spinning cotton and weaving Khadi? We were doing that anyway. Picketing was being done in front of liquor shops. Some girls from our hostel were taking part in the underground movement. We could make out from their secretiveness and their furtive movements. After all Preetilata Wadeddar herself was staying in a hostel nearby, at that time.[5] In spite of my secret sympathy for them, I never joined those movements, as I did not want to disrupt my studies. Moreover, though student unions in other colleges called strikes, Bethune College did not have a student union.

Our Principal, Rajkumari Devi, was very strict, she never allowed any break in the academic routine. Besides, I was never one to break rules. I wouldn't even skip classes. The fact that we were not financially independent as a family, I think, preyed upon my mind. I did not want to do anything that would endanger my mother's position in my mama's house. I felt that my primary duty was to complete my education with as much seriousness as possible. So, even if I secretly harboured political inclinations, I did nothing that would disrupt my studies. Wearing Khadi was the only personal statement of political protest that I allowed myself to make. The other thing I did was to continue with the Girl Guides. I had already joined the Girl Guides before coming to Bethune College (see Chapter

5), though I never imagined then what a major role it was to play in my life in later years.

I worked very hard but do remember one or two rare occasions of playing truant. On a day when the practical classes were simply dragging on, Dada arrived at the College gate and said, 'Let's go off for a picnic.' 'But what about my classes?' I protested. 'Why, excuse yourself for one day,' advised Dada and I obeyed him. And then Dada, Anubha and I went for a ride sitting in the upper deck of a double-decker bus as it meandered through the busy streets. Dada had brought some sardine and cheese sandwiches. What a fine picnic that was, eating sandwiches under the open sky, ambling along in the bus! That was the first time I tasted cheese.

In Bethune College, we had at least eight to ten programmes of song, dance or drama every year, such as Foundation Day, and the pujas, though Saraswati Puja was not celebrated. Besides, there was a drill teacher who taught us exercises, tennis, badminton and other games. I took part in sports, drill, cycling and drama. During my first year in Bethune, a pandal was set up in the grounds and we enthusiastically put up a play, *Grihaprabesh*, in which I had the role of the naughty nephew. In the following years, we staged *Chirakumar Sabha* and *Shesh Raksha.* I was comfortable acting in social dramas and Rabindranath's plays, but not in historical dramas. I could never deliver dialogues in the mandatory exaggerated, singsong fashion, so I never acted in those.

When my Intermediate Examinations were over, I went to Delhi after a long time. It was wonderful meeting my childhood companions, those uncles of my age, Nikhil and Anil after a long time. Under Nikhil Mama's guidance, I started reading great English authors such as Bernard Shaw, Lytton Strachey and D. H. Lawrence, whose books I had seen in my mother's bookshelves, but had not touched so far. For the first time, I was exposed to Shaw's critical, analytical mind, his philosophy of progress through conflict and evolution. I was also deeply interested by Lytton Strachey's historical writings. But I cannot say how far I was personally influenced by them, as I was after all, a science student.

When Mejodadu heard that I was thinking of studying medicine, he proposed that I should be admitted to Lady Hardinge College in Delhi. But Ma wanted me to come back to Calcutta. Perhaps she was thinking of my marriage at that time. However, I was adamant about studying further. I had even got a seat in the Calcutta Medical College, but it was a five-year course. Because of our continuing financial constraints, I finally decided to study pure science with mathematics honours. Again, between Scottish Church and Bethune College, I chose the latter because the fees for Scottish were Rupees Twelve, while at Bethune I would have to pay a mere four rupees! I was awarded the Duff scholarship as well as a merit scholarship after the Intermediate examination, but in those days that did not mean that I would not have to pay any fees.

My college years started me thinking about women's lives. Why were they not free even if they were educated? As I grew older, I began to notice the paradox of a woman's life: how her husband and children imprisoned her in a life of total submission and non-identity, so that she had no life of her own. Even if the children grew up and went away, the husband would never allow her to be free. On the other hand, widows or unmarried women or women without children might have this independence, which Ma called *nirankush jeevan.* They might be unhappy but at least they were free. This idea made a strong impression on me. However, I was to find that in my own life, I was extremely fortunate that I did not experience that bondage and was able to carry on with my work in spite of a strong-minded husband and small children.

Notes

1 Established in 1879, Bethune College is the first women's college in India. Its history is linked to the history of Bethune School that was founded in 1849 by a group of Englishmen and Bengalis, and named after John Drinkwater Bethune who was the Law Member in the Viceroy's Council, and who gave a large sum of money and property to the school. In 1883 Kadambini Bose and Chandramukhi Bose, students of Bethune College, became the first women graduates of India, the University of Calcutta thus offered women degrees well before Britain did.

The college's alumni were distinguished pioneers in social reform movements.

2 Bina Das was the daughter of an educationalist, Benimadhav Das. She attempted to assassinate Jackson, the Governor of Bengal. She failed to shoot him but was caught and sentenced to several years of imprisonment. She was released in 1938.

3 Kamala Dasgupta was a Gandhian who was arrested and in jail for a number of years. She lived and worked as a committed social worker to the end of her long life.

4 A committed communist (1910-87) who mobilized many ordinary women to join the Atmaraksha Samiti that helped women during the Bengal Famine, 1943 and Partition, and also took part in the Tebhaga. She rose to be the Deputy Leader of the Opposition in the West Bengal Assembly in the 1950s. She left the party because of its increasing corrupt practices and loss of idealism and also could not accept it splitting into the CPI and the CPI-M. See also her memoir, translated from the Bengali: *In Search of Freedom: An Unfinished Journey* (Kolkata: Stree, 2001).

5 Preetilata Waddedar (1911-1932) obtained a BA degree with distinction and became the principal of a girls school at Chittagong. She was a member of the Surya Sen (Masterda) terrorist group that took part in the Chittagong Armoury Raid in 1930. She led the attack on the European Club in June 1932, killing herself to avoid capture.

Seven

A New Beginning

It was over the matter of my marriage that I came to realize how modern my mother was. For quite some time, many relatives had been pressing her to arrange my marriage. After all, there were two other girls 'to settle' after me, and so on. Ma always replied that I should be allowed to complete my degree course, and that only if she found a 'scholar' would she agree to a match for me. Finally, one of her cousins, and thus a mama of mine, wrote to her that there *was* such a young man. His name was Saibal Kumar Gupta and he was the Sub Divisional Officer at Kanthi, and he had actually read her essays and was interested in meeting her. 'Think of Ashoka,' wrote Panchugopal Majumdar, 'I shall bring him over during the Pujas.' I wonder now what made Ma agree with such alacrity.

So in 1932, when I was twenty, Saibal Kumar Gupta came to our house with Panchugopal Majumdar. He was thirty years old, a member of the Indian Civil Service and an Ishan scholar.[1] We were all introduced to him, Ma, Didima, my mamas who were there at that time, and me. They were soon busy chatting. I also joined them, and after observing what was going on for some time, I said 'namaskar' to him, picked up his teacup and left the room. Much later, in a letter, he wrote to me that he thought I was dismissing him with a 'namaskar'.

The conversation that day centred on Gandhiji, of whom my future husband was a great devotee. We were discussing what would happen if Gandhiji actually fasted to death. I said that since Gandhiji had openly and forcefully resolved to do so, it was quite possible that it would happen, for the political situation was not really in the hands of any individual, or even of the masses. My answer was quite unpalatable to Mr. Gupta. He was extremely worried about what would happen to the country if Gandhiji did die. The rest of the conversation was about whether we used Swadeshi goods or not, and our political convictions. In the latter sphere, I must admit to some ambiguity on our part. We as a family were extremely politically conscious: we attended the meetings of Subhas Bose, had attended Gandhiji's meeting at Sodepur and others as well, we discussed such issues and Ma wrote about them, we wore khadi, but that was about all. Probably, our financial position and our dependence on Ma's family made us all wary of political commitments.

Mr. Gupta came another day and we had a long conversation. As he was leaving, he told my mother that he might visit again during Christmas. On 27 December he arrived, quite late in the evening, at about seven or eight, without any prior notice. He came on the following three days and sat talking to me and other family members. My mamas did not quite like that, they felt first he should make up his mind concerning me, whereas he was more keen to get to know me before all else. He asked me whether I had read Bertrand Russell. I had to reply in the negative, but I hastily added that I had read Thomas Hardy, D. H. Lawrence, Shaw, Strachey and others, though perhaps I knew little of their philosophies. I was thinking that had he asked me about Newton's law of gravity or atomic theory, I would have had much to say! But somewhere amidst all this serious talk, he suddenly said that he had asked my mother to correspond with his father. I asked him, what about and he stammered, about us. I gathered that he was talking about our getting married. I asked him how could he have made up his mind in such a short time. It was such a serious matter! He said, 'I will not disclose that!' I repeated, 'Suppose your im pression about me is wrong? I don't want you to regret it later, I don't want to deceive you.' He replied confidently, 'I am quite sure I will not regret it.' Later he told me that he had been deeply affected by this conversation. Of course, he did not ask me about my im pression of him, which I was also not willing to disclose then!

He went away one day after that and shortly afterwards, wrote a letter to my mother. He wrote, 'I am sending you the letter I have written to my mother. Please see it, and decide upon the next course of action. It would be best if you wrote to my father, Sri Rasiklal Gupta.' The letter to his mother contained all sorts of details about me: my name, how old I was, what I studied and such things. He had included the words, 'she appears to be quite good-looking'. That I had grown up in a joint family in my mama's house and, therefore, probably our circumstances were straitened, was also mentioned. It was a sort of summing up of pros and cons, done by a very analytical mind.

Ma sent her letter of proposal around 11 or 12 January, and my future father-in-law immediately sent a reply saying that he would come on 21 January and perform the *ashirwad*–the ceremony of blessing me which would signify our engagement. He had found his son to be so recalcitrant in the matter of marriage, that this open display of interest had led him to seize the opportunity of finalizing the details at once. So I was formally engaged on Saraswati Puja day, that is, 23 January 1933.

In the intervening period between my engagement and marriage, we did meet occasionally. My fiancé came to us during the Id, Good Friday and Dol holidays and spent the whole time in our house. Once our marriage was fixed, my family did not disapprove of our meetings, though others would join us. So we were given some freedom that let us get to know each other and we did not feel constricted in any way.

At this time, we also exchanged letters practically daily, with my mother's consent. She told me, 'In this way, you will come to know your own self and each other better. So, you have my permission to correspond.' This was the beginning of something that became a lifelong habit with us. Whenever we were apart, even later, for example, when my husband went to England, we always wrote to each other daily. Nothing extraordinary, perhaps: just an exchange of news of our daily activities, a sharing of thoughts and views, yet it brought us very close together, for many things can be written which cannot be expressed verbally. And so it was, that whenever we were physically separated, mentally we were closest to each other.

It was through this correspondence before our marriage that we really came to know each other, and exchanged our views frankly and openly. My fiancé found that I was 'able to think independently and able to express [my] views articulately–not one to say things only to please others.' In another letter, he wrote that he had found me to be 'neither excessively exhibitionist, nor inordinately shy in your reactions to me, you have been yourself.' Gradually, we were losing our hesitancy and were able to express our feelings for each other, lay bare our weaknesses and faults as we perceived them, without the fear of rejection, secure in the knowledge that our regard for each other was strong enough to make such anxieties redundant.

At the same time, we informed each other about our respective families, the circumstances we had grown up in: the attitudes and situations that had influenced our characters and personalities. From my fiancé, I came to know about the vast family in Bhola, in Barishal, in today's Bangladesh, which would be my future home, of the responsibilities I would have to shoulder. He was in a way letting me know about his enormous commitment to his family, his sense of duty towards them, and preparing me to share this aspect of his life as an equal partner, which I did joyfully.

When I consider how conservative society actually was in those days, I am amazed at the progressive attitude of my mother. I would tell her what I had discussed with my fiancé during the day, and I can only marvel at the sensitive yet skilful manner in which she seemed to direct our thoughts and feelings. There was no embarrassment, yet both of us found a way to ascertain our feelings. There is no doubt that I was deeply impressed and also moved by my fiancé's sensitive, deep vision of life, his intellectual abilities, his extraordinary mature personality, which were being revealed to me through our discussions and correspondence. At that time, I used to think that such close mixing was common in our social circle but as I grew more experienced in the art of arranging marriages for others, I realized how rare it actually was. Where did Ma get her modern outlook from, I wondered.

Note

[1] A candidate who obtains the highest marks in the Humanities in the B.A. Hons examinations was called the Ishan Scholar of his year.

Eight

Our Wedding

Our wedding took place on 27 April 1933 and went off with all the confusion and clamour that is common to such occasions. My father-in-law brought the *barjatris*, twenty-five or so persons who made up the groom's party, from Bhola, their village in East Bengal. A house was hired for them in Calcutta, not very far from where we lived. On the wedding day, the *adhibas tattva*, the customary gifts sent to the bride by the groom's family, arrived from their house. A huge fish, half a maund (about 20kg) of curd, thirteen enormous earthen pots of thirteen different types of sweets that had been brought all the way from Bhola. This created quite an uproar in our house. Where would we store it all? There were no refrigerators in those days! The sheer amount of the sweets and fish in the tattva held us speechless. The customs of the two Bengali Hindu communities of East and West Bengal were very different. The passage of time has muted these differences, a trend begun with Partition when the great bulk of the Bangals, as the East Bengali Hindus were called, crossed the new border to seek refuge in West Bengal. At the time of our marriage the differences were much more striking. Their tattva was certainly very different from the tattva we Bengalis of West Bengal were accustomed to: there was no decorative element in it, just bulk. There were two sets of clothes for me, one for the adhibas that included the fish and the sweetmeats, one for *gaye halud*, or the bride's ritual bath with turmeric. But since we were unable to send a well-decorated tattva to Bhola ourselves, I suppose I cannot complain. All the gift items were simply packed in suitcases and sent off with us when we left Calcutta!

The wedding ceremony itself did not pass off very smoothly. My husband considered a marriage to be a solemn sacrament and really disliked the lighthearted revelry, the rustic rituals, the noise and clamour that accompanied the average Bengali wedding. The shehnai was playing when the groom stepped down from the car. He asked that it should be silenced. He also refused to wear the conical wedding-cap, the *topor*. He had said that only the *yajna* should take place, but by that time, the ladies' party had taken over, and my husband was forced to go up to the terrace against his wishes. I took the seven steps round him and we exchanged garlands, but only once. Somehow, these rituals were done with and we then sat down for the *sampradan*, the giving away of the bride, the *saptapadi,* when the bride and the groom go round the fire seven times, and the yajna. Now, the situation turned just the opposite. The entire yajna was performed with great care and attention to details. A relative who was also a Sanskrit scholar and a professor of Presidency College, Hemchandra Sen, sat next to us, explaining the mantras. If the priest made any mistakes with the Sanskrit, either my husband or his mentor would correct him and give him the proper mantra. The whole exercise was like a Sanskrit lesson and quite amusing, and this part of the ceremony took twice as long as it should have!

I, however, was going through conflicting emotions. I quite agreed with my husband that the unnecessary and indecent clamour during a wedding was most unseemly. In fact, during my children's weddings, I was very strict about this aspect of the ceremony. On the other hand, the yajna took so long that I was getting rather restless. I had invited many teachers from my school, the English and Scottish ladies were all sitting there, and I was wondering whether they were being properly looked after. My husband's friends had also come, as part of the groom's party. One of them, Mr. Karuna Kumar Hazra, told my husband, 'I'm going upstairs for a while.' My husband replied, 'Go ahead. As you can see, I am a little busy.' This raised a huge laugh. I was wondering whether the guests were eating properly or not. Also, there was limited sitting space, and people thronged all around, pushing and shoving, blocking the doorways, trying to get a glimpse of the ceremony. So, the solemnity of the ceremony was lost and I must admit, this distressed me.

Finally, the ceremony was over. Then all the family had gathered for the *bashor*, when the newly wedded couple spend the night accompanied by relatives and friends, intending to stay up with us all night, laughing and joking and making merry. But my husband said that he was tired and wanted to rest. So, there was no night-long revelry. We remained in Calcutta the next day and the *phulshajya* or the bridal night, so-called because the room would be beautifully decorated with flowers, took place here. On the following day, we went off to Bhola, my husband's home. Much of the trip was made by steamer. First we went by train to Khulna, from there to Barishal by steamer. This was my first journey by waterways and I was enchanted by the beauty of the river—the banks edged by rows of coconut and betel palms, the vast expanse of blue waters on which danced mauve flowers that rested on floating green leaves. My husband told me that those were water hyacinths, and they were choking the rivers of East Bengal. The picturesque little villages that we passed by had such strange names: Jhalkathi, Patar Hat, names totally different from those we were used to in the lands I had known! It was a wonderful trip. There was an excellent dining room on the steamer where we were served a three-course meal, starting with soup, in proper English style. We were travelling alone, the rest of the wedding party had already left for Bhola. On reaching Barishal, we were met by my husband's second eldest brother, Mrinal, and three children: Gouri, Kanu (Ashok) and Bolu. We spent the night with my Mejoja, Binapani Devi, the wife of my husband's second eldest brother, Mrinal. We boarded the steamer again the next day, this time bound for Bholaghat. We had the choice of a boat or a car, to reach home, but my husband's eldest brother, Utpal, who came to receive us, suggested that we should go by car as going by boat would be uncomfortable.

And so, at last the new bride arrived at her in-laws' home. What a scene that was! We were not expected before evening, and here we were, getting out of the car at midday! It was just like a scene out of a story or a novel by Bankim, or Romesh Chandra Dutt! All the people of the village heard the sound of the horn and dashed helter-skelter to the house. People came running, from all directions, running along pathways through the fields, the women still holding their Khuntis or cooking implements, running to see the bride!

The car stopped near the baithakkhana, where my father-in-law was busy with his clients, and we got down. My husband got down and started striding quickly towards the house, quite oblivious of the fact that the new bride ought not to walk so fast! And who would help me out of the car and escort me inside? Since we were there before time, nobody was around to greet us with the usual ceremonies. Finally, I got down by myself and hesitantly stepped forward, barefoot, having left my chappals in the car. Then my husband's youngest sister, Himani, and Aruna, the daughter of his eldest brother, Utpal, came and led me inside. All the while, my better half continued to stalk forward, leaving me to wonder whether he was ashamed of the strange creature he had brought home!

At last we reached the house. Preparations for welcoming the bride were almost complete, but the *alpana*, the rice flour designs on the floor, had not yet dried. My mother-in-law, Matangini Devi, came forward and performed the rituals of greeting and blessing the new bride. After that, I was made to sit in a room full of children. Soon, I realized that my role for the next few days was to be that of a baby-sitter!

The first meal I took in the house of my in-laws was a novel experience for me. I was asked in a whisper by my mother-in-law, 'Will you eat with the others?' I said, 'Of course.' My husband's cousin, Birendra Kumar, had married two weeks earlier and his bride, Madhabi was present and thus there were two new brides in the family. When we sat down for lunch, I found that not only were we going to sit together, but also that we would share the food on the same plate. A big brass plate was brought with the rice, vegetables, fish preparations and other items. Rani Boudi, another cousin's wife, mixed the rice with the vegetables and other items of food. Then the three of us—the two new brides and Rani Boudi—shared food from the same plate. I found this most amusing. As far as I can remember, I had never shared food from the same plate since I was five or six years old. Perhaps this was a ritual of bonding with the new family. However, in my subsequent visits to my husband's home, this ritual was not repeated.

The ways and rituals in my in-laws' house were totally different from those we were acquainted with in Calcutta. In Barishal the *boubhat,* the feast to welcome the bride, was in the morning. Everyone was extremely busy with the preparation and serving of a grand feast, and with looking after the guests. Nobody had much time for me or the other bride. We soon realized that all the women in the family, my mother-in-law, sisters-in-law and others, were fully occupied with the cooking and so, the duty of looking after the children came to us, that is, the two brand-new brides. Indeed, such was the pandemonium that mothers were forgetting to feed their own children, so busy were they in the kitchen. Bidyutlata, my Boroja, that is, Utpal's wife, and Bibha, my husband's second sister, and thus my nonod or sister-in-law, both had children barely a few months old. To my amazement, and also amusement, I noticed that my Boroja had in a hurry, picked up Bibha's child to breastfeed her. Then the child's mother rushed up, crying, 'Boudi, whom are you feeding!' Nor had I ever seen food being prepared in such large quantities. The clients of my father-in-law brought a large number of huge fish to the house and all the ladies fell to work, cleaning, skinning, cutting and cooking the fish.

During the boubhat, the focal point of the ceremony was the afternoon meal. A few hundred people were fed in batches in two or three courtyards. The people of this part of the country were indeed very fond of food, and were proud of being hearty eaters. Nor were the womenfolk any less proud of their culinary skills. I watched in frank astonishment as the guests consumed large amounts rice with three different kinds of dal, then with a couple of vegetable and mixed vegetable curries, before moving onto the two or three kinds of fish cooked in a variety of ways, followed by equally large quantities of mutton curry with polau or pilaf and chutney. And to round off the feast, they were served a generous helping of payesh or rice pudding, which they called mishtanna.

So busy were they all with the preparation of food and its serving, that the new bride was totally neglected. No one had the time to dress me up. Someone casually mentioned that I should wear a pair of bangles and a nice sari, but nobody helped me to select my clothes or ornaments with care. I felt very embarrassed, took out whatever was in front of me and felt quite unlike a brand-new bride. I do not suppose I looked like one either! I was not wearing any jewellery. It was also the boubhat of the other bride, Madhabi. Our respective husbands com pleted the ritual part of the ceremony, handing us plates with a little food and a sari, symbolically promising to take care of us for the rest of our lives. Then the two of us, the brides, sat in one corner of the verandah, folding betel leaves and minding the children. And those who wanted to have a look at us, came to us and talked to us. I received over a hundred saris as gifts, most of which I gave away later.

Nine

The Early Years of Our Marriage

From my earlier life as a carefree student, I plunged headlong into a sea of domestic responsibility. My new family was large and closely bonded. My husband's five brothers, their wives who were my jas, and children, his three sisters, who were my nonods–the older two, Tarulata and Bibha who were married and had children and the youngest, Himani, who was unmarried–and various cousins, formed a traditional joint family in which my parents-in-law were the undisputed heads. The married sisters and the older brothers lived away from Bhola, which was definitely the nerve-centre of the family. Crises like illnesses or celebrations like social events or festivals were common occurrences. In such a large family, even the everyday meals or the education of the children needed skilful management and organization. The different brothers had different levels of earning, different attitudes and viewpoints. Yet they were emotionally close and the family lived on the basis of sharing their lives, their joys and their sorrows.

It was my husband who tutored me on my role in the family. He was uncompromising in his notions of family duty. He had told me, not once but often, that his father regarded him as the one who must support the family and take care of all their needs. And he made it clear to me that responsibility towards his family must be my first and foremost concern. Given the sheer size of my new family, this was a mammoth task, but I slipped into my role quite easily, thanks to my husband's guidance. Did I feel at all resentful of my new role? I do not think so. After all, my own upbringing had taught me similar lessons. Had I myself not been brought up in a family where bonds and duties took precedence over all else? Had my Dadamashai and mamas not borne such responsibilities cheerfully, uncomplainingly? Indeed, in those days, such values and norms were the rule, not the exception. Hence, I too accepted my new role as natural, and did my best to live up to my husband's expectations.

My husband left for Faridpur four days after our *boubhat*, to rejoin his official duties as Additional Judge. I remained with my in-laws until 17 May 1933, and as I have said earlier, it was a vast family made up of my jas—the wives of my husband's brothers—the children, as well as my husband's unmarried sister and various cousins. The whole day flew by cooking for the family, feeding them and in talk and more talk. Then a decision was taken that my parents-in-law would come with me to Faridpur. As was the custom, I called them Baba and Ma, just as my husband did. While Baba was ready, Ma just could not find a suitable date for she wanted to complete her Shashti puja, in Bhola.[1] Eventually tickets were bought for my father-in-law, Himani, a sister-in-law, myself, two nephews, and a muhuri[2] and we set off for Faridpur. At midnight we got off the steamer got on another one and then and boarded a train. At Rajbari, in the morning, my husband was waiting for us with a car. My mother-in-law joined us at Faridpur after sometime.

We spent only a few months in Faridpur and then my husband was transferred to Calcutta, as Additional Judge, Alipore. There we hired a house on Rashbehari Avenue and we all lived together, the two of us, my parents-in-law, the nephews—my eldest nonod's son, Debiprasad, and Mejda's son, Ashok—and Himani. In July I went back to college. We had a sudden bout of fever, all of us fell ill except my parents-in-law and my husband. There was no one to nurse us. My mother came to stay with us for a day and supervised the nursing. I had missed many classes of the BSc course and became nervous because I felt I would not fare well in the approaching exams. So I went home with Ma and stayed for about ten days so that I could prepare for the exams without any disturbance.

Before the ten days were over, on 10 December 1933, my father in-law suffered a cerebral attack, and everything went haywire. I had to return to Rashbehari Avenue. All my five jas and my two married nonods and their children came to be with my father-in-law. The house was very large, with ten rooms, so accommodation was no problem. But that was the end of my preparation for the BSc examinations. Two more uncles-in-law had come to stay with us with their wives. They were also ill and under medical treatment. The responsibility of handling many tasks fell on me: looking after the smooth running of the household, meeting the countless visitors who came to call on my father-in-law. I had very little time to myself. I would finish my work and retire very late at night, too tired to sit up and study. The only time I found was early in the morning before breakfast, when my mother-in-law attended to my father-in-law, and my husband read the morning newspaper. My studies really suffered and I soon realized that I would not be able to retain my honours in mathematics. It was a great disappointment. By this time the practical classes had begun and I went to attend them, perhaps a little against the wishes of the family.

As can be imagined, a life of unbridled domesticity began to pall somewhat and I attended Bethune College with great enthusiasm, for it provided me some respite from my household duties. Another classmate had also got married, and the two of us were the centre of attention for all the other girls. My husband often came in his car to pick me up after college, and all the girls watched us with great curiosity. I remember a special occasion, a college outing which we all attended to bid farewell to Rajkumari Das, our princi pal, who was retiring after many years of service and we gave her a suitable farewell. Our new princi pal was Tatini Das. She organized a steamer-party for the students, professors, everybody. We had a delightful time. Ultimately, my examinations were over and I was awarded the BSc degree with distinction, having got very high marks in all subjects. Though I had had to give up the honours in mathematics, as I had feared, I was awarded the Basanti Devi Gold Medal for the highest marks in chemistry.

My son, Partha, was born in Calcutta on 5 August 1934. At the beginning of 1935, orders for my husband's transfer came, and it was back to Faridpur for a second time as a District Judge. By this time, my father-in-law's condition had stabilized, and it was decided that he would go back to Bhola, and in February 1935 his eldest son, Utpal, came to take him there. All the other relatives had gone back to their own homes, and it was one of the rare occasions when my husband and I were by ourselves. We packed with the help of Bonbihari, a Harijan lad whom my husband had brought up since his days at Contai. We went and set up home in the new official quarters. In April, Himani joined us from her college hostel, as did Debi prasad, a medical student, who now had holidays.

Life in Faridpur was a novel experience for me. For the first time, I became part of an official circle and a somewhat different lifestyle. This circle consisted of the District Magistrate, the Superintendent of Police, and my husband, the District Judge. We used to go to the Club. We met Kabiruddin Sahib, the father of Professor Humayun Kabir, who was the president of the Club. I began to play tennis in the Club, with the encouragement of Kabiruddin Sahib, and we would practise every morning. My husband's cousin Nihar Kumar Gupta was the District Agricultural Officer at the Agricultural Institute near Faridpur. We loved visiting him and his wife, Rani Boudi, whom I remember as being a very accom plished housewife. Faridpur was a very cheap place. One could do one's entire shopping for the day's meals with one rupee—fish, eggs, vegetables, milk and mutton—and still have six annas left. Our household consisted of ourselves, a couple of servants, Bonbihari, Himani and the nephews when they were on holiday.

One day we had a surprise visit from Gurusaday Dutt. This was in 1935 and he had still not retired from the ICS. He was most upset to have arrived unannounced in the middle of our lunch and refused to join us at table. When we finished our lunch and came and sat with him in the sitting room, he told us that he had come to Faridpur in order to start the Bratachari movement there.[3] He insisted that I be the organizer in the district. When I told him that I was involved with Girl Guides and could not do anything else, he just would not accept my 'no'. He kept pressing me to take the Diksha, the special vow of the Bratachari movement. When at last he realized that I would not be moved, he wanted to initiate my son, who was not even a year old! In spite of this, we later became very good friends. His wife, Sarojnalini Dutt, who had already died by then, remained an inspiration to me as a selfless partner in her husband's committed social service.

Among the host of illustrious people we met at this time, was Prafulla Chandra Ray, the eminent scientist. He was staying at the Circuit House, but after a visit to the agricultural farm, went to stay with my sister-in-law, Rani Boudi. My husband already had some slight acquaintance with him. When we heard he would be having a meal with us, we were very pleased, but also slightly apprehensive, as we had heard that he was tremendously finicky. We had heard that he referred to tea as a poisonous drink! We did not know what to serve him. But when others were drinking tea, he made no comment. When my husband asked him what he would eat, he replied he only ate thick rotis and muri or puffed rice. But next morning, we found he was eating everything without any fuss. Rani Boudi had sent a large tiffin-carrier full of mishthi or sweetmeats—she was an expert in the art of making them—for him. When I expressed my doubts about whether he would eat them, she said firmly that he ate everything. And we too discovered it to be true, though he ate with moderation. We found him to be a simple, good-hearted person.

The Jubilee Celebration of Queen Victoria was being organized in Faridpur at that time. All the memsahibs, the officer's wives and some distinguished Indian ladies were on the Entertainment Committee. They decided to feed schoolchildren. I protested against this decision. I said we should feed the poor and destitute children in the slums. The others were aghast. They said how would you keep count of such children in slums and bazaars? They would turn up in the thousands! I was suitably abashed.

My academic career ended after my graduation, and I was never able to hide my disappointment over this fact. In those days, we were not concerned about building up our individual careers. In fact, we thought that women went to work only out of financial necessity. Even I had never realized then, that taking up a job could give one's life a sort of fulfilment. I had sat for my BSc exam under extremely difficult conditions, and as time went on, I became more and more immersed in my domestic duties. On the other hand, my husband began to press me to continue my studies. He suggested that I should do an MA degree in economics, as I would not have to do practical classes if I took up this subject. Finally, I decided to give it a try. When Partha was around six months old, I started studying again. My husband was delighted and enthusiastically began to tutor me. He brought me many books and recommended many things I should study. Unfortunately, I made no progress. The fact was that, though my husband was a brilliant student and a com petent teacher, I was not an ideal student. I was used to attending classes, assimilating the material, reading up and analysing it on my own, and I had never had tutors. For six months, we struggled on, my husband and I, but ultimately I had to give it up. My husband was transferred to Howrah, and we all left Faridpur and came away to Calcutta.

We stayed for about a year in Calcutta this time, in a rented house on Lansdowne Road. My husband would travel to Howrah every day. Partha was two years old at that time. Then we went to Rajshahi for a brief two months, followed by about nine months in Calcutta and after that, another year-and-a-half in Rajshahi. It was during this second stint in Rajshahi in 1936 that my husband decided to go to England. It was also at this time that my father-in-law passed away in Bhola. We went back there from Rajshahi, for the funeral and other related ceremonies.

After my father-in-law's death, I brought my mother-in-law to live with us in Rajshahi. She was still very grief-stricken and I tried to look after her as best as I could. I had noted what her favourite dishes were, even the kind of plates she liked to use, and I tried to do everything according to her taste. She was naturally very pleased. That summer, my sisters, Anubha and Anju, came to stay with me, and my husband's sister, Himani. The girls wanted to learn cycling. I used to take them to visit different places of interest. We would go down to the river Padma, and run around in the sandy riverbed. I was expecting my second child then, but that did not stop me from playing tennis, or running about with the girls. I remember one particular day when there was a bore tide coming up the river, and I raced home with Partha in my arms. What a race it was, between the tidal wave and me!

In Rajshahi, we faced many other adventures. Once, while going to the *bawarchikhana*, as the kitchen was called, which was a little far away from the main house, I found a cobra with a raised hood directly in my path. I was terrified. But to my relief, it slithered away. Then I noticed that there were scores of baby snakes crawling at the base of a large tree, each one with its hood erect. We were literally walking on a snake's nest! I called my servants, gardeners and others and they sprinkled acid on that spot. Still, the big snake had to be dealt with. Finally one day, it was spotted in my mother-in-law's kitchen, quietly coiled in one corner. We could neither approach it, nor would it move away of its own accord. Finally, we called up the police lines and two men came with their guns and shot it.

In spite of such adventures, we had an uncomplicated life. There was no electricity and we used hazack lamps and moved about with the help of torches. I do not remember our movement being hampered in any way. There were big gardens and the children had plenty of space to play. My husband used to play football in Rajshahi, and I continued with my tennis. There were some foreign missionaries there, who were also sportsmen. One Mr. MacLeod was a gifted footballer. The missionaries and other officers would often invite us for dinner and occasionally we would also invite them. So I continued to gain experience in entertaining in the Western fashion. We never served alcoholic drinks, which we did not stock in the house. We would inform our guests about this and warn them that we would only be offering sherbets. We faced this problem only with British colleagues, the Indians in the official circle straddled both worlds. So we would serve soup and polau or fish-head curry, or both, and both items were equally appreciated! We were all adopting certain anglicized ways, such as visiting clubs and having British people over for meals. But for me, that was the limit. I went to the Club to play tennis. I did not take to talking in English, nor did I pick up any other habits. And that is why I occasionally fell into error. Once, I offered my British guests cigarettes out of a tin, without realizing that I should check the tin for mildew. The guest quietly disposed of the one I had offered and lit one of his own. Later, I realized what had happened. No one smoked in our house. I had got the tin for a party some weeks back, and put it away. When I took it out for the guests after a prolonged period, obviously, the damp air of Bengal had done its damage!

Towards the end of 1937 I came to Calcutta for my second confinement, my husband's term in Rajshahi also ended and this time, he was posted to Dacca. When my baby daughter, Shakuntala, was three weeks old, I too went to Dacca, taking my nonod Bibha and her children together with my own. We had to go to Narayanganj via Goalanda by steamer and then we drove from there. My husband was very fond of his sisters. He felt that they had a very hard time in their in-laws' homes, so they should come to their paternal home to relax once in a while or failing that, at least to our home. We were in Dacca for about nine months, until 1938. I found Dacca quite crowded, though the area where we stayed initially was beautiful. It was called Segunbagan and was very green, full of trees. Our driver taught me to drive the car, and I drove extensively in Dacca, in the Court area, and also in the markets, the busy part of town. But I was very careful, as I did not have a driver's license as yet. After leaving Dacca, I did not drive elsewhere.

People said things were cheap in Dacca. At least, Bibha, who stayed with us for five months, said so. But I felt Faridpur was cheaper. A wide variety of fish was available in Dacca. So many types of fish would be bought from the market including of course, the famous ilish (hilsa)! And in such large quantities—whole basketfulls of kholshey or a large number of koi, pabda or prawns. Fortunately, Bibha was an expert in cutting up, cleaning and cooking fish and her family was very fond of fish, as was my husband.

During the monsoon, there was tremendous rainfall, and the whole countryside was inundated. I came from the hot, dry area of Jaipur and Delhi, I had never seen anything like it. I persuaded my mother-in-law, to take me on a trip to the family's ancestral home in Madhyapara. Made entirely by boat, that trip was a unique one for me—something I've never forgotten. We hired a boat in Dacca, went past Narayanganj, into Munshiganj district, to the village of Madhyapara. At Narayanganj itself, we found that the river was swollen with rainwater. The fields and roads on either side were all under water. When we came close to Madhyapara village, Ma began to point out the landmarks—the Daroga-bari, someone's house—and so we realized that we were in the vicinity of the village. Ma could make out where the main roads were, but of course, I could not. Eventually, we reached the family home. Water had entered the house and we found it practically impossible to go from room to room. Then Himani found a novel way of paddling along in a makeshift boat, actually an enormous mud tureen or pot. I had learnt a little swimming in the pool of Hedua in Calcutta, and I too swam about, using the floating mud vessel as a sort of buoy. We went in this way to the potter's house and picked up some beautifully executed clay toys, dolls and statues of gods and goddesses.

The next morning, we took our boat to Outshahi, and later to my mother-in-law's natal home. This house was situated next to a large tank and I had been particularly keen to see it. We spent some time there. An uncle of Ma's, who had earlier lived and worked in Rangoon, had now come and settled down in Madhyapara. He invited us to his house, and we went there too, by boat. What a huge house he had built on the bank of the pond, that too, a proper, permanent structure, standing on a high foundation next to the large tank. Rohini Dadamashai, as we called this uncle, had probably been a businessman in Rangoon. He now lived in this house with his two sons and their families. His eldest son had died, his widow too had remained with them. Rohini Dadamashai showed us around his house very happily.

This house was the only pucca or permanent house in the whole village. All the other houses in the area were made of a sort of bamboo matting and they could be dismantled and set up elsewhere in the event of floods. A little like the houses in Shillong. My in-laws had many houses in Madhyapara, occupied by the members of the vast extended family. These had three courtyards, with four rooms on four sides of the courtyard. Ma told me that many pujas would be celebrated here. Though it was August, the potters had begun preparations for the coming Durga puja.

This was my first experience of staying in a village in East Bengal, even though it was for a short time. I was most intrigued by the way the people here adjusted to the difficult conditions: travelling by boat during the monsoons, living in movable houses. Their simplicity and affectionate nature was very appealing to me. Their deep family ties and sincere love for their large, extended family was very moving. In happiness and sorrow, especially in times of trouble and adversity, they helped each other out with true solicitude. My mother-in-law used to come here every year during the Pujas and lived right royally, like a queen, as was the custom for the head of the family. Those memories were too painful for her in her present widowed state, and she refused to come for the Durga Puja that year, and the family felt very dejected as a result.

The countryside was beautiful beyond compare. Such large rivers, an abundance of lakes and ponds—the countryside of East Bengal enchanted me. We have seen the villages of West Bengal in films like *Pather Panchali,* but I do not recall many movies displaying the beauty of East Bengal, except perhaps, the films by Ritwik Ghatak. Had I ever been asked to make a personal choice about the place where I would like to settle down, it would have been East Bengal: Jessore, or perhaps Faridpur. Perhaps even Chittagong, which I felt was a bit like Assam. Hilly, and beautiful. I would not have chosen Calcutta, where we came ultimately out of necessity, not choice, as a result of Partition. I even liked Krishnanagore better than Calcutta in those days.

Notes

1. Falls in the month of Jaistha, mid-May to mid-June, when prayers are offered to the Goddess for the welfare of one's children.
2. A lawyer's clerk.
3. Conceived by Gurusaday Dutt, this was a movement for the regeneration of the village, and members took a 'brata', or a vow, to commit themselves to self-reliance and to be of service to the nation. It was mainly village-level work, and its ideals were akin to the Scouts and the Guides.

Ten

Ghare, Baire: Working at Home and Venturing Outside

It was in Dacca, in 1938, that I came into contact with a host of women's organizations such as the All India Women's Conference (AIWC), Dacca Branch, Ananda Ashram, Leela Nag's Dipali Sangha, and the National Conference of Women in India (NCWI). Each of them had a separate organization, but that year, they had decided to raise funds jointly and then divide the money among themselves. Ashalata Sen and Charushila Devi were in the forefront of those organizations.[1] I was roped in somehow; I was to direct a cultural programme and to raise funds. This was to be a variety programme. One group decided to perform a Radha-Krishna dance, another staged

'Karna-Kunti Sambad' and so on. Then children and young girls too put up some items. Dacca was culturally a very progressive place, and had developed its own style, very different from the style of Santiniketan and getting performers and stage items was not a problem. My main task was to coordinate the whole show and prepare a two-hour programme. As for the fund-raising, my unit had managed to raise the maximum funds. The tickets were a mere two rupees and we had collected five hundred rupees. It was quite a substantial amount in those days. We also raised some more money through exhibitions of craft items made under the banner of the women's groups, and through food stalls. When I handed over the money my unit had collected, and stated the accounts, I remember that I was given a big hand of applause.

So that was my first formal venture into organizational activity. I had learnt a lot from it. I learnt that dividing up the workload makes for less pressure on individuals and brings better results. I realized that when many groups work together, a greater body of talent and expertise can be tapped. Most important, I found that I had come into contact with a wide variety of people: singers, dancers, talented people, whose friendship enriched my life. I was greatly impressed by the cultured ways of the nawab family of Dacca. I also saw for myself the tremendous skills of women from the underprivileged sections of society. I began to comprehend that these very skills could be harnessed to set them on the road to financial independence

Gradually, almost imperceptibly, I was being drawn into a variety of activities. Initially, the chores of looking after a large and bustling household had kept me fully occupied. There were children to be kept engaged, older nephews and nieces whose higher education I organized, and even tutored when necessary. There were the usual clutch of family crises like illnesses and medical treatments to be attended to. Added to these, there were the social duties of a District Judge's wife. I do not think that I was consciously looking for things to do outside the home, my life was a constant stream of continuous activity. After our time in Dacca, I found myself getting involved with organizations and activities that were strictly outside the domestic purview, though in content they might have been no more than an extension of the kind of work I was already doing for the family.

Looking back, I see that the days before my marriage were the last days of a carefree student life, a life without stress or anxiety. Even though I was unable to perceive it immediately, after my marriage, I gradually became immersed in responsibilities, so heavy, that under their weight, my untroubled existence vanished forever. There were no more days of light-hearted gaiety, of laughter and enjoyment. I became involved in a huge household of numerous members and vast responsibilities. I was not able to free myself from that duty-bound life from the time of my marriage in 1932 to 1992. It continued to bind its fetters round me. For over sixty years, had I been able to spare a thought for myself even once? Had I felt 'This is *my* household! This is *my* life?' even for a day? Instead I had to think of others in the household: their needs, their requirements. Such questions drift through my mind but I cannot find an answer. The mind is filled with tiredness, with despair. Do one's own desires have no value? Does desire get guided by some unknown force—Fate—or whatever we might call it? I never found real pleasure in mere household duties. I often could not find a meeting-point between them and my innermost desires. Yet that is what I had to occupy myself with for a long time. And it was not *my* household. Rarely have I lived alone with my husband and children. As I look back, I wonder in all that I did so dutifully, almost mechanically, was I really under a sense of obligation that these tasks must be carried out by me? Have I received what was due to me? My debts to Life I have probably repaid in full measure. But did I get my true dues? Perhaps I did not. And that was why I finally stepped outside the home.

Note

[1] Ashalata Sen (1894-1986), a Gandhian social worker, freedom fighter and writer who remained in East Pakistan after Partition and was a member of the East Pakistan National Assembly. She later came to India in the 1960s. She is still remembered in Bangladesh today for her work amongst women. Charushila

Devi was the daughter of Paramananda, the founder of Ananda Ashram, which she took over after his death and maintained the same high level of social service to the community, particularly notable during Partition and its aftermath.

Eleven

My Life as a Rover

The early years of my married life were rather like a rover's. We moved from town to town, according to my husband's postings, and I got to see the greater part of undivided Bengal, before Partition and independence. I was also becoming an expert in the cumbersome business of packing and moving an entire household, sometimes within three months of arriving at a place! Of course, those who are acquainted with the British administrative system will understand the reason behind my husband's frequent transfers. They were absolutely political. While he had gained a reputation of being an extremely upright officer, his political sentiments were perhaps too patriotic for comfort. He expressed his views in a forthright manner, and refused to administer harsh or unfair sentences. Nor was he willing to consider patriotism to be a crime and punish his countrymen for it. Instead, it was he who was often 'punished' with sudden transfers and obscure postings.

In 1936, I became very busy with another 'first' in my life—arranging and organizing the wedding of my niece Aruna. I was trying to do this alone in Calcutta. The initial steps I took ended in disaster. The marriage had already been arranged and the date of the wedding had also been fixed, but the prospective bride and groom had not met! My niece was not in Calcutta and the groom too was away on work. Both my husband and his third brother, Anil, who was a civil surgeon, were in Rajshahi while Aruna's father, Utpal, was at Bhola. I was the sole person dealing with the groom's family. When I suggested to them that the wedding should be postponed till the boy and girl met, they became furious and threatened to break off all negotiations with us and look for another girl. I sent a telegram for the consent of my husband and Aruna's father at Bhola and they agreed that the marriage should not take place then but should be postponed. The marriage was called off just a week before the wedding date. Aruna's uncle, Mrinal, was very annoyed with me.

After the fiasco, I joined my husband in Rajshahi, and took Aruna with me so that she could continue her studies in Rajshahi College. She was a good student, and began studying for her I.Sc. I used to tutor her in maths. Very soon, her marriage was arranged with a fine boy from a very distinguished family in Rajshahi itself. Both the families had similar views about dowry and there were no demands from either side. So, it was an excellent match. The wedding would take place in May 1938.

Later I returned to Calcutta to make the arrangements for the wedding since the family elders and Aruna's parents remained in Bhola. Starting with the bride's trousseau–her saris, her petticoats and blouses, her jewellery–I had either to buy or prepare every little item. I stitched some blouses and petticoats for her. Then came things like designing the wedding cards and getting them printed and going around inviting the guests. Fortunately, I knew Calcutta fairly well, and my mother's family was a great help to me. Then I hired a house, a school building, near Jadu Babu's Bazaar, where the family members who were travelling to Calcutta for the wedding could be put up. We had to hire everything, from mattresses and sheets to crockery, glasses, serving dishes and spoons. Then I had to hire a cook and his helper. Gradually, the house filled with people: my sisters-in-law and their families, the relatives from Madhyapara and the bride's maternal family. Now, there was the added responsibility of organizing the meals for this large group of people: fixing menus, getting the commodities from the market, the cutting and chopping and cleaning of vegetables and fish, the serving of the meals—quite a major task. By the time the bride's parents arrived, all the preparatory organization was complete. Aruna's mother, Bidyutlata, and her maternal relatives took the pressure off my shoulders by taking charge of the kitchen. They were very good at that. But I still had my hands full with what was almost my speciality—managing the children. I would see to it that they ate their meals on time. I looked after them during the day, and baby-sat when their parents went out shopping or to meet their own relatives. It was something I enjoyed, and they did too, so it was no problem. My husband kept track of the accounts. At the same time, though we had divided up the chores, the final responsibility lay with me. My duties ended when the bride went to her new home and the wedding guests departed. I was only twenty-five at that time and this was a major test of my abilities. I worked very hard to make this occasion a success, and I admit that I learnt a good deal about the nitty gritty of organization, and this has stood me in good stead later in my life.

In 1938, at the end of our time in Dacca, my husband decided that he would go to England to sit for the Bar. He had to sell his beloved car to find the money for his fare. We packed all our furniture and other belongings and loaded them onto a huge luggage-carrying boat, called 'jewellery boat' in the local language. This boat had a large hold beneath the planking in which the goods were stored. As our furniture was being stored, we found that ultimately, there was no place for my four dining chairs, which we then auctioned off at the pier itself! All the luggage was sent by river to Bhola. My mother-in-law and I went to Bhola. My husband left for England in September 1938.

In 1939, my Dada, Arun, was getting married. I was at Bhola with the children. My mother wrote, saying that I must come to Calcutta, as she would be unable to organize my brother's wedding all by herself. So I came prepared to work hard, secure in the knowledge that I had already completed one such assignment successfully. There was, however, little for me to do, for Ma had made all the arrangements with the help of my mamas. Dada had chosen his bride himself. She was Suhasini Dutt, whom I had known in college, and she was working with the revolutionary students' organization. It was an inter-caste marriage and her family was not in favour of it, so her colleagues Kalyani Das and Bina Das were arranging the ceremony. My mother too had initially been upset, not because Dada was marrying outside our caste, but because she had already chosen another girl as his bride, and she would be breaking her word to this girl's family. Later, she came round and blessed the couple. My father's brothers too attended the wedding and took part in the ceremonies.

Another new experience occurred at this time when I substituted as a teacher in Suhasini Boudi's school for about a fortnight. Dada and his bride went off to Amritsar for a few days after their wedding. She taught at Romesh Mitra Girls High School and requested that I take her classes during her absence and I agreed with alacrity. But once I went to the school, I found that I would have to teach science and maths in Bengali. This was difficult for me as I did not know the Bengali terms for English expressions such as 'theorem' and 'parallelogram'. I was pleasantly surprised to find that the students themselves helped me out! Who was teaching whom, I wondered.

While I was in Calcutta for Dada's wedding, my eldest sister-in-law, Bidyutlata, fell ill and I had to look after her. My plans of joining my husband in England had to be scrapped, and instead, I hired a house in Calcutta and set about arranging for my sister-in-law's treatment. Soon my mother-in-law arrived from Bhola with Himani. I alone was responsible for the family's well being–from nursing Bidyutlata, to going to the bank, keeping accounts, seeing to the daily marketing, teaching the children and keeping them occupied–everything was my responsibility. As a widow, my mother-in-law would not let anyone else but me cook her meals. Himani had got a job as a teacher, so she too left the house after breakfast. The only help I received was from Ma, who supervised the Brahmin cook's work, and my sick sister-in-law who kept Partha and my baby daughter, Shakuntala (whom we called Kunta), busy. To top it all, once we had set up an establishment in the city, many relatives from Bhola came over for various kinds of medical treatment. More often than not, I had to organize all that as well. People came to visit my mother-in-law. Our house was like a constant merry-go-round. In spite of all the stress and anxiety, some good certainly came of it. I am convinced that these domestic duties played a great role in training me for my later endeavours in the field of social work.

Towards the end of my stint in Calcutta in 1938, I witnessed the historic Congress Session where the scene of the contest between Subhas Bose and Pattabhi Sitaramaiyya took place. There was a great rush to buy tickets for that session. I too got myself a ticket. It was a time of great political excitement. The session took place in Wellington Square. Many leaders of national importance were present. I remember seeing Nehruji, Purushottam Das Tandon, Rajendra Prasad, and of course Gandhiji himself, Sitaramaiyya, Subhas Bose, Sarat Bose and a host of other Congress leaders. They all arrived in a huge procession, as was the custom of the Congress. Gandhiji had managed to negotiate for the release of the revolutionaries who were still in jail, so they were there in full force in the visitor's gallery: Bina Das, Kamala Mukherji and Kamala Dasgupta and others. Leaders from Dacca, like Ashalata Sen and Bhupen Dutta were also present. I was full of curiosity. Such a large organization! Such tremendous excitement! I had never attended such a large meeting before.

It was like a drama unfolding before our eyes. Everyone knows what happened in that session. How Subhas was elected President and he came to preside. But Gandhiji said, 'This victory is my defeat,' and Subhas immediately responded with his resignation. What was amazing was the way in which a candidate was removed, with such twisted words! As soon as Subhas offered to resign, Rajendra Prasad immediately got up and proposed the name of Sitaramaiyya. Someone else seconded it at once and the whole thing was done! Just like that, before our eyes! Then Subhas left the Congress and formed the Forward Bloc. I watched the whole episode with astonishment, and I must say, with fascination as well, as I belonged to neither party, I was simply an observer. My husband was still in England at that time, and I came home and wrote to him every evening, reporting the day's events. I would even cut out the reports from the newspapers and send them to him, for I knew he would not get to see them otherwise.

In August 1939 when my husband returned from England, he was posted in Jessore. The political situation was quite tense on the eve of World War II. The first thing that happened in Jessore was that Partha fell ill with jaundice. We had an anxious fortnight, trying to keep him in bed. I called my mother to stay with us and she would keep him company. We had to be very careful with his diet. We had a very large house to stay in. My own children were of school-going age then, and there was always a bunch of nieces and nephews who came to me in their holidays. Add the neighbours' and other officers' children, and it was large enough for me to run a school! In fact, I had transformed one of the rooms into a kindergarten, put up charts and pictures and I would teach the children there. There too, I put up many children's plays, I even wrote some myself!

During the Durga Puja vacations that year, my husband chose to go to Bhola, but I had spent four months there in his absence, so I stayed back in Jessore with the children. The usual lot of children arrived to spend their holidays with me; this time, the children of my youngest brother-in-law, Birendra. There was a *dighi*, a big tank, behind the house and we spent long hours bathing and swimming there, though, of course, these activities were limited in September. It was in the following summer that we really used that tank to our full advantage. I taught Gita Roychaudhury (later Mukherjee) and her aunt, Anila Devi, an active All Bengal Teachers' Asociation (ABTA) leader, how to swim. Gita later became well known as a communist M.P.

In 1940, during the Puja vacation, my husband suggested that we should take a holiday in the western part of the country. We had relatives in Jaipur, Delhi, Agra, Amritsar and Lahore and he proposed that we should visit these places. I was delighted. We had been married almost eight years but we had never gone on such a trip. So, the two of us, Partha and Kunta and two servants, made up a large party and ventured out. Our first stop was at Delhi, where we stayed with Mejodadu. He was very pleased to have us and was very hospitable. His son Nikhil showed us round all the interesting spots of Delhi, including the historical monuments. Partha loved visiting these sites, and the evening before visiting any place, I would tell him stories and historical anecdotes about the place. Delhi has many such spots, interwoven with the history of the Sultans, the Mughals, and I told Partha all these stories. He loved them. He loved exploring these historical spots. Perhaps that was the genesis of his interest in history though he was only six at that time. Much later, he admitted as much to me.

The next stop on our itinerary was Amritsar, where Dada stayed. We stayed there for a couple of days and proceeded to Lahore. Our friends, Bhabesh Sanyal, the eminent artist, and Mr. Amar Sengupta who worked for Shalimar Paints, were in Lahore then. We stayed with the latter and spent two fun-filled days in Lahore. Then I wanted to spend some more time with Dada, so I decided to go back to Amritsar. This time my husband and I went separately. I got down at the station in Amritsar with the children and went to Dada's house. I went and sat with Dada, chatting away. It was very hot. So I bathed, changed, took off all my jewellery. I never wore too much jewellery. But on this trip, I was wearing quite a large amount—fourteen pairs of bangles, a pair of bracelets, gold necklaces, heavy earrings—a lot of gold. I had taken off the ornaments and placed them on the bed and loosely covered them with a towel. In the meantime, Dr. Girija Nath Sen, my youngest mama, called to say goodbye and I went to him to touch his feet. I had left Partha in the room. As I went to Mama, I noticed that the servant was entering the room. He was leaving when I went back after seeing mama off. Then I lifted the towel and found–nothing! Not a single ornament was there. I asked Partha, 'You were sitting there, didn't you see who came in?' Partha said he had followed me out of the room. I ran to Boudi in the kitchen. 'You're playing a trick on me,' I accused her, but she assured me that it was not so. Dada came in, sweating profusely by now. He kept calling the servant, but there was no answer. The fellow had obviously fled, taking my ornaments.

We were supposed to join my husband on the train passing through Amritsar, and leave for our next destination. But we went to the station, told him about the theft, and made him get off the train because I insisted that we must file a report with the police.

Once again, we faced difficulties. My husband wore khadi. That itself made the people in the thana, the police station, look at him askance. He went to the District Magistrate too, but a khadi-clad ICS only aroused his suspicion! After filing the report, we returned to Dada's house. My husband was clearly annoyed with me for my carelessness. In the middle of the night, Partha slipped into bed with me and said, 'Ma, here is my gold chain, please wear it!' I was so touched! I still feel moved when I think about it now, all these years later. I had lost my ornaments and his father was upset with me, so here he was, the six-year-old, trying to console me by giving me the necklace I had given him for his *annaprashan,* his rice-eating ceremony!

To Partha's father's surprise, I slept well that night, though he did not. Next morning, he even commented on the fact. But the truth was that I was not unduly distressed to lose my jewellery. It's not as if I did not regret my carelessness, or that I forgot such an unfortunate episode. But I did not sit moaning and groaning for my lost ornaments.

Partha was at this time, a little bit in awe of his father, though very fond of us both. Sometimes, my husband would ask him which of his parents he loved more. The little fellow, hardly more than five, was diplomatic enough to say, 'Both equally'! As he grew older, there would sometimes be a conflict with his father's views. But where I was concerned, though I too was a strict parent, he knew that I would yield to his wishes if I understood them. That was probably why he once said that while his father was as hard as iron, I was more understanding. On the whole Partha was a self-reliant boy, unlike Kunta, who as a child liked to sleep with her arms round me. It was only when he was sick, that Partha really needed his mother. But even then, he could be induced to stay quietly in bed, if I gave him an illustrated cookery book to leaf through! He loved going over and over the pictures of Mrs. Beeton's cookery book!

We completed our journey by making a trip to Kankhal and Haridwar and other places of interest in the hills. Finally, we visited Agra where my uncle, Keshab Mazumdar, professor of history, greeted us most affectionately. Then we returned to Jessore.

Twelve

Jessore and Krishnanagore

At this time, we were anxious to find a suitable groom for Himani. She had already completed her MA and was teaching in Calcutta, and had also enrolled for her Teachers' Training Course. This time, I took the lead in negotiations. I came to Calcutta, stayed with my mother and set out seriously to make a match. There was not a single advertisement that I did not answer, not a lead that I did not follow up. I went all over town, sometimes taking my brother Amitava or younger brother-in-law, Amal, with me, sometimes going alone. Finally, I ended up in the Kankulia Road home of Dr. Shibnarayan Sen. The prospective groom himself opened the door. He was shaving, and had got through only half his beard! I met his mother and liked both of them. I invited him to Jessore in order to meet the girl.

After matters were settled, Dr. Sen came to Jessore. He arranged for Uday Shankar and his innovative dance troupe that had stunned Europe with its brilliance to visit Jessore on their way to Kalia, the original home of the Shankars. It was a large group, including Zohra, Uzra, Simki and Ravi Shankar. We requested them to put up a show in Jessore and they did so. There was no electricity then, and they used hazack lights. In spite of the difficulties, the show was excellent—mesmerizing. We could only wonder at it. Later, we felicitated Uday Shankar. He was garlanded and given a citation by Mr. Keshab Chandra Roychaudhury, the grandfather of Gita Mukherjee. It was a very pleasant occasion.

Somewhere amidst all this, Himani and her prospective groom had met and approved of each other. The marriage was fixed for January 1941, and in the meantime Dr. Sen returned to Nepal, where he worked as the curator of a museum. The wedding took place in Calcutta, where we hired a house for the occasion. This time, I can say that the whole affair was my doing—from the negotiating stage to the final day of the wedding ceremony. As in the case of our niece Aruna's wedding, earlier, I got the trousseau ready and attended to all the other arrangements. Himani insisted that she would be married in white, like a Christian bride, and I even managed to find her a white Benarasi sari with gold embossing. While making ornaments for the bride, the subject of my own lost ornaments came up and my mother-in-law kept saying that I should make some for myself as well. She gave me a pair of her own bangles so that I could have something made for myself. Because we fell a little short of the required amount of gold for Himani's trousseau, I used the bangles for her. My mother-in-law was a little annoyed with me. As for my husband, he never had the slightest perception of my needs and requirements though he was always so perceptive and considerate about everybody else. And as for myself, I really had no hankering for gold and was really glad that we could provide well for Himani. Was I the slightest bit aggrieved with my husband's attitude? Perhaps! When the wedding was over, I began to feel that I had been able to fulfil all my duties towards my husband's family.

After the wedding was over, we returned to Jessore. This time, we had a group of extremely distinguished writers as guests at our home: Sajanikanta Das, Bhibhuti Bhushan Bandopadhyay, Satyanarayan and Probodhendu Tagore. They were on their way to Sagardari, the birthplace of Michael Madhusudan Dutt. We found a place for them to stay in Jessore and also organized their trip to Sagardari. I was unable to accompany them, for I had to make all the arrangements for them.

I enjoyed our stay in Jessore. It was not such a cultural centre as Dacca or Krishnanagore, but it was not lacking in cultural activities either. Jessore was a serene place and had its own charm. We came into close contact with the families of Jibanratan Dhar and Keshav Roychowdhury. We met Haridas Mitra, the revolutionary, and his wife, Bela Mitra, a niece of Subhas Chandra Bose, who later led the Rani of Jhansi Brigade, the female wing of the Indian National Army, alongside Shahnawaz. Bela was a very talented singer. And I continued to play tennis in the club here, though the facilities were not very good.

The only act of public work that I was involved with was raising funds for a women's hospital. There was a string of child-deaths and the Civil Surgeon requested that we should do something. There was not even a clinic for women over there. Then I got involved in raising funds for a clinic. The others working with me were the officers' wives. I had met my old school friend, Anjuman Ara. She also joined me during the fund-raising drive. A lot of people used to tell us that we could have given the money ourselves. But my answer was that a joint effort was always a good one when everyone gets involved. We called this the Child and Female Welfare Society.

Soon thereafter, orders came for my husband's transfer to Krishnanagore. I was sorry to leave Jessore. I had enjoyed my stay here and we would miss our many friends. My mother-in-law went back to Bhola for the time being and my husband and I moved to Krishnanagore with our children. At that time, there were no students from the greater family staying with us. However, very soon, my household expanded to include Ashok, the son of my elder brother-in-law Mrinal. This boy, Ashok, whom we called Kanu, had run away from home to become a fighter pilot. He was brought back and admitted to a college in Barishal. But he was just not able to get on with his father and was miserable there. So I suggested that he should stay with us in Krishnanagore to do his ISc. His father agreed and soon Ashok came to stay with us. Then my eldest nonod, Tarulata, also sent her daughter Annapurna to us for the vacations. My mother-in-law joined us. It was good for all of us. The children had company, the students had a disciplined environment. It became a regular practice on my part to invite all the children of the neighbouring slum, Bunopara, on my children's birthdays and give them a hearty feast. Often, these children would come and play football in the grounds of our house.

I had always been good at handling children. Members from the extended family came to spend some days at Bhola whenever they wanted, as many of them as they wished. We too would go there two or three times a year. Bhola was the place where we spent our vacations. The children would go as soon as their vacations started. I looked forward to teaching them swimming, to putting up a drama, to organizing all sorts of celebrations and, generally, I got involved in many types of activities. My father-in-law was always very happy with my activities. Once we had staged a play about lawyers taken from a story of Rabindranath. I also adapted the poem 'Abhisar' into a dance-drama and staged that. I taught the children the dances and songs. Aruna was a very good dancer, I gave her the role of Basavadatta. We did many such programmes in Bhola. I revived this practice in Krishnanagore and together, the children and I put up many such plays. The children too looked forward to all the new activities I introduced. I was always very interested in games and sports and tried to give them as much opportunity for sports as possible. It was as if a fresh breeze was blowing, something unknown, hitherto not experienced, was being done. They would often tell me, 'Kakima, things have changed for us since you've come. We have got much freedom which we didn't have before.' 'In what way?' I would ask. 'We've been given a lot of independence, we've been allowed to wear modern clothes!'

Our days in Krishnanagore were very pleasant. We found a very mixed group here. There was the usual official circle, to which was added the circle consisting of the college principal and professors, and the missionaries of the huge church establishment. We indulged in a variety of activities. Both my husband and I were able to indulge in our fondness for games. The people here had a spontaneous, lively involvement with cultural movements, and we found a unique cultural atmosphere in the town. Many musical soirees and programmes took place. We were living in an immense, eleven-roomed house, right near river Jalangi with our own private pier. Long walks along the river bank were among my favourite pastimes.

One of my most pleasant memories of Krishnanagore was the time we performed a skit which was a caricature of the officialdom of the times. We had become very close to the District Magistrate, Sushil Dey and his wife. Mr. Dey had written this skit, *Panchakeya Naksha*. He took the role of the District Magistrate himself, while his wife played the Magistrate's wife. They persuaded my husband to portray the District Judge. I too acted in the skit. Others did the roles of a headmistress, lawyers, junior officials, even peons. About sixty years ago, we were putting up this satire on how we talked inside the club and outside it, our relationship with different classes of people: sometimes respectful, sometimes contemptuous or disdainful; and the power wielded by the lowly peon. Asok Mitra, who was Assistant Magistrate then, did a marvellous job as the peon. On the whole, it was a wonderful production and brings back some very fond memories.

Thirteen

The Quit India Movement and the Bengal Famine

By 1942, the situation on the war front had become very serious and by August the Quit India movement had begun in right earnest. It was a direct attack on the British government. Many people became involved in that movement. And imperceptibly, I too became involved in peripheral activities. So many people came to my husband for advice, which he gave to the best of his ability. Some came to us for help. If an activist had been jailed, his family might approach us for aid, and I would do whatever was in my power. Annada Prasad Choudhury of Abhyashram would distribute leaflets and handbills carrying the words, 'Do or Die'. We would all do our bit, but very secretly, for example, I would pretend not to know how the handbills had got to my house. Once they were there, I too would secretly distribute them.

I must say that my husband was in a dilemma at this time. As a passionate follower of Gandhiji and also being deeply imbued with patriotic fervour, the Quit India movement cast him into a morass of indecision and unhappiness. His immediate wish was to give up his job and plunge into the agitation that was brewing all over the country. On the other hand, there was a large family that depended upon him, financially and morally. The dependents were not only his wife and children but also his mother and the other members of our extended family. Finally, on the advice of his brothers he gave up any plan he might have made in this regard.

At this time, the Japanese were coming closer and closer to India. Suddenly one day in December, Calcutta was bombed. The bombs fell on Hathibagan, close to my maternal family's home. We soon got news of the death and destruction that had taken place in the locality. My mother sent word that she wanted to send my younger sisters and the family dog to me here. There was a sort of panic-stricken exodus from Calcutta, into which I was drawn willy-nilly. Practically every day, families that were either related to us directly or had been given our address by others arrived by the morning and evening trains, and asked for shelter. Some of them would stay with us till we could make arrangements for them. A large number of them were on their way to relatives in other places such as Murshidabad, and our house was a sort of transit camp for them. We became preoccupied with feeding this steady stream of guests, or arranging for them to stay somewhere, or sending them off to wherever they wanted to go. Our house was always full—the ground floor was overflowing with people.

Many organizations in Calcutta began evacuating their institutions and I was left with the added task of finding suitable premises for them. Lady Abala Bose contacted me from Calcutta to find some space for her Nari Shiksha Samiti, Shilpa Bhavan that was headed by Amiya Pal, the daughter of the nationalist Bipin Chandra Pal. Sarojnalini Dutt Memorial Association came over with the Training School and set up its establishment in a rented house. Similarly, the Calcutta Blind School, the Brahmo Samaj Training School, Sachindra Prasad Nari Shilpashram along with Geeta and Dipti, the granddaughters of Dwijendranath Tagore,and many others moved to Krishnanagore. The big schools of Krishnanagore, such as Don Bosco and others, accommodated many such schools. My husband and I helped them in many ways to find alternative space, and work smoothly. We were made committee members in some cases and patrons in others. Again, this was a learning experience for me. I observed the different ways in which organizations worked, some for women and children, others for social uplift, yet others for shelter and rehabilitation. But even here, I was more a student than a worker. Sudha Sen, the wife of the Principal of Krishnanagore College, was our chief organizer. I followed her lead rather than working independently.

We stayed in Krishnanagore for about two-and-a-half years. This was one of the most eventful periods of my life, for here, I began 'working' for a cause for the first time. Whether it was resettling the institutions from Calcutta, or rehabilitating the evacuees, or supervising the production of khadi material in the villages, or furthering the cause of the Quit India movement, I was in the thick of all this activity, more as a trainee than as a leader. But my involvement in so many different spheres of activity would not have been possible without the unconditional support of my mother-in-law. As I became more occupied outside the house, she took charge of my children and the running of the house. Never did she resent my outside activity. On the other hand, she herself was an exceptionally generous and compassionate person. Often, she would do whatever she could to help people in distress, or get me to help them. She was genuinely pleased when I did succeed in doing something for others. She has been more than a support. She has been an inspiration for me.

The war had been going on for three years now. The shadow of impending famine was stalking the land, though none of us had any idea about the seriousness of the situation. Already, we had become aware of spiraling prices and the growing misery of the common man and woman. Women would be seen on the streets, carrying sacks of rice on their heads. We would ask, 'You are selling your whole stock of rice, what will your family eat?' 'We eat spinach and other greens, and collect roots and such things,' they replied. This meant rice was already a scarce commodity for them. I would buy the sack of rice at perhaps thirty rupees, thinking that this would help the poor woman. In any case I needed to keep extra stocks of rice and lentils because of the continuous stream of people we had coming to stay with us. Moreover, I would occasionally arrange a good meal for the children of the Bunopara slum, and their mothers came too. So, keeping some rice in stock was always a habit with me. Now the black market came into existence. Then there was talk of a rice bank and mortgaging one's crop. Anti-hoarding drives began, and houses would be searched for illegally hoarded rice. The farmers were not allowed to keep their stock of rice. There was no end to the sufferings of the common people. It was in Bankura, which was our next place of posting, that we actually witnessed the famine and the consequent starvation with our own eyes.

The transfer to Bankura had taken place in the middle of the school year and Partha had already missed some months of school. I was very worried about his promotion to the next class. But the princi pal of CMS school, Mrs. McArthur, said that she would send me a question paper, so that Partha could take the test at home, and then there would be no problem for his promotion. When we came to Bankura from Krishnanagore, we found that it was a very pretty place, a little hilly like Chota Nagpur, and very green. The monsoon had been good, and plenty of rice was available, at fairly cheap prices. A local strain called Danaguri was really excellent. This was the first time that we had electricity in the house. Earlier, we had always had to use hazacks at night. This was thrilling. But the bathroom remained the old-style service toilets. Our official quarters were very large and sprawling. My husband had come in the place of Annada Shankar Ray, who had just been transferred. We soon settled down in our new home.

Gradually, I began to notice a swelling tide of villagers, moving towards the town. Initially, I saw, perhaps, one or two families, going towards the hospital by the road next to our tennis court, and from there, to the town. The number increased every day. We watched people collapsing beneath trees, unable to go any further. And where were they to go? We had people working in the house, whose homes were in those villages. They told us that entire villages were getting em pty, as people moved towards the town. The government had bought up all the available rice, and there was nothing for them to eat. And this was in September, when the paddy fields were doing fine, the crops were in the fields. But they could not be harvested before mid-October and the peasants were leaving their land and going away.

One day, Usha Haldar, the wife of the Commissioner, came to me and said, 'Have you seen how many people are camping in our clinic?' I was horrified at what I saw. The clinic was just a small one, where pregnant women came for delivery. Next to it was the Dufferin Hospital. The clinic was full of women and children. They had nothing to eat and nowhere to go and had taken shelter there. That was when we decided that we had to feed these people–we would have to give them at least one meal a day. We, the officers' wives, and other local ladies, formed a Relief Committee. So we started a big kitchen there, a sort of gruel kitchen, where khichuri was cooked for these people. We were given some rations from the government stocks. We were able to feed about a hundred women and children here everyday. Very few men came to this kitchen. Most of the menfolk went towards the town in search of work. We decided that a relief camp was not enough, we ought to set up a home for these women.

Suddenly, we found ourselves in the middle of a lot of publicity. We heard that Vijaylakshmi Pandit wanted to visit our camp. Renuka Ray sent me a telegram, 'Will you put up Mrs. Pandit in your house?' My husband sent me a note from the Court, 'They will come to Bankura. Get two rooms ready.' Thus members of the AIWC, such as Urmila Mehta, Renuka Ray, and Phulrenu Guha and its president, Vijayalakshmi Pandit, came to Bankura. I was in a quandary, what sort of food should I serve them? Everything was available, for a price of course, but I had certain misgivings. If I gave them good food, that would be a problem, and if I did not feed them well, that would be a problem too! Finally, I kept the meals simple. They were vegetarians, so we served some rice and dal, a dish or two of vegetables and some rotis. They would have their breakfast and go off for their surveys, returning much later for lunch.

I had arranged a room for the guests, but had not entered it after they occupied it. I simply asked them whether they were comfortable.

Next day, Partha told me, 'Do you know, Ma, there are so many bottles on their table! Go and take a look.' So I entered Mrs. Pandit's room and really discovered an array of perfumes and cosmetics on her dressing table, at last about a dozen of them. Of course Partha was amazed, because he had not seen much more than a bottle of coconut hair oil on my table! Even I was a little disconcerted. I hardly spent any time on my toilette–used a little coconut oil, quickly combed my hair, no li pstick for me, applied sindur, perhaps some powder in summer, for both the children and me, prickly heat powder. No doubt, there were differences in our lifestyles, but our ideas matched where work was concerned. Mrs. Pandit filled us with enthusiasm and encouraged us. We organized a meeting, where all the local dignitaries were present, and she attended it. A local gentleman donated one lakh of rupees for our work and Mrs Pandit was delighted. She said her work had been successful.

I had already joined the AIWC in 1936. In Dacca, I had done some fund-raising, but I began to work seriously now for the clinic through the AIWC. Its Bankura branch, called the Nari Sammilani was already very active, doing a great deal of work like running a small private hospital. It was a strong body with a proper constitution. An earlier president, a very progressive woman, Sudha Majumdar, had set out a body of rules and regulations, which we found extremely useful. That small booklet laid down guidelines of how the President should be chosen, how the Secretary and Treasurer and other office-bearers should be elected and what their duties were. I was first the Treasurer of the Relief Committee, which we had just started. Later, I was put in-charge of the project. Usha Haldar was Patron and the District Magistrate's wife was the President. The wives of Dr. Durgadas Gupta and Dr. Anathbandhu Ray were members. We all worked together so enthusiastically, that it is a mystery to me how the organization broke up and disappeared later.

This was how I got seriously involved in social work. By this time, my son was in school, Bankura Zilla School. Kunta was also going to a small primary school nearby. My mother-in-law was there to look after the home, so I put my free time to the best possible use. My husband would leave for the Court in the morning. There was no petrol, so he would cycle all the way, while we women volunteers went on foot. Once in a while, the Commissioner or the District Magistrate might provide a car. Then we would go to the villages and see what the situation was like. If we found an old woman all alone because all the younger people had left, then she would be brought to the clinic. I regard this period as an apprenticeship in how to run an organization. My mentor and guide was Usha Haldar who was a very experienced social worker. She had begun the clinic in 1934, which had been inaugurated by Rabindranath Tagore.

When I stepped out of the home, when I trained my vision on the outside world, I came face-to-face with such a terrifying reality that I was thoroughly shaken. It was 1943. Babies were dying in the great Famine, along with so many others, in Bankura. I thought could I remain aloof, uninvolved, do nothing? How could I simply sit at home, busy with my own small household when people were dying outside my doorstep? As I have related, it was Usha Haldar who drew us out of our sheltered existence to work for others. Looking back, I think that that was the first time in my life that I had a taste of freedom, of independence, which inspired me to serve my country. When I began to work for the country's welfare, I felt I was able to discover myself. I found my path. I thought, those of us who are so busy with home and family, should we remain forever entangled in domestic ties? Surely we could make some time—certainly we could. Amidst all the chores of the daily routine, all the work that was performed for oneself, who would not like to do something for others? It was hard work, helping the people in the famine-affected areas. But the happiness I derived from saving the child orphaned by the Famine, bringing back a smile to her lips—such joy I had never experienced while serving, feeding and looking after my husband's clamorous family. This work, looking after the helpless, serving society, united me with a similar band of workers. This is what gave me tremendous self-satisfaction and joy, and brought peace to my mind. At last, I felt that I had found something meaningful and a sense of direction that continued to inspire me, through the terrible days of Noakhali, Partition and beyond.

Yet with the sense of freedom that I experienced, I wondered whether it meant that everything I had done before was somehow meaningless? Was it a fruitless task? That too was not true. I had served that vast family of my in-laws with much love and great labour. During the pujas, I would stitch a large number of clothes for the nieces and nephews. I looked after their studies, successfully carried out all the arrangements for two marriages. I had to arrange for the medical treatment of those family members who were ill and came to Calcutta for operations. I even became a skilful nurse, having learnt to administer dri ps and assist the doctor during deliveries. We would be transferred every few months, perhaps after a year. I became adept at packing and moving house—no mean task. I had to run my household with great care, for we were always a little short of money. After my marriage, my father-in-law fell seriously ill and we had to bear the expenses of his treatment. When he returned to Bhola, it was his long-standing dream to build a large, pucca dalan, a paved courtyard, which my husband fulfilled for him and my father-in-law was able to spend his last year in that house. Then, there was the expense of bringing my ja, Bidyutlata, to Calcutta for her medical treatment and setting up what became an enormous household in Ballygunge Place.

It soon became clear that I was to bear a greater degree of responsibility for the family than others, and I often wondered why this should be. Was it because, by virtue of being acquainted with Calcutta from my student days, I was the one, more than others in my in-laws' house, who knew how to get things done in Calcutta? Or was it because my husband, in his letters, would always stress that his father had laid the responsibility of maintaining and looking after the joint family on him? And thus as his wife, a great part of the burden was borne by me. Why did I accept it? Perhaps I always felt that since the responsibility was my husband's, I had to be at his side, as his partner. I too had to do my share. This is what gave me the inspiration to work in the way I did. Even though my husband never said it openly, I know that he too appreciated me for my efforts, and as for the family, I have received as much love from them as I have given them myself. I remember when we were in

Calcutta during Bidyutlata's illness, a relative asked my mother-in-law how things were being managed, since none of her sons were there at the time. She replied, 'My sons aren't here, but Ashoka is here!' I felt truly proud that she had equated me with her sons! Most important of all, I discovered that I had a great deal of ability and originality. I had organizational ability. These had been honed and sharpened during the early years after my marriage. They stood me in good stead ever after.

Fourteen

The Bengal Famine Unfolds in Its Ghastly Way

Mrs. Vijayalakshmi Pandit told me that as President of the AIWC she was organizing a conference in Delhi and I must go there to tell the members about our experiences. So I went to Delhi for her meeting. That was the first time I attended such a large meeting. I was asked to narrate my experiences, and I spoke about the terrible sufferings of the people in Bankura. Then Mrs. Pandit advised me to start an institution for the orphans. We could train the women in different kinds of vocational work, she suggested. So I hired a house in Bankura and we started an institution called Shishu Sadan. We had at least fifty children there. We used to receive funds from Delhi, from Mrs. Pandit–five hundred rupees a month. With that I managed the food, clothes, medicines and even some basic education for the children. Next year, Mrs. Kamaladevi Chattopadhyay came to visit our Home, for she was then the President of the AIWC. She came to see the way we were conducting the orphanage and she stayed with me.

Strange are the ways in which coincidences work. Mrs. Chattopadhyay would go to the villages with us to review our work.

And at the entrance of a hut, she noticed two tall, beautiful terracotta horses. She liked them so much that she wanted them. The peon, whose hut it was, was astounded. He said they used the horses for their pujas. He could not imagine what she wanted them for. But she insisted, and he got hold of a pair of terracotta horses for her. She used them as the logo for the Cottage Industry Emporia, and of course, now those Bankura horses are eagerly sought by connoisseurs everywhere.

During that trip, Mrs. Chattopadhyay collected a lot of samples of local craft. Lots of terracotta and clay things were made by the local potters, and the handloom textiles of Bankura were also of a very high quality. One particular item that fascinated her, was the tiny metal *kunke* or stick that women use for applying sindoor, and the figurines of Manasa, of which we now have a large one on Calcutta's Eastern Metropolitan Bypass. She took the kunke and figurines with her when she went to Delhi and then she sent a volunteer to collect more samples. This was a woman who was absolutely indefatigable, cycling from village to village in search of samples, making a survey of what were the articles that were produced, which villages specialized in what sort of craft, who were the artisans, and gathering such information. Thus this was the genesis of the Cottage Industries organization, pioneered almost single-handedly by Kamaladevi Chattopadhyay.

I found the whole experience fascinating. We would go from village to village, stopping in the potter's section. Where they used wheels, they made symmetrical pots and urns and glasses, and then perhaps, one item which was different, unique. Kamaladevi would at once pick that up. The menfolk worked with the wheel, the women made things with their hands—the Manasa figurines or lamps, the *panchapradeep*. Once they had been shaped, they would be dried, then burnt. It was an arduous process and many broke in the process. Most of these craftsmen belonged to the Kumhar and Lohar communities. We had two peons from these communities and they took us to these localities. Or the little boys who acted as the ball pickers in our tennis-courts would take us to their homes or those of their relatives. That was how we managed to collect so many samples.

All these unique craft items were made in the villages, but urban people had not been made aware of them so they were not noticed nor was there any demand for them. They were rarely sold. Now Kamaladevi organized the marketing of these things, so that very soon, a demand grew for them in the towns and they began to be sold in large numbers. And at last, the village craftsmen could earn a little from their traditional skills.

There was a locality called Christiandanga in Bankura, clearly a Christian locality. I noticed that in spite of the famine and starvation, they were extremely clean and disciplined people. They were always dressed in clean clothes. They got some help from the church, but they still wanted work. Then, I suggested that they could use a room in my house and start doing some stitching and embroidery. Their work was exquisite, be it embroidery or drawn thread work or stitching. They had been trained by the missionaries. We, that is the families of the civil servants, had been provided with some material, 15m per family, which was neither suitable nor sufficient for our soft furnishings. So we began experimenting with dyeing, printing and decorating that material and using it to make napkins, serviettes and a variety of such things. The women began to do all this too. That was how my office room was converted into another social service centre. We had a charka centre there, and some girls worked with khadi. And others sat with their embroidery. I would buy whatever was made and then hold exhibitions. I would get my family members to market these items. The other officers' wives worked with me. Bankura had plenty of rich people and a prosperous Marwari community. So usually, all the things sold well. Those who worked in the charka centre did not earn very much: perhaps four or five annas. They were the poorest section of the people. But those who did the embroidery earned quite well. And what lovely things they made!

I began to learn how to coordinate the various branches of activity I was involved in. For example, I kept poultry so that eggs could be supplied to the children of the Shishu Sadan. And if my children's schools needed anything my girls could supply, I could request the authorities to take the articles from them. Things began to move fairly smoothly. I got a lot of help from the women of Bankura, who were very progressive. Most members of Bankura Women's Conference were middle class. The wife of the editor of the newspaper *Bankura Darpan* would regularly publish articles about all our activities. As a result, we even got a lot of publicity. Mohanlal Gupta, a local man, donated a lakh of rupees to us for our work.

Shishu Sadan flourished. Dr. Maitreyi Bose came from Calcutta to inspect it, and she was very pleased. But she pointed out a major flaw: there was no bathroom or lavatory! The children still visited the fields in their time-honoured fashion. Dr. Bose told me that I must immediately get toilets made and of course, I did. The children studied, spun thread on the charka, and looked after the cows and poultry we kept there as part of their 'basic' education. They did some gardening: grew some vegetables and looked after some flowering bushes. I was overall in charge as organizer and treasurer. There were so many sides to running a home like this, looking after the health, the education of the children, and moulding their character as well, imparting a sense of responsibility, developing them into good human beings. I realized that the last was the most important. I also saw that my band of workers and I were receiving excellent training through this work! The children called me 'Ranga-ma'. I was their confidante, their friend. Whenever I meet any of them, even now that they are elderly, they still address me by that name and fondly relive their days in Shishu Sadan. Guiding a child to grow up to be a responsible, independent adult gave me utmost satisfaction.

Here too, we organized cultural programmes to raise funds. The Ganguly family was well educated and known to be very talented. They were related to the Tagore family. We asked them to put up some items, and they organized some dances, a performance of Rabindrasangeet and a sitar recital. We wanted to include the children we were working with, so we brought many Santhal children from the Santhal locality of town and they too sang some of their songs and performed a local dance. Bankura had a very mixed community and we wanted to please them all. One day, there was a Krishna-Radha Leela, which appealed very much to the Marwari community.

There was an evening of folksongs. Those were the days of famine and Communist activity, so the popular song about the peasant sharpening his sickle was also performed. Everybody participated, Communist or otherwise, Bengali, Santhal, middle class and orphan, in these programmes. We raised a sizeable amount of funds which went to the AIWC's kitty. We used the money to sponsor the education of our Shishu Sadan children.

The Quit India movement died down by 1943, and now we were following the exploits of Subhas Bose and the Indian National Army, the INA, which was aiming to free India from the British yoke militarily. We used to listen to Subhas' speeches on the radio. When we were in Chittagong in 1945 we heard that he had reached Manipur. The government was evacuating Chittagong. The army was being pulled out, trains were being stopped, boats were being sunk, so that Subhas' army could not establish a firm foothold there. However, the situation changed very rapidly. The war came to an end, and it seemed to be the end of a chapter. It was at this time that we noticed a rapid deterioration in the character of the people. It was no longer possible to comprehend people's motives. It was difficult to say who was working with the country's interests at heart and who was guided by political theories. We could not make out whether people were truly concerned about the issue of Partition. We noticed that they were more concerned about how to make a quick fortune, how to grab some property, how to secure some personal business opportunities in their own government departments rather than being guided by any altruistic motives. The moral fibre was being destroyed. We could not keep ourselves safe from greed. Violence was on the rise with rioting and killing going on unchecked. It seemed to us that Gandhiji's principles were no longer applicable. Since we had noted this transformation, we were extremely worried about the state of the country, and particularly about the condition of those who were weak and exploited. We were determined to face the situation and stop the decline.

It is interesting to note the role played by the Atmaraksha Samiti, a branch of the Communist Party at this time. When this organization was first established in 1942-43, it was certainly involved in social welfare, but that was only one area of its interest. There was another item on the agenda of its members: 'people's war'. Therefore, a far more political angle was involved. In 1942, they were cooperating with the British war effort, not because of concern for the country but because Russia was engaged on the side of the Allies. They attempted to ensure that the British were not unduly disturbed by the Quit India movement, that they did not face any real trouble. This is when we realized that the Samiti and the AIWC were on different lines. For example, during the terrible famine of 1943, the Communist Party and the Atmaraksha Samiti put in all their efforts to maintain harmony and discipline. There was to be no looting, no public upheaval, whereas we felt that in such a desperate situation, people should take the law into their own hands! Let the people loot food, if they had to. Our role was to see that the common people found some relief, some amenities.

Around this time, the Bankura branch of the Atmaraksha Samiti came into being in our town. They were organizing a sort of parallel body. They would attend all our meetings. They had made most of the villagers into their members and they would bring them to our meetings. They wanted us to admit those girls into our ranks, but we felt we could not do so. At the AIWC we were doing a lot of relief work, but we did not let any politics enter our activity. The Atmaraksha Samiti, however, was much more political in its approach. They were training the women to be politically conscious and to agitate on various issues. They were even trying to enter organizations like ours, so that they could use them for their political ends. And this is where we faced differences with them, hence some tension occurred. The AIWC focused totally on welfare work.

Those who worked for AIWC, never took any money from the organization for our travel or any work-related activity. It meant that only upper middle class women, who had the means, would work for AIWC. We also had a four-anna membership charge. But many housewives joined the organization, and every one worked according to their abilities and aptitudes. In Bankura, we had a group of women with sound education, strong common sense and a genuine desire to serve, to improve the lot of those less fortunate than themselves.

In our clinic, rather than em ploy nurses, we trained the mothers to look after the children. We trained young girls in Home-nursing and First Aid. Later, on the advice of Usha Haldar, the wife of the District Commissioner, S. K. Haldar, we got the doctors of Dufferin Hospital to train some girls in basic healthcare and hygiene and midwifery. In that way, the entire community benefited. We conducted craft classes, trained girls to make things and tried to set up a marketing structure. We raised money through programmes and functions for no funds came to us from the government.

Another area of our work was with the tribals, the Santhals of villages like Shaltora, Ranibandh, places which are today tourist spots. We were dumbstruck to see how these Santhal women had to labour just to eke out a living. They would walk miles to sell sal leaves, and for practically no money at all. We found their condition to be deplorable. The land was like Birbhum, very picturesque, quite fertile, the climate was good but for the tribals, the situation was bad. An added burden was the widespread prevalence of leprosy. The tribals had an unusual, though humane custom. They would segregate the persons who had contracted the disease, they made separate huts for them on the outskirts of the village, but they did not callously abandon them. They continued to supply food and other necessities to them. The government had also built many such small but sturdy huts for them. This was called Leprosy House and the government doctors attended to the patients here. We began to work among the lepers. The Sammilani's hospital, a private hospital, would treat them with great care. We would send them the patients and the testing and treatment would be done there. We also realized that children of leprosy patients might contract the disease more easily and needed to be segregated. So we arranged for such a place in Bankura. There was already a home for such children in Jamshedpur and missionaries were working among the leprosy-afflicted people of Purulia. I do not know whether we were able to spread the awareness among them that leprosy is curable, but we did whatever little was possible.

In 1944, after Kasturba's death, Gandhiji asked his followers to form the Kasturba Trust, dedicated to women. Women would work for and among women. When that Trust was organized, I was deeply interested to work for it. I had already met Sucheta Kri palani, Mridula Sarabhai and Aruna Asaf Ali when I had gone to the AIWC conference in Bombay. I was staying with Mridula Sarabhai. The others were underground at that time, but they had come to Mridulaben's's house and spoke quite openly with me. I always kept up a correspondence with them later on, from Bankura.I now began to take their advice on how I could follow Gandhiji's guidelines. Lila Ray, the wife of Annadashankar Ray, had already begun a khadi center in Bankura, and Bankura Abhay Ashram was also doing commendable work in this field. I went on a survey of the villages, and I found it was possible to do excellent work in the villages itself, there was no need of coming to the towns. I visited the centre of a renowned worker, Nanibala Akui. She was a child widow. She was running many work-centres, and the girls working under her loved her and trusted her fully. She would organize their daily work, and see to it that at the end of the day, they received their four to five annas, their food- rations and their yarn. So, in those terrible times, these girls at least had food security. I thought the policy 'you weave, we shall buy' a very practical method of work. I began corresponding with others, planning to set something up.

In the midst of so much happening in the world outside my home, our daughter Kasturi was born in December 1944. Our third child, we named her after Kasturba Gandhi, whom we revered and who had passed away that year. At this time we were transferred to Chittagong. Kasturi was just five months old when we moved to Chittagong in 1945. I was a really sorry to leave. Partha was in Class Seven, Kunta too was happily going to school. She was very attached to me and at night would sleep with her arms around me.

We had a cultural organization called Rabichakra, where literary discussions and dramas were held. Bankura was not as culturally progressive as Krishnanagore, one had to motivate the people, but we had been able to do so. But most im portant, I had learnt how much work there was to be done, and how I could do it within my limited scope. It was the place which provided the foundation for my lifelong involvement with relief activity and social work. These three years, 1942 to 1945, have a special place in my memory.

Fifteen

Chittagong and Communal Riots in Calcutta and in Noakhali

We travelled first to Calcutta, then to Goalanda by train, from Goalanda to Chandpur by steamer, and finally the last leg of the trip to Chittagong was by train. The-Goalanda-Chandpur stretch was the famous steamer journey everyone talked about. It was a breath-taking experience over the rivers Padma and Meghna, the landscape on their shores, the subtle and vibrant colours, made it so utterly beautiful that it has never been surpassed in my mind.

We reached Chittagong in May 1945. There was heavy, torrential rain throughout June, and I had never experienced such rainfall. The house that would have been given to my husband as his quarters had been taken or requisitioned by the army and we were given alternative accommodation. The war had just ended. But the place was full of soldiers: Amèrican, African and Indian. After all, Chittagong was very close to the war front. There were so many jeeps and lorries running on the road that it was difficult to cross it. The house we were supposed to live in had been allotted to some members of the Women's Auxiliary Corps India (WACI) and Army nurses and it was a year at least before we were given possession of it.

Himani was expecting her first child so I brought her over to Chittagong. We had heard that Dr. Anil Bhowmik, a renowned doctor whom we knew, was posted here, so we placed Himani confidently in his hands. My son joined Class Seven in the local Municipal School, and continued there till the Partition in 1947. There was some uncertainty over finding a school for Kunta. The famous Khastagir School of Chittagong had been evacuated to Dacca, and for five months, I taught Kunta at home till it was brought back to Chittagong. The principal, Suprobha Dasgupta, with whom we were acquainted and called Minudi, told us to admit Kunta and we did so.

It was an excellent school. By this time, I knew the workings of several missionary schools as well, and I still feel that none could match the Khastagir School of Chittagong. The academic side was as good as was its discipline. The campus was tidy and attractive, which attracted the students. And it had such a dedicated band of teachers as I have rarely seen elsewhere. One particular incident remains etched in my memory. When I went to work among the riot-affected people of Noakhali, I had left Partha and Kunta at home with their father and they continued going to school. One day, Kunta's principal and a teacher came home to see how they were all getting on. At that time my husband was struggling to plait Kunta's hair and was obviously not doing a good job of it. When the two women asked him to allow them to help, he refused, saying, 'No, no, I can do it very well.' They did not say anything further, but the next day, they arranged that Kunta should take a change of clothes to school. They would help her change her dress in school, tie her hair, and get her ready before sending her home. Such thoughtfulness touched me deeply and made me feel that I had a solid support system behind me. As for the teachers, they felt that I had gone to serve the riot-affected people, so it was their duty to look after my children and relieve me of my worries about what was happening at home.

In Chittagong, I began working under the auspices of the AIWC. Nellie Sengupta was its president at that time.[1] I worked for the women who had been affected by the famine and displaced because of the war. All food items were rationed then, and many people did not have access to steady rations. There was a group of English ladies, mostly officers' wives, who received grains at a cheap price and they were looking for people to distribute these among needy women, and I got involved and distributed the grain in my neighbourhood. The grain was stored in my house and I measured it out for the women according to the size of their families. We kept cards which had all their details. Once, some of the Ladies' Club members came to inspect my work. Then they began to check whether the ratio of the Muslim and Hindu recipients was equal or not. I was naturally incensed by this deliberate attempt to politicize the issue. As it happened, there were more Muslim women on my rolls than Hindus, but to me, these were destitute women in need of aid, not the members of a particular community. Had they all been Hindus, I would have served them; I would have done the same had they all been Muslims.

Meetings were held in Nellie Sengupta's house. From May 1945 to May 1946, sporadic riots were taking place in many areas, and we would get to hear the news. It was the Great Calcutta Killing that began a new chapter of violence.[2] A relative of mine, an army officer, had gone from Calcutta to Chittagong at that time. He found it practically impossible to return to Chittagong. When, finally, he did fly down, he brought to us many tales of horror: how the bazars in Calcutta had been looted and there was no food, no vegetables to be had anywhere. Chittagong was famous for a root vegtable called ole, a kind of yam, which keeps for months. I sent as much yam as I could find to Calcutta. Our relatives wrote to me to say that at last they had something to eat with the rice. Even finicky gentlemen who never touched yam otherwise thanked me for sending it.

There were other troubling events taking place in Calcutta. People were leaving their homes and migrating to what they thought were safer parts of the city. A friend of mine moved from Park Circus, a predominantly Muslim area, to Kalighat, a predominantly Hindu one. Calcutta was reeling with distress, and we would get the news. But till October, nothing happened here. The riots erupted in Noakhali on 10 October. Initially, we did not come to know about the riots, though the Divisional Commissioner was posted in Chittagong. But very soon, people from Noakhali villages began arriving at the railway stations.

We set to work at once. A meeting was called at Nellie Sengupta's house, where we decided to set up a Relief Committee. I was made the convenor of the committee and I had to find others who would go with me to Noakhali to do relief work. Initially our task was to distribute relief materials, medicines and clothes among the people who were escaping from their own villages. They needed food, for themselves and their families, and clothes, for most of them had fled empty-handed, carrying nothing with them. We collected relief material, organized ourselves into groups and went into various districts: to Feni or to Ramganj or Choumuhani. We would discover the routes by which these refugees were fleeing, and hand over the material to them. But that was all. We tried to persuade them to return to their villages, but they refused to do so.

We linked up with other branches of the AIWC and also with other relief organizations and set up a relief committee. The branch members of Dacca, Chandpur, Comilla, Calcutta and Chittagong met and we often went into the interiors. Choumuhani was the centre closest to Noakhali, so many people had collected there. In the beginning, we went for a couple of days, did some distribution, then returned to Chittagong. On the way, we might meet some other group going towards Choumuhani. In this way, a continuous network was maintained.

Kasturi was only a year-and-a-half old, and I used to feel very distressed at leaving her at home and going off, but I had no alternative, especially as I was determined to help the people affected by the terrible communal riot. Soon, I became fully occupied in trying to rescue the abducted girls. I wondered how traumatized they must be, how desperately they would be praying for someone to rescue them and that their families would take them back. Nor could I understand the mentality of the abductors. I felt it was unjust to point a finger only at Muslims in their attitude to women, for Hindu society too was guilty of terrible ill treatment to women. If once a Hindu girl had gone against the accepted norms of Hindu society, she would be treated like an outcaste, beyond the pale, whereas, in Muslim society, a woman could marry two, even three times. Upper caste Hindus did not generally allow widows to marry again, and condemned them to a lifetime of celibacy. So the debate over which society was better left me cold. It was the thought of the mental trauma of the poor tortured young girls and young women that haunted me. I remember that at this time, I had a very illuminating conversation with one Mr. Jacob, a Christian. My husband and I sat talking to him, while his 14-year old daughter played badminton with my 12-year-old son. Mr. Jacob said, 'Suppose someone abducted my daughter, wouldn't she believe with her whole heart that I would be looking for her, that I would find her and take her home? Can you imagine her feelings if she thought I would abandon her?' I was deeply moved by those words. I thought that if a girl were physically tortured, and her family refused to take her back, she would develop hatred not only towards her family, but towards society as well. So I resolved to rescue abducted girls and to persuade their families to take them back.

On 20 October, I went to talk to the District Commissioner on this issue. I requested him to provide protection to our volunteers for this work. He replied, 'It will take time. It may even take years. How can you rescue so many girls?' I was furious. What sort of administration was he in charge of that it could not rescue abducted girls? We were determined to stick to our planned path of action regardless. On the same day, we heard that Acharya Kripalani, the Congress president and his wife, Sucheta Kripalani, were coming. I went to meet Sucheta and told her that we wanted to do more than relief work, we wanted to rescue the abducted girls. We wanted to bring them back and unite them with their families. We asked for her help. Her answer was not encouraging. She too said that taking search parties and hunting out individual girls would take a lot of time, it was next to impossible. But she would try, she promised and asked for our cooperation. I told her that we were not worried about conversion, for religion is born of one's own faith. But it was the indignity, the sheer humiliation of abduction and rape that distressed us.

By 26 October we had begun to go in batches into the villages of Noakhali, distributing relief material in the stations, looking for abducted girls, listening to the people's accounts of the happenings and preparing a list of the affected villages. The army maintained a very tight grip at this time, and would not allow us to go into the villages in the interior. But when the Kripalanis came, Carter, the Commissioner of Chittagong Division, was forced to allow them to enter Noakhali under armed escort. The eyes of the whole country were focused upon this part of the Bengal and there would have been a great uproar if they were prevented from going on their tour of inspection. Things had reached a nadir. Houses were being burnt in an organized fashion. The Hindu houses were being looted;

everything, from grain to clothes was stolen, the families under attack had nothing to eat, no extra set of clothes to wear. The abduction and torture of women continued unabated. Men and boys were forcefully converted. We heard all this from the fleeing people we met in the stations, and in the places we went to distribute relief material. But we had only heard about all this, at this time we had not seen any of it, as we had not been allowed into the interior. Acharya Kripalani and his wife were allowed to make a tour but we were stopped.

On 7 November Gandhiji came to Chandpur. On a sudden impulse, I decided to go and see him. At the station, we were told that Gandhiji was coming by a special steamer that would not come up to the jetty but would remain anchored mid-stream. Partha, Kunta and a couple of co-workers were with me. I still marvel at the steps that I took. I was so keen to see Gandhiji that I got into a boat with my group and reach the anchored steamer. I saw Arunangshu babu, someone I knew, standing by the steamer's railing and hailed him. He was very kind and got permission for my son and me to attend Gandhiji's prayer meeting on the steamer. We climbed onto the steamer and sat with the other members of the prayer group. I was so moved that I could not speak. With the children and my colleagues I went to the station and got onto the train which would take Gandhiji to Choumuhani. Every compartment of that train was overflowing with people who had come to be with Gandhiji, people who wanted to get a glimpse of him. Only his compartment was empty. The train stopped at every station, and everywhere silent crowds craned their necks for a glimpse of Gandhiji. Many other members of the AIWC branches of Calcutta, Comilla, and Chittagong were also in the train.

At last we reached Choumuhani, and were taken to the house of a prosperous rice trader, Jogendra Kumar Majumdar. He had arranged to provide meals for Gandhiji's huge entourage and to look after everyone. In the evening, Gandhiji held another prayer meeting in a large open compound. He spoke to everyone and said that they must not be afraid. He said that there was no point in leaving the country and fleeing. Yes, a terrible thing had happened, a great disaster, but people must put it behind them, and the volunteers should work together in an organized fashion. Then, about twenty to twenty-five of us, mostly AIWC members and the Kasturba Gandhi National Memorial Trust (KGNMT) volunteers, went to talk to him about the way we should organize our work. Renuka Ray spoke on our behalf. Gandhiji said that we would have to go and live among the people for whom we were working—one or two workers per village. Unless we did that we would not know the real condition of the people, their actual losses, their mental condition. We should try and rehabilitate the abducted girls, bring them back to society. We should not concentrate on the same area, but select separate ones and work there individually. I decided to go to Lakshmipur Police Station area. Both my husband and my mother in Calcutta supported my desire to be part of the relief activities, though I suspect none of us realized at that time, how long, how weary, how difficult would be the days ahead.

On one of my trips, I had a very unpleasant experience. Once, when I was going to the interior, I saw a jeep approaching us and was told this was the vehicle of Ghulam Sarwar; the latter had been associated with the riots. The jeep blocked our path and some persons started interrogating us, 'Where are you going?' I indicated that I was going to distribute relief material. I had two boys with me, carrying clothes, medicines, and so on, and also armed guards. The people in the jeep were very aggressive and would not let me go. Later, a local MLA came along and threatened that I could go alone, but not with my boys. I put forth my views very strongly and would not back down. He swore that I would not be allowed to go to the villages in the future. On that occasion I did go and I distributed the relief material. But when I returned, I immediately sent a report to Gandhiji and Professor Nirmal Bose.[3] I had noted that this time, it was the local Muslim leaders who were unwilling to allow us to go. The local leaders, like that MLA, and, of course, Ghulam Sarwar's men, were afraid of us. If we took volunteers, they suspected them. We went during the daytime, we could not make out when these opponents were going into the villages. Probably at the dead of night—we met them while they were returning. I met Sucheta Kripalani and apprised her of the situation as well. Her advice was that all the relief material should be kept in the office of the Congress, or of the Noakhali Rescue and Relief Committee. As I was talking to Sucheta Kripalani, my attention was attracted by an inconspicuous khadi-clad gentleman. He introduced himself as Dr. Nripen Bose, a worker of Abhay Ashram. He told me that they had established a camp at Baralia village in the Ramganj thana. He advised me to bring the relief material packed in such a way that we would not require vehicles and it could be distributed, if need be, by his volunteers.

We were beginning to feel quite frustrated at this time. We did little more than distribute relief material. We did not really get a chance to talk to the affected villagers. We never found the abducted girls. How well organized the villagers were! Where had they taken the girls, where had they hidden them? Had they taken them to other villages, to other houses? There was no way for us to know. The local people did not trust us, nobody told us anything. And if ever a girl did return, she claimed that she had escaped unscathed. No girl was ready to admit to being raped simply because of the fear of social stigma. At the time there was so much public uproar over this issue of abduction that all over the country, people were willing to take these tortured girls back. There was strong denunciation of forced conversion. Rigid orthodox customs like 'purification' were being thrown to the winds. There was a wave of sympathy and compassion for the sufferers. Young men wrote to us, offering to marry them. But in reality, few of these girls returned. If they did, they always claimed that they had escaped being tortured. I know of only one case, where a young policeman married an abducted girl. He said, 'It wasn't her fault!' They married, and lived happily. I met them many years later in West Bengal and was delighted to see that they had such a happy marriage. But that was the only case I know of a marriage of an abducted girl.

Notes

[1] The British wife of J. M. Sengupta, a leader of the Bengal branch of the Indian National Congress, who had made India her home. She was later elected the

leader of the Bengal Congress. After Partition, she lived on in East Pakistan and became a member of the East Pakistan National Assembly.

2 On 16 Aug 1946, M.A. Jinnah as leader of the Muslim League called for Direct Action Day to establish the demand for Pakistan. The protest soon turned into a wide-ranging massacre of Hindus while the Mulsim League government of Bengal and the British authorities took no steps to restore law and order.

3 A well-known pioneering Indian anthropologist who worked as Gandhiji's secretary at one time.

Sixteen

Living and Working in Noakhali

After a month of making these short tri ps, distributing relief material, trying to discover the condition of the people and rescuing abducted girls, we began to feel that all our labour was sim ply in vain. Perhaps we did manage to rescue an abandoned infant or send an elderly woman to a home. But we were unable to prevent people from leaving their villages or to persuade the evacuees to return. Quite disheartend, we wrote to Gandhiji and got permission to meet him in Sriram pur, where he had established his cam p in a burnt-down house. I went there accom panied by my husband, my colleague Phullarani and her husband, Ranen babu. We told him how we wanted to do justice to our work, but felt we were achieving nothing at all. Bapu gave us a patient hearing. Then he said that working for a few days, then returning home, would bring no results. Any sort of work that one undertook, must be done with com plete concentration and involvement. So, if we thought that we would do the work without our wholehearted commitment and smugly collect the total rewards, we were mistaken. We must go and live in the villages and give moral support to the villagers. Only if we ourselves had the courage to face the dangers of the situation, and lived continuously in the villages over an extended period of time, would the local people be assured about our commitment and return to live in their own homes. For, courage, like fear, was contagious. Just a single example of a courageous deed would act like a beacon of hope and would arouse the bravery and self-confidence of the local people.

I told Bapu that my husband and I were unable to agree upon my future course of action because of our little daughter who was less than two years old. Gandhiji suggested that we should be ready to take our children to the village with us. If we went to stay there with our own children, we would be able to convince the villagers that nobody could harm them without first harming us. This would prove our sincerity. Gandhiji warned us that we must have real courage, for any false bravado would immediately be detected by the villagers. They would see through us and despise us. We could go to the Harijan villages, as few workers had gone to those areas. He told us that we could work under Thakkar Bapa, the President of the Harijan Sevak Sangh, who was looking after the relief work in the Harijan villages.

It was my husband who now expressed reluctance. He said my life was obviously my own and should I wish to endanger it for the sake of the country, there could be no objection to it. But did I have the right to endanger our daughter's life? Mahatmaji's eyes twinkled wickedly. He said to me, 'See what your Lord and Master says!' My husband at once offered to put an end to the controversy by giving up his official duties and joining our work. But Gandhiji said, 'Now I require only your wife.' Then, Bapu himself settled our differences in his inimitable way. He said that at this age, a child needed her mother more than her father and thus our daughter must go with me. My husband was speechless! After prolonged discussions, it was decided that I would take along a young playmate for Kasturi with me, who would stay in the camp with her during the times I had to be away. There would be many others working with me and

I would not find it difficult to take care of my daughter. Until my job was completed successfully, I would not think of returning home.

My husband had never stopped me from working for the relief and rehabilitation of the victims of the riots. Instead, by taking the responsibility of Partha and Kunta, and for my official correspondence, he made it possible for me to be away from home for this long period. But he was naturally anxious about my well-being and now, the worries about Kasturi became an additional burden. However, he bore it very well. Whenever he had some leave, he would try to visit me, or, if he did not have enough time, at least, to go as far as Thakkar Bapa's camp to see the situation for himself.

Phullarani and I took our youngest children and went off to camp. First, we went to Parbatinagar. Soon things fell into a routine. We would get out in the morning after a good breakfast. We would carry some relief material and select a house in a locality that acted as our base for the day. We would meet the family of the houseowner, then go around to other houses and meet the other families. We returned in the evenings and held prayer meetings. At this time, many distinguished people visited our camps. We knew Kamala Dasgupta had come to Noakhali, we heard that Bina Das was expected. I would plan and prepare our tour-charts. Phulla and I worked for more than a month in Parbatinagar and Majupur. We found that most of the locals were weavers. Their houses had been burnt, their looms destroyed. They had been attacked in such a way that it would be difficult for them to be rehabilitated, to start working again. It was terrible.

I felt it would be better to set a base for myself, from where I could do more constructive work. After a while I met Thakkar Bapa and with his blessings, set up camp in a Harijan village called Tumchar, with my colleague Sneharani Kanjilal. The most prominent family were the Talukdars. I went to meet them. What a charming house they had! A large central courtyard was flanked on either side by six rooms. A large pond lay at the back of the house, with a path leading to it, and adjoining it, screened-off bathing areas. Their kitchen was to one side of the house. We built our camp next to the pond. We put up a kitchen for our use near the pond and screened off our own bathing-hut. We dug three trench-latrines, one for the men, one for the women, and one more for visitors. Our camp had quite a few workers. We followed Gandhiji's method. Each latrine had sand and ash piled up. After use, one would dig them up, so that the ground was covered by a fresh layer of soil and there would be no flies or dirt. During my schooldays, we had learnt to make similar trench-latrines in our Girl Guide training. So, that training came in useful again, after so many years.

Labanyalata Chanda, who was working with Abhay Ashram, sent us a camp box which would have put Robinson Crusoe to shame. From string and rope to candles, a torch, a saucepan, a knife, a pair of scissors, a mosquito net, some sugar, tea leaves and milk powder, soap, towels, medicines and a First Aid kit—even a small shovel that we found very useful for digging our trenches—everything was so neatly packed in it that we were not inconvenienced at all. Labanyalata Chanda was at this time, the sanchalika or organizer of the Kasturba Gandhi National Memorial Trust. She was running a school in Comilla, and many people were sending their young daughters and wives to Comilla. They believed the women would be safer there than in the villages. In spite of the uproar all over the country and promises of support, nobody believed that abducted girls could be rehabilitated at that time.

Our arrival in Tumchar seems to have given the local Hindus some courage. The Talukdars showed us where a cow had been slaughtered in their house, where beef had been cooked, which they had been forced to eat. The young girls of their family had been all sent away. Though the local Hindus were gradually feeling a little encouraged by our presence, they did not have either physical or psychological strength. There was no stock of food—everything had been looted. There was no place to work and earn something. We saw that the family with whom we stayed had only the fish of the pond, and nothing else. Plenty of relief material was coming at this time, through the Union Board as well as through the AIWC or the Congress and other organizations. We distributed whatever was needed in our area, and also sent the extra material to other areas. We were not only giving material to persons affected by the riots, but also to the Muslim poor. We had a doctor in our team. We had begun to rebuild the destroyed houses. A lot of work was being done. There were about 33 different organizations working in Noakhali at this time, and we coordinated our efforts through Noakhali Rescue and Relief Committee so that each one of us took up a separate line of activity.

At this time, I wrote a letter to Sachin Mitra, the Secretary of the Harijan Sevak Sangh, saying that I felt we were unable to win the confidence of the people. They were repairing their houses, but they seemed unable to make up their minds to stay. They were merely biding time. The two communities had made no overtures to each other. We found that Hindus came and attended our prayer meetings, because they were hoping to get something. But Muslims did not care to come to them at all, or their attendance was lackadaisical. Muslims were very suspicious of us. They seemed to think all our work was only for the Hindus.

At all times, I tried to keep Gandhiji informed about our activities. The few meetings I had with him, the hours spent in his company, are unquestionably a treasured chapter in my own life. I was able to witness not just his moral strength and courage, but many other facets of his character, some amusing, some even disconcerting for us. Gandhiji was a stickler for discipline. His famous pocket-watch was a source of terror for all of us. Woe betide us if we were late for a task or an appointment scheduled for a particular hour! Similarly, his legendary passion for cleanliness also kept us on our toes. He had set certain standards for the toilets in our camps. Once, while visiting the camp of Bijoynagar in Lakshmipur Thana, he found that the arrangements were less than satisfactory. How sorrowful he was, that his own workers had fallen short of his demands on cleanliness! How could they teach others if they themselves remained ignorant, he lamented.

Much has been already written about Gandhiji's spare and very selective diet and the problems it created for those who looked after him, and, indeed, I myself have experienced this. During his visit to Bijoynagar, Kamala Dasgupta, who was in charge of the camp, found she was unable to procure nanny goats which would provide milk for Bapu's consumption. So I was asked to take along two or three nanny goats with their kids from Tumchar to solve the problem. With great difficulty, I managed to persuade some people to let me have two goats and their kids for the duration of his stay. Then came the job of transporting two full-grown goats and four kids to Bijoynagar, nine miles away. Sneha and I went on foot, accompanied by a man carrying the kids in a basket on his head, and another leading the nanny goats. What a sight our party must have been! We realized this humorous angle after being repeatedly stopped and questioned on the way. Once we reached Bijoynagar, I was determined to photograph Gandhiji with the goats. As soon as he realized my intention, he started running, and I could not get a proper shot of him with the goats. Gandhiji laughed with child-like glee. 'So, you want to photograph me with goats!' he said. 'Why not?' I asked. 'They are yours; after all, you are drinking their milk!'

In our early days in Tumchar, for a month we studied the Koran with a maulavi who wanted us to understand the principles of Islam. He was a follower of Gandhiji, and I later saw him at a prayer meeting. Describing Islam as a religion of peace, he told Sneha and me that according to Gandhiji's principles, everyone must respect the religion of others, but how could we respect Islam if we did not know its tenets? This seemed logical to us, so we agreed to study the Koran under his tutelage. Sneha and I got up early in the morning, walked a mile or so to the maulavi's house and began our study from seven-thirty in the morning. My husband however was not so ready to approve of my action. He wrote to me saying that some orthodox Muslims had written to Gandhiji saying that no non-Muslims had the right to read the Koran. Since I was surrounded by fanatics, he was worried that our seemingly harmless and conciliatory move might be misinterpreted and I might find myself in the middle of a dangerous controversy. Thankfully, nothing like that occurred.

After that month of study, I came to the conclusion that the *Hadith* was rather didactic. In the *Hadith,* one is told what to do and no one can use his or her discretion. In Hinduism, one can follow any of the various paths of worship, or meditation, or nothing at all, whatever one desires. But in Islam, one must follow its precepts quite rigidly. Women must follow purdah. Men too have to abide by many set rules. That did not appeal to me. The thought that one cannot make up one's own mind, or decide for oneself what is acceptable and what one wants to discard, did not appeal to me. For exam ple, my mother had observed purdah in Jai pur in her youth. But I also knew many Muslim officers who did not enforce it in their homes. So, I always felt that the freedom of choice should lie with the individual and that a person should follow his or her own conscience, not be dictated to. Of course, I realized that at the time when the *Hadith* was com posed, social conditions had made it necessary for Hazrat Muhammed to im pose these diktats perhaps to protect women..Hindu society too was in dire need of further reform. It was dominated by tremendous orthodoxy and narrow-mindedness, which had resulted in its decay, and in spite of many reforms, I could see the drawbacks in front of my own eyes. Even now, many Hindus did not accept the girls we had rescued, if the slightest suspicion of rape occurred in their minds.

In certain areas, the Koran has given more rights to women that what the Hindus have, such as the right to property, to trade, to a part of their paternal property, and so on. Hindu women only got such rights after Partition, after the enactment of the personal law governing Hindu society. Each religion has bound the womenfolk within its purview to some extent, and the only way out for them is the Common Civil Code. Parsi women were always ahead and since independence Hindu and Christian women too have progressed greatly. The only way Muslim women can do the same is by stepping out of the shackles of Muslim personal law or the Shariat.

Islam does give women full control over the household, but the woman is always subordinated to the man. This is not unlike our traditional Hindu joint family, where the head of the house decides the future career of the younger generation, or the marriages or other major decisions. The subordination of women was very much present among the Muslim women in the villages too. But as we went round the villages, we discovered that they were very free among themselves.

They talked to us quite freely. They often asked us, 'Why have you come here?' 'To talk to you, to get to know you,' we replied. 'Would your people marry one of us?' they quipped.

Three months passed in this way. We organized medical teams, rebuilt houses, set about repairing roads, communicated with the local people and wrote our reports. We visited villages and camps, we held meetings. At that time, Gandhiji was staying in Haimchar. Before the end of February 1947 he called a meeting of the workers in the Harijan villages. He would hear our reports and decide which way to go after that. Sucheta Kripalani picked us up in her car and we started out for Haimchar in the morning, thinking that we had plenty of time in hand. But disaster struck when the wheels of our car got stuck in the slushy mud of a road under construction, and the Muslim construction workers realized that we were relief workers and simply refused to help us. At last, a road supervisor who had known me earlier, spotted me, and organized some men to help us. But by the time the car was pulled out of the mud and we were on our way again, it was very late. We did not manage to reach in time and Gandhiji was very displeased with us. We learnt that he was now moving onto Bihar. We were so disappointed. We had wanted to show him all the work we had been doing in the camps: the construction of the new houses, the cleaning of ponds, the building of roads. His presence was a major source of inspiration and reassurance for us. Bapu saw our distress and tried to console us by promising that he would soon return. His work in Noakhali was now complete, he said. He advised us to continue in the way we were doing.

Some of the advice Gandhiji gave us that day, has remained fresh in my mind even today. He said, 'You women must be like Mirabai. If, like her, you truly believe that the path you have chosen is the rightful path, then you will also take everyone around you on that path. You will never look back.' Giving us the example of Kasturba, he said, 'It is through sacrifice and self-discipline that our bond became deeper. I have often heard her say that the happiness she felt when we were together was far exceeded by the deep happiness she felt in our being involved in the same course of activity.' I can never forget that by removing us from the narrow, self-centred sphere of family life and flinging us into the world of social work, Gandhiji showed us how women could fulfil both our duty towards the family and responsibility towards society without creating a conflict. If a conflict were to rise, then it would be our mission to walk undeterred upon our chosen path, overcoming all obstacles and difficulties.

Seventeen

In Noakhali without Gandhiji

I recall that when my stay at Bijoynagar Camp was over, I left for my own camp, Tumchar, on foot. That pleased Gandhiji very much. He always told us that if we had to work for the villagers, we should live like them. He blessed me whole-heartedly. We did see him again before he went away to Bihar on 1 March 1947. By this time, riots had started in Bihar. Muslims were being killed there in the same way in which Hindu had been butchered in Noakhali. It was a retaliatory movement, an act of reprisal. Gandhiji had received a letter from one Syed Ahmed Khan, asking him to go and see for himself what the situation was like. He met us on 28 February and left for Bihar the next day and could not come back to Noakhali again.

I reached Tumchar Camp to find that a Government Order had arrived advising that the relief officer would distribute the compensation money in cash for the riot victims in March. I immediately went to Lakshmipur, where I met many other colleagues. We were all worried about the extremely vague terms of the Order.

The Muslim League government of Bengal would give every household 250 rupees per holding as com pensation, and 200 rupees to every weaver, fisherman or peasant for his tool and im plements, of course, on the furnishing of proof. It seemed to us that this order was most unsatisfactory, given the nature of the Hindu joint family. So next day, I went to Noakhali. I wanted to meet Mr. Akhtaruzzaman, ICS, and Additional District Magistrate, to explain the loopholes in the order and get a proper official briefing on the terms, so that no affected person was left without proper com pensation. I had to wait the whole day as he was on tour. But, though he returned late at night, he courteously heard me out, and typed the necessary document himself, then and there. In all the years of my life, I have rarely seen such a sincere and efficient officer.

We made a brief visit to Kazirkhil Cam p which was managed by Satishchandra Dasgupta,[1] hoping to persuade him to bring Gandhiji to our side before he went to Comilla. Satishbabu used to direct Gandhiji's movements. But we learnt that Bapu's route had already been fixed and could not be changed. In spite of the failure of our mission, it was extremely instructive to visit such a highly efficient and well-run cam p and to see for ourselves Satishbabu's innovative filtration plant for filtering water.

Back in Tumchar, I had the pleasure of a sudden visit from my husband and Mr. Kanjilal, my colleague's husband. The Talukdar family, with whom we shared our kitchen, was very excited and most anxious to provide the best possible food they could. Ultimately, they killed two ducks and I had to leave all my work to cook the meat! When I asked my host why he was making such a fuss for the sake of the two husbands, when nothing special was ever done for us, he replied, 'Ma, you are our very own, but these are guests!' After a grand dinner, we had our usual prayer meeting, where many voices joined in to sing. When Sneha Kanjilal sang '*Moder Garab, Moder Asha,*' the crowd, mostly peasants and villagers, joined in enthusiastically. The next day, we moved to Charamandal, where the relief officer would come to disburse the com pensation. Thakkar Bapa had a cam p here. After he left, it was managed by Bina Das Bhoumik. It was a Harijan (Namashudra) village. We all sat together in their huge kitchen for a meal—an excellent meal of dal, rice, fried and curried koi fish. Once again, my husband and Mr. Kanjilal received special treatment. As the two of them left for Chittagong, their parting shot was, 'You live in great style, we find! This is like a picnic!'

That very day, Mr. Rahman, the relief officer arrived, bag in hand, with another hanging from his shoulder. A canopy had been set up and one by one, the members of each holding were called, their goods and belongings including cattle, and so on, were enumerated and the compensation was given. Our workers were there with their own lists, checking carefully so that nobody was left out. The Union Board members were also keeping an eagle eye on the proceedings.[2] Mr. Rahman returned with us to Tumchar that night, and the same work continued there the next day. Even now, suspicion and mistrust, hatred and crookedness were in evidence. Those who had suffered were quite skeptical about the real goodwill of the Muslim League government. The President of the Union Board had enormous clout—he could even cancel holdings. This had happened in my camp, in the case of a widow. The President refused to recognize her claims, saying that the surviving family members would look after her. But she had had a room, she had also possessed a cow. It was her cow that had been killed, then cut up, and fed to the family as a symbol of conversion. We took up her case vigorously, and ultimately, they were forced to backtrack. The relief officer gave her compensation, which had created quite an uproar then. Thanks to Akhtaruzzaman Sahib's order, the compensation was given quite fairly.

Gradually, with the resources in hand, a few huts began to be mended, with some new sheets of tin, some old, burnt material, some bamboos. Both Thakkar Bapa and I had noted in our reports that these so-called low-caste Hindus were hard-working, peace-loving and God-fearing. They had been terribly distressed by forced conversion, the brutalities perpetrated on them and the abuse of their women. They might tell us their woes secretly, but they would not go to the police station—where nobody took their statements, where they were threatened with reprisals. Moreover, in these terrible months, they had become extremely weak, both physically and mentally. After the destruction of their homes and families, they had been unable to earn a living, just somehow managed to survive. All the while, they were traumatized by insecurity and the fear of further attacks by the majority community of Muslims. Most of the Hindus were so weak physically that they could do no hard labour. We found that when we looked for men to carry our heavy sacks of rice, or to row our boats, or for road-building, the Hindu men were quite unable to bear the burden of hard work. In contrast, their Muslim neighbours were strong and hefty and, therefore, they were hired and received the substantial wages for labour. No wonder, the Hindus still felt nervous. On the other hand, inflammable speeches were often made by the majority community. There were many incidents that pointed to the harassment of the minority community of the Hindus, such as making a road right through the middle of the arable field of one Gouranga Sarkar, at the insistence of the Union Board President.

I had found countless such instances during my survey. From the morning, I would start visiting villages and localities according to my list. Entering houses, of both communities, I would talk to the womenfolk, try and find out how they were, the condition of the children, and so on. In Hindu families, there were hardly any women or children around. In Muslim families, the women sometimes com plained that we worked only for *them*, that is, the Hindus. We explained that we went first to whoever had been affected by the riots, but we also gave clothes, medicines and other necessary items to the Muslim households. We offered to send our cam p doctor and help them in other ways. We found that even if the Muslim women sometimes took up our offer, the men were supremely indifferent to our appeals for peace. As for the Hindu women, they were so happy to see us, so embarrassed that they had nothing special to offer us. They would offer us the fresh coconuts from their trees. When we declined, they said, '*They* take them anyway, without asking, and we are too scared to say anything. It would make us happy if *you* took them!'

We remained in our relief camps for three more months. We were working as before. But the work of fostering communal harmony just did not make much progress. We wanted people to come back to their homes and live in peace. We wanted to see the establishment of communal harmony, the feeling of amity between Muslims and Hindus. Gradually we realized that it was not going to succeed. I have often wondered, why was it so? The violent hatred, mistrust and anger, these were not one-sided. There was hatred on both sides, ill feeling on both sides. We might be eating, working, sleeping and living together, and yet this mistrust persisted. This was because of a basic distance between the two communities–a distance caused by the orthodoxy that existed in both communities. These obdurate, negative attitudes were present in both, only one side could not be blamed. Isn't this where human beings can make a difference? I often wondered then if someone were being murdered in front of me, would I stop to ascertain whether the victim were Hindu or Muslim, or would I rush to save the person regardless of her or his faith and creed? And the answer was obvious. Faith and creed were not important to me in the face of her identity as a human being. It was at this time that I really understood what 'human rights' meant. Why could we not think of human rights, why could we not observe certain simple humanitarian principles? It was so obvious that our failure was wreaking havoc on our country.

Now I began to understand what my mother wrote about: why the physical violence that men perpetrated on women was psychologically so destructive for women. Why so many women refused to admit that they had been physically tortured. Most women do not want to admit such nightmares–they want to forget them. I had stayed in a house where a young woman with such experiences constantly reiterated that she had escaped, she had hidden submerged among the plants and hyacinths covering the pond. She would not admit the truth and nor would the family. Firstly, there was embarrassment. Then, there was the fear that the neighbours and others would ostracize them or force them to send the woman away. And this was true in most of the cases of abduction. Only about 25 percent of the girls who returned admitted to physical torture. But whether they admitted it or not, their distress was there for all to see. It was extremely upsetting that we could do very little for these traumatized young girls and young women. We could provide some physical relief for those in the camps. But what could we do about their agonized, traumatized minds? What they really needed was counselling, but only those who would admit the truth could be counselled. Those who denied it could not be counselled.

As I have said earlier, When a young girl had been abducted and violated, whether she was thirteen or fourteen or twenty-four or twenty-five or older, she often disavowed her traumatic experiences and was accepted by her family, by society. In such cases, I felt that the situation was positive. It was in the countless other cases, where the families rejected a girl who had been abducted and raped, or where such a girl was unable to overcome her trauma, that both the girl and her family needed counselling. Very rarely were we able to succeed in such situations. One case stands out in my memory as a bright example, which too I have mentioned earlier. In a village, a Hindu couple, a young man and his wife, came to us. The girl told us that even two months after the communal riot, she was being taken away every night, sexually abused, and returned the next morning. Their very fear for each other's safety kept the two from reporting the case. They absolutely refused to file a case in the thana. Finally, there was no way out for them and they escaped from the village. What I found very heart-warming, was the fact that the husband did not abandon the girl. He kept repeating, 'It's not her fault, what is she to do?' And what about all those who never came back—not to their homes, not even to the relief camps or thanas? We shuddered to think of their fate. We had been able to do nothing for them.

As the summer approached, our schedule became more busy. In those days, we had no cars or jeeps and I would be walking eight to nine miles from one village to another, often carrying Kasturi. Once we had gone to visit a work-centre in a village in Ramganj Thana. I had taken Kasturi along with me that day as we had a vehicle with us. I left her with a family and went off on my survey work. The womenfolk of the family, all elderly, were delighted to have her with them since they had sent all their young girls away. I went round and saw the new building that had been built in place of the school building which had been burnt down, the new looms, sewing machines, and so on. Everything was ready, but there were no students or young people left in the village to take advantage of the work-centre. It took us all day to complete our survey. It was evening by the time we returned to the village. We all climbed into the car and set off merrily. After going a little way, it was the driver who reminded me, 'Ma, you haven't fetched your daughter!' We turned back to fetch her and I was very embarrassed at the amusement of my colleagues Pyarelal and Bhupen Dutta. As for my child's hosts, they had heard the car going away and were quite prepared to look after Kasturi for a long time if I had really abandoned her!

As my workload increased, I could not be as regular in writing to my husband as earlier, and rarely had time to write to my elder children. My husband's letters reflected his anxiety over the fact that the two elder ones were deprived of their mother's attention and care. In one letter he wrote that if I returned to find my children thin and weak or if Kunta's skin had become dry or Partha had a bad cough, I shouldn't blame him, as he couldn't possibly take care of my children properly, all alone! He wrote that he would watch them carefully to observe whether they were depressed by my absence. Of course, they were occasionally upset by it. I got a letter from my elder daughter, written in her childish hand, scolding me for being a naughty mother, entreating me to come back, sending me a thousand pranams in return for the promise to return. Partha was older and more aware of the situation in the country. From my husband's letters, I came to know that he occasionally went to political meetings and was forming his own opinions. My husband once wrote that Partha appeared a little depressed, which worried me.

As for himself, my spouse was battling with loneliness in my absence as well as struggling to check his growing anxiety about me, given the political situation of the country. On 9 February 1947, he wrote, 'As the days go by, I am getting pessimistic, for the situation in the country is gradually getting worse. I don't know whether you have access to newspapers, but if you read them you'll know that the policies of the Muslim League can catapult the country into a civil war at any moment.' Naturally, my being in Noakhali was a source of extreme worry for him. He warned me against being thoughtless and impulsive and against taking risks. He even wrote that if I did not immediately promise to obey his instructions, he would be forced to resign from his duties and join me in Tumchar Camp! He worried about me over-working, about my health, about my walking long distances every day. Having seen our camp for himself, he worried about the primitive conditions in which little Kasturi lived. Increasingly, his letters reflected a deep unhappiness about our forced separation, and the uncertainty over how long it would continue. He repeatedly wrote that he felt an awful sense of guilt at living a life of physical comfort when I was bearing such hardship in the camp. This was indeed one of the most difficult periods in our marriage. Never did my husband stop me from my work, or question my involvement in it. On the contrary, he did all sorts of work for me, like looking after my official correspondence. Moreover, he smilingly bore the responsibility of looking after Partha and Kunta on his own. Yet, there was a deep undercurrent of dissatisfaction with our present arrangements that was very evident in his letters. Once, he wrote that he felt like just leaving everything and coming away to join me! As for me, my worry and anxiety for the other half of my family were not any less, but my intensely busy life and my deep commitment to Gandhiji's words made me determined to complete my work and not think of returning home as yet.

In mid-April, there was an outbreak of cholera in our area. Dr. Palit, who used to stay in Ramanandi village, was unfortunately a victim. I went to Dattapara to collect medicines and request that a team of doctors should be sent to carry out inoculation and treatment in my area. The doctor there told me that they had just returned from a trip and they would only be ready to go with me the next day. But I had left my daughter Kasturi in the camp and I rushed back. The next day, the medical team arrived with the supplies.

While we were busy managing the cholera epidemic, repairing old houses and building new ones, sinking tube-wells, getting the villagers their new charkas, their fishing nets and steadily rehabilitating them, unknown to us certain political changes were occurring in Delhi. We did not have radios nor did we have access to newspapers. We were as if cut off from both Delhi and Calcutta. As a result, we did not realize exactly what was going on in the corridors of power. We had no clue that the country would be divided, that Pakistan would come into existence, that one would not be able to enter the other country without a passport. When we first heard the news, we could not comprehend it. How could this be? Perhaps I was like the one-eyed deer—I was so busy dealing with the problem in front of me that I had no time for reality! I sent my reports to Sucheta Kripalani regularly. When she heard about the outbreak of cholera in my area, she wrote to my husband from Delhi,

> 'Ashoka is unable to understand. The Partition is inevitable. You must bring her and your child back from Tumchar. I will tell Bapu.'

In May, we received the news that my husband had been transferred to Calcutta in order to work for the Partition Committee. He would have to leave for Calcutta. How would Partha and Kunta manage all alone in that vast house in Chittagong? I was desperately needed in Chittagong. I sent a telegram to Sucheta Kripalani to come and attend to the remaining details of winding up the camp. When Gandhiji heard of this, he told her that I could be persuaded to stay on for some more time. Sucheta apparently told him that she knew I would never have contacted her but for an emergency. I had by this time built up a wonderful relationship with Sucheta, whom I admired very much. Even now, I consider her to be the most remarkable woman amongst the many outstanding women I have worked with. She was very sincere and unswerving in her commitment to her country, and she never spared herself while performing her duties. Her self-sacrifice and unselfishness were tremendously inspiring to the rest of us.

At last, I too set about packing, to leave for Chittagong. I had been living in the camp for almost seven months and it was not a small job, distributing all the material left with me, the clothes, medicines, everything. We were still sinking tube-wells in some villages. We had more or less completed the task of inoculation, and my area was comparatively safe now. Most of the camps were being closed. The Noakhali Rescue, Relief and Rehabilitation Committee was winding up many camps. Abhay Ashram was only keeping its Dattapara centre and sending its other volunteers away. Kazirkhil Camp of Satishchandra Dasgupta was one the of the very few camps to continue functioning. On my last day, Sarat Talukdar, the head of the family with whom I had been staying, came to see me off at the ferry jetty. Many pairs of eyes were full of tears that day. This sorrow was something we would have to learn to live with.

Notes

1 He lived and worked like Gandhiji, following his ways so faithfully that he dressed and walked like him and was known as 'Banglar Gandhi' (Bengal's Gandhi).

2 The police stations were divided into unions where people's representatives and nominated members and circle officers (civil servants) sat every month to consider the needs of the area, somewhat like today's panchayat, though the latter is an elected body.

Eighteen

The Partition

As Partition loomed ahead, men like my husband who were government officers, that is, who ran the administration of undivided India under the British, were asked to opt for either independent India or the newly created nation of Pakistan with its two wings separated by India: East Pakistan (old East Bengal) and West Pakistan (that also contained West Punjab, the old state of Punjab being divided between the two new countries). My husband decided to opt for West Bengal, and thus India. Neither of us imagined that Partition would create such a gulf, such a total divide between people who had earlier lived as part of one large diverse society consisting of Hindus and Muslims and many other smaller communities like Parsis, Jains, Sikhs, Christians, and so on. The Partition Committee began to divide up the property, the country, the districts, the population. Most Muslim government officials opted for Pakistan, many Englishmen also chose to stay there. Others like my husband chose India. Those who were leaving packed for their new destination, while those who had chosen to remain, helped them in many ways. All hearts were heavy. The residents of Nandan Kanan, Andarkilla and the Brahmo Samaj area of Chittagong, who had opted to remain, were all worried about their future. Amidst my packing, I was busy organizing little details, such as money for those children whom I had rescued and sent to Prabartak Sangha as I did not want them to get into difficulties after my departure.

As I completed our packing, Partha gleefully wrote out the labels, CHANDPUR TO KULPIGHAT-VIA-CHANDBALI. In between chores, we looked up old friends, comrades, relatives. God knew when, if ever, we would meet again. Many people invited us for a last meal together. Mrs. Karim, the wife of the district magistrate, said, 'You'll be leaving on the third or fourth of August? Will you take your meals on that final day with us?' I suggested instead that if she could cook something and bring it to my house, I too would do the same, and then we could meet a much larger number of people for the last time. We arranged for another twenty or twenty-five families to join us. On that final day, we had the strangest possible farewell party. It was difficult to understand who was taking leave of whom, who was bidding farewell. My husband too had arrived that day. We gathered together in our house at the bottom of the hill Hindus, Muslims, Sikhs, English, civilians and army officers, a group truly representative of the diverse strands existing in this country, India. What a heart-rending occasion! Had anyone present there ever thought such an unimaginable situation would actually happen—something so painful, so heartbreaking? Mrs. Azim, the wife of the barrister, had made a cake for our journey. She came to the station to deliver it to us. That was the last time we boarded the steamer from Chandpur and sailed over the majestic Padma. Then we caught the train from Goalanda to Calcutta, travelling to an uncertain future.

When we reached Calcutta, there was no place to move to because of a delay in the allotment of our official quarters. I went to stay with my mother in 2D Kartik Basu Lane in north Calcutta. My husband put up in the house of a police officer, Pranab Kumar Sen, in Lalbazar, for in those dangerous times, there was so much violence on the streets that getting to his office at Writers' Building would have been difficult. Lalbazar was next door to Writers'. From 6 or 7 August 1947, there were continuous riots in Calcutta, in spite of Gandhiji's arrival in Calcutta on 7 August. On the night of 15 August, all this suddenly seemed to stop. Hindus and Muslims embraced in public, covered each other with attar, rode together in lorries. Gandhiji was staying in Hydari Manzil in Beliaghata, the large house of a prosperous Muslim family who had left for Pakistan. Suhrawardy and his ministers took Gandhiji by car to all the riot-affected areas, Beliaghata, Kankurgachi and Metiabruz under heavy police escort.[1]

I went to see Gandhiji at this time. It was difficult to get there because it was very dangerous to travel about. My husband was too busy with his duties to take me there, besides, he could not come all the way to Beliaghata from Lalbazar. Finally, on 8 or 9 August I went to see Gandhiji. Though he was weak and fasting, he was very happy to see me, and spoke as if he had suddenly felt very encouraged about the possibilities for peaceful coexistence. He asked us to organize a women's meeting. In spite of Partition, the Muslims must not leave India. That was his message. We could only organize this meeting after 16 August, when India and Pakistan were already independent. It was held in the University Institute, and the hall was absolutely crowded. Everyone had come in the hope of seeing Gandhiji. When the audience saw that Gandhiji had come in the company of Suhrawardy, the mood changed completely. There was such an outpouring of hatred, of scorn and contempt as I had never

Killarney Lodge, Darjeeling, 1975 ~ (from left) Narayani, Partha, Kasturi, Palti, Shaibal, Ashoka, Kunta; (in front row from left) Himadri (Partha's son), Srirupa and Nilanjana (Kunta's daughters)

(from left) Arun, Anju, Shakuntala (standing), Rita, Suhashini, Jyotirmoyee Devi, Bhashkar

Chittagong, 1946~Partha, Shakuntala, Kasturi

Rajshahi, 1936 ~ Shaibal Gupta

Hungerford Street, Calcutta, 1951~Family group from the extended family of Bhola with mother-in-law, eldest brother-in-law and eldest sister-in-law

Oxford, 1956~ Partha

1971, Apala

1957, Shakuntala

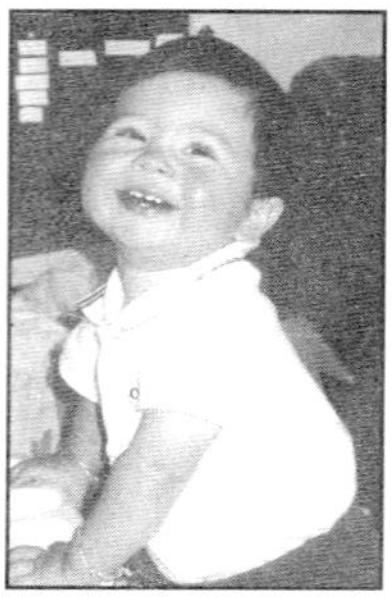

Robi David, great-grandson (Srirupa's son)

1948, Kasturi

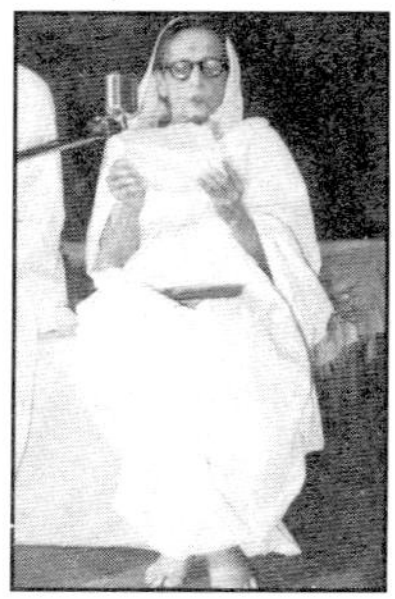

1973, Rabindra Purashkar ceremony, Jyotirmoyee Devi

Calcutta, 1999 - Narayani, Partha, Raghubir (Kasturi's son), Kasturi, Apala; (in front) Niharika (Partha's daughter), Conrad and John (Apala's sons)

THE NEW MEXICAN 5A
Friday, October 5, 1956

Girl Guide From India Visits Here

An interesting and interested visitor to Santa Fe this week was Mrs. Ashoka Gupta of Calcutta, India. Mrs. Gupta is state commissioner of the West Bengal Bharat Scout and Guides and a member of the national council of the Bharat Scout and Guides.

USA, 1956~Ashoka's visit to the USA reported in newspaper

USA, 1956~Ashoka (right) with others at a girl guide camp in western uniform

Ottakamund, 1932~Ashoka with others at a girl guide camp

Petrapolis, Brazil, 1962 - Ashoka at the International Conference of Social Work

1963 - Ashoka at Bhanshi camp, Dandakaranya, Madha Pradesh

West Bengal, 1961~Ashoka with Lady Baden Powel and others visiting a refugee camp

Calcutta, 1990~Ashoka with the All India Women's Conference Reception Committee

Maldah, 1962 - Ashoka beside (right) Swami Lokeshwarananda and others from the Samajkalyan Board

New Delhi, 1989, Parliament House ~Ashoka (at the podium) with Rajiv Gandhi, then Prime Minister (sitting second from left) and Shankar Dayal Sharma, then President (sitting third from left)

Noakhali, 1947~Bejoynagar Camp (left to right) Bela Mitra (5th), Shah Nawaz (6th), Jeewan Singh (9th), Kamala Dasgupta (7th), Sneha Kanjilal (8th), Ashoka Gupta and others

Noakhali, 1947~With Gandhiji's team (photograph taken by Ashoka)

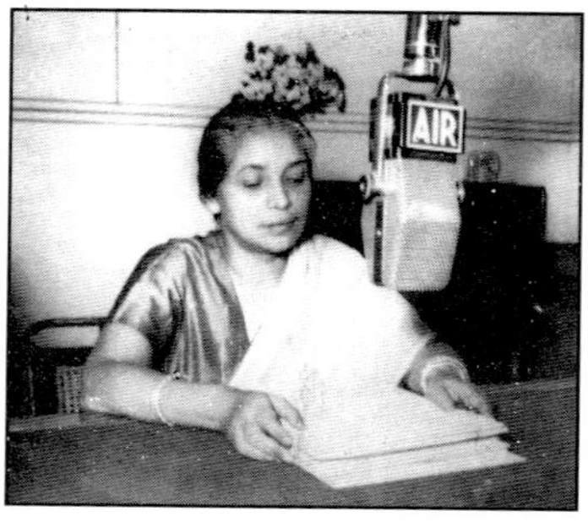

1953~Renuka Ray, then President of the All India Women's Conference and also an MP

seen before. Suhrawardy had been the chief minister of the Muslim League government of undivided Bengal when the massacres in Calcutta of Direct Action Day, 16 Aug 1946, and Noakhali, Oct 1946, had taken place. The women began to scream in anger. Gandhiji begged them to quieten down, but his appeals went unheeded. Dr. Maitreyi Bose, the labour leader, tried to calm the crowd, but she too failed. Suhrawardy was so terrified that he cowered behind Gandhiji. We tried to calm and bring about order by singing the familiar bhajans but we could not silence the crowd—nothing worked. With great difficulty, Gandhiji said a few words. He said that the only thing he wanted was Hindu-Muslim unity. This was why he had come. He said no Muslim should leave India and no Hindu should leave Pakistan. He said peace must be maintained in this land so that there might be peace across the border. After that he left the meeting. He gave us one last instruction: we should patrol the streets in groups. We need not go far. But we should try to ensure that every locality remained peaceful and that neither community indulged in acts of violence.

Most of my colleagues from Noakhali were here in Calcutta and we decided to have peace marches. Sachin Mitra said he was going to organize a peace march. On 1 September he was leading his peace march to the Nakhoda Mosque area with boys from his group of volunteers. Someone stabbed him with a knife. He was taken to Medical College Hospital immediately, but there was such profuse bleeding that he died two days later. On the day of his death, 3 September, it was raining so heavily that the city was waterlogged. We had been given a house next to Presidency General Hospital, an area that got flooded very quickly. There was so much water that it was difficult to get out of the house onto the street. Somehow I managed to reach the Medical College Hospital. I found Sachin's wife, Angshu, standing outside in the verandah. She told me he had just passed away.

The death of Sachin Mitra was a dreadful loss to us. I had known Angshu from our college days. Though she was a year senior to me, we had acted together in plays, and had become close friends. I had been a guest at their wedding. Then, during our days in Noakhali, I had come in very close contact with Sachin. I would often write letters asking for his advice: how should we proceed, how would we solve a particular problem, and so on. He was full of energy and enthusiasm, as well as idealism. He seemed to be a little like Subhas Bose. It was terrible that such a sincere, idealistic young man should die in this way. Angshu and Sachin had no children, and she would now be alone. Later she trained in the management of child-care programmes at Wardha from Asha Aryanayekam and worked as a schoolteacher. After Sachin Mitra's death, Gandhiji wrote to Angshu, 'Do not grieve. There is no solace for this grief. He has become a martyr, his death was a hero's death.' But that was no comfort to us.

Gandhiji now began a fast unto death. All the requests, entreaties, pleas of officials, ministers, party workers, ordinary men, could not make him break his resolution. At last, the rioters laid down their arms, and he was persuaded to end his fast. He was now a broken man, lost, his faith in human beings destroyed.

He said he would return to Noakhali, but that was not to be.

Communal riots broke out in Punjab. The two communities were now divided by tremendous suspicion, hatred and mistrust. Relationshi ps between the two had gone terribly wrong, and there was no meaningful communication between ordinary people on both sides. Now that Partition had taken place would anything change? What would be the political ramifications? In the villages of Noakhali I had mixed with everybody, talked to everyone, and the actual nature of the divide had not been not clear. I had no way of knowing that I would be shocked and deeply grieved by the subsequent events. That lay in the future. It was not quite so evident then. Those of us who had lived in East Bengal faced absolute, devastating changes after Partition, which was such an overwhelming phenomenon that it could not quite be grasped, let alone analysed. We sim ply floundered and groped in the dark. We were not really prepared for Partition, though it was not as if we were caught unawares. We knew that Partition would happen, that changes would occur. What we did not know was what form it would take–we could not conceptualize what life would now turn out to be. It was a time of panic and of paralysis. My husband was a government servant and we opted to be posted in West Bengal. But those who owned property in East Bengal, who had lived on the land of their forefathers for centuries, for them, leaving the land was unacceptable. As for those of us who had left old East Bengal and come to India because our fathers, husbands, brothers or sons had jobs in West Bengal, we had no houses or homes of our own to go to. Until an official quarter or housing was allotted to us, we had to put up with various relatives or friends, here and there.

Those who left East Bengal as refugees came almost empty-handed. Let me give the example of my husband's family, which consisted of six brothers and three sisters. The two eldest brothers, Utpal and Mrinal, decided to stay on in East Bengal; Mrinal remained in Banishol, while Utpal stayed on in the ancestral house in Bhola. The two middle brothers, Anil and my husband, were in government service and decided to opt for India. The two youngest brothers, Nirmal and Amal, were working in West Bengal and they remained here. In Bhola life was very different. Our family owned a lot of land in Bhola, and my younger brother-in-law used to look after the cultivation of the fields. A lot of grain was grown in the riverbed near Bhola. Practically all the paddy needed by the family was grown on our own land. Occasionally that rice would be sold and a better quality of rice would be bought from the markets for our use. Those who owned land were not dependent on others. They grew their own food, lived off the land, and on large properties, there were coconut palms, betel nut palms, plenty of fish in the ponds. Thus for middle class families there was no shortage of food and basic needs were fulfilled. People might have been short of ready cash, for instance, if someone was planning to make a trip somewhere, he might have to worry about getting hold of the necessary funds. In other words, there was enough space for everyone to live comfortably and there was more than enough food for all. As I have mentioned earlier, during the vacations, many people would gather there—all the brothers' wives, the married sisters with school-going children, older nieces and nephews. I recall time happily spent playing with the youngsters, or getting up plays and dramas. It was a unique way of life. Such a way of life, of close, easy family reunions, or even the life of a large extended family that had based its well-being on its land or some other property, was the casualty of the Partition. I did not quite understand what had happened in 1947 then. By the next year, another picture began to emerge, and I realized that a new way of life was taking shape.

The house we were given was opposite the Race Course, very spacious with about twenty rooms. Soon, the greater family converged there and I was managing a household of almost forty people! In 1948, my third eldest brother-in-law, Major General Anil Kumar Gupta, came to stay with us together with my mother-in-law. Then, my younger sister-in-law, Sulekha, who had lived in Dinajpur (now in East Pakistan), joined us with her little child because her husband worked for the LIC in Nadia. Then, Amal, the youngest brother-in-law who used to live in a mess came to live with us. The eldest nephew, Pronab, who was staying in the hostel of Presidency College also moved in with us. All in all, it seemed to me that my house, though not exactly a boarding-house, was one where a large wedding party had assembled. People had come from everywhere, just as they do for weddings, but the difference was that they stayed on! And of course, the largest share of the responsibility lay with me, for I had to organize their meals according to their tastes. In those days, rice, sugar and various other necessities were in short supply. So managing the kitchen required delicate juggling. I would instruct Sulekha to take care of the visitors, to preside over the vegetarian kitchen, and other duties. My husband would leave for office by eight. There were servants to help, but to arrange for the meals of such a large number of people was in itself a massive task, more so because of the strict traditions that were followed in those days. Then, there were other responsibilities: getting the children admitted to schools, or fixing up medical treatment for those who needed it. In those days these were quite onerous tasks and they all fell on my shoulders.

My most important duty at this time was to set up a stable home. Partha was admitted to Class Nine in Ballygunge Government School. Kunta went to Loreto House, a Catholic convent school. I was a little worried because she did not speak English and was told that she remained absolutely silent in class. She gradually picked it up quite well and had no problems in school. I would have liked to admit Kasturi to the nursery section in Loreto, but I could not afford the fees, which were twenty-five rupees. So she went to the nursery at Sakhawat Memorial School, where her monthly fee was one rupee! Himani's daughter, Ajapa, was also in the same nursery. It was quite convenient for us, really, because the school was close to our house. Bula, another niece, joined Sakhawat Memorial as well, and was admitted to Class Nine. The school routine now fell into place, with the children leaving by ten and returning by four.

Yet another heavy responsibility was now placed on me. I had come into contact with many people while working at Noakhali. Many of them like Dr.Prafulla Ghosh or the workers of Abhay Ashram or members of the Congress now joined the Government of West Bengal. I knew them well and they began to involve me in their work, which meant that I was busy with outside activities as well. A reception centre for refugees was set up in my house, and we began to record who was coming from where, where he or she would go, all particulars about each person–not like the record that refugees had to fill in at Sealdah Station. This was different. Someone known to us might be in some sort of trouble and arrive suddenly without warning. Someone might need medical aid, another might have come to look for a relative; in another case, the older couple had stayed back and had sent the youngsters–many such people came to our house. It was a floating population. People came there and stayed for a few days, while making enquiries about relatives or friends, or while looking for work. Most of them were young people without guardians and, in effect, we became their guardians.

East Bengal had become East Pakistan. The shape that society would finally take was still not clear. Many people were coming away. The passport system had still not been introduced. People were crossing over, but they had begun to face considerable harassment at the border. They were subjected to minute questioning, all their belongings were inspected, and they were made to give up their money and jewellery. As late as 1948 or 1949 talks were still going on about what people could bring and about passports. Yet by this time in Punjab the situation had become quite stable. Houses had been built, refugees had shelters over their heads. But in West Bengal there was nothing. No houses had been built for the newcomers. They were putting up with their relatives, but how long could such a system continue?

Between 1947 to 1949, there was no real influx of refugees to West Bengal as there was later. Many people did come, and they came to stay with families like ours, so they did not possess the characteristics of refugees. In truth they had come on 'reconnaissance missions' rather than to stay. They still had a part of their family in East Pakistan, they had come to explore the situation or to gauge opportunities and their chances of building up a new life, or to see how much help they would get. They were not entirely helpless, nor were they totally dependent on others. After the Noakhali riots of 1946, there was an increasing feeling of unease or uncertainty among the Hindus of East Bengal. Often, the women or the younger children might have been sent away to this side, which was felt to be safer. But Bengal was still not a house divided, as happened later. That is why the 'transfer of populations', that occurred in the two Punjabs, had not happened here. Many Muslim families remained in West Bengal, many Hindu families remained in East Pakistan. However, this situation changed in 1950.

Political trouble flared up during the years 1948 and 1949 in the milieu of refugee ingress into the country. The Communist Party tried in many ways to harass the new government and it was declared illegal. Many of the communists crossed the border into East Pakistan. We knew about this but it did not bother us very much, because after all, we were not working for a political organization. We were doing social service and trying to see whether the destitute could be supported in any way. It is difficult now to know exactly what went wrong. The correspondence between Nehru and Jinnah and the correspondence of people like Fazlul Haque or Suhrawardy point to the fact that seeds of distrust and fear still existed. But Nehru openly disclaimed such doubts and his views were echoed by the ministry of Prafulla Ghosh, the first chief minister of the state of West Bengal, who said Bengalis loved their hearth and home, they would not move! In 1950, however, steamers began to arrive with their macabre load of corpses, followed by the terrible riots of Barishal. This time, the Hindu Mahasabha became vocal and active here, as did the Muslim League in Pakistan.

At this time, there was some amount of correspondence between Nehru and Bidhan Chandra Roy, who succeeded Prafulla Ghosh as the chief minister, on this matter. Dr. Roy stressed that in spite of the comparative peace and harmony in Bengal, we too should be ready for all eventualities. But he and Prafulla Ghosh both reiterated that they were sure that there would not be an influx from the other side. But, suddenly, there was news of a riot. My experience of Noakhali in 1946 did not hold good this time. Despite the horrific communal riots the Hindus had not fled to West Bengal. The poor, tortured people of Noakhali were mostly Namashudras or Scheduled Castes. As cultivators, they were not willing to leave their land and go away. In 1949, we heard of riots in Khulna, we were extremely surprised . Khulna was a peaceful area, predominantly Hindu. What could have caused the riots there? Were the Hindus being forcibly evicted by the Muslims? Was there a plan to that effect? We had not begun to think in that way then. The refugees from Khulna reported being subjected to great violence, a tremendous degree of torment. Soon after these riots were controlled, we heard of incidents in Barishal. A whole steamer-full of Hindus had been tortured, their goods looted, and their women raped. Then people started escaping from Barishal. For Bengal, 1950 was a year of unmitigated horror. The authorities in East Pakistan, headed by Fazlul Haque did their best to control the situation there, as did Dr. Bidhan Roy, now the chief minister of West Bengal, here. They tried to start an open dialogue. Nehru and Liaquat Ali, the prime minister of Pakistan, too held talks and came to some sort of an understanding, which we call the Nehru-Liaquat Pact. This took place in 1950. It was hoped that the flow of refugees would be stemmed somewhat after that, and indeed this did happen: 1951 and 1952 were much quieter years. Then in 1953 about 3,00,000 to 4,00,000 people migrated to India, and a tremendous effort was made to manage the unprecedented crisis. A huge centre was set up at Sealdah Station.

Government organizations and many social workers of different institutions did what they could to feed and find shelter for these unfortunate people.

Moreover, the situation was uncertain because no one had an idea about how long the influx of refugees would continue in this way. After the Khulna riots, things suddenly took a political colour. There could be two kinds of riots: either spontaneous or instigated. The Khulna riots were certainly instigated. Many people now believe that the International Communist Party was behind them, though I have no idea what their motives might have been. Even in the case of the Noakhali riots and the Calcutta riots, we may say that there was instigation, though we did not realize the true situation at that time. Noakhali used to be a very peaceful area, neither was Calcutta particularly violent communally. Bihar had been quiet for a long time. The riots were instigated. The Muslim League leader Suhrawardy was to blame for the Great Calcutta Killing and Noakhali riots. In the case of Bihar, it was revenge, a sort of tit-for-tat. Perhaps it was more spontaneous than the others. But after 1950, the situation became very unstable and the refugee influx continued year after year, with 2,00,000 or 3,00,000, or even more, seeking shelter annually. We began to experience a crisis situation. There was no space anywhere. There were no facilities available. How were we to house and feed these lakhs?

My brother-in-law Mrinal, a lawyer in Barishal, had a leaning towards the Hindu Mahasabha. His wife decided to wind up her establishment in East Pakistan. Many others began to seek temporary shelter in our house. The situation in Sealdah Station was chaotic and Mira Dattagupta stepped in to set up an efficient system to help the incoming refugees. She more or less lived in the station, taking her baths and her meals there. She worked with the government relief officers who were also based at the station. They took statements from the refugees. Such work was also going on in the border areas. Members of the AIWC also went to work at Sealdah Station. A roster had been drawn up and we worked according to it. Leaders were appointed, and the volunteers worked in groups under those leaders, of whom Mira Duttagupta was one and Snehalata Kanjilal, who had been my working partner in Noakhali, was another. Charushila Dhar who hailed from Jessore was working in Bongaon and volunteers would be told to go and work under her supervision. This team work was very efficient, particularly as there was no political interference, no political overtones. We had no political affiliations at the AIWC. It was easy to work under those circumstances, and it was enjoyable as well. We were fortunate in receiving the guidance of Renuka Ray who was the minister in B. C. Roy's cabinet. Though Dr. Prafulla Ghosh ceased being chief minister after five months, Dr. Bidhan Chandra Roy, who had outstanding abilities, succeeded him—the post was now called chief minister—soon joined the rehabilitation effort. He had paid great attention to the task of refugee rehabilitation, and did everything with enormous care. Hiranmay Banerjee, ICS, was appointed the Relief and Rehabilitation Commissioner and he guided us at every step.

Notes

1 Vice Princi pal of Surendra Nath College, a dynamic activist and Congress worker who was also a member of the AIWC.

Nineteen

The Grief and the Trauma of Partition

East Bengal fascinated me on my very first visit. What a strange and beguiling country I found it to be. I loved seeing boats flashing through the waves, and I loved travelling by steamer. I would reflect on water and its relationshi p with land—so much water everywhere, and I would ask, did the trees too rise out of water? As I have said before, I found the names of the jetty stations to be quaint and amusing–Patarhat or Jhalkathi–what kind of names were these? My husband would ask what should names be like? Like Kanpur, or Jai pur or Mirzapur, I would reply laughingly, these are proper names. It was an altogether different land, so different from the drier places of North India where I had grown up. My enchantment with the rivers, the water, the water hyacinths–even now, those pictures float before my eye. The land is no longer ours. Why did that happen when it was very much the land of our forefathers!

My love for East Bengal, indeed my fascination with it, has continued to this day. Even now, aged nearly 93, I wish I could go back there! There was a pleasant relationshi p with friends and neighbours, a friendly social intercourse between the communities, which was sadly destroyed by the Partition, and which gives me immense pain now. I knew at first hand of the depth of attachment that bound the average East Bengali for his native land, his home, his fields. Yet at the time of Partition, communal hatred, or even distrust of the other community, was strong enough to im pel thousands of people to abandon their homes! We kept a record, which provides us with statistics of the people who were crossing the border, in 1950, in 1951, or in 1952. In many cases, whole families had crossed over, with the exception of the old parents, who had remained behind in order to protect the family home. Or a young brother might have been left behind for that purpose. But no one would leave behind a young daughter or a wife. This fact itself paints a dismal picture of certain social realities of the time. It was as if one way of expressing communal hatred was through the torture and rape of women. We had already noted during previous riots that women were sexually abused. But now it became a sort of policy in the context of Hindu-Muslim differences. If a family had a young female within its ranks, she was not safe. This became a deep-rooted belief. And indeed, many women did disappear during this period.

It might be appropriate to mention a short story, *'Akjat'* written by my mother, Jyotirmoyee Devi. It is about two girls who were fleeing East Bengal in 1971 during the War of Liberation to escape capture by Pakistani soldiers. One girl was a Muslim, the other, a Hindu. One had some bread with her, the other carried some chira or dry rice flakes. After a while, they sat down for a rest, and the Muslim girl took out the bread she was carrying with her while the other girl took out her chira. Then they decided to conserve the chira, which would not spoil, and eat the bread first. At that particular moment, they were not thinking of caste or community, both belonged to the female community, both were vulnerable to male attack. They were looking for ways to escape safely. Were a man to catch one of them, there would be no way of escape from torture and humiliation.

This was a story. Yet this was also the truth. This brutality occurred on both sides of the country: Punjab and Bengal. On our side, there were many more incidents of women being kidnapped or raped. This was why people crossed over, anguished and terrified. Even now, the pattern remains the same. If a person wants to flee in the dark of night, he needs the aid of a neighbour. There is some hope if the neighbour is truly a good man. Otherwise, he might well kidnap the girl who is with them. Hindus in Bangladesh worry, if their sons continue to stay on there, they might have to convert to Islam. The peculiarity of the situation experienced by the people of East Bengal is this religious coercion which finds expression in forcible conversion, being forced to eat what is prohibited by the Hindu religion; the humiliation, the kidnap, torture and even rape of women. Unlike Punjab, where there was open killing or abduction followed by marriage, here, often the kidnapped women were not killed but kept alive in utter humiliation and unspeakable torture of the flesh and the spirit.

Nowadays, there is much discussion about women and violence. The truth is that domestic violence was as rampant in both the communities then as it is today. For example, in Hindu homes, women were beaten up, brides were tortured, men married many times, very young girls were prey to molestation in large families. What happened after Partition was something different. It was as if the basis of society was changing, the class structure itself was being shaken up. Many Muslims considered to be their social inferiors by the Hindu middle classes were now making a bid for higher status, trying to engage on equal terms with their Hindu neighbours in a way that had never been done before. There is an insightful account of this in Hiranmay Bandopadhyay's book, *Udbastu.* He had asked a certain Hindu migrant, 'You seem to have been well off, why did you migrate?' The answer was,

> 'Those who used to work in my house would usually be asked to sit in the outer areas of the house. Now they were now coming inside the house, into our bedrooms and asking, "Can we sit?" If I replied, "No, let us go and sit outside," "What's the difference?" would come the answer. "We are all equal now. Let's sit here."'

He continued,

> 'This was the first step. We accepted it. The second day, when the women of my family were bathing in the pond, they started baiting and abusing them. This too we bore silently. After this, we found that both the Muslim men and the Muslim women were freely going in and out of our inner apartments. We began to feel that we were not secure. So, we bought a house on this side.'

When asked whether he would return to East Pakistan some day, he replied, 'No. We shall not be able to maintain our dignity or our status over there.'

This sort of social division is prevalent in both Hindu and Muslim societies. Those considered to be social inferiors are not given any license to behave as they wish. In both communities, there were certain social rules: some people could only be greeted in the courtyard, others could be brought to the formal sitting room, but only a few had access to the bedroom. Since many felt uncertain about their ability to protect their social position or security, they decided not to remain in their old home. It was not a fear of life, but of one's social dignity or status that drove many Hindu families to leave their hearth and home and migrate to India.

After Partition, this communion, this link between the

communities disappeared. The Hindus and Muslims had been living not just in harmony but also in friendship. There was plenty of give-and-take, inter-dining, sharing of social occasions, of celebrating festivals together. This was true of both Bengal and Punjab. The vegetables that grew in one's kitchen-garden, the fruit, the fish from the ponds would be exchanged. When we came away in 1947, we did not realize what the impact of Partition would be. It was in 1950 that we saw it for ourselves. I had never before seen such a vast tide of humanity as at that time. It was the same at all the borders: at the Bongaon border, at the Gedey border, at the Darshana border or at Sealdah. Even during the riots of Noakhali, I had never seen such crowds in the stations. The largest number of migrations was from Jalpaiguri, Dinajpur, Rajshahi, Malda, northern Bengal. In the new situation some of the old districts (such as Dinajpur and Malda) had been divided between East and West Bengal, whereas Rajshahi was attached in its entirety to East Bengal. As a result, the well-to-do Hindu families of these areas crossed the border to this side. But this was more or less covertly done, because most of them had relatives on this side who helped them to rehabilitate. And such families never approached the government for help. Neither here nor in East Bengal—they just did not ask for any aid. Hence, there are no official records of their status as refugees. If there were 10,00,000 refugees, then only about 3,00,000 were in the records of the government. The government has no idea about where the remaining 7,00,000 have disappeared. They have either mingled with their own relatives or they have settled on the land here, set up home and hearth afresh.

There was a tremendous degree of difference in the way Partition affected Bengal and Punjab. In Punjab, first a west Punjab and Sind were carved out, which together with other provinces became Pakistan. The Partition was a one-time affair for Punjab. There was a greater degree of exchange of population in Punjab than in Bengal. In Punjab, entire families moved from one side to the other at one go, be it from India to Pakistan or vice versa. Many families were completely destroyed: many Hindu families and many Muslim families. Trainloads of people were massacred. Many families who went from

India to Pakistan were brutally murdered; the same was true for those who came to India from Pakistan. These were not routes to be covered on foot, these were all train routes and those who availed of them were the most vulnerable. On the other hand, those who came walking from East Bengal were often saved by the very fact that they came in scattered groups, and they could escape from mass attacks. In Punjab, often the attitude of the other community was: here is a trainload of people, let's finish the whole lot! In East Bengal, there was less of this mass killing: some died but many survived.

In East Bengal, the riots took place, as we saw, first in Noakhali in 1946. We were then working in the relief camps. People were already moving away then, for the sake of safety. As yet, they were not leaving the country but going to other districts for the sake of security. Some moved to Assam, others came to Calcutta or went to Tripura, across the zilla or district borders, on foot or by train or steamer–whichever option was available to them. Sections of a family were already getting separated; that is, the women and the children were being sent away for the sake of safety, with the old parents staying back to watch over their property. Sometimes even the young men stayed back. The old men and old women stayed because it was most difficult for them to leave. Thus even before the formal partition, the families were facing division. This had not happened in Punjab. There, the whole family moved together at the time of the Partition itself. If they decided to stay back, the whole family stayed back. But in East Bengal, you might still find some who had remained behind in 1947, though the rest of the family had migrated. Even now, after over fifty years, a handful of families are there, who have been somehow able to save a couple of empty rooms. Perhaps an old couple remains somewhere in a village of East Bengal. But they live in fear, in anxiety–they do not know when they might have to leave. Those who have come away have been scattered all over this enormous subcontinent of independent India. Unlike the Punjabis, the Bengalis did not get any evacuee property as very few houses or properties of Muslims were available in West Bengal.

In the 1950s, communal tension reached a peak. People had been just cut to ribbons in the steamers. Since the highways for travel were all waterways, things became even more difficult for the refugees. People depended on boats, on the steamer. If you wanted to hide, you hid among the water hyacinths in the ponds. If you started walking, it would take a long time, you would need an escort, for you would not know the way. In East Bengal, even when we went from one village to another, we had to walk alongside the ponds, go through forests, skirt woods and copses. There was no way of avoiding the water. On the western border of India with Pakistan, because it was over land, people could come away overnight. Whereas in the eastern border there were so many water bodies. How were they to be crossed? Someone with a boat must help out. This was a terrible drawback. Many people were killed while making their way to this side. Or, all their valuables were looted. It was very difficult to find food on the way. What do people eat over there? A little fermented rice, or some moistened chira. There were very few shops on the way. The journey to the border was fraught with unimaginable dangers.

As the tidal wave of refugees began to crowd our side, that is, West Bengal, relief work had already begun on a small scale. People were already being directed to different relief camps: those from Jalpaiguri to one place, those from Dinajpur to another, and so on. Refugees from 24- Parganas, from Bongaon, from Khulna were being sent to various camps. Those who came to Calcutta often had relatives here, or they too were sent to Burdwan or Birbhum. This enormous task of organization had already begun but as time went on, we began to feel that our efforts were inadequate. At the same time, there was no real readiness for refugee rehabilitation in West Bengal. That is why those who came did not even have a roof over their heads and often resorted to forcible occupation. Perhaps they had to be content with a ten-foot-by-ten-foot cubicle, though they had left behind a veritable palace, or an enormous property.

Moreover, they had not been able to come with their money or jewellery, nor did they get any monetary compensation here. Not only that: in West Bengal a list had been compiled of what each family had left behind. Thus all had thought that a record would be kept. But we know that although these papers might be found in the archives—piles and piles of papers—no one has even bothered to go through them. It was the government that had made this provision. When one crossed the border, one had to fill in a questionnaire: name; the village you belonged to; where do you wish to go: what have you have left behind; what losses have you suffered: who is the head of the family: and so on. Many such documents had been prepared. Those refugees who had filled such documents had kept them carefully for a long time. I know that for a fact. Then, they must have realized that such records are completely meaningless and destroyed them. Much research is being conducted about such matters now. But at that time, it was the actual anguish faced by the refugees that we found very distressing. The record in itself might not be an important document. But what those people lost, what they got in exchange, how they conducted their lives in the next half-century is glimpsed through these papers. Since every twenty-five to thirty years adds a new generation, there is a new post-Partition generation now whereas about 75 percent of the older generation is no more. The new generation has no idea of what has been lost as they themselves have seen and experienced nothing. Thus they do not feel very emotionally upset about it, though they must have heard the tales of the great bounty of East Bengal and its beauty and how much their older relatives grieve over their departure and exile. Among the old, those of us who are still alive, who still remember, we know what we have lost, and we still feel the anguish after all these years!

Twenty

The Inequities between Bengal and Punjab

I plunged deeper into social work. Dr. Prafulla Ghosh, the first chief minister of West Bengal, asked the voluntary organizations to set up a samiti or a committee which would coordinate the movements of the refugees from East Bengal, specially women and children so that they would be looked after properly. Another task he gave us was to knit woollens for all the refugees in Punjab and elsewhere who were cold and without warm clothes in the winter. Mr. Casey, the former Governor of Bengal before the Partition, sent many bales of wool from Australia, that we could knit and make woollen garments. There were eighty organizations, like the Punjabi Mahila Samiti, the Gujarati Mahila Mandol and the Maharashtrian Mahila Samaj apart from the AIWC and the All Bengal Women's Union (ABWU). We met and coördinated our work. C. Rajagopalachari was the first Governor of West Bengal after independence. He allotted space for us in Raj Bhavan, to work as well as to store the materials. Truckloads of wool were being sent–where would they be kept? It was due to Rajaji's cooperation that that a Central Room was established for stocking in Raj Bhavan. Rajaji helped us so much that we had no difficulty in carrying on our rehabilitation work. Dr. Prafulla Ghosh was with us for only five months, from August to January 1948. But within that time, he gave us a car twice a week and that facilitated our work greatly. Our workers would distribute the wool among the various organizations and collect the completed garments the following next week. There were camps in Sealdah Station too. We brought all their materials over to our office as well. There was a forty-foot-long verandah in my house where the wool would be piled up and some women would work there. Others took the wool home. Later, all the material was sorted out here and packed. We would meet at Raj Bhavan twice a week and practically every day at my house. I also employed a couple of girls who wanted to participate in the work. My mother-in-law was most supportive and this proved to be invaluable. She would keep people informed of my whereabouts and when I would be available at home.

The tasks were multi-dimensional. Twice a week, I had to go to Raj Bhavan, and Rajaji's daughter would always be present. Every morning I went out to distribute the material. Then perhaps a certain organization needed my advice on how to proceed with its work. So I would go there along with my colleagues. I would make a round of the various organizations, setting up their work-teams, explaining how things were to be done, giving them samples, weighing out the materials and distributing them. Some would take the material from the Central Office. Many people brought their personal problems to me—perhaps small, but always innumerable. Someone might be worrying about an aged mother he had left behind. Another had two young girls in his charge and wanted a small room for them. A meeting would be held every Tuesday where I made the final decisions. We might decide to send a person who was completely without friends and family to the AIWC Centre at Bethune Row, or to the Nari Seva Sangh, or to the ABWU. If a refugee had a place to stay, he or she had to be sent there. We arranged to send the girls to the women's camps that had been set up in Titagarh or the Refugee Colony. We had to put the younger ones in school, to find work for the older ones. We started adult education classes. When land began to be forcibly occupied, many persons from that area would come to seek our intervention. Our work was not on a large scale, not a massive venture. There were these eighty organizations, as I have already said. If even ten members of each were busy, that meant about 800 persons, who all worked hard and sincerely, doing our best to help the people who looked upon us as their only succour.

These eighty organizations were all small and some were long established registered societies. The AIWC had been established in 1919, a full twenty-eight years before the Partition. There were many types of organizations: some dealing with education, others with craft, yet others working for the welfare of exploited women. At that time, each of them came together on one grand common programme. Even cultural organizations like the Gujrati Mandal and Kerala Mahila Sangami were eager to raise at least a hundred rupees. I remember that the women of every state came up with their own schemes and proposed to put up a cultural item for a show, which was held under the auspices of the AIWC. How well I recall the spirited performances: Punjabi women singing with dholaks, white-haired Parsees dancing the garba with sticks, the women from Kerala performing the Onam dance in their white sarees. The Marwari women put up a monsoon dance. A school sent its team to organize various functions. It was a wonderful show. In those days, New Empire Theatre was the only place where such shows could be staged. It was full from top to bottom. And, we had raised 9000 rupees by that show, which is probably closer to 90,000 rupees now! It was the first time that we all worked together under the banner of the AIWC, rather, the West Bengal Women's Emergency Relief Committee, to raise funds. This was in 1948. None of the participants took any money for the items they staged. The whole thing was done in such a delightful way, with great verve and joy. Every participant put her whole heart and soul into the show, there was no sense of rivalry or competition. The whole atmosphere was permeated by a sort of joyful enthusiasm, though we were actually trying to mend a sorrowful situation.

Even when we sat knitting in Raj Bhavan, we kept chatting with each other. There was a group of Assamese women, among whom was Debbala Chaliha, the mother-in-law of Jaya Chaliha.[1] Assam too had lost Sylhet because of the Partition, and there was great sorrow over this. But at that time, we were knitting for the refugees of the Punjab. We still did not feel that the problems of the Partition were very desperate on our side, and indeed it was not so until 1950 because so far those of us who had come had managed to resettle, the refugees stayed with their relatives or in the refugee colonies; Sealdah Station had begun to overflow with people, but the forcible occupation of land and houses had not begun. In Calcutta we were still providing help for the refugees of Punjab as we did not consider that the situation in Bengal was all that serious. Even at this time, the Indian prime minister was telling us that in spite of the Partition, Hindus would remain in East Pakistan and Muslims would continue to live in West Bengal, as there was no real enmity between them. So we had to do our utmost to maintain peace and communal harmony here. In Bengal the problem was not one of rehabilitation but of confidence-building, whereas in Punjab it was one of population exchange under the most violent circumstances. Therefore, much of our attention was turned towards working for the Punjab refugees.

As mentioned earlier, all that changed in 1950. Now we were forced to take note of the gravity of the situation. Governmental organizations and numerous voluntary ones did all they could to feed and find homes for these unfortunate people. Some were relocated in houses rented or built by these organizations, they were given training and work was provided. The AIWC played a major role in trying to rehabilitate single girls and women. Ananda Ashram of Dacca had moved to Calcutta and the AIWC rented a house for them in Nalini Sarkar Street. I was at that time a member of the standing committee of the AIWC and the convenor of the relief committee. The Calcutta branch of the AIWC was doing several types of work at the time. Many women linked to various political parties were also involved with it. I remember that Renu Chakravartty, Suhasini Ganguly and Manikuntala Sen were among this group.[2] They were members of the Communist Party, and had gone underground after the Khulna riots. After the Communist Party was banned, its members assumed other names and lived in secrecy.

The Nehru-Liaquat Pact had been concluded rather secretively. Suddenly we found that India's official policy was that the border would be sealed and the passport system would be introduced. There were immediate repercussions. We felt it immediately, because at this time, my husband was obliged to go to his paternal home, now in East Pakistan. My husband's eldest brother, Utpal, was stricken with cancer and was seriously ill. My husband needed a passport. My brother-in-law's eldest son, Pranab, who was in India could not go because he did not have a passport. That was when we realized how things had changed. Though the Nehru-Liaquat Pact had said that people could take some of their belongings and some amount of money to the other side, now new rules were made. We found that people were not allowed to take more than 50 rupees. But what could be done with that amount? Now we realized that the country was well and truly partitioned. The tidal wave of refugee influx could not be stopped even for a day. And in 1953, 1954 and 1955, the influx continued unabated. We have figures for 1954 to 1956. Every year over 2,00,000 people would enter West Bengal. They came in so many ways, using such ingenious methods! Some went into the camps. Other went into Tripura and Assam. There was enough empty land available in those areas and settlements came up there. It would have tremendous political repercussions later when the original inhabitants reacted violently against the hardworking and enterprising newcomers who seemed to have taken over their states. Some refugees went into Bihar, into places like Betia. But it was Calcutta that actually faced the problem, with its population trebling in this period.

This was a time of terrible crisis. These newcomers did not know where their next meal would come from. Many women and girls took to other means to earn some money. We used to hear that in these colonies, girls could be picked up at any hour. I did not see this myself but we heard about it. What I do know is that girls were really tortured and exploited. We tried to rescue some of them. We organized vocational training, gave sewing lessons and other such training to give them a respectable means of earning their living. But the truth was how much money could something like sewing bring in? Especially when one's very sustenance, the medical treatment of one's whole family, depended on it? I feel the decline in moral character that I noticed at this time was all related to this question of survival. Women took to an immoral way of life, and generally, in society, the tendency to cheat and defraud also seemed to be on the rise. There was no increase in looting or burglary, but the moral rectitude of the nation had taken a downward plunge. There was much trafficking of women and young girls.

We became involved in all kinds of welfare work. The school and college certificates acquired in East Pakistan would have to be revalidated here. Then, many new schools had to be set up. The cases which were referred to as 'permanent liability' (PL), that is, old people, or families headed by women and having minor children who were sent to separate camps, now marked a new departure and signified that society was changing. This was the beginning of the break-up of our traditional joint family. Perhaps the nucleus of the son and his wife stayed together with the aged parents, after all, where were they to go? But the unmarried sister or widowed aunt was sent to another camp. This aspect of the rehabilitation work really upset us. This is when old-age homes were started in Belur and Kashi. Camps for the aged was set up by the Government of West Bengal in Dhubulia and in Rupasree Palli. Still others, who could not be resettled anywhere, were sent to camps in large tracts of empty land near Jhargram. In places like Kalaikunda and Dudhkundi, where there were airforce bases which were empty now, old-age camps had been set up. I have toured these camps and seen all the steps which were taken. And I will always believe that much more could have been done with better planning. There was too much difference in the allocation of resources between the west (Punjab) and the east (West Bengal), much inequity in the level of rehabilitation work, in funding, and living conditions between the two parts of the country. Renuka Roy wrote about this in her memoir, *My Reminiscences,*[3] where she talks of her struggles to get equal treatment from the union ministry at the centre, which consistently thwarted her efforts and those of others.

At this time, I visited practically each and every refugee camp in our side, in order to survey what were the facilities that were being given, what was the condition of the people, their state of mind, their level of awareness. Starting from Cooch Bihar to Jalpaiguri and Siliguri, though there were just a few there, going onto Dinajpur and Dhubulia, where there were many, and Nadia, I toured all the camps. I made a survey of what was being provided by the government and what was being done by other organizations. It was not as if there was no organizational framework at all. There was indeed one, and it was quite a good one for the PL group. But our administration did not have much power. The superintendents of the camps had no authority at all, all they could do was to write to their superiors who would petition further higher-ups, and so things went on. If the superintendent asked for some relief material, there was no surety that he would get it. They might get two mats per three families, or a blanket which would have to be shared by three persons. So at this time, many other organizations stepped into this field, working individually a well as in tandem with our emergency relief cell. We apportioned the work according to need and convenience. For instance, local organizations, like the one in Nadia, would be told to provide milk and other supplies to the camps, while we provided them with the wool and other articles so that people could earn some money.

Notes

1 She belonged to a family that was socially prominent and politically influential; her brother-in-law, B. P. Chaliha, was a long-serving chief minister of Assam.

2 Renu Chakravartty was a niece of Bidhan Chandra Roy, the chief minister of West Bengal. She became a Communist as a student at the Unviersity of Cambridge, and a member of the Communist Party of India. She was an MP for many years. She was married to the journalist and fellow Communist, Nikhil Chakravartty. Suhasini Ganguly was a senior Communist leader from East Bengal.

3 Renuka Ray, *My Reminiscences: Social Development in the Gandhian Era and After* (Kolkata: Stree: 2005).

Twenty-One

Squatters' Colonies

In the first three years after Partition, about 70 percent of the refugees were rehabilitated on their own. Perhaps they had relatives, or found help from people they knew. The remainder found their way to relief camps. But what they got from the government were like crumbs when compared with what the refugees from West Punjab received.

They were given a loan of Rs. 250 for house-building, a loan and not a grant, that too, in three instalments, Rs. 50 per instalment. So, the first time, they might buy some bamboos, then some other materials with the second instalment, and with the third, a couple of sheets of tin for the roof. But the hut just could not be raised, and this is something I have witnessed. No one could complete the hut. Had they been given the amount altogether, they might have been able to do so, and make some headway. The system of distributing funds, the planning for rehabilitation was quite different for Punjab and for Bengal. There was a great deal of disorder and confusion in Bengal where, in fact, there was no system at all. If some villages had been set up, or a couple of small townships been founded, the task of rehabilitation would have progressed greatly.

In the report that I submitted later, I wrote that the refugees were living here in camps, under the most difficult conditions. Many simply stayed on the platform of Sealdah Station, where khichuri would be distributed for everyone, just like a langarkhana of a gurdwara. People would be served from about 11 in the morning, their khichuri being handed to them. No one kept track whether the children had eaten, or whether the old people had had a satisfactory meal, or indeed, whether the food was edible or not. Mothers did not know whether the children could be sent to school. Old people were extremely upset. There were no facilities at all. I have minutely inspected all the camps, one in Titagarh, another in Ranaghat, another in Dhupguri, an old people's camp, and many others. There was nothing in these camps. Just a roof put up overhead somehow, nothing else whatsoever. A weekly dole would be handed to the refugees. Eight rupees for the children, twelve for the adults. A single family got eighteen rupees. But no constructive measures had been taken for them.

In the Punjab, since the main bulk of refugees arrived in 1947 itself, the authorities there did not have much time to prepare schemes of rehabilitation. Yet, everything was done in a very organized fashion. Houses and townships like Faridabad were built, factories were set up and people were given work. The property and bank accounts of the Muslim families who had left India had been properly recorded, so the newcomers were allotted this evacuee property in exchange. A large number of Muslims had migrated to Pakistan from Bombay and Uttar Pradesh and quite a few from the Terai region. A lesser number had gone from Madhya Pradesh. So, there were complete evacuee property lists with the government, even of those who had migrated from West Bengal. This property was distributed among the Punjabi refugees, and they got a roof above their heads. The rule of 'a house for a house' was maintained, as far as possible. But there was no forcible occupation. The refugees only occupied property with the permission of the government. Suppose someone had come from Sindh and he wanted to relocate in Bombay. He was given property in Bombay. Punjabis who might not want to go far from Punjab were given property around Delhi, if not property, then at least land. Many statements were taken from the refugees as to what they had left behind. Perhaps the father made a statement, 'I've left behind a house'. The son made a separate statement on similar lines. So, both received evacuee property. Such cases too were not rare. They were asked whether they had bank accounts and what their income was. They were given compensation. This was a tremendous achievement under the circumstances. After those terrible riots, with thousands being killed on either side, there was no time for thought, for proper planning. Yet, camps had been opened on both sides of the border, which accurately recorded information, according to which the relief measures progressed. The building of townships was equally helpful. It was amazing how the township of Faridabad came up from scratch in the plains near Delhi! I still remember the energy and zeal with which the minister, S. K. Dey, would personally inspect the construction work, from the mixing of the cement to the final structure. After this, proper rehabilitation measures took place in Bombay, in Gujarat. Many Pakistani Muslim families also relocated to Bombay and Uttar Pradesh, to Madhya Pradesh and the Terai.

At this time, having observed the inequalities in the rehabilitation efforts and schemes, at our insistence, the Ministry for Rehabilitation set up a committee for rehabilitation, just as had been done for Punjab. Mrs. John Mathai was the head of the committee in Punjab.

So we said we also wanted a similar committee. A committee was set up here under the leadership of the minister, Meher Chand Khanna, and many others, including Purabi Mukherjee, Deputy Minister in the West Bengal Ministry of Refugees and Rehabilitation, and I were made members. It was called the Committee for the Resettlement of the East Bengal Refugees. We surveyed the camps, to see what steps were needed. There was a cell in this committee for the 'permanent liability', as mentioned earlier, women who had no family, or old people who had no relatives, those who could not be rehabilitated. I was appointed the head of that cell. Mrs. John Mathai was my counterpart on the other side. She had set up many schemes, had organized everything so skilfully that we were full of admiration for her. Mr. Khanna and Mrs. Purabi Mukherjee were our leaders. In our committee meetings, there would be representatives from West Bengal, Tripura and Bihar. We would discuss and compare the situations in West Bengal and Punjab and wonder why things were so different on the two sides. We wanted to see for ourselves what steps had been taken for women's rehabilitation. Ultimately, Meher Chand Khanna was forced to set up a committee which I headed, for such a tour of inspection. The other members were Bina Das, Sheila Davar, Sudha Sen of the AIWC, Amarkumari Verma and Suniti Pakrashi, Deputy Director of the Women's Cell, Government of West Bengal. We went to Punjab to see what kind of relief measures had been taken there and held discussions with Mrs. Mathai and other members of the other committee. We also visited many places: Panchkula, portions of Kashmir, Jalandhar, Dehra Dun and many areas in and around Delhi. We saw, how easily people had just crossed the border and settled here. How many facilities there were in the girls' camp! The older children, boys and girls, were going to school and the women cooked food in the rooms allotted to them. Whereas in Bengal, there was no proper place even to stay. People were living out of trunks and boxes, the way people somehow stay on railway platforms. They spent years like this. There was no privacy and there was a clash of interest. When we returned from the tour, we made a report, which clearly stated how, from both the financial angle and that of amenities, these people on this side, were being deprived; whereas adequate space, money and financial assistance had made all the difference in Punjab.

The main difference was that on our side we were unable to provide homes. Everything remained at the level of camps, and as I have said earlier, it was like living on a railway platform. If we had made it compulsory that every family would be given a house, and an occupation, then each family could have settled down. Even if they had provided individual tents to families, some of the problems might have been solved. But that did not happen at all. When the refugees entered Bengal, they received no help whatever. Or if they received anything, it was minimal. But in Punjab, we found they were living in proper houses. They had a roof upon their heads—no matter where they were quartered, they had been provided with a room and a verandah. They could use the verandah as a sort of kitchen. They too were deprived people, the houses were tiny, perhaps, the older generation was not present and the young people were living by themselves. But, whatever the case, they lived together as a family, they knew they had a brother or sister, or someone to fall back on.

In Punjab, the whole family lived together. There were schools in the camp itself. They would hear the bell ring and go off to school by themselves—boys and girls. They would return home to eat their lunch of dal-roti. But it was not like that in Bengal. There was no school on the camp except a primary school. Boys and girls were kept in separate camps. Suppose a boy lived with his mother in a camp from the age of twelve, after four years, he would be shifted to the boys' camp, and he would spend many years there. Even if the parents wanted to educate their children, how were they to do it? Where were the facilities? Therefore, the girls had to be sent elsewhere; perhaps to the Ananda Ashram or the Nari Seva Sangh, and the boys to the Boys' Home set up by the Ramkrishna Mission and other organizations, where they were properly looked after. The tragic results were that because of the separation, the family could not be easily brought together later. Sometimes a mother did not recognize her son since he had grown up away from her. As these boys had no money they could never visit their families. Such was the degree of mismanagement. That they managed to survive under such horrendous circumstances is, I believe, a great credit to these courageous refugees.

We began organizing classes for the education of the children. The AIWC, ABWU and many other organizations formed groups and went off to various camps to conduct classes. There were separate classes for older people and young children. The government provided us with vehicles, that was the sum total of its help. All the other expenses, that of books and materials and whatever else was needed, was borne by our organizations. Every Thursday, we would go off to our appointed camps. Not only would we get hold of textbooks, teach the children and set homework, we would also appoint suitable persons in the camp who would carry on the classes on other days. This is how our work began in Titaghar and Chamta Camp and elsewhere. We began to work well, in an organized manner, and we developed close bonds with each other, our various groups soon became very close. But just as we were learning to work systematically and well, we found there was extreme chaos in the rehabilitation department.

Gradually, thereafter, schemes for rehabilitation began to be devised. Schemes for the education of the refugee girls, whether they would attend school, who would bear the expenses of their schooling, and so on, began to be put together. These were milestones that had already been crossed in Punjab. There, as pointed out earlier, both boys and girls were going to school, and staying with their parents, whereas in Bengal the family had been being broken up. The girls remained behind with their mothers. Then, the older girls were sent away also, to various training centres, and the mothers were left alone with their infant children. A feeling grew up that these women were not capable, or perhaps not suitable, for rehabilitation. Boys and men were given opportunities, they received plots, but not the girls. If an eighteen-year-old boy could be regarded as a suitable candidate for receiving a plot of land, why not a girl, who could then support her mother? We had to fight long and hard against this discrimination. Ultimately, through the efforts of Shanti Das, 20 plots were given to women in Bauria in the district of Howrah. In another area next to Bauria, women were given plots as the head of the family. Girls brought their mothers and younger siblings over and set up their homes.

Boys were already being given plots then. Some had taken their mothers away from the camps to live with them, some had not. Now schemes were begun to train the mothers to earn a livelihood. Women took up various types of training like canteen management training. Boys learnt farming, but this training was not imparted to the girls. For the girls, there were schemes such as fruit preservation, which was seasonal, and stitching and embroidery for a diploma. Much more was needed for proper rehabilitation. The rehabilitation work suffered because there were not enough proper schemes. In the meantime, Meher Chand Khanna came to the rescue of P. L. camps. He tried linking up with Ramkrishna Mission and Ananda Ashram. Large plots of land were now given for training boys and girls; these large technical training institutes we see nowadays had their genesis at this time.

It was around 1957, we began to hear that the refugee colonies had become squatters' colonies, and that none of the refugees wanted to leave their camps. So they were to be forcibly evicted from the camps. Now the weekly dole they were given would be discontinued. They were told that they could go to Dandakaranya or somewhere else. As many as 7000 to 8000 persons volunteered to go, and a list was made out. Arrangements were made to send these people to Dandakaranya gradually.

Now squatters' colonies began to come up in and around Calcutta where the Army had camps or on runways or airstrips. Refugees decided that since land was lying vacant, they would raise their homes there. Why should they remain in distress? The government was obviously not able to cater to their needs. Those who had gone to the camps were those who were truly destitute and with no resources of family support at all. There were some who wanted to try their luck in other ways. So, they began to try and locate space for themselves in empty areas with the help of their friends and family members. That is how the squatters' colonies began. It was at this time that another very significant incident took place. A delegation from Punjab visited us, among its members was Rameshwari Nehru. She was an experienced activist and former President of the AIWC and had worked with the Punjabi refugees. Ajit Prasad Jain was also present. He was a minister who had been in the post of Minister for Rehabilitation before Meher Chand Khanna. The latter was a man of no vision and had no sym pathy for refugees. People declared that much was being done in the west, what were the people in Bengal getting? If we put up the orphan boys in homes, what would they be given per head? What about homes for the girls? The funds were so inadequate, how were we to provide clothes for them? Now they had just one set of clothes. I asked the minister why the same facilities, that were being given in the West, could not be provided in here.

During the discussion, which became very animated, I said that though the social workers and the Ramkrishna Mission and other organizations were doing their best, we were in a tight corner and but for the monetary support of the common man, nothing would have been possible. The government funding was so limited that there was no money for the refugees to find fuel to cook rice. Then I requested Rameshwari Nehru to come with me and survey the squatters' colonies. I wanted to show her what the people could do by their own efforts. I had already seen some of these squatters' colonies coming up. The refuges had got hold of bamboo and other materials, cut them to size and somehow managed to raise their huts practically overnight. The question was not whether we were in favour of forcible occupation of land. I just wanted to show that this was the way rehabilitation should proceed as surely people must be given a roof over their heads. And Rameshwari Nehru also showed an interest in the matter. This was not done officially because it was not an official tour of government inspection. But when she expressed her desire to see the colonies, the government did not refuse either. I did get hold of official conveyance though, and took her to the Bijoygarh Colony. This had earlier been an enormous airstri p. That had been used as the main thoroughfare and the houses had been built on both sides of it. None of the houses were pucca, they all had earth foundations and walls of bamboo matting. The colonists themselves had divided up the plots into two cottahs each and allotted them to each occupant. Shops had come up. A school, a hospital and a clinic had also come up there. Mrs. Nehru seemed quite impressed by the refugees' efforts. She was in fact very impressed by what she saw and asked me why were we not supporting this venture, since these were truly the genuine efforts of the people themselves. I did not tell her then that these were actually instances of forcible occupation. But I myself was of the opinion that if the government could provide no help, then this was the only way out. Either the voluntary organizations should step in to provide people with these facilities, or they should take such steps themselves.

The other thing I thought was that these refugees were not weak or helpless by nature. They were hardworking, they had initiative, skill and the ability to plan. Neither were they lacking in intelligence. These small colonies that came up almost overnight were a testimony to their courage and resourcefulness. Many political parties, especially the Communists, were also supporting these activities of the refugees at this time. The ban on the Communists had been lifted by this time and Rameshwari Nehru was on very good terms with them. I believe that if this forcible occupation had not taken place then many people would have actually met with their deaths. It is not important now to remember who supported this venture, who went against it. What is important is that with their own efforts, people found a way to survive. Of course, if I were to lose a house of my own to forcible occupation, my reaction would certainly have been different. But since these colonies mostly came up on empty land, this was the best solution to the problem. There was plenty of land available in West Bengal at that time. If the resettlement of the refugees had been done with proper planning, it would have been far better. Many more people could have been settled, cultivation too would have increased. In many places such as Dhubulia, Jhargram and the lands beyond Jhargram, there was much land belonging to zamindars and former British companies that lay almost empty, with empty houses–property which had been left lying since the departure of the British. These had not been allotted or used. If this had been done in an organized way, the refugees would not have faced so much trouble. Later the United Council of Refugees was set up by the Government of West Bengal in collaboration with voluntary organizations and chaired by Justice B. K. Guha, ICS. It was given an office in Raj Bhavan's garage.

Around 1957, the refugee camps were being closed down, all except a few, at Dhubulia and Rupasree, and Cooper's Camp. The old people were kept in these three camps. Their children would grow up some day and take them home, or else, some arrangements had to be made for them. It was the Central Government's responsibility but nothing effective was done. There was discrimination and total lack of organization, total chaos, though people were eager, ready to start rebuilding their lives. But the same authorities who had drawn up a policy of rehabilitation and had done such a wonderful job in West Punjab did not cooperate. They were questioning all our demands. If the people in the west were given three blankets, those of the east must be given one only, for it was less cold here, they said. Some of the officers from West Bengal, who also served the same department and looked after the affairs of our refugees, were forced to resign and come away. The Centre did not look after the humane side of our rehabilitation efforts. They were only concerned with saving expenditure. Only about one-third of the amount spent for the West Pakistani refugees was allotted for us.

Twenty-Two

Dandakaranya

The next stage in the story of our rehabilitation efforts is set in Dandakaranya. Ten full years had passed since the plans were made for rehabilitation at Dandakaranya. It was in 1957, ten years since the Partition that it was announced that such huge numbers of people could not continue to stay in the camps, they would have to move. The government began to move the people in 1960. They were almost like the American pioneers who moved westwards to settle beyond the prairies. The refugees were equipped with little more than a lantern, and a plough, accompanied by a wife and minor children, for the older children were not permitted to go with them. It was a nightmare! For each holding, there was one adult male, his wife and small children. The difficulties these families had to face! If the women sat to cook with the help of the lantern, the old people were left in the dark. If the man took his plough, there was no one to take his cow to the fields. After reaching the dark forest, Dandakaranya, thirty families were assigned to one village, the group moving together, each with a cow, the men followed by the small children, all walking along, with nothing more than a lantern. What would they do in this wilderness? What would they eat? Of course, initially they were given three months' rations. Later, also a tent. That was their sole security.

If we just think, even once, of Faridabad, or Delhi, Uttar Pradesh, even Bombay, we can then comprehend the plight of the refugees who went to Dandakaranya. In Punjab, the refugees got readymade houses to occupy. After all, if there is a roof overhead, then the menfolk can go out to make a living, leaving the women behind. But in the forests of Dandakaranya how would the men go off to begin cultivation leaving the women behind unprotected? The forests were infested with wild animals. There were no buildings, just tents. If a cheetah or a bear attacked them, who would protect them? There was no end to dangers: be they snakes or scorpions or tigers. When you clear a prime forest area to create a human settlement, a jungle which has stood for thousands of years, there is no guessing what kind of creatures might emerge, apart from frogs and scorpions. There was no rain and no water: what misery for people used to a land of rivers and much water! Perhaps there was just a single tube-well in the camp, and that too did not function properly.

These people, who had come all the way from East Bengal, needed water to drink, to cook their food! It might have been a better idea to excavate a few ponds and then make arrangements for human habitation. The terrain, too, was difficult. In some places, even cutting ponds would not have helped, for they would have found no water. Elsewhere, dams had been erected to divert a canal towards a settlement. It was not as if the situation was equally bad everywhere. For example, there was water in Parolkote, and there, the refugees could settle. We heard that canals would be dug. But when the refugees first went there, there was nothing! Malkangiri was a really arid locality. When the villages were initially founded, everything looked pretty as a picture. The land was divided into plots and the plots were distributed among the families. Initially, everyone had liked the set-up. But after three months, they were at starvation level. I am speaking from first-hand experience because I did visit and stay in Dandakaranya. When you went there the first day, you were served with khichuri. Fine. But you had to make your own arrangements from the second day. There were no plates or bowls or buckets. There was no water, no cooking utensils or arrangements, so how was one to cook? I have never seen such a terrible lack of infrastructure before. It was all at the behest of Delhi, so naturally, people were very angry. And we had also seen the situation of the local authorities, they too were very unhappy at the situation. Thus, what had been possible for rehabilitation of the Punjabi refugee had not been possible here. Nothing was pre-planned, or organized despite the fact that the refugees came to Dandakaranya only in 1960 and there had been three years' time to plan and organize. Had some steps been taken in those first few years, they would not have faced such terrible problems.

The migration from East Pakistan has been a continuous flow from the 1940s right down four decades, though the flow has been in the form of waves, sometimes a tidal bore, sometimes a lean trickle. In reality, right from the time of the Bengal Famine in 1943, people had been coming over to West Bengal, which was not a migration, for they were moving from one part of the country to the other. The real exodus began from August 1946, when the first fearsome riots took place, riots the like of which we had never seen before. The next lot came in 1950. From 1950 to 1956, so many refugees came that the situation of West Bengal was quite chaotic.

They seemed too many in number wherever we sent them. However, in Andamans, the rehabilitation work was proceeding quite well. The refugee camps were closed in 1957. There was a lull of three years after that. But during the China war in 1962, again an influx took place. In 1963, so many people were coming in that they were sent straight to Dandakaranya. The place had been geared to serve about 7000 refugees, that was how it had been planned, now the whole thing was thrown out of gear with this new wave of migration. This was like the great influx of 1950. The movement across the border did not end ever; there was a constant trickle at all times. During the Indo-Pakistani war of 1965, the trickle again became a wave.

Twenty-Three

Our Children

In 1953, our youngest daughter, Apala was born. This was most unexpected and I was somewhat housebound. I remember that when the Congress session was held in Kalyani that year, my baby daughter was just six months old. I could not go out much, but I could organize the canteen at Kalyani by telephone. I also managed to get all the news of their plans and decisions. I got so much help from Rammohan Singh of ABWU and Karuna Kana Gupta of AIWC that there was never any difficulty in continuing my work. I was so busy with my relief work that this unexpected and enforced period of seclusion would have been very upsetting had I not received the fullest cooperation from my family. I might well have had to forego any plans for future activity for quite some time but for my mother-in-law and younger ja, Sulekha, and elder ja, Bidyutlata, who took charge of the daily running of the household. Moreover, our eldest daughter, Kunta, then aged sixteen, was like a little mother to her baby sister, Apala. It was she who really brought up Apala and saw to all her needs during those years, leaving me free to carry on with my work.

Kasturi, aged nine, was studying in Loreto House. All our children were very good at their studies, perhaps because of their regular habits. My husband had made it a rule that no youngster should be outside the house after six-thirty in the evening. After that from 7 p.m., he would sit with them and supervise them if necessary. He looked after their needs in English and Bangla, while I taught them chemistry and mathematics and other science subjects if they required help. We did not need to em ploy tutors because the schools provided excellent guidance, and by doing their home-tasks regularly, the children got along very well. When my nieces and nephews did need extra attention, I myself tutored them. But we did encourage the children to pursue their interest in extracurricular activities. The girls, especially, attended classes for drawing, singing and dance.

The aftermath of Partition meant that Calcutta was still not very safe, and we had a few anxious moments with the children. Partha used to take the school bus. Once, I remember, he did not return even much after his actual time, and we were very worried indeed. We took out the car and went to look for him. We found that the bus had broken down and all the boys, including Partha, were pushing it! On another occasion, I was late in picking up Kunta after school and when I did not find her waiting for me, I was absolutely panic-stricken. But when I came back home, I found she had returned by a rickshaw, payment for which was made by my cook Ram and Partha gleefully frightening Kunta by saying, 'Mother will give you a thrashing', where as I was congratulating Kunta for being clever! I think I still remember these incidents because even such small things caused absolute panic in those days.

There was quite a big bunch of children growing up together because our nieces and nephews were there in the same household with our children, and that was one reason why they did not feel bored, or even mind very much that I was so busy with my relief work. Both Partha and Kunta had been exposed to political discussions and debates from a very early age, and were well aware of what was happening in the country. Both of them, and even Kasturi too, to some extent, had been also exposed to the different way of life in the districts and small towns of Bengal and so they knew all about village life and the rural side of our country. They learnt much more about the country than they would have had we lived in a city all our lives. Having been brought up amidst books and a lively intellectual atmosphere, they acquired a taste for literature, both Bengali and Western, and an appreciation of the arts, which remained with them always. My mother's influence on them was also strong, since she always played the role of storyteller when she come to visit us.

The children displayed different personality traits right from the start. Partha had inherited his parents' quick temper, but Kunta was always very calm and serene. Even as children, Partha was the more bookish one, while Kunta was much more curious about the world around her, and quite eager to carry on her own experiments. We noted with amusement that while Kunta studied all about cows and goats from real life, Partha preferred to gather his information from books! She also had pets: goats, hens and ducks. But Partha was not as fond of animals as she was. From her childhood, Kunta was very interested in household activities. When we were in Krishnanagore, we used to sleep on the terrace. Once, we woke up to find Kunta missing. She was then five years old. After a while, she came up to the terrace with an armful of flowers that she had plucked from the garden. We thought she would set about arranging the flowers into posies, but we were amazed to find that they were actually ingredients for her make-believe cookery! The marigold was her turmeric, the red hibiscus, her chilli powder, other flowers became 'vegetables' that she cut up and cooked!

One particular thing about Kunta that I look upon with pride even now was her willingness to always help me around the house. I did not ever employ sweepers to clean our bathrooms and we cleaned them ourselves. When we were staying in our Race Course residence after 1947, I cleaned my own toilet, the boys cleaned theirs, and Kunta was in charge of cleaning the toilet used by the other people in the house. She was supposed to finish the job before going to school, and she performed the task faithfully every day. One day, she must have forgotten, or perhaps she was in a hurry and had not cleaned the toilet. Partha spilt the beans and I made the poor girl com plete her chore as usual. I told her that she was not to leave home till her task was done! And she did indeed do it!

The environment of a convent must have affected Kasturi unconsciously in more ways than one. Once, when my mother-in-law were busy performing some puja and offering flowers to the deity, she astounded her grandmother by asking, 'Won't you offer flowers to my goddess, Mother Mary?'

I had always been fond of sports, and was quite good at various games. During our postings in the districts, I used to enjoy going to the Club with my husband, to play tennis. My husband was a fine sportsman and a keen footballer. He used to play football regularly in his younger days. We were all very fond of swimming. When Partha and Kunta were small, we used to take them to the Club so that they too could take part in games with us. In that way, we spent a lot of time with the children, by sharing their recreation as well as their study hours. In Calcutta, there was less chance of sports and games except for badminton in the lawn. Partha and Kunta were in higher classes and more busy with their lessons. Other extracurricular classes took the place of the regular evening games. Our bond with the children was maintained through supervision of their studies, something which today's parents seem quite unable to do! We also had regular family outings like visits to the zoo.

During the Quit India movement, there were heated political discussions in our house, some of which centred on whether my husband should give up his job in response to Gandhiji's call. Partha was often present at these meetings. Later, when I was away at the Noakhali camp, Partha used to attend political meetings. This was not uncommon in those days, and, in fact, once a nephew of mine had been hauled up before the Police Chief in Krishnanagore on charges of attending a seditious meeting. How surprised the officer had been to hear that the boy was the nephew of the District Judge! Most of the people who came to our house were freedom-fighters and were given due respect. My husband himself was a follower of Gandhiji and wore Khadi. Self-sacrifice and building the nation were the two favourite topics of conversation in our house in those days, and no doubt Partha was greatly influenced by such talk. Later on, when he became a historian, he took the addresses of many freedom-fighters from us, and met them for the sake of his research.

Partha topped the Matriculation examination in 1949. I remember that his school principal, his teachers and some of his friends all came home to dinner to celebrate his success. He stood sixth in the IA examinations and joined Presidency College with history honours. Perhaps his father would have liked him to study economics, but he had made up his mind about history and now stood firm in his decision. I believe that it was the atmosphere in his own home that inspired him to study history. After his school-leaving examination, he went to Pune to visit his doctor uncle Anil, my husband's third eldest brother, to whom he was very attached. He also had to undergo some treatment as his knee was swollen at this time. When he returned from Pune, we found that his mind was quite made up about studying history. Here too he emerged as the university topper and was declared the Ishan Scholar of his year, as his father had been in his time. He went off to pursue his postgraduate studies in Oxford in 1953.

Kunta too was a very good student. When she left school, she was keen to study medicine, but being underage, she joined the BSc course with physiology honours. She too was a gold medallist and a first class first. Even after her graduation, she wanted to study medicine, but her father did not encourage her in this. He was keen to get her married. Kunta did her masters in physiology and later joined the academic profession as a lecturer in Science College.

Of my four children, it was Kasturi who was the most athletic and good at games. She played basket ball, volley ball and table-tennis. She was also good at rowing. Though Kunta was quite a bit older than her, she and Kunta were good friends. I later heard from Kasturi that when Kunta was in college, she would sometimes pick up her younger sister from home on Thursdays, her weekly School holiday, and take her for an afternoon show at a nearby cinema. Then, they would come home separately, so that their parents might not suspect that they had been playing truant! On the rare occasion when their father did catch one of them coming home late, a small white lie would save them! So strict was the half-past-six-o' clock rule in our house that the children ganged up to break it!

My mother-in-law's presence in the household was very beneficial. She was a wonderful person, full of love, kindness and compassion. Not only did she love her sons, her daughters and her family, her affection encompassed animals, outsiders, the whole world! The servants and their children received as much attention from her as did the abandoned kitten she rescued. She bound us all together with bonds of love. It was because she provided unstinted support that I was able to spend long hours away from home. She was unfailingly supportive in my work as well. She always had a kind word or some encouragement to give to all the distressed people who came to our house. It is from her that I learnt tolerance. Since I had left the financial management of the kitchen to her, I could be secure that the household was running on oiled wheels under her guidance.

Moreover, she taught us all some very valuable lessons. She did not permit any discrimination over food where the servants were concerned. All those who worked in the house or came to serve us in any way would eat exactly what we did. Once during the mango season, there were not enough mangoes to go around easily. I suggested that the mangoes should be served at table and the servants could have their share the next day. But she disagreed and at once started cutting up the fruit and apportioning equal amounts to everybody. 'These people come to look after us, shouldn't we look after them as well?' she said. My husband too followed the same rule. When the bearers served the fish or meat curries at table, he would insist on being shown whether there was an equal amount set aside for them.

Another rule in our house was that the children of the servants, the driver, for instance, would sit with us at the dining table and have their meals with the family. I remember an incident from a much later time. A Dr. Mrs. Ruth Glass from England used to come to our house for discussions with my husband on matters concerning the Calcutta Improvement Trust. Once she had a meal with us. As she sat down at the dining table, I introduced her to the others of the family. Finally, she pointed to two little ones at the opposite end of the table and asked, 'Who are these?' I told her their names, and said they were the children of the driver and the cook. She laughed and remarked, 'Mr. Gupta, I see that you are a real socialist!' We were not socialists in the political sense, but we did believe in the dignity and equality of all human beings and tried our best to translate such beliefs into actual practice as best as we could. Whoever came to the house on whatever mission was treated with dignity. My husband took care of a Harijan lad called Bonbihari, and we were all very fond of him. While my husband bought him his two sets of clothes annually, it was I who got his shoes, shawls and other necessities for him, sometimes, in the earlier days, even with my scholarship money. Thus, all of us tried to do whatever we could for those dependent on us.

Twenty-Four

Making Friends and Forming Networks

My interest in relief and rehabilitation work brought me into contact with a wide circle of extraordinary personalities. Much of our work was to do with coordinating with official and non-official relief bodies all over India. I was fortunate in having senior colleagues like Sucheta Kripalani, Sushila Nayyar, Lakshmi Menon and Renuka Ray who taught me a great deal and served as my guides. They were truly remarkable women who had a vision for the future and dedicated themselves to working selflessly for the attainment of that vision—the vision of a better India. The 1940s and the 1950s were also a turning point in our social history. There was an all-round struggle to sweep away the old and iniquitous social and economic systems, a conscious effort being made to reform and rejuvenate a traditional and moth-eaten society. This movement touched the heartstrings of all communities, all creeds, all sections of society. Maharashtrians, Gujaratis, South Indians, Parsees, Sikhs, Muslims, all communities in all corners of India responded to this urgent call for change. Calcutta had always been a cosmopolitan city with a large and active population of non-Bengalis, most prominent of whom were the Marwaris. Perhaps because of my upbringing as a *prabashi*, or perhaps because of my links with Jaipur, I was very close to many non-Bengalis, and had a large number of Keralite, Punjabi, Parsee and Marwari friends. I witnessed the amazing movement for reform that was taking place among the Marwaris at this time.

It was at the time of the Quit India movement that many Marwari men and women got together under the leadership of Sitaram Seksaria, to start the Samaj Sudhar Samiti. Under the guidance of the very progressive and dynamic Sitaramji, this samiti took up the cause of modernization and called for *ghungar karo:* bringing women out of seclusion. Sitaramji wanted the Marwari community to come out of their traditional orthodox way of life and participate in the mainstream of national life. Many others joined him: Bhagirath Kanoria, Basantlal Murarka, Ishwari Prasad Jalan, Debi Prasad Khaitan, to name a few. The Marwari Balika Vidyalaya and later Sri Shikshayatan School and College were set up to encourage the education of Marwari girls. Another premier institution, Abhinav Bharati, grew up under the guidance of Gyanvati Lath, Shanti Khaitan. Pratibha Agarwal and others, a group of progressive Marwaris established the Anamika Kala Sangam, where Marwari girls acted together with the men and staged some wonderful plays. I often visited their rehearsals at Muktaram Babu Street. This group became actively involved with the Quit India movement as well. Later on, after independence, they maintained their social service and cultural activities and their progressive attitude. Not only did I make many friends here, some of my most active colleagues were from this Marwari group. Sushila Singhi was one of them. The story of her life was quite extraordinary. Widowed as a child, she went to stay with her grandmother in Vrindavan, but was brought back to Calcutta by her very progressive father. She started studying at Beltala Girls' School and later completed her graduation. She met Mr. Singhi, a Marwari widower with a son, both of them were involved in the freedom struggle, and they decided to get married. Sushila was involved in education and social welfare and was a member of the AIWC and the Women's Coordinating Council and was also very active in the Family Planning movement.

A large number of Sikhs who migrated from Pakistan rehabilitated themselves in West Bengal. There were quite a few Sikhs already settled here, working as mechanics, drivers of buses and cars. They gave shelter to all their refugee relatives. In the Jagubazar locality, each large garage gave shelter to many families. A huge Sikh community grew up in Calcutta at that time. A large gurdwara was built in Chetla. A group of Sikhs will set up a gurdwara wherever they go. I have visited the one in Chetla and eaten its free *langar* meal. We had a lot of Sikh friends since I was brought up in Delhi and had roots in the west and also because my brother lived in Amritsar, and my mother was with him. I was very close to many of them. I have seen how they helped out their refugee relatives. In each household, entire families would occupy single rooms which they had curtained for privacy. They had not yet received any house allotment or compensation and were living with their relatives. Later, they received compensation in such a way that it was easy for them to set up their transport business or any other business they chose. They settled down, established themselves, even found the means to set up their gurudwara as a community. The present generation of Sikhs in Calcutta is the second generation of those refugees. My mother especially was quite close to the community, she felt a sort of affinity with them because her roots were also in the west.

Many Sikhs spoke excellent Bengali. They still do. My mother wrote an essay called *'Badrinather Pathey'*: while visiting Haridwar with two girls, she had lost her tickets, and was in great difficulty, for unless they purchased fresh tickets they would not be allowed to come out of the gates. A Sikh gentleman sitting there said in perfect Bengali, 'No, Ma, you don't have to buy fresh tickets.' So many people had learnt Bengali and sang Bengali songs beautifully. Punjabi-Bengali marriages did take place in those days. Take the case of the royal family of Patiala, which later converted to Christianity. Rajkumari Amrit Kaur had a Bengali mother; a girl from Keshav Chandra Sen's family had married into the Patiala one. Since Partition, Calcutta's Sikh population has increased.

There were various international organizations like Friends Service (Quakers) that had come to India during World War II and now joined our efforts at rehabilitation. We had started 'Save the Children' committees in 1943, taking in the children orphaned by the famine, the war or the Partition. There were many old organizations like Nari Siksha Samiti, Nari Seva Sangh and the All-Bengal Women's Union which set up homes for young girls who had been rescued from exploitation, where we housed many adolescent girls. At this time, my experience with the Girl Guides stood me in very good stead. Romola Sinha of the All Bengal Women's Union also had begun to work with the distressed girls since 1933.. The AIWC also trained volunteers for rehabilitation work, under the guidance of Renuka Ray, and Karunakana Ghosh was very active in this area. Our branches all over India also helped us very much. We even had a branch in China which was working with us. We set up committees in Calcutta and in every district to coordinate the relief work. The United Council of Relief and Welfare was trying to coordinate the work of these various groups, and also to bring in the organizations set up by the refugees themselves. As members of the AIWC we tried very hard to get the women's groups together and received considerable support from the Governors of the state: Rajagopalachari, Katju and Haren Mookerjee. Their commitment was absolute. They opened up Raj Bhavan for us, set up many kinds of committees, often guided us and explained how things should be done.

After 1955 a Social Welfare Board was set up which did not focus on relief but on constructive work. It was more interested in drawing schemes for women, for making them independent, so that they could stand on their own feet. The Board was modelled on the Kasturba Gandhi National Memorial Trust of Gandhiji, which he had set up specifically for women. It was to be administered by women, for women, where women would take care of rural women. Starting from delivering children to educating the girl child and adult education, it was a complete scheme for total female uplift and independence. These schemes for the self-reliance of women began with the Kasturba Trust. Once the Social Welfare Board came into being, it more or less followed this model. The only difference was that it divided its work according to areas. Committees were set up on the basis of districts. That was how one group of workers who had been unacquainted with this field became involved in social work. Often, we would make the wives of government officials part of committees or their heads. Initially they might have been full of trepidation, for they had never worked in this field before. But after two years, when they had to leave for another place, they would tell us, 'Didi, thanks to this work, I came to know my own country. If you hadn't brought us out of the domestic confines we would never have known the actual state of our country.'

Twenty-Five

Girl-Guide Training in the United States of America

Girl Guides was a novel feature that I, as State Commissioner, Guides, had introduced in the rehabilitation camps. My purpose was to give the young girls some recreation, a taste of enjoyment and freedom. Their studies were not progressing, they were getting no vocational training, they were not able to go out, visit places, see the outside world. These were their formative years, yet they were suffering from a lack of goals and from disorientation. I was thinking of ways to train these girls. So I wrote to the International Headquarters of the Girl Guides for some help, asking if they could provide training for at least one person, who could then impart it to others, which would be of great benefit to us. They agreed, and they also invited me to study their system of work. Because the girls I was working with had special needs as they did not have the benefits of a 'normal' existence, like their counterparts in the USA or the UK, the organization agreed that we should include an Indian adult leader as a trainee who would proceed to the UK. She was sent in 1956 for Girl-Guide training, so that she could train girls here, this brought us good results. We could set up training centres in each and every camp. Miss Pakrashi, deputy director, Department of Relief and Rehabilitation, Government of West Bengal, helped us tremendously in setting up these girls' companies. In the camps of Nadia, Burdwan, 24-Parganas, Medinipur, the girls received excellent Girl-Guide training.

Thus in 1956, in the middle of the refugee crisis, I went off to the USA for a few months to study the working of the Girl Guide organization. This was my first trip abroad. My youngest daughter, Apala, was just three, and I left her behind in the care of my mother-in-law, her aunt Bidyutlata, and her eldest sister, Kunta. I was with a group of international representatives, about fourteen of us, from all over the world. There were representatives from Malayasia, China, the Middle East, Pakistan, Mali, Korea and other countries. Our objective was to study the organization and programmes of the Girl Guides and the 4-H Youth Clubs, to see how these organizations involved the youth of the country in development work. We went to New York and then toured the whole country, attending meetings and conferences and observing the organizations. I stayed in the west for three months. Then we were sent to Texas, where we spent almost a week. There was a regional conference there where we met girls from all sorts of backgrounds. We were also scheduled to go to Mexico, but unfortunately, I was unable to get a visa. After that, we were off to the Mid-West where there was another regional conference. At this conference, guides, scouts and their captains had assembled. They showed us around and explained things to us with great enthusiasm.

My tour was not only interesting, it was also extremely educative. My hosts had organized everything meticulously. I attended these big conferences, but I found it most helpful to meet people in small groups, many of whom I had addressed at the large conferences. It was in these small meetings that the networking took place, for there was opportunity to interact then. Our programme was packed. We would return from a meeting in the evening, then leave to attend another meeting. In the morning we would be off to the next place on our itinerary. Or a group of Girl-Guides would come to meet me. Small villages, hamlets, towns, even forests, we went all over, to many kinds of venues.

One of the high points of my trip was a visit to an American Indian reservation. We actually stayed right in the middle of one. These were the native Indians, most of whom had already been decimated in the previous century. The remaining few had continued their attacks on the white Americans and the outcome would probably have been total extinction of the Indians. But the solution that was found was this Indian reservation: a sort of fixed area within which they were confined and not allowed to come out. They maintained their traditional lifestyle inside these reservations, somewhat like our own tribal people, marginalized from the fast path of industrial development. Of course, the analogy is not exact. For when we went into their huts, we were surprised to see that though they looked like thatched huts from the outside, inside they were the quintessential American home, fitted with TV, fridge, heaters and all modern amenities! How interested we were to meet the American Indians and they too watched us with a curiosity matching ours. We also participated in a special programme, where we representatives put up a show. The American Indians wore their traditional dress, and they put up a wonderful show for us.

After this, we were taken for three weeks to Syracuse, for a particular training programme in social service. The director of our training programme was Dr. Kindlesberger. While working on this orientation programme, I was most amused to find what a motley group of students he had! There was a lady from Philippines who was middle-aged, and I myself was 42 at that time. But many of the group were very young, boys and girls who were seventeen and eighteen years old. As a result of this training course, we came to know America, came close to each other and explored ways of moving ahead together. We were to meet up with Dr. Kindlesberger again when he and his family came to Calcutta in 1960.

After these three weeks of training, I visited the Niagara Falls and then went to Chicago. I went to the Ramakrishna Mission in Chicago and told the director of my desire to see the building where the Parliament of Religions had been held in 1893, the venue of Swami Vivekananda's famous lecture. Surprised, he asked why I wanted to go there so late at night. I told him that it mattered to me even though I would only get a glimpse of the house. I requested him to send someone with me, as I had been provided with transport. So, I went with the escort he provided. He took me around the building where the famous lecture had been delivered. It was just like any other building, but to me, a precious site. Since it was closed, I tried to peep inside through the glass panes. Then the caretaker arrived and offered to open the doors of the hall, but I stopped him, I took a good look at the hall through an open window. I can still feel the thrill I experienced, a sort of enchantment to be on that spot, the spot hallowed by the footsteps of Swamiji, the place where, with his oratory, he had won the hearts of all, scored an international victory! It was an exhilarating experience, indeed, and I felt that this was a meaningful pilgrimage.

Something strange occurred at the Ramakrishna Mission that I remember still. Swami Bishwananda said to me, 'I see you are a devotee of Swamiji.' I replied that I could not say that, but my mother was, and because of that I have read a lot of his works, and indeed there are many of his books at home. He then said, 'There's a lady who writes for our magazine, *Udbodhani*–Jyotirmoyee Devi. Do you know who she is?' So I told him that she was my mother. He laughed a lot, remarking on how small the world is. He said he had read an article by her even in the most recent issue of the magazine. He began to quote from many of her works to show me how well he was acquainted with them! I told him how much I had learnt from my mother, how we had read so much because of her. In fact, the set of Swamiji's works which my mother had bought is even now with me. Bishwananda said he enjoyed Ma's writings. I promptly came back to the hotel and wrote to my mother, describing the whole incident to her. I told her that I was thrilled to find that she had devoted readers of her works in the USA, and, in fact, I teased her that she was world famous!

Los Angeles via San Francisco. My hosts told me that I should break my journey and make a halt in order to see the Grand Canyon as not everyone got the chance to see it. So we went by plane to Santa Fe, halted there overnight, before going next morning to see the wonderful sight of the Grand Canyon. We took many photographs. It was a memorable sight. After coming back to Santa Fe, a very interesting incident took place. A young man, around 35 years old, suddenly arrived there in a jeep, saying that he had heard that someone had come here from India. I told him I was from India. He said he had been in India during the war and asked where I was from. When I said that I was from Bengal, he asked, 'Do you know the place called Jhargram?' When I told him that I did, he asked me whether I had ever been to the Agricultural College where Dr. Pabitra Sen was the principal. It turned out that the man wanted to award a scholarship to a particular student over there, and asked me whether I could go and meet him. I told him that this would be quite easy for me, but I wanted to hear his story first. He said that he had been posted in India and had been in Kalaikunda for a long time. There he had got into an intimate relationship with a young woman. I think his conscience demanded that he should do something for someone there. He wanted to provide the tuition fees for a particular student. I could not tell whether the boy was his son. He was obsessed with doing something for somebody. I feel something must have happened for which he wanted to make amends, and coming to terms with his conscience. The gentleman spent the whole evening with me. We had dinner together. When he was leaving, he gave me his address and told me that I must meet his protégé, find out about him and give him all the news. The boy used to write to him, he said, and had even expressed his desire to go to the USA, but he felt there was no need for that. He should study and try and improve his situation. That was what the principal also felt, he told me. Subsequently, the principal told me the whole story, saying that the boy did indeed want to go abroad, but he did not have the abilities that would help him to do so and that the American would send his tuition fees and all kinds of material help.

The man showed a desire to raise a child. This was not uncommon at that time. After World War I, many illegitimate children were born as a result of the liaison between soldiers and local women, and these 'war babies' were abandoned thereafter. In fact, the Kalimpong Homes had been set up to look after such babies and did a commendable job. It was only later that the home was opened out to all children. We too looked after war babies in our Save the Children Committee, the children orphaned by the Famine and by the Partition. During World War II there were again children born of involvements between local women and soldiers. Many of those soldiers did contribute heavily to our children's funds, like the man from Santa Fe.

From Santa Fe we came to San Francisco, and we were shown round the city and the surroundings. After that, there was a month-long camp in a place called Fresno. I stayed in a guesthouse and worked with a group was called ELOWIN. We stayed together, attended the camp, even went on trips together. In the weekends I would spend time with an American family, a very nice family. They had a son who would take me around everywhere and show me the sights. He was very interested to know where I had learnt English, and from whom, since I myself spoke a different language. They showed me around the Big Tree Region, the Yosemite Forest. The trees were huge! An opening had been cut out at the base of one giant tree-trunk to make a sort of tunnel, through which our car passed, with the remaining portions of the enormous trunk standing like walls on either side. We visited many other places with interesting sights, such as hills of volcanic lava.

One day, in the hotel, a guest came up to me and asked where I had come from, was it Calcutta? I said perhaps my looks betrayed that I was from Calcutta. He replied that it was not my looks but my *sindur* which had told him where I was from. This gentleman was a tourist. We met Bengalis, suddenly, in strange places. I met Triguna Sen this way. I was attending the Sunday service at the Ramkrishna Mission in Berkeley. He was listening with great concentration to the speech, his eyes were closed. But when the service was over, he did not look around, just walked out swiftly. Later, I asked him about that occasion, he said he had indeed been in Berkeley that day. He had also noticed that there was a Bengali lady in the audience, but that was all. I teased him about his amazing lack of curiosity. Didn't he wish to take a second look, to see whom it might be, whether he knew her or not!

At Berkeley I met Krishnakamini Rohatgi who later married Dr Sushil Mukherjee. We had boarded the same aircraft when leaving India a few weeks ago. I had got off at Rome while she went straight to America. She was going on a Fulbright Scholarship. I had taken her address in case I found an opportunity to visit her hostel. She was so happy to see me. We were meeting after two months. I asked her why she was looking so pale, and she replied, 'Didi, there's nothing for me to eat. I'm starving!' I teased her, 'This is a land of milk and honey! So much food is available and there's none for you? What will people say?' She said she lived on milk and ice cream and fruit. 'Can one survive on this? How much bread-and-butter can you have?' She was a Gujarati, used to dal-roti and rice, and she was also a vegetarian. Really she was having a terrible time. She was so happy to see me, almost as if I was a member of her own family! Such a brilliant student, but she was practically starving and strangely did not use her initiative and cook for herself!

Prabha Ghoshal, whose husband, Umesh Ghoshal, was an ICS officer and a colleague of my husband, also came to meet me. Her husband had brought some things from the Girl Guide office in India, which I had asked for. I had wanted some literature and some friendship bags, for I was visiting many places, many people, and I wanted to gift some tokens or small souvenirs. I also visited the branch of Ananda Ashram that had been set up here by Swami Paramananda and Sister Charushila Devi, the director of the Calcutta ashram, had given the address. Mother Gayatri Devi was the administrator of the American branch. She had been brought over by Swami Paramananda and had taken charge after his death. The ashram was in La Crescenta, California. I rang her up and told her that I had two free days. She asked me to spend Kali Puja with her. So I requested my hosts to drop me at La Crescenta on the way to Los Angeles, where I would spend two nights before rejoining them. The people at Ananda Ashram were very pleased to see me and I was equally happy to speak Bengali after all this time. I spent the day there. They were celebrating Kali Puja in the ashram, and had even made the image of the goddess themselves. I did not offer puja, that is, I did not fast till midnight and do puja. But a lecture-discourse was held at night. It was attended by many persons. I attended the function and found that it was full of Americans and that I was the only Indian. At dinner luchi, cholar dal and khichuri were served. It was a very enjoyable experience for me.

Next day, I left for Los Angeles. There too I visited the Ramakrishna Mission. I had taken all the addresses from Bharat Maharaj here. The swamijis there asked me to have lunch with them. So, I completed my programmes with the Girl Guides and came back there for lunch. How thoughtful, how caring were these swamijis! They had heard that I was from Hooghly and they had cooked the favourite dishes of the people from there: kalai dal and posto. When I asked the monks whether they felt homesick, living so far away from their country, they replied that it was because they missed their own land so much that they ate Indian food! Swamiji asked me about my connection with the Ramakrishna Mission. I told him of my meeting with Swami Bishwananda, and about my mother and also about my connection with Bharat Maharaj. My brother-in-law, S. N. Sen, Himani's husband, was closely linked to the Mission, and my mother-in-law had also accepted their vows. No wonder I was close to the Ramakrishna Mission!

Next on my agenda was a three-day long camp at Los Angeles, which was a big affair. After that I would leave for Texas. So far, I had had a wonderful tour, covering almost the whole of the USA. From New York in the east, all of the north, including the Niagara Falls, then to the west, to San Francisco, having taken in the Grand Canyon in the centre, and now I would see the south. I toured all of the USA. and met many people. And all my hostesses were wonderful people. My hostess in the USA was Peggy Delano of the New York World Association of the Girl Guides and Girl Scouts.. She would write to at my various addresses and forward my letters to me. She also asked me if I had enough money, or if I needed anything in particular.

Americans were indeed a very friendly people. But when I took the first course, I felt that they were rather domineering. At that time, during Jawaharlal Nehru's days, we were very heavily indebted to America and were taking a lot of wheat from them through the PL 480 scheme. When I remarked once that we were taking the grain as a loan, they looked at me in a very arrogant fashion and said, 'Gift. It's not a loan. It's a gift.' I was very angry and retorted, 'Surely not.' What lay behind their domineering attitude was that they were helping us, and I did not like it at all! But I enjoyed discussing the history of India, explaining how the Aryans had come here, how gradually the various people of various communities had settled down together. An American was present who would assert the superiority of Americans, which did upset me. Some of the members of the audience would ask about Partition, and I would tell them that my Girl Guide cam ps were a part of the rehabilitation effort. That through such activities, I wanted to train these homeless, rootless refugees, make them forget their sorrows over whatever they had lost, and give them stability and a sense of belonging.

After Houston, I went to Florida. This was the only state where fruits like mangoes and bananas were grown. They treated us to these fruit with great enthusiasm. At that time these were not grown locally but came from Hawaii. What they did grow in large quantities were apples and grapes. In one of the places I had put up, there were vast vineyards on both sides of the house. I thought one could very well live on those grapes alone. The people there would tread all over the grapes which were strewn on the ground, and all I could think was that grapes are so expensive in India! I wanted to go round the vineyards. My hostess was taking her car out of the garage, but I told her I wanted to take a walk around the fields. Americans hardly walk! This hostess was a Jew. I found her setting milk for curds, and I asked her how she made curd. She told me that she curdled the milk with a little sour curd. We compared notes and I was delighted to find that our methods of preparing curd were the same.

I would often demonstrate our Indian cookery, either in the camps, or in front of a group of girls, or even for our hostesses. Usually, I made luchis. I would quickly knead the flour with some salt and shortening, make the balls, roll them into circle and then deep fry them. As they puffed up, my audience would be wonderstuck. "What's inside?" they asked. 'Nothing,' I answered, 'just air!' They would add, 'It's very tasty. What do you eat this with?' 'Fried potatoes,' I said. Sometimes I would make finger chips with the luchis, or perhaps a spicy, stir-fried potato dish. The other thing I used to make was the Bengali sweet dish, pantuas. I asked them to get some cottage cheese, which must not be sour. I mixed it with a little flour, kneaded the mixture, made small balls and deep-fried them, having made the syrup ahead, and would drop the fried balls into it so that they would soak for a while. Then they were ready for eating. They loved them. They were used to cakes and biscuits, this was something absolutely new for them. I had even managed to fill the centres with small bits of sugar candy so that it looked like elachdana, or the little grain of cardamom that we would otherwise have put in them. My audience loved the taste. Once, I had made 120 pantuas in one and a half hours!

The other thing I had to often demonstrate was how I wore my sari. American women were most curious about it. There's no belt, how do you keep it on? Why doesn't it fall off? I would often have to unwind my sari and show them how I tucked it into my petticoat or made the pleats. Then sometimes, some of the ladies would want to try out a sari. Sometimes they made me wear their clothes.

All this was fun. But the training in the guide camps was often quite difficult. We had to work very hard. We had to learn how to pack, how to set up a camp, how to dig the ground, so many things. In the camps, a girl would be appointed quarter master. She looked after us a little. In the morning, she would ask, 'Ashoka, what will you eat?" 'The same as everyone else,' I replied. She brought me a carton of cold milk. But I did not like that and asked her if the milk could not be heated a little. When she asked why, I said that I did not like the taste of cold milk. It was so strange, the Americans loved their milk cold. Even in hot coffee, they mixed some cold milk! So, a few days later, the quarter master came with a saucepan of hot milk for me. 'Ashoka likes hot milk,' she remarked. But what was really interesting was the way she kept the provisions cold. She dug a hole in the ground and kept the cartons of frozen milk, ham and other things in it. When she took out a carton of milk, it was still ice cold. This method of refrigeration was something I learnt from the Girl Guide camps. We were also taught how to keep food hot.

The World Association really looked after us very well. When I had taken the Pan Am flight from London to New York in August 1956, I was quite apprehensive as I knew no one in America and it was my very first visit. How would I go anywhere? I had received a letter which told me to 'look out for a green uniform'. So, when I disembarked, I looked around, and then I saw a woman wearing a green uniform. Peg Delano had come to the airport to receive me. and I had no trouble whatsoever. She took me to the Headquarters and I discovered there that they had chalked out my entire programme. I was to catch a train alone the next day. When I told them that I needed an escort, they assigned this duty to a girl guide. My hotel was very close to the United Nations office. Kamala Mukherji, a worker of our Ananda Ashram, was now in New York, her husband had set up a business there. She was a very good poet. She came to see me and took me to her house for the night. Next morning, I found two girl guides waiting to put me on the train. I asked them to have breakfast with me. They took me to a drugstore, where I saw that we would find not only drugs, but also food–cakes and biscuits, breakfast, tea, coffee, whatever you wanted. I asked the girls what they wanted to have, and treated them to a meal. Then we went to the station. It was not at all like the stations here, where there are coolies to carry your luggage and put you on the train. We had to carry our luggage ourselves and I had quite a load. Suitcases in one hand, a bag in the other, another slung on my back, and a small shoulder bag. We proceeded down the platform, till we came to the train for Washington D.C. The girls wished me good-bye and went off. When I got off at Washington, there was another green uniform, so I had no difficulty in finding my guide. I too was dressed in my uniform of Bharat Scouts and Guides, a blue sari, which was easy for them to recognize.

At Washington, we attended our first course, which was a week-long course. This was conducted, as just mentioned, by a very arrogant person, who tried to tell us how great the Americans were, how generous, how wonderful their country was, how there could not be a country as great as the USA. He also implied that we, who had come from these various countries, were inclined to beg before them. They had no problems at all, whereas we were riven by communal divides and such evils. I did not like his attitude at all. Incidentally, I became very friendly with the representative from Pakistan. She wore a green salwar-kameez as her uniform, whereas I wore a blue sari. Coming from the same subcontinent and being able to converse in a common language, Hindi, created a bond between us.

We received very extensive training at the camp at Edith Macey Training College in Pleasant Valley, New York, so that we ourselves could train girl guides back home. Getting up at dawn, we would start the day with prayers, then, after finishing our ablutions, light the campfire. I learnt to chop wood. They took photos of me chopping wood, dressed in my sari. We had to chop up a large block of wood into small pieces, otherwise we would not be able to light the campfire at night. And of course I had to take my turn. It was not easy cutting up a log of wood, but I managed. We stayed in cottages which had two or three beds. But the bathing was done in an open space, a sort of community space and that posed quite a problem for me. There were no curtains, one went there, undressed, had a shower and came out. No one had any qualms about undressing openly, but I felt quite awkward. I would wait for everyone else to finish their shower before I went for mine! There were two washbasins for washing one's clothes. We took our soap, our washing, soaked them in the hot and cold tubs, wrung them out and hung them out to dry. Another problem that I faced was with the uniform. The American Guide Camp uniform was a short skirt to be worn with high-heeled shoes or shoes and socks. That too was a problem for me, because my underwear was knee-length and I needed shorter ones to wear under the skirt. How would I wear the skirt? The situation was only resolved when my room-mate lent me two sets of her undergarments!

During the three weeks we spent at this camp, I made many friends and learnt many new things. There were two Japanese girls from Hiroshima, who had been badly affected by the bombing. Their skin was all wrinkled, like monkey skin, they looked as if they had aged prematurely. We became very close. I had taken many photographs of them. They used to wear kimonos most of the time. I too wore my saris. We played many kinds of games. Most of them were group games. And of course there was the singing round the campfire. The Japanese girls taught us their songs, I sang Bengali songs. The Brazilians sang their songs.

It was at this camp that I learnt a novel method of serving a large number of people in an orderly fashion. We would sit for our meals at long tables. There would be a Head at each end of the table. All the food was placed before her, she would serve equal portions on each plate and the plate would be passed down from hand to hand to the end of her row. In this way, each person at the table was served. The helpers kept the serving plates full, and brought her fresh plates as needed. The Head would finally take her plate when the whole row was served. I tried this system out in India and found it to be excellent. It was not a buffet, so people were eating in a regulated manner. All had equal helpings, everyone had to eat everything. No one could take more than her share, or take only what she liked, disregarding the whole group. The Heads were very experienced, often grey-haired ladies who were now trainers. But they were very smart, in their uniforms and boots.

The American ladies I met at this camp, who were also availing of this training programme, were very fine people. Most of them were housewives. Some said they had adolescent daughters, for whom they conducted guide camps, and they wanted to learn the ropes properly. They were good, sincere women, and it was this sincerity that led them to take this training. This training was not in itself anything spectacular. All of us were housewives and we knew how to cook, how to run our homes, to look after our families. But the point here was, how to get the young girls interested, how to engage them and involve them in such activity. This was the main thrust of the lectures that we attended. Many outside speakers also delivered such talks.

Most of the Americans I met were so caring that I was quite overwhelmed. I also tried to give them some little gifts. The Americans loved our handicraft items and I had taken a lot of those. The children loved sandalwood penknives, or a tiny row of ivory elephants. I had taken many small curios made of sandal-wood, brass and ivory, which had not been banned then. There were many people with whom I became very close. For example, when I came to Houston for the camp, I found I was to stay with a lady whom I had met earlier at a previous camp. It was the same in Chicago and at many other places. I came to realize that racial differences were quite intense in American society. I came in contact with many black girl guides, and while going about with them, I found that racial discrimination was a reality. It was not as if we would find a notice saying 'Blacks aren't allowed here'. But the fact that in some establishments, we saw the notice, 'No discrimination, you can come in', made things clear to us. When we went out with the coloured girls, they often refused to go to certain places. Perhaps they were afraid of being insulted. But I never faced any such discrimination myself. In fact, in Texas, there were instances, when a friend took me to a restaurant, and said, 'I've brought a guest from India,' and the answer was always 'You are our honoured guest.' In some places, I was declared a 'citizen of Texas', or a 'Big Chief of Houston', and so on. This custom was common all over the USA, but we rarely ate out. We were mostly entertained in people's homes. The Americans' courtesy to a foreigner was truly heartwarming. Aside from the kindness we had found in America I recall, at the end of this trip, a wonderful guide camp that was held in Yokohama, in which all of us participated. I had reached

Yokohama late at night and spent two days there. Our hosts were incredibly warm and hospitable. I was sitting all by myself in one corner when they made an announcement, 'There is a delegate from India.' I stood up and folded my hands in greeting and there was a warm applause. I still cannot forget how spontaneous, how natural was the treatment we got at Yokohama.

One advantage that I had in the United States was that because I knew English I could mix with the people very easily. I could understand their customs, their ways, even their jokes and it was as easy for them to make out what my needs were. This was the major difference between my trips to the United States and my later trips to the USSR and to Germany, where the language barrier really created many difficulties. In the United States, I could convey my preferences. For instance, I would tell them, I would not eat beef and wanted lamb. If I wanted some soup, I asked for it and got it. Elsewhere, I might ask for soup and get tea!

I learnt much from my trip. The first thing I saw was that there were girls as well as boys in the Scout companies, there were no companies exclusively for girls. They suggested we should introduce the same rule in India. After all, families contained both girls and boys. Why should parents neglect their daughters? I maintained that the needs of boys and girls were different in the adolescent stage. I was not sure how far it was feasible for boys and girls to mix together, to stay in camps together during this period. Yet they asserted that there was no need for this segregation. Hence, in a way, my training was not only for the girls. After I returned, the Bharat Scouts and Guides also merged into a single unit. Pandit H. N. Kunzru, the National Commissioner, felt that we should not divide the organization into two separate wings for boys and for girls.

In the Punjab, we saw how in the refugee camps, boys and girls were not separated as had been done in Bengal. Boys and girls in their teens stayed together and attended the same schools. Coeducation had become quite common there, but it was not much in practice in Bengal. Before Partition, perhaps Scottish Church College was the only coeducational institution. There were hardly any coeducational schools, as far as I know. That is why, I wanted to have two separate sections in the camps, one for boys and another for girls. But my proposal was not accepted because the others said we were being old-fashioned, maintaining purdah! I said it was not so, but I had certain reasons for my demand. I certainly feel that there is need for boys and girls to mix with each other at a certain age, but I also feel that there is a need for privacy as well, which we usually fulfil in our daily lives. In offices, we have separate lavatories for men and women. In public buses, seats are reserved for women, not because of any forced convention, but because a woman carrying a child in her arms needs a little extra help. So does an old person. A strong young boy with no load in his hands should allow an old man to sit. These are simply good manners.

On reflection I would say that there is a need for separate space sometimes, as there is for reservations, like seats for women in public transport, for men will not give up their space to women. Nor will men give up their rights, not if they have once grabbed them! They will in fact take even more, if they can! There is also the need to work together in the same space, to share it with boys and men. After the merging of the Bharat Scouts and Guides, I saw that though the women's movement should proceed separately, there was also a space where they would both have to work together, whether at home or in the field of welfare. Today the world has changed and I feel now that certainly, boys and girls should study together, they should understand each other, they should also understand that they have equal rights. There should be no discrimination between them, especially where education and such rights are concerned.

By November I had spent four months away from home and it was time for me to return. I made a slight detour on my return trip, just as I had done on my way out to America. I had begun my trip with a stopover at London. Partha's birthday was on 5 August. At that time, he was in Oxford. I planned my trip in such a way that I could spend the day with him. From India, I first went to Switzerland where a small camp was being held at a place called The Ark. It was very popular with guides from all over the world. After attending that camp, I went to Switzerland proper and spent a day at the Girl

Guide Centre, The Ark. From Switzerland, I flew to London. On 2 August Partha came to receive me at the airport, with Amitabh Gupta, the son of a friend of mine. Partha took me all around London, showing me the sights. We went to Madam Tussaud's and many other places. I asked him what he wanted for his birthday, and he asked for a camera. So I bought him one for 5 pounds and he was to take many lovely photographs with it. Next day, I went to Oxford by bus. One of Partha's friends called Shyamalendu put me on the bus and Partha was there at the other end to receive me. Since it was his birthday, I asked him what special dishes he wanted to eat that day and he said,'Cauliflower curry and rice'. In India, he had been very fond of meat, but there, he was pining for vegetarian food! We went out to a restaurant. I spent the night at Partha's lodgings and next morning, left for London, to catch my flight to New York and begin on my training.

On my way back, I returned via London and Paris. I attended Partha's convocation at Oxford. Then he joined me for two of the three days that I was in Paris. I had called him up earlier and told him about my plans. I had asked him to come to Paris since I did not know French and it would have been more enjoyable with him. He said he would be able to come if I sent him his fare, which I did. I was alone for a day in Paris, before Partha arrived. He had told me not to go out alone, since I would have language problems. But in Paris, though few people spoke English, there were signs in restaurants indicating where English was spoken. I stayed in the Girl-Guide Centre and Partha stayed in a hotel next door to it. We went all round, seeing the Louvre, and other places. Partha left for London before I left Paris. It was then that I faced a major difficulty. I was booked on a hopping flight which would go via Rome and Athens. But when I went to the airport, I was told that the plane was not going to land at Paris at all because of bad weather and heavy cloud formation. I was in a real spot as the airlines people refused to make arrangements for me for a break journey, although I had a major argument with them over this issue. In desperation, I rang up the Indian embassy, but got no response from them either. Finally, I rang up the Pakistani embassy. I was in for a real surprise. The

Pakistani ambassador, Prabhat Mukul Choudhury, was actually from Chittagong and very well known to me. He told me that he would at once bring me to the embassy from the airport. But I said that my problems would have to be sorted out first. The airlines people were going to give me a ticket via Karachi, but I had no visa for Karachi, and since I did not speak French, I was unable to explain what my problem was. He promised to settle my visa woes.

He and his wife came over and took me to the embassy. That night, they threw a party for me, at which many young Bengali men were present. They were so pleased to meet me, to talk in Bengali with me! Though it was almost a decade since the Partition, they were even now full of nostalgia for their land and their language. I spent the night with the Choudhurys. At night, Mr. Choudhury brought out his official seal and stamped my passport, so that I would have no difficulty in Karachi. This was indeed a pleasant experience for me.

But that was not the end to my troubles. When we landed at Karachi airport the next morning, something went wrong with the BOAC aircraft, and it would not go further. I would have to board a flight to India next morning at six. But I was on a transit visa and it would expire at 2 a.m.! Once again, it was an old friend who came to my rescue. I remembered that Mr. M. H. Khan, my husband's colleague, whom we had known very intimately in Krishnanagore when he was the Superintendant of Police, had opted for Pakistan and was based in Karachi. When I asked about him in the airport, they said he was a very senior intelligence officer, and they rang him up so I could speak to him. Mr. Khan was delighted to hear my voice and told me that he would 'arrest' me from the airport and take me home. When I told him that my transit visa was valid only till 2 a.m., he promised to get me to the airport by that time. There was a mighty uproar in the Khan household when I arrived there. Mrs. Khan set about preparing a lovely dinner. We had a lot to say to each other. Our sons were practically the same age and they used to play together, act in the same dramas, in Krishnanagore.

Because I was worried that I had not been able to inform my husband of the change in my programme from Paris onwards, Mr.

Khan rang up Calcutta and my husband was on the line. He was obviously astounded to hear my voice. He said he was about to leave for the airport to pick me up. I told him that according to my new schedule, I would reach by about 2.30 in the afternoon, the next day. Then my husband had a chat with Mr. Khan as well. Very soon I was back in Calcutta, but Fate had given me a fine opportunity to catch up with two good friends, who had extended invaluable help when the Indian embassy had failed me.

Twenty-Six

Our Children Grow Up

Partha spent seven years in Oxford, from 1953 to 1960. By that time he had completed his Ph.D. In 1956, I had attended his Convocation in Oxford. We had also spent some time together in Paris. In 1957, 20-year-old Kunta went to the Windsor Camp of the Girl Guides in London. At that time, she too spent a few days with Partha. He had settled down quite well in England. My husband kept up a very regular correspondence with Partha, writing long letters to him every Saturday. In contrast, I wrote less frequently, perhaps once in a fortnight. We felt that he was not averse to settling down in England, though we, his parents, never wanted that. But it was his uncle, whom he called Runu Mama, who took a decisive step in this matter. Runu Mama, a doctor, had married an Englishwoman and settled in England. He convinced Partha to visit us once before taking the final decision. Partha came to us in 1960, and decided to stay here, and we were happy with his decision. Partha was very attached to the extended family, especially his elder uncle Anil and his cousins.

After a brief stint at Burdwan University, Partha moved to Delhi, where he filled in a leave vacancy for Tapan Raychaudhuri in the School for African Studies at Delhi School of Economics. Later, he joined Delhi University, where he remained throughout his career. At this time, he was considered to be a very eligible bachelor and we received many proposals of marriage for him. However, soon afterwards, he met Narayani Menon, a brilliant student of history, who was preparing to go to Oxford after her masters degree. Mr. Bisheshwar Prasad introduced the two of them, thinking that Partha might be able to advise Narayani about her plans to go abroad for study. However, a romance soon blossomed. They were engaged before Narayani left for England. At first, they did not want us to make their engagement public. But we kept getting many proposals for Partha. On one occasion, we were invited to tea by a very respectable family in Maurice Nagar in Old Delhi, expressly for this purpose. After that in order to avoid further embarrassment, Partha asked us to announce his engagement to Narayani.

Partha and Narayani were married in 1966. We were very happy with the match. Narayani had been born in Patna and spoke Bengali quite well even before her marriage. Her background was similar to ours, for her father, V.K.R. Menon was also an I.C.S. officer. As a family we tried to be as broad-minded as possible and had told our children that we would not select partners for them. They should find their own partners, and we would host the wedding party! So we did not mind in the least when Partha chose to marry a girl of his choice. My mother and mother-in-law were equally delighted. Later, Pulak, my brother-in-law Mrinal's grandson, decided to marry a Muslim girl. My mother-in-law had blessed the couple, saying that since marriages are made in Heaven, why should we make a fuss over the girl being from a different community? When the son of my nonod, Tarubala, announced that he wanted to marry a divorcee, Ma said that she had no objection whatsoever. After all, did not widows remarry? As for my mother, her attitude was that such marriages broke down prejudices and bias. So, we all welcomed the brides with open hearts.

Partha and Narayani's wedding was conducted in the traditional Nair style. Narayani's father and uncles, dressed in their starched white mundus and angavastrams, appeared so handsome and distinguished! Of course, our custom of sending a *tattva* with fish threw them into confusion because they were a generally vegetarian family. But apart from that, there were no problems. The bridal couple exchanged garlands after the bride had gone round the groom three times. It was a small, neat affair followed by the yagna or fire ceremony of the Bengalis.

Kunta's marriage was more traditional. She was acquainted with Kajal Das Gupta through her friends at Science College. Her father and I approached his family with a formal proposal. The marriage was celebrated with all the customary fanfare. Because of her marriage, she lost the opportunity of studying abroad with a state scholarship. Kunta began her career as a university lecturer in 1962. She also became an external examiner with various other universities. She was very active in Girl-Guide activities.

By the end of the 1950s, the various branches of our extended family were gradually getting settled, some in Calcutta, some in places like Krishnanagore. At that time we lived on Hungerford Street. After years of carrying the responsibilities for all the family-members, I suggested to my husband, that my elder ja, Bidhutlata, could move to Krishnanagore with her children, and my mother-in-law could live with another son for a while. But my husband was nor willing to allow Ma to live anywhere else. As for my sister-in-law, Ma had a special affection for her, since she was the first daughter-in-law to enter our house, and since she had come as a very young girl. So, when we built our own house in Gol Park, we planned it in such a way that my mother-in-law, sister-in-law and her children had adequate space to themselves. We held the *grihapravesh* ceremony for our new house on Apala's birthday in 1960. I missed having a study or at least a corner to myself, where I could keep my papers, my correspondence, and so on. Often I would spread out all my papers on the dining table. But since adjustment had been a key word in our family life all along, this too became a part of my schedule.

At this time, my mother, Jyotirmoyee Devi, was at the height of her reputation as a writer. Earlier, she used to live with her sons or daughters, as each one took up a job and settled down. In 1961, my mother who had a plot of land in Hathibagan wanted a house for herself and my husband helped her to build one. She now enjoyed a much more settled life. She had published her first collection of stories. *Raj-jotak,* much earlier, with the help of Sajani Kanta Das through my efforts. Eminent litterateurs like Prabodh Kumar Sanyal and Sajani Kanta Das and my brother-in-law Goshtho Bihari Chatterjee were very appreciative of Ma's works and she also had a faithful following among *prabashis*. She had been a part of the literary circle popularly known as *prabashi sahittiks* (Bengali writers from outside Bengal) like Suresh Chandra Chakrabarti, the editor of *Uttara*, and was close to many other writers like Sita Devi, Shanta Devi and Anurupa Devi. It was Kanti Ghosh who introduced her to the authors' circle in Calcutta, and soon she established herself as a forthright, observant writer. I often accompanied her to various meetings and even to political meetings.

Among Ma's close friends were Radharani Devi, the famous poet and writer, the mother of the writer Nabaneeta Dev Sen, and Charulata Mukerjee, a well-known social worker who had also served the AIWC as its Patron and was the mother of Renuka Ray, with whom I had worked earlier (see Chapter 24). She too was an admirer of my mother and would invite her for various meetings. In 1975, a conference on the legal status of women was organized by Renuka Ray, in which the victims themselves spoke about their experiences in the presence of women judges. Sankar Prasad Mitra, Chief Justice of Calcutta High Court, presided over the conference and Padma Khastagir and Manjula Bose, women judges, were invited to hear the speakers. Renuka took my mother to the conference as an honoured guest. It is from experiences like these that Ma continued to study the social situation, which formed the background to her stories and novels.

A major achievement on our part at this time was editing Ma's writings and publishing a complete set of her works. Partha and the noted writers Bani Roy, Gour Kishore Ghosh and Mahasweta Devi helped me a great deal with this project. Ma received accolades from many quarters for her writings, and was given many awards. The Parisad Padak (medal), the Ladies Study Group Cash Prize and the Bhubanmohini Padak. More important, the children inherited from their grandmother, a love of books, of literature and the Bengali language, which I feel have been a major influence on all of them. Two of our children had married and moved away and the family had shrunk. I now began to get more and more involved with the world outside the home.

Twenty-Seven

My Visit to the USSR

In 1957, the USSR invited a delegation from the AIWC for a month-long tour organized by the Soviet Women's Committee. The AIWC's chairperson, Lakshmi Menon, nominated me as one of the six members. My youngest daughter, Apala, was still small but I could not resist the desire to see the USSR. The other members of the delegation were Tapati Mukherji, Nirmala Desai, a Gujarati, and Vishalakshmi Narayan Swami from Andhra. Our delegation was led by Mitha Lam, an eminent barrister of Bombay, and Masuma Begum was the deputy leader. She knew Arabic and Persian very well, which was a great advantage. When we went to places like Uzbekistan, she would give a vote of thanks in Persian, which was generally quite well understood in those places, and it gave us a sort of link with the local people.

Our delegation did visit many institutions so that we got an idea of the way organizations worked and how society functioned, and we did some sightseeing too. We were taken round many interesting places including Leningrad, Tashkent, Samarkand, Uzbekistan, the Black Sea coast and Tajikistan. In Moscow we saw the Lenin Mausoleum and found the embalmed bodies of both Lenin and Stalin displayed there. The bodies were so lifelike, they looked as if they were merely asleep! When I visited the museum a second time in 1988, the body of Stalin was no longer there. By that time, Stalin had lost his place in Russian history as one of the architects of the nation, and his body had been removed from its position of honour.

Our Russian tri p was very interesting for many reasons. We had interpreters, and had no real difficulty. Besides, the people were warm and friendly. We found their hospitality very appealing, especially in Uzbekistan and Tajikistan. I found the people of these areas very similar to our own, open, hearty, fun-loving people like the Punjabis. Another thing I found very amusing was the fact that many words in their language were common with our own. They too called raisins 'kismis' and 'tarmooj' and 'kharbuja' were also the same. The names of the fruit Babur had brought to India from here remain common to both our countries. The food too was similar. They served us tandoori food, naan and pilau. They would organize parties for us, and really exerted themselves to entertain us. We found that their notions of hospitality were very similar to our own. So much food! We would go for lunch, and there were so many kinds of fruit and kebabs, we would be quite full eating all those items. Then, mounds of meat and biriyani would appear. The Uzbeks and Tajiks also love music and dance. They sang Hindi songs for us. When we asked them how they came to know these, they said that Raj Kapoor had gone to Russia once and taught them these songs. In one place, we also heard a Bhatiali song. We enjoyed hearing our songs on their li ps. Their music, accom panied by mandolins, is also lovely.

Russia is a land of very mixed cultures. These places, such as Tajikistan have a pronounced oriental influence, which provides an exotic touch, and makes them appear closer to us in affinity. But when I went to Moscow, I sensed the difference. It was like being in a different country. Moscow was much more European. I had heard so much about Moscow. I found that it was a very old city, with beautifully preserved old buildings. They obviously loved marble, which they had used extensively in their architecture. Plenty of people here spoke English. But where food was concerned, it was monotonous for the vegetarians among us, because they had little choice apart from yogurt and salad. If they asked for soup, it might be made of beef stock. Vegetables served to them might have been taken from a meat stew. It was difficult to explain to them our concept of contamination of vegetarian food when it was cooked with non-vegetarian food. So the vegetarians stuck to yogurt and salad. When we sat for meals, we were divided into our two groups: Mitha Lam, Masuma Begum, Tapati Mukherjee and I, the non-vegetarians, and the other two who maintained a strict vegetarian code. When we were on the last leg of our journey after visiting Moscow and Leningrad, Tapati Mukherji fell quite seriously ill. We were on a quick tri p to the Black Sea coast and the sea air must have disagreed with her. She had such a very severe attack of asthma that she seemed to be at death's door. We were advised to send her away from the coast as she was probably allergic to something in the atmosphere. She left for Moscow and began to recover almost immediately.

Our delegation was a very effective one. We had Mitha Lam, one of the foremost lawyers of the day. Tapati Mukherji was a writer. She was also excellent at reciting poetry and would often recite her own as well as Sarojini Naidu's poems. Masuma Begum, with her fluency in Persian, was able to create an immediate rapport with her audience. Pooling all these talents together, we effectively explained to our hosts how changes were being introduced in the legal framework of our country, the work we were doing at AIWC, our social service programme. We also invited them to visit our country.

The first thing that I noticed as we arrived in the USSR was that the faces of ordinary people, especially young girls and women, appeared sad. One of the air hostesses on the flight from Kabul to Tashkent was practically in tears when I asked about her children.

She had had to leave a sick baby and come on this trip and there was no possibility of taking leave because she had just a limited number of days off. One day from my Hotel Sovietskaya I saw that an elderly man took keys from a woman attendant who worked on our floor. It turned out that when she came to the hotel to work, he would be at home and vice versa. This was how they managed to catch up on news or talk about something important. Both appeared to be sad and grave. I realized that the Soviet system gave no importance to individuals and everyone had to put in the compulsory eight to twelve hours of duty come what may. In the crèches too the babies were taken care of efficiently but there was little emphasis on being loving and affectionate. The caretakers seemed to do the work mechanically. When I asked one of the attendants which babies she took care of, she said that all took turns with the children and no attachment was allowed to develop. I thought of how each child needs mothering and needs to develop a sense of attachment for psychological security, which was being disregarded.

Though we were shown round the places no one was allowed to interact with us freely or to ask personal questions. At the Trade Unions too I saw that the Unions were geared to making the workers reach the maximum targets. No one was allowed to raise a voice. The leaders added that in order to fulfil the requirements of the state there was no question of permitting strikes or raising wages. The state's needs would be put first. Our visits to hospitals showed us that these were of high quality and were very clean. About 50 percent of the employees were women but they were at the lower level and most of the higher posts were held by men. There was certainly a strict hierarchy amongst the health workers with doctors, specialists and managers at the top and the nurses, attendants and cleaners below. When we visited the farms we were told that everything grown in the community farms went to the state owned warehouses and cultivators could not keep anything for themselves. They were given about an acre to grow what they wished and rear cattle or poultry. I saw that there was certainly a lack of freedom in the USSR and it caused me much pain and many questions remained unanswered. I had to admit, though, that the country was progressing but it seemed to be at the cost of human rights. The people did get work for eight hours and were economically better off, but they had no freedom of speech or no control over their lives and that certainly bothered me.

The very next year, the Soviet Women's Committee came to India on our invitation. By that time, no new relief camps were being opened in West Bengal as the government was not going to give any loans. We took the Russian delegation round to the Udayvilla Camp, where the director at the time was Bina Das. This camp was famous for all the various types of handicrafts the inmates produced. They engaged in knitting, weaving, printing, painting, and even ceramics and everything was of such good quality that there was a heavy demand for them from all over India. The Russian team was served a meal on ceramicware produced in the camp. They were really astounded at the beauty and variety of the things available there. We held a party for them on behalf of the Social Welfare Board. Another reception was organized at YWCA, where Rajaji was present. He was not posted in Calcutta then and it was purely by chance he happened to be there that day. All the women's organizations got together and accorded a warm welcome to the Russian women.

Twenty-Eight

Travels to Brazil, the USA and to Japan

In June 1962, S. K. Dey, Minister of Community Development, sent a letter asking whether I was willing to go as a non-official delegate to an international conference on social work to be held at Petropolis near Rio de Janeiro. It would be a one-and-a-half month long tour. After attending the conference, we would go to Mexico, and then onto many centres in America. We were to review the working of the 4H Youth Club programme, to study their programmes for girls, to see how they developed their projects and what problems they faced. So I packed my bags again.

Our trip took place in June 1962. This time our group consisted of three members: B. S. Murthy, the Deputy Minister for Health and Social Welfare, was the leader of the delegation; a young man, M. G. Nanavati, an official of the community development programme was in charge of our schedule, and I was the non-official delegate, the deputy leader of the delegation. We had to take shots for yellow fever, since we were stopping in Dakar. Then, after a stopover in Italy, we landed in Rio de Janeiro. Since our own delegation was so small, I had no idea that the conference would be such a large one with perhaps ten thousand delegates. We disembarked at Rio and were taken to a place about 40 to 50 kms away called Petropolis. We were put up at an enormous hotel. There were so many rooms in that hotel, that but for the reception people, I would surely have been lost. Strangely enough, there is a street in Rio de Janeiro named after Mahatma Gandhi. And just before our trip, the Indian ambassador had been B. K. Acharya, ICS, who had made a great effort to bring Indian culture to the people of Brazil. Unfortunately, he had moved out of Rio by the time we went there. We had quite some difficulty with languages there. Very few people spoke English, most of them spoke Portuguese. When I went to my room, I found there was no soap, though they had provided towels. So I went to the Reception counter on my floor and asked for soap. They could not understand what I said, so I pretended I was washing my hands. But still they did not understand what I was trying to convey to them. Next I tried rubbing my palms together, but no one could make out what I was trying to say. Suddenly, I had a hunch and said the word *sabun*, the Hindi for soap. 'Oh, you want *sabun*,' they exclaimed and brought out a cake of soap! The same incident was more or less repeated in the case of a measuring tape. Unable to make them understand the word 'tape', I said I wanted a *phita,* the Bengali equivalent, and they immediately understood. I realized how our vocabulary has been enriched by words from Portuguese. And just as in the case of the Russians, here too I found that some words for fruit and vegetables that had been brought to India from Portugal were common. They too used words such as 'papaya' and 'ananas', as we did.

The landscape of that part of the land was also familiar, with its profusion of coconut and areca palms. You could mistake it for West Bengal or East Bengal. I found it fascinating. And while going round the country, I actually came face to face with another aspect of our own history: the faces of the people, their physical features and their general appearance, seemed familiar and I realized how deep was Portugal's influence upon our own country. They had left many descendants in India. We all know about Goa and Diu and Daman, but we hardly realize that the Portuguese influence was equally strong in Bengal. On seeing the people of Rio, I felt that I had seen many similar faces in Chittagong and Noakhali. The names Gomes and Fernandes, which were quite common in East Bengal, were proof of the fact that the Portuguese had married local women and sired many descendants. Luchi and malai curries, cooked with coconut milk, were also proof of their influence on Bengali life, apart from the many words that entered our language with their advent. They left churches in many parts of the country, including in Bengal, where their religious literature and books were distributed, and I have seen these books in Cox's Bazaar . Though the predominant foreign influence of this period has been that of the English, the Portuguese influence is not negligible either. It is the French and the Dutch influence that have been comparatively marginal.

Portugal's Indian connection made itself felt in many unexpected ways. During our stay in Rio, we were sometimes invited to the homes of the local people. We were surprised to find that we were served with luchi and paratha of the kind we make at home. Their pulao was no different from ours, the curries were the same. In fact, the word 'curry' is Portuguese as well. On one of my flights, I noticed that they were offering something called 'Prawn a la Bengal'. Out of curiosity, I ordered it, and was not really surprised to find that it was nothing but prawn malaikari. The hospitality of these people was also exemplary. They made us feel very much at home.

The conference focused on rural and urban development. A working party had met well ahead of time to prepare a statement designed to clarify the ideas of the conference at Recife. The working committee has studied: *(i)* theory of community development; *(ii)* human factors involved; *(iii)* practice of community development; and *(iv)* the future of community development. The committee gave the delegates the following to consider: (*i)* Should community development be initiated and run by the government or other organizations or both? *(ii)* What should be the function of community development in the formation of local government bodies where these do not already exist? *(iii)* What would be the relationshi p between community development and local government in the field activities? *(iv)* How would effective coordination be carried out? *(v)* what is the administrative structure required? Should the primary responsibility be vested in the Council of Ministers under the Prime Minister or President, with im plementation through the various technical ministries? Should there be a separate administrative body, as in India? Should it be given to existing technical departments? *(vi)* Is community development a distinct technical field requiring a specialized disci pline or what should be the content of the training? *(vii)* Should 'mulitpurpose' workers be trained at the field level and what would be the function and content of training auxiliary workers in community development and in specialized technical fields?

The conference was divided into five Commissions and seven Study Groups in addition to eight Plenary Sessions presided over by eminent social workers. At the Plenary Session there were papers on rural and urban community development by highly experienced people but there were no discussions nor were recommendations presented at the closing session. The five commissions dealt with: *(i)* unity development and organization and was chaired by Charles Hendry, Dean of the School of Social Work, University of Toronto. The vice chairman was Husain Bin Isa from the Ministry of Rural Development in Malaya; *(ii)* interrelationshi p of social work and other disci plines and was chaired by our leader, B. S. Murthy and the vice chairman was Guiliano Mazzoni, Institute of Social Service, Rome; urban community development: *(iii)* special needs and characteristics was chaired by Robert Leaper, University of Swansea, Wales and the vice chairman was Mercedes Esquerra from Chile; *(iv)* rural development and its special needs was chaired by Sybil Francis of Jamaica from the Ministry of Housing and Social Welfare and the vice chairman was Victor Lopez from the Ministry of Social Welfare and Health from Venezuela. *(v)* Development Training and uses of leadership resources was led by my old friend Dr Kenneth Kindlesberger, Dean of the School of Social Work, University of Louisville, Kentucky. I had worked with him in Syracuse in 1956. In addition there were seven Subgroups and one of them, Role and Training of Professional Social Workers for Community Development was led by Herman Stein of the USA and M. C. Nanavati, the Indian delegate. I was the vice chairman of the Subgroup dealing with development of family and child welfare services within a community development programme. It was chaired by Dr. E. S. Mendoza from Venezuela and consisted of over 40 people and we were divided into two language groups, Portuguese and Spanish under Dr Mendoza and the other in English under my charge.

Except for the Plenary Sessions, all Commissions and Subroups met at the same time and so participants could not attend other groups or sessions. Moreover because the final recommendations of the groups never came up before the Plenary Sessions, each Subgroup and Commission had to be satisfied with the findings of one aspect of the whole theme. However we were informed that the conference had evolved this method after considerable experience gained in previous conferences and the main purpose was to provide an opportunity for persons with common interests to come together and receive guidance from the experienced and exchange ideas. During the discussions we learnt that there were indeed common problems but that the method of solution would differ from country to country. I found at the end of the conference that there were a dozen people I exchanged addresses with and kept in touch with but the rest of the 2200 people remained as an indistinct memory.

The best speech was that of Julia Henderson, Director of the Bureau of Social Affairs, UN. She gave a brief history of community development and paid tribute to India for pressing the need for it as early as 1948 and focussing the attention of the UN on it in 1952. B. S. Murthy had read out a paper on India's achievements in this sphere in one of the Plenary Sessions. The President of the Conference, Dr. Lester Granger, handled it very ably and his wife was very popular with everyone. We felt the conference had been a great success and parted with tears from our Girl Guide friends.

One incident that still retains its brightness in my memory was of an evening towards the end of our stay in Rio. It was the last day of the conference and each country gave a show or sang a song. Mr. Murthy who was a good singer was tired and had retired to bed. We were asked to sing, and though I was not a good singer I could not refuse and finally sang Dwijendralal Roy's '*Dhana-dhanya-pushpa-bhara*'. What was astounding was that when it was time to sing the refrain, the entire hall joined me. Nanavati sang the main verses along with me and as for the rest, we all sang the chorus verses together. It was wonderful. I was so delighted! I also sang Rabindranath Tagore's song '*Momo Chitte Niti Nritte Ke Je Nache*', clapping my hands to the rhythm. The people were genuinely interested in hearing an Indian song, and how well they responded when I sang! It was a most heart-warming experience. The next morning, I related the whole story to the minister. He was quite sorry to have missed the fun, since he was a good singer. And I had had to fill his place with my thin voice!

We came to the end of our trip and were ready to go onto the next part of our journey, but the minister fell ill. We had to get him admitted to a hospital. Then, since we had a lot of free time on our hands, Nanavati and I went sightseeing all over Rio. What I remember most was the imposing statue of Jesus Christ on a high column, facing the harbour, his hands stretched out to the sea as if he were greeting all newcomers. I bought a small replica of that statue as a souvenir as well as photos of it. This was the time I had my first ever ride in a cable car. I will not say I was not at all afraid, but I enjoyed the experience too.

When the minister recovered, we left Rio. We were to go to Mexico, but the flight to Mexico was cancelled on that day. We boarded a plane for New York. We were to attend a big party on arrival, but when we got off at the airport, the authorities asked us to wait. We had already boarded the car, and they made us all get off and called us inside. I thought that some of our papers might not be in order and I was about to send Nanavati when they insisted that we all come inside. They took us to a room, put us inside and locked the door. We were horrified. We did not know what was happening. Later, we were told that a child on our flight had been afflicted with a rash. They were verifying whether it was some kind of pox or not. Though we had taken all our shots, we were all to be quarantined. So we were kept imprisoned there and of course the embassy officials who had come to receive us were quite panicky. After much confusion, we understood that we would be released only after receiving the vaccination, and the fumigation of our belongings. By the time we were released, the party in our honour was almost over. Finally we were taken to our hotel. It was not before the next day that our suitcases reached us after the clothes had been taken out and fumigated. By that time, our programme had been quite upset.

This time, my time in New York was spent more in sightseeing than in studying. First we went to see the Empire State Building, the tallest building then, and the Statue of Liberty. In the evening there was a discussion with the social welfare groups. After finishing the day's work, I contacted the Girl Guide office. They took me out to dinner that night in an exotic revolving restaurant, and sitting high up there I had a glimpse of New York by night. They invited us to a party the next day, where the minister was also invited. They really treated us both with great warmth and hospitality at the party. After New York, wherever we went, Washington, Chicago, everywhere I would contact the Girl Guides and we would get the same terrific reception. One day the minister told me, 'I see that you're quite an international figure!' I replied that I was certainly not an international figure but that my Girl Guide organization was one.

The next day, we flew to San Francisco. Our hotel overlooked the Bay, and it had a wonderful view. I was thrilled to see so many penguins. The whole scene appeared unreal somehow, like a dream. We saw the famous Golden Gate Bridge and all the sights of San Francisco. I found my friend's daughter, Chitra Rao Bose, waiting for me in San Francisco. When I asked her how she knew I was coming to the city, she said her mother had written to her, telling her that she had sent a parcel for her with me. The next day, Chitra came to see me at my hotel. I took out the huge parcel of blouses her mother had got stitched for her. Then she went through my saris. When she came to know that my trip was almost over, and I would now only visit Los Angeles and Hawaii before returning home, she said, 'I'll take all your saris and pay for them in dollars.' I was really indignant. 'Why must you pay me?' I asked her. 'My trip is financed by the Government of India. Take the saris that you like!' So she selected all my new saris and one old one as well. I gladly gave them to her.

Chitra took me to her flat for lunch. She asked what I would like to eat. I said I would have whatever she cooked. 'But I won't cook!' she said. I was puzzled. What were we going to eat, I wondered. She showed me a number of packets marked 'Monday', 'Tuesday', 'Wednesday' and so on. She said she did all her cooking for the whole week on Sunday and kept the food packed and frozen. She asked me which day's food I wished to have. I said we should have the food reserved for that day. I do not remember what day it actually was, but she insisted we take out the packet in which there was fish, and also another day's packet. When I protested that her schedule would be upset, she would not listen. Her husband came home for lunch, and also the daughter who was with them. Their other child was probably living with her grandmother, Amal Prabha Bose, in India then. We had a delicious lunch. I was much impressed by the systematic and efficient way the girl young woman managed her home and her career, neglecting neither. She was working in a hotel at that time. Later she dropped me at my hotel. My next stop was Berkeley. After that we went on to Los Angeles. Everywhere, we visited the 4H clubs and welfare organizations.

The next place on our itinerary was Hawaii. As we approached the islands by plane, we were amazed to see a series of huge gaping holes like craters appear in the ground, which had all been caused by earthquakes and volcanic activity. Yet people also lived here. I have never seen a lovelier place than Hawaii. As we came out of the plane, we were greeted by young girls who garlanded us with marigold leis. Our minister was beaming—young girls garlanding him, some even biting his small finger gently according to their custom! We were put up in the East-West University of Hawaii. Our hostess, Mrs. Watumal, had invited us for dinner that night, but unfortunately, I slipped and fell and hurt my knee so badly that I could not attend the dinner. The minister of course was delighted to go, and he had a good time at the party, what with the songs, the dinner and the night clubs. I missed that experience. Next day, Mrs. Watumal came to see me. She told me that I should have informed her about my accident and she would have found a way of getting me to the dinner. I replied that I had not wanted to upset her. But we became very good friends. She gave us a lot of literature, showed us around the university. There was an exchange programme for students of Hawaii to come to India and for Indian students to go to Hawaii. She told me that when I returned to India, I must look out for good students and get them to avail of the exchange programme. Mrs. Watumal and I kept up our friendship for many years. She is now no more, but the East-West University of Hawaii is still going strong.

Our next destination was Philippines but our plane was unable to land there because of a terrible typhoon. So we landed in Tokyo instead. And what a time we had at the airport itself! The Japanese are such a polite people that their very politeness threatens to choke you! They bowed to us and we bowed back, they bowed again and so did we, and this went on ad infinitum. They shuffled backwards and forwards and we tried to take a few firm steps, but could not even inch forward! When ultimately these courtesies came to an end, we finally came out of the airport. We were taken to the Imperial Hotel. We observed that the terrible scars of World War II were still all to a evident. Any mention of Hiroshima or Nagasaki still brought tears to their eyes. The was had brought untold misery to them, had brought death and destruction to a degree almost unthinkable. But how bravely they were rebuilding society and state! They showed us around many organizations, including some vocational training centres for girls. We noticed that in Japan, girls also worked professionally.

At our request, they took us to see a residential training institution for girls. When I asked the girls how they felt about their situation, we were told that there was plenty of discrimination against women in Japanese society. The girls felt that they were treated as inferiors. All the benefits went to the menfolk, the girls did not receive even a quarter of them. They did the same jobs but they did not receive equal pay. What was worse, when they went home, they had to cook and clean and look after their menfolk and children single-handedly. The husbands would come home after work, eat their dinner and go out for the rest of the evening. Visits to nightclubs and geishas were common. The men would not help their wives to look after the children. It seemed they were the responsibility of the women alone. The girls said they realized that though they too went to school and had all the advantages of an education, they knew that the boys had a higher place in society and women were supposed to serve their menfolk. The more senior an official, the more liberties he took, with nobody to reprimand him or say anything. The men had no respect at all for the women. I listened to the complaints of the young women and thought that this injustice, this exploitation, was not visible. These women were all so pretty, so soft and dainty, that it did not appear as if they suffered from any sort of exploitation.

We attended a Tea Ceremony and found ourselves at the receiving end of their amazing hospitality. Everything was bound by formal rituals. The first half hour was spent by the hostesses daintily wiping the teacups and saucers with napkins, while we became so impatient that we felt absolutely exasperated. By the time the tea came, it was almost cold. We sipped it slowly, holding the cup with a napkin in both hands, just as we saw the others doing. This was my experience of a genuine Japanese ritual. Apart from this, we visited many stores, exhibitions and institutions. Having talked to many girls, I came to the conclusion that girls in Japan were in no better a position than girls elsewhere. Compared to their Indian sisters, they might have more exposure, more freedom to venture into the outside world, whereas Indian women were far more cloistered. But where attitudes were concerned, the treatment they received from society was no different from us. They were definitely not regarded as equals by the men. In spite of their working outside, they had to bear all the responsibility for the family themselves. The link between family members appeared to be quite strong. They too had close bonds with parents and children, though the joint family system did not exist there.

There were still many 'geishas' in Japan, though not as many as after World War I. It was at that time that many women had taken the occupation of entertaining men, since they had no training for any other kind of job. Many men had died during the war, and these women had to find a way to support their families. The situation of these girls was no different from their poorer, more distressed Indian sisters in the same profession. The Japanese geisha might have earned more, she might have been more refined and better dressed, but psychologically, their situations were the same. I spoke to some of them who knew a little English.

The next day, a Japanese gentleman came to help me buy a camera. I really wanted to buy a camera and Japanese cameras were known to be the best then. So we bought a famous camera, and the gentleman showed me how it worked. But I made the mistake of not taking the receipt for the purchase. This was at the final end of the journey, after this we would be going home. We flew to Delhi via Hong Kong. When we were flying over Calcutta, I felt so sad that we would first be going to Delhi, though Calcutta was so close! My son had come to receive me at the airport. The customs authorities had a look at the camera and asked for the receipt. I said I had a tax exemption as I was a tourist. But since there was no receipt, I had to pay a fine. That too amounted to 50 rupees, but I only had dollars with me. Partha heard the fracas from afar and came up and paid the fine. So finally I brought my five-hundred-rupee Japanese camera to India with a fifty-rupee fine. Then I came out of the airport and sighed with pure joy. What a wonderful feeling to get back to one's own land! Partha was teaching in Delhi at that time, at the Delhi School of Economics, and I stayed with him that night.

Before I left Delhi, S. K. Dey, the Minister for Community Development, had invited us for lunch and had asked us what we had learnt on the trip. I told him that the conference on International

Projects on Community Development in Rio de Janeiro had been very successful and we had met many people from all over the world. Indeed we had garnered much rich experience. We had also described the measures and the projects we devised here and their outcome, using our system of Panchayeti raj as an exam ple and our audience too had felt that we had been able to make progress. Because of my work with the Social Welfare Board (see Chapter 30), I had coordinated programmes with the community development programmes, so I had first-hand experience of the work, and had noticed the outcome of the changes we had introduced. During the earlier projects, the boys and girls used to work separately. But now, there were joint projects. When the Panchayet called a meeting, the speaker would sit on a charpai, the others would sit on mats or carpets spread all around. The women would be in the background, near the walls, and they would have their faces covered, but they would be present. They would take an interest in the proceedings. They would prepare the refreshments. Neither did the men treat them with disrespect. There was a friendly, open air about these meetings.

In the countries we visited, we had found there would be a community centre at which these community programmes would be held. All the people came there, converged there and sorted out their projects and programmes. What we saw there was the inclusion of the adolescent group through clubs like the 4H Club, which had no equivalent in India. Moreover, in India, young girls and newly-married women had no place or organization of their own, though the older women all partici pated in community programmes. These were the differences I had noted in our situation, and I had liked the new things we had seen. We had indeed learnt a lot from the various places we had visited. We had also carried back a lot of literature. The Rio organization continued to send us literature in large quantities, but since it was all in Portuguese, it was not of much use to us

I was eager to get onto the first possible train for Calcutta. Kunta's wedding had taken place just before my departure on this long tri p and I had left with my house in disarray. As we were leaving for the station, my brother-in-law, Nirmal Sen Gupta, my cousin Deepali's husband, arrived with a ticket for the train to Calcutta. How happy I was! He saw me off at the station. That first meal in the dining car—in those days there used to be dining cars equipped with tables where meals were served—consisted of nothing more than dal, vegetables and rotis, but it tasted heavenly to me. I still remember my feelings of that time, my sheer joy at being home and tasting Indian food.

My husband was at the station to receive me together with my nephew Pranab. As soon as we reached home, we went to see Kunta in her new home, for I had gone away just a few days after her marriage. My two daughters at home were Apala, then nine or ten years old, and she was very happy to see me and Kasturi, who was nearly twenty, a student at Presidency College, studying for her BA Hons degree.

Twenty-Nine

Dandakaranya Again

In 1962, the refugee problem became acute once more. There was a major influx across the border. At this time my husband was offered the post of Chairman of the Dandakaranya Development Authority. He stipulated specific conditions: he would only take up the post if certain powers were given to him. The government agreed, but verbally, and later he faced many problems because these powers had not been given to him in writing. My husband joined his new post in November 1963. I too was to go along with him but I was delayed because of the marriage of Baromama's youngest daughter,

Sheela, who was staying in our house while the arrangements were being completed.

My brothers, sisters and I had grown up under Baromama's care. He was the Accountant General of the state of Jaipur, and had inherited Dadamashai's estate and responsibilities along with it. My siblings and I had very strong bonds with our mother's family. Moreover, Sheela was almost like a daughter to me, since she had been born just the day before my daughter Kunta's birth. I had been instrumental in arranging the match and the ceremony took place in my house. Roghu, Sheela's brother, who had just finished his studies abroad, was also staying with me, and Baromama was about to come from Jaipur to perform the wedding ceremonies himself. I was therefore not free to go to Dandakaranya before the wedding was over. I would like to add that these ceremonies and social duties that we performed, though quite complicated and involved many people, did not seem onerous because we had grown up within the joint-family system. We did not really regard them as mere duties, to be finished off as a routine affair, or as casually as possible. To us, these were the expression of our true ties with our families, things we did because our family was something we cherished. If I came to hear of an eligible bachelor, I would at once inform a relative with a daughter of marriageable age. We did these things, took up these responsibilities not because of vague notions of family duty, but because we genuinely wanted the best for our family and had strong family relationships which were important to us.

After the wedding was over, I joined my husband in Dandakaranya. It was a vast area, located mostly in Orissa, a portion of it was in Madhya Pradesh, and some in Andhra Pradesh. There were three main centres, Malkangiri and Amarkote in Orissa and Paralkote in Madhya Pradesh. It was a densely forested terrain, and each centre was far away from the other. From the Headquarters at Koraput, the distance of any of the camps was not less than 90 miles through dense forests. Though the Godavari River also fell within this belt, no camps were situated on its banks. The camps were set up on the banks of the Shavári and the Tamasha Rivers. Because there were no rivers and streams in that stretch of Madhya Pradesh, a tank was excavated. The main camp here was near Jagdalpur, that is, almost at the end of the Chhatisgarh area. There was another unit near Raipur, which was in the middle of a thickly settled tribal belt. Amarkote in Orissa was also part of a tribal area. But Malkangiri was situated in a totally unpopulated area, an area so arid and difficult that it was unimaginable that people would actually settle there. It was near the famed Malyabangiri waterfalls, but the falls were completely dry now. The very fact that no human settlements came up here demonstrated the wretched condition of the refugees. Only those with no other alternative would even try to eke out a living for themselves in such terrible circumstances.

If we had to go from one centre to another, we would be driving through completely unpopulated areas. So, when we started out in the morning, I would carry an Icmic Cooker, complete with some rice, potatoes and eggs. We had to drive for about five to six hours to reach our destination, and the roads were of course terrible. Where would we find food in those places? So I would light the Icmic cooker, and soon, a simple meal of rice and boiled eggs and potatoes would be ready. This was sufficient for our needs. If we managed to get a chicken, we might have a simple chicken curry at night. Greens of any sort were just not available in those days, as tribals do not eat those vegetables. It was the Bengali refugees who gradually began to grow pumpkins, gourds, spinach and other kinds of vegetables and greens there. So, while out on work, we more or less lived on boiled rice. And how handy my Ickmic Cooker was! However, most of the forest bungalows were equipped with pressure cookers, water filtres, some utensils and other necessities. We often stayed at these bungalows, but even here, it was easier for me to cook the boiled rice meal in my own cooker rather than in the kitchen of the bungalow.

Food was the least of our concerns because neither my husband nor I were fussy eaters. My husband never complained about what he was eating, and was happy to have a simple meal. Nor did he demand changes in the menu. The same was true for me as well. And when we saw the miserable condition of the refugees, our food was like a feast. More to the point, neither of us had even the time to consider the unsatisfactory state of our diet. We were too busy attending to the work at hand. We got out early in the morning and once we reached the unit, my husband began to attend to the people. Their petitions had to be reviewed. He had been assigned two assistants, both South Indians who had held jobs in the Punjab rehabilitation offices, who were no longer required there and were then posted to Dandakaranya. They did not know Bengali and could not communicate with the refugees. Moreover the other office staff had a sort of derision, even a loathing for these people. So, the Dandakaranya Development Authority (DDA) staff were hardly the right people to interact with them.

The refugees were not a pretty sight. Their condition was appalling. Their daily struggle for survival was so awful that they did not even have the power to express themselves clearly. They could not tell us what they wanted in materials, because their existence was so insecure, almost animal-like. Living in tents, with no lights, just one lantern; constantly at the mercy of wolves, jackals, even cheetahs, no water, no amenities–how were they to live? All they had was a plough and a cow. How would the cow live? What would it eat? Where would it find water to drink? The central authorities felt that having transported the refugees, sent certain goods and implements, their job was done, now these people just had to cultivate the land and get on with it. Large sheets of tin had been dumped in the camps, but how were the settlers to make fences, walls, houses? For how long would army tents protect them against the creatures of the forests? How would they get the kerosene for their solitary lanterns? How would one lantern suffice for the needs of a family consisting of the husband-and-wife, minor children and aged parents? If one of the two tube-wells in the area went dry, how would so many people manage with only the other one? They had been herded into trucks and packed off to the forests. But after that, what would they do for food, drinking water, utensils? With the best will in the world, crops cannot be grown with bare hands, a spade is required. A man would have to travel 95 miles just to get one! The head of the spade would be available, the handle he would have to make. If they had to catch fish, first they needed to weave nets. The thread for weaving the nets would have to be brought from the headquarters. The nets were not ready in the monsoon, when fish were plentiful; by the time the nets were ready, the winter had set in and the waters had dried up, the fish had disappeared. So many difficulties in everyday life! I found people there had even lost their friendliness, and they were no longer good-natured.

If medicines were available, there were no cups or saucers in which to take them. If the camp was close to a stream, there was no pot to fill water in. It was very hot in the morning but very cold at night. No roof over their heads—how indeed were they to live? I had never before seen such lack of facilities or concern—it was as if, having provided the barest minimum, a dire skeletal structure, the Centrehad fulfilled its responsibility. We too had looked after refuges in Bengal, but we had treated them better. Of course, there can be no comparison with Punjab at all, but here, the plight of the people had fallen to an impossible nadir.

Adequate clothing was urgently required. There were no weavers so that cloth could be woven. Weavers were taken and settled there. Thread had to be brought from Bengal; it wasn't supplied from Raipur. The Khadi Commission had made a scheme for weaving. The cotton wool, that would be spun and made into yarn, was to be supplied from Gujarat. But it was observed that not everyone could do this work. After that centres for weaving were set up in Dhamtari in Madhya Pradesh, and the Harijan Sevak Sangh went to Dandakaranya with the mission of setting Gandhian principles into practice. But they found the situation to be quite terrible. The people could not be self-sufficient. Every refugee was treated as equal to the other; no one was to be superior than the other in any way. The land given to all was equal in size. All were to grow crops and make a living. Yet the basic necessities of a farmer's life were not supplied by the government. For that reason, though there was enough land, there was very little that could be cultivated.

My husband had to constantly maintain a dialogue with the government, explaining which scheme was practical and humane, which was not. The government could not understand that a woman could not manage with only three saris; that one blanket would not be enough for an entire family. If the family consisted of husband, wife, children and the husband's parents, were all of them to huddle under one blanket? They were supposed to be given a set of bedding com plete with a blanket and a mosquito net, pillows and mats—but the things given to them were of the worst possible quality. It is not cold in Bengal, but Dandakaranya was com paratively much colder—how would a family of even three manage with just a light blanket? This is what brought on quite a confrontation between my husband, the late Sukumar Sen, ICS, and the Ministry of Rehabilitation.

Because he was from East Bengal himself, my husband felt a special em pathy with the Bengali refugees of Dandakaranya. They had been forced to face a climate and a terrain they were com pletely unfamiliar with. From the land of rivers and abundant rainfall, they came to a dry, parched area. Used to eating rice and fish as a staple part of their diet, they now found they had largely to do without both. When we asked them what they ate, the refugees said they boiled some barley and mashed it up for their meals. As for fish, they got it once in a blue moon. From a life of sim plicity and security, they were suddenly uprooted and planted in alien soil, in adverse circumstances. One could not but feel sym pathy for them! I myself remembered the tension I had had to face when I went to East Bengal as a bride, and had to adjust to a way of life com pletely unknown to me. But then, I made my adjustment happily, out of choice, but there was no choice for these unfortunate people!

At this time, I was a member of the Central Social Welfare Board. The Social Welfare Department and the voluntary organizations had to fill the lacuna caused the shortcomings of the Central Government and I got much help from Mrs. John Mathai and Soundaram Ramchandra of Gandhi Gram in Tamil Nadu. When refugees faced official problems which the government was hesitant in solving, the Social Welfare Department came to our rescue. Dr. Sushila Nayar of the Indian Red Cross not only gave us powdered milk and provided us with nurses, but also helped us to train volunteers for our work. Many voluntary agencies came forward to aid us by providing a great deal of material help. People were eager to help with money and services. However, the government response was poor. So, it was left to the Social Welfare Board or the Ministry of Health or the Red Cross to build the bridges.

My work was both official and non-official. I would accompany my husband into the interior on his visits to the camps. Then, while he went about his official duties of listening to petitions, organizing his officials, and overseeing the official work, I went around interacting with the people, inspecting their camps myself, finding out what their pressing problems were. Sometimes, when I was not able to go with my husband, I had to find other means. The co-ordinator of the Social Welfare unit was Bhupendrakishore Rakshit Roy, a famous revolutionary of yester years. I would sometimes accompany him on his tours. His job as a social worker was to see whether the supplies were coming, to locate lost persons, and so on. Mr. Roy would read out the letters written by men, and I would read out the letters written by women. We came to know about all sorts of problems and discord and tried to sort them out. Occasionally, I accompanied Dr. Shankar Ghosh Dastidar, the local medico, on his rounds. While going with him to the patients' tents, I saw for myself not only the problems of the patients but also of the doctor. He attended to the patients as best as he could under those primitive conditions. He helped us tremendously in our work as well. He has left memoirs of his work in Dandakaranya from which we get an insight into this whole episode. These people played a heroic role in somehow keeping the camps going.

I would go around talking to the women, to see whether the sick were getting medical attention. Some women were pregnant. There were many aged persons who had arrived at Dandakaranya. This was the second phase of refugee resettlement. During the first phase, a strict weeding out had been done of the old and the infirm, mainly because there were no facilities in these camps to look after them. Also, only close nuclear family units had been allowed to stay together. In this second phase, this rule too had not been maintained. Thus, large extended families arrived in batches and scattered here and there, and there was the added problem of people trying to locate their distant family members. However, there was a positive side to this situation. There were more working hands within one unit, and they took their own measures to try and rehabilitate.

Just one example is sufficient to give an idea of how poor were the conditions in Dandakaranya. While out on a day's work, my driver and the others were desperately hungry and looking for some food. Ultimately, they found a place where some food was available, a sort of hotel. When the rice was served, it was simply covered with flies. I almost puked at the sight of it. My companions offered some to me but I said I was just not hungry. Indeed, at the sight of those flies, my hunger had vanished. But what surprised me even more was that my companions and others were actually spending their money to buy that food! The memory of that meal remains with me even now.

The government's policy in Dandakaranya was not only lacking materially, it also fell short of understanding the psychological and human needs of the refugees. As it is, their day-to-day life was so difficult. Was there no need to take care of their minds, their emotions? No plans had been made for education or entertainment. In fact, we used to find that the people loved celebrations. In the month of Falgun (mid-Feb to mid-March), there would be a series of such festivities. What were they celebrating? Nothing in particular, it was just an excuse to get together and make merry. Different families would organize feasts for all their friends and neighbours. Then, in the evenings, they would get out their *khols* and *kartals* and start singing *kirtans*. The whole village would assemble for this. These people were mainly Namashudras and Vaishnavs. The singers would wear the traditional sandalwood-paste markings on their foreheads. God knows where they got their musical instruments from. But this certainly gave them great relief and joy. Later, they began organizing Durga Puja in their camps. These were their means of recreation. But the government never understood their need for learning, for recreation or religion and took no steps to foster such development. That is why Dandakaranya remained such a lop-sided project.

Somehow we got through till September 1963. But my husband was finding it increasingly difficult to work under such circumstances.

He demanded that he should be given more concrete powers, otherwise he would leave. While the matter was being sorted out, the responsibility of Mana Camp was given to another unit. My husband strongly voiced his opinion that the Mana Camp should be developed as a proper township. The people coming here were not just evicted peasants. They would need proper houses, schools, training colleges, hostels for students, and such facilities. He proposed that such a plan should be drawn up and only then would he be willing to take charge of it. The resettlement work under Koraput, that is, the Malkangiri, Amarkote and Paralkote camps, was going on as before. The whole thing was a mess. Completely controlled by Delhi, the work had come into the hands of unsuitable people . Most of the officers were the riff-raff from the Punjab sector—those who were superfluous there and were kept on the rolls by being given jobs in the Dandakaranya Development Authority. They neither understood the language of the refugees, nor their needs, and worse, had not the slightest compassion or sympathy for them. The examples were the two secretaries from Tamil Nadu assigned to my husband. Delhi's failure to understand the needs of the Bengali refugee actually strangled the Dandakaranya scheme. Had there been greater decentralization or independence, had the Bengal government been put in charge and also given the necessary powers, I believe we would have done a much better job of it. The outcome was that since my husband did not get the powers he sought, nor was the planning to be done according to his advice, he resigned his post and returned to Calcutta.

After we came away from Dandakaranya, I used to miss it. It may be that my nostalgia was based on the fact that this was a unique period of my life in more ways than one. This was perhaps the only time in my married life that my husband and I really spent a few months alone together, sharing our thoughts, our time, even our work, in a way we had never had a chance of doing in our busy life. We were no less busy in Dandakaranya than we had been in Calcutta, but here, the demands regularly made on our time by a large and dependent family were not there. Isolated from our household, we were so happy to be working together!

Back in Calcutta, I would wonder how things were going on in Dandakarnya. I wanted very much to go there again. I found a way of doing so by organizing a Girl Guide Cam p in the refugee cam p. Dr. Parimal Das and I took a group of guides and held many educative and entertaining programmes for them, which were a huge success. At that time, I often sli pped away and took a round of the villages as well. This time, I was going on my own, not as the wife of the Chairman of the Dandakaranya project, and I moved with far greater ease and freedom.

Kalyani Bhattacharya, the elder sister of Bina Das, told me that she had seen the kind of work we were doing in Dandakaranya and she was interested in carrying it forward. Naturally, I too was very enthusiastic about it. We went together to the cam ps, and set up our first Mahila Mandal in Kondagaon. For the first time, a batch of girls did a condensed course and passed the Matric examination. The amazing thing was that there was no plan for generating any kind of em ployment for such girls. To Delhi, all rehabilitation meant was providing the families with land and plough. There were children growing up here, and a primary school and a centralized High School had also been set up. But after that? Where would they find work? Dandakaranya in my opinion was just like a concentration cam p at that time. Or like the tea gardens in olden times, where the children of the workers never went to school unless it was in the estate itself, and where they had no em ployment avenues except on the estate. But our Mahila Mandal created a way out of this maze. Gradually, organizations like Khadi the Commission, the Harijan Sevak Sangh and others set up centres where em ployment was provided to the refugees.

Through our Mahila Mandals, young girls were given vocational training, Girl-Guide training and the condensed course of study. Two other Mahila Mandals were set up in Amarkote and Paralkote. These were all managed by Kalyani Bhattacharya and her aide, Amiya Sen. Amiya has written many articles about her experiences of this time, the help she received and how her work progressed. My role was to find money and materials and send them to Dandakaranya. Not just Calcutta, many other places also sent a large volume of relief material. In fact, so much cloth went from Bhilai and Raipur that we did not know what to do with it all! Distribution, I discovered, was a tricky problem. When the government agencies did it, there was sure to be something wrong. Either there would be no uniformity, or there would be inefficiency. Some received too little, some received things of low quality, it was never evenly and justly done. Yet this same work was done by Bharat Sevasram and Ramakrishna Mission so efficiently! My own view was that the need of every member of a family had to be addressed—there should be at least one set of clothes for everyone. And women and children had to be shown extra concern. A man could go around in just a lungi but a sari was not enough for a woman, she needed a petticoat and a blouse as well.

At this time, we received a lot of aid from the Red Cross, and other international relief agencies to whom we appealed. Often the quality of these foreign materials was so good that the refugees themselves sold them for a high price, remaining quite content with the old stuff they managed to get and that extra bit of money. I also instructed the women's organizations to make parcels consisting of two large kanthas, some small sheets and six sets of clothes as 'baby-packets'. We distributed these to mothers with newborn children. So much foreign material came in at this time that we could do a very good job of distribution. I myself visited the distribution centres and made sure that every inmate of every camp got his or her share of clothes.

I still have the vouchers and receipts of that time. When I go through them, I marvel at how low the prices were at that time, and at how much we had done. And yet, it was not enough. The condition of the refugees was never satisfactory. They never had enough for their needs, they never had a satisfactory life. There were certain places where they were better-off than in others. Their condition was certainly better in Maharashtra. Many had also settled in the Terai and in Bihar. But the same could not be said of Dandakaranya. We kept up our links with them for quite some time. The people kept up a regular correspondence with us and so we kept in touch. This went on till about 1966. They would write personally to me, much more to my husband, for they still hoped that he would go back there and do something for them. But that was not possible. Many of these refugees entertained the hope that they would return to West Bengal some day. That did not happen. Nevertheless, the next generation of the original settlers seem to have built a better life for themselves. Many refugees who settled elsewhere got citizenship certificates and made something of their new lives. Some even became Members of Legislative Assemblies. But the refugees of Dandakaranya have not received their *parchas,* the documents for land given to them even today.

Thirty

The Central Social Welfare Board

The year 1960 was an eventful one. The refugees were still arriving and there was no proper rehabilitation work going on. At the same time, I was moved from the State Welfare Board to the Central one. Durgabai Deshmukh, who was Chairman of the Central Social Welfare Board decided she wanted some of us who had three or four years' experience at the state level to be on the Central Board. This was also the recommendation of the Study Team on Social Welfare which was led by Renuka Ray and had submitted its report in 1959-60. By sitting on the Central Board we would be in a better position to present the state's problems. So, I joined the Central Board, while Phulrenu Guha, who was my Vice Chairman at the State Welfare Board, took my place as its Chairman. Labanyaprabha Datta who used to be a member of the Central Board came and joined the State Board. So in 1960 and 1961, not only was I busy surveying the work of various State Boards, I was also working for the community development and social welfare boards.

I acquired valuable experience while working with the Central Welfare Board. I was assigned to the states Orissa, Tripura and Rajasthan—possibly because I had grown up in Rajasthan. I had to tour these states once a month to survey the work that was being done by the state boards. I was also put in charge of the Andamans, but never went there on tour. Mohanlal Sukhadia was the Chief Minister of Rajasthan at this time. He showed us around many parts of Rajasthan. The strange thing was that Rajasthan was a wealthy state, so the backwardness of the people remained concealed from the eyes of the casual observer. Only if one went into the interiors and actually visited the people's homes did one experience the backwardness. At this time, the community development boards and social welfare boards were jointly formulating coordinated programmes under what was then known as the Panchayeti Raj. These programmes were sort of blueprints for women's development programmes. The minister of Community Development was S. K. Dey, the famed builder of Faridabad, under whom the rehabilitation programme of Punjab had progressed so magnificently. Even now, I cannot help wishing that he had been assigned to Bengal during our crisis period with the Bengali refugees because he was a man of ideas and of action. He never prevaricated or vacillated. He worked hard himself and also made others work.

In my tours of inspection of the Social Welfare Boards I found that in Tripura relief and rehabilitation and women's development had progressed very well. Though it was done under the agency of the Government of India, there was the proper attitude of compassion and sympathy. Since there was enough land available as well, the projects progressed successfully (though we were unaware that later the indigenous people of the area would feel swamped and resent the hardworking refugees). In Orissa, I inspected the work being done by the Block Development Officers or BDOs through the Social Welfare Departments or Community Development Boards. I also surveyed the work being done for refugees. I found certain discrepancies in the work undertaken for different categories of people. For example, the work for local people progressed much better than that for the refugees, who were facing some measure of neglect. Then, there was some tension between the refugees and the tribals. There was a difference in the outlook, for the refugees were uprooted people of the plains whereas the tribals did not have skills that were available to the new settlers. The tribals had learnt many new means of cultivation and other things from them, yet a conflict came into existence.

Rajasthan, which I also visited in the course of my work, provided a different set of learning experiences. Mrs. Sukhadia, the chief minister's wife, took a lot of interest in welfare work and was specially concerned about the rehabilitation of the girls of the red light areas. In many places, she had begun centres called Roop Mahal, where these girls were taught various handicrafts and they could make an independent living, thus giving up their earlier occupation. Workshops were set up in unused mansions and the girls made bangles, all kinds of costume jewellery and the various kinds of handicraft that Rajasthan is famous for. Mrs. Sukhadia had herself shown me round many of these centres and I was most impressed. She had great concern and also, a vision, many ideas about rehabilitation which she put into practice successfully. The advantage she had in Rajasthan was that many Marwari families had migrated to other parts of the country in pursuit of their business interests, and their enormous mansions were all lying empty. Such beautiful mansions, marble floors, solid doors and windows. Quite a few of them were used to house schools or such organizations. Education and welfare measures really progressed in Rajasthan. We could take Pilani, a premier college of science and engineering set up by the industrialist family of the Birlas, as an example.

I loved visiting Rajasthan, because of my childhood memories and because I felt a special affection for the place. I do not speak the language as well as my mother did, but I felt very comfortable with the people there, as if they were my own people. At that time, we did not have many AIWC units in Rajasthan. Our usual method was to involve a group of women who would provide leadership to a much larger group which would actually provide the grassroots support. But conditions were not conducive for the AIWC's work on legal rights in Rajasthan at that time. The women lived in mohallas, and though they engaged in a variety of craft, the quality of their work varied, and they hardly got any money from it. Instead, through the Kasturba Trust we began to reach out to the village women, providing training so that they could make beautiful objects of a high quality. We taught them to choose good materials and finish them well. We also provided the knowhow for proper marketing, so that these articles would fetch a good price. Then women could make a proper living from them. This project was quite successful, for Rajasthani handicraft is much in demand all over the country and even abroad. They are justly famous for their textile weaving, printing, dyeing, embroidery, their costume jewellery, metal-work, their Rajasthani paintings and many other kinds of delicate and intricate craft.

I was thus very busy with my duties in the Central Social Welfare Board. Even though I did most of my work from my house, I did have to go to the office of the Board once in a while, to get my letters typed, for instance. I would also go to the Girl Guide office regularly. By this time our Girl Guide organization was working very well, training many guides all over the state, and developing many projects. That too needed my attention. Moreover, many people would come home, wanting to consult me on various matters. When I became a member of the Central Social Welfare Board, I had to tour the three states, Tri pura, Orissa and Rajasthan regularly. This meant I was away from home on an average of seven to eight days a month. This could have caused a problem on the home front, as Apala was just seven. However, that did not happen because of the extended family. By this time, we had built and shifted into the Gol Park house, which had a large household: my mother-in-law, Bidyutlata, my eldest ja, and all the children. My elder sister-in-law took charge of the day-to-day running of the household, and that left me quite free to pursue my other responsibilities.

The first time both my husband and I were away together for a long time, was when we went to Dandakaranya in 1962. This was surely a trying time for little Apala, as she had to not only do without us, but also Kunta, who took care of all her needs, was now married and away from home. But we managed somehow. Kunta used to come to visit at least once a week. We came home whenever we could. If I had a Welfare Board meeting in Delhi, I would go via Calcutta and spend a few days at home. My husband did the same. The children came to us during holidays. I found that one could run a household in this way, even while being constantly on the move. We all wrote a lot of letters to each other. Now, sometimes I go through the old bundle of letters and find them to be most amusing.

Phulrenu Guha served as the Chairman of the West Bengal Bengal Board till 1965, and was followed by Dr. Sarala Ghosh. Gradually, things were changing: appointments began to take on a political colour. Phulrenu Guha joined the Congress. Till 1967, West Bengal had a Congress government. But after that, the United Front government came in and the posts of Chairman and Secretary went to their party people. Even the general workers were political people, as if the department had come under the purview of a political party. This was a sensitive department, with three MLAs and two MPs attached to it, and it controlled such portfolios as health and education. Swami Lokeshwarananda and Mother Teresa were members. However, eventually, it did not remain apolitical.

When Renu Chakravartti was Minister of Social Welfare in 1969, she appointed a commission to survey the social welfare projects being carried out in the state. I was appointed by her as a member of that three-member commission. So, almost ten years after my tenure as Chairman of the Board, I went on a very extensive tour to each and every part of the state. Orphanages and homes such as the Liluah Home, women's projects, refugee rehabilitation, Girl Guide projects, we had to examine everything. Of all these departments, refugee rehabilitation was the most im portant. I would count our Guide training programme as one of our most successful projects. Many people have the urge and the time to serve, but not the training. Again, some others might have the monetary backing, but without proper training, nothing is of value. This task of training personnel was being performed beautifully by the Girl Guides' trainers of the Kasturba Gandhi National Memorial Trust.

Thirty-One

Reflections on Social Work

Over the years, a change has come about in the very nature and quality of social work. It is today a career option requiring special training and managerial skill, and such a career is often well paid. Social work is regarded as a stepping stone to politics or a way of occupying oneself. Politically minded people lobby to fill important positions. However, in our time, we were motivated by a simple philosophy of social need and compassion. We did this work because we believed it was our duty to serve the less fortunate, to find solutions to their problems. I was never motivated by any particular political ideal. I had no illusions about wanting to reform society. What was much more important to me was the distress faced by individuals, and the need to alleviate that distress. Raising slogans or leading processions meant nothing to me, but if I could help even a single woman, I felt great satisfaction. I devoted myself to discovering the root of individual problems and finding solutions for them. I strongly believed that if I could set an example through my individual effort, then ten others would feel inspired to come and help me.

Moreover, there was no need for incentives or rewards; there was no hunger for power or recognition. We were drawn to social work out of a need to find a sphere of activity outside the confines of the home, to 'do something for the country' and for people less fortunate than ourselves. We had just emerged victorious after a struggle for independence, but we knew that the economic and social needs were extremely serious. Many women like me had been exposed to these ills as the wives of government servants. Sarojnalini Dutta, the wife of Gurusaday Dutta, ICS, and Usha Haldar, the wife of S. K. Haldar, ICS, had carried out pioneering social work in the districts where their husbands had been posted and were like shining examples before us. Others like Sucheta Kripalani and Renuka Ray had been actively involved in the freedom struggle. How could we just let go of our ideals and commitment?

At that time, social work was not seen as a career. At the AIWC, we met our travel expenses ourselves. We got no 'perks'. I remember that while going to the Guide office I would often carry my 'bundle' on a stick and walk down to the office. It was no hardship! Moreover, our AIWC sessions were like enormous get-togethers. Whichever region hosted the session showcased its cuisine, crafts and culture for us. Thus, while getting acquainted with the specific problems faced by women in that area, we also got a chance to learn more about the place and the people. A strong bond developed among us: it might even be called a 'sisterhood'. We were colleagues and friends, always ready to help each other out. Thus our work was also our recreation, our sphere of learning, our window to the world. I feel what I derived from it, in terms of personal satisfaction, exposure, experience and friendships, cannot be measured in any way. It was like a treasure, something that gave meaning and richness to my life.

Today, a salaried social worker will wind up at six in the evening and offer to meet the distressed person the next day. It is a nine-to-five, paid job. We did this work because we believed it was our duty to serve the less fortunate, to find solutions to their problems. We would attend to a person in need, whatever the hour, whatever the place. If someone turned up at my house at ten at night, I would hear her out. I would contact the police at midnight, if need be. If a girl who had been assaulted or raped or was in any other trouble sought shelter, my own doors would be open to her. Many girls came to us for help, girls who had nowhere to go. We fed them and took care of them ourselves till we could find solutions to their problems. We were guided by a desire to understand the situation of the distressed persons and see things from their viewpoint, not ours. I find that this attitude is missing among the new generation of social workers.

We have seen that in this field action cannot be postponed. The situation usually needs immediate attention. A molested woman needs immediate shelter, needs to be comforted, helped to overcome her trauma. If a girl has been beaten up, she at least needs to spend the night in a safe place. She needs at least 24 hours of care. My sister Anjali Chatterjee, a member of the Kasturba Gandhi National

Memorial Trust and a teacher, told me about a woman who was sitting on the jetty on the bank of the Ganga. She was weeping. She did not get up for a long time. My sister managed to persuade her to come home with her, gave her something to eat, made her spend the night with her. That girl was contemplating suicide. At least that was one life saved. These are the kind of cases we have to deal with. Therefore, a clinical, professional approach is not always a progressive step.

So many people came to me, so many wrote to me, refugees, non-refugees, people who had been separated from their families, girls facing exploitation, women looking for jobs. I tried to do my best for them all. I found jobs for the girls. On principle, I gave jobs to girls, not boys or men. It was not that I could not find jobs for the boys, but I had a very simple philosophy. I believed that many will help boys, but very few would help the girls. Moreover, men are much more free, much more mobile than women in our society. So, the women are in a vulnerable position and I tried to help them. If a mother came asking for a job for her son, I would tell her I could help her, but not her son. I believed that if I helped the mother, the family would be saved. Whatever a woman earned would be used to bring up and educate her children. A sister would help her siblings, a daughter would help her parents. This does not always happen in the case of boys. They tend to become self-centred. Especially if they've grown up in boarding schools, the ties with the family are weakened, and they are not willing to take responsibility for them. We noticed this in the refugee camps as well. The boys went away and made a life for themselves, began earning, but a good percentage did not come back for their parents. There's a saying, 'a son is a son till he gets a wife, a daughter is a daughter all her life.' Girls are generally more tender-hearted and compassionate. I will not say that all men are inconsiderate and selfish, but it really depends on how close they are to their families. For all these reasons, I tried to help women with all my ability.

Of course, women are becoming increasingly independent these days, and looking forward to independent, unencumbered lives of their own. While I agree that this is necessary and desirable, I feel that they should think of those who were behind them, those who put them on the road to success. If the younger generation neglects the older one, I believe it will highlight an immense failure of the social and cultural training we have given them. There is a definite place for older people in society. They have the ability to work, they have strength and wisdom. It is up to the youngsters to recognize these strengths and abilities, and make a space for the elders that will make them feel happy and fulfilled.

If more women's organizations come up, they will be of immense help to women. Short-stay homes are an absolute necessity for abused women. If women could find a means of supplementing the family income through some sort of handicraft like knitting, weaving, spinning or embroidery, this extra income would be spent on their family. There are so many women whose husbands are drunkards and do not earn, their entire family depend on the women's meagre earnings. Therefore, the financial independence of women is of vital importance. I do not say this from the point of view of the feminist movement. I am talking here of female empowerment, of *stree-shakti*, something which has always been there in society, but which needs to be used properly to give women a better future and allow them to take care of their families themselves.

I speak of the importance of financial independence from bitter personal experience. It has always been a matter of deep personal regret to me that I never held a paid job, never earned money myself. The regret is firstly on the question of self-esteem: I never realized how much fulfilment women could find through their jobs, how much they gained in selfhood and confidence. Secondly, a woman can be truly free to follow her own wishes only if she is financially independent. People might wonder why I had such a feeling of dependence and inferiority, coming as I did from a good family and having been married into another fine family. Indeed, I often felt that I had nothing! I never considered my husband's income to be my sole preserve, nor could I demand that I wanted this or that, or that such and such was my share. Why could not I do so? Because it was my belief that my husband's income belonged to his family and not to me. Since I always felt that my husband's income was his own, to be spent at his own discretion for the extended family, I could not ask for anything. If there was money left after meeting the needs of the family, surely my needs would be fulfilled, but only if all prior obligations had been met. Similarly, my children could not lay any claim on my husband, for like others in the family they too were its ordinary members.

I have faced great financial hardshi p all my life. Even as a student, I chose the college which asked for lower fees. Later, after marriage, our income was limited and the extended family was very large. Though things were cheap in those days, our expenditure often exceeded our income. We had to bear enormous expenses during weddings and other social occasions. I remember many an occasion when, having organized the wedding ceremony and borne the cost of the festivities, I had no money to buy a personal gift for the girl or groom whose marriage I was organizing. Surely it was a glaring omission on my part, but I really did not have the means! I have already mentioned the medical expenses and the educational expenses of various members of the family. I did not begrudge these expenses, but the truth was that they left me with absolutely no money for myself. I do not think my husband realized my plight. There was a time when he would give some pocket money to his sisters, but he did not consider it necessary to give me any!

I do not remember ever buying a sari of my own choice for myself. One particular incident has remained firm in my memory. I once bought a jar of cold cream for myself out of the wedding budget of my husband's niece Aruna. Then I forgot about it and could not balance my accounts by six annas. When my husband asked me about it, I had no answer. When I did remember, later, I felt very embarrassed and ashamed that I had spent six annas outside whatever I had budgeted for. Perhaps this is just a small event, nothing extraordinary, the outcome of my own psychology. But that feeling of shame and helplessness remained with me for a long time.

Often, I felt that my children suffered because of our financial circumstances and that really upset me. They had to make do with two sets of school uniform, though three would have been ideal. Where other girls wore a blazer, my daughters wore cardigans, because they were cheaper. When Apala was going to Loreto House, she had to use public transport as I could not arrange for a car. But she was small, and I used to worry about her having to cross the Park Street crossing on her own. Where their studies were concerned, we were lucky as the children did not need tutors. Moreover, wherever they needed help, my husband and I took the trouble to study the subjects ourselves and tutor them.

I feel that had I been able to earn, I could have shared my husband's responsibilities. I could have done extra things for my children that were left undone, which in itself would have made me feel happier, more content. Yet, where was the time to look for a job? I was busy with household activities from morning to night—cooking, teaching, nursing, looking after, organizing. Moreover, I had three daughters who could not be left unattended. In such a situation, the very fact that I was able to step out of the home and offer my contribution to the world at large, was of course quite something. However in this day and age, it is imperative that women should become independent. Many years later, when my daughter Apala was about to go abroad to study, a Punjabi lady asked me how I found the courage to send my young girl out alone into the unknown world. I told her then that if we had the courage to loosen the ties and give our daughters some independence, they would prove themselves to be the equal of our boys. And I know this is true, not just for my daughters, but also for many, many young women these days.

Thirty-Two

A Visit to Germany

In 1969, I went to Germany with a delegation of six others, to see the work the German government was doing for youth. We were shown many clubs and organizations, where the girls were given many types of education and training so that they could stand on their own feet. We also visited a convent and met the nuns. We found that it housed girls from all over the world. There were many girls from Kerala in that convent. I noticed that these girls were in the basement doing the menial jobs like ironing, washing clothes, cooking, and so on, whereas, those who were upstairs did the jobs like teaching and administration. These were mainly the white girls. When I asked about this discrimination, I was told that these girls who worked in the basement needed to complete their education before they could be given work such as teaching, and that they were studying as well. They attended classes and did their lessons, and in the remaining time, they worked in the basement.

Germany had a structured educational system that sorted out children by aptitude. When I questioned them, I was told that this kept the drop-out rate really low. Within the first few years of school, a child displays signs of deep interest in studies or otherwise. Those who have no inclination for studies are taken into other fields where they are given specialized training. This is done right after Class Five. Those who continue their studies might go in for higher education or opt for white collar jobs. Another interesting thing was that teenagers up to the age of eighteen were not allowed to stay outside their houses after six. There were very strict rules regarding this, and those who broke the rule might even be locked up by the police. They spent their evenings doing their homework. I found this system of training their youth quite excellent, something which other nations would do well to pick up. Indeed, the situation in the United States was just the opposite. There the children would just not come home in the evenings and the pressing problem before the parents was of finding a way to induce them to stay at home. They would either be out on dates, or in the field, playing or fighting or passing time in some other way, but very reluctant to come home. Thus, American mothers would often say that TV was a blessing in disguise. It was only after TV became a fixture in American homes that the kids remained home in the evenings. They did not mind staying home and doing their homework as long as they could do it in front of the TV!

Once again, food posed the usual problems during our trip. The vegetarians in our own group found that if they asked for 'vegetables', they would be served the vegetables in a meat stew! But by now, we were getting used to these things.

Thirty-Three

Changes in the Family and My Work Expands

Kasturi completed her MA in English and then applied for the post of Lecturer in Indraprastha College in Delhi with the encouragement of Narayani who was already teaching there. Kasturi taught there for a few months and made a name for herself as a good teacher. Prior to that she had sat for the civil services examinations and qualified in the Indian Administration Services (IAS), the successor to the ICS. The results came out while she was teaching in a temporary vacancy in Indraprastha College. This was in 1969. She left for the National

Academy of Administration, Mussoorie, that year. My mother-in-law had passed away in 1967. With my mother-in-law's passing, a chapter in our lives came to an end. Now our family consisted of my husband and me, Apala, my elder sister-in-law, Bidyutlata and her son, Pranab, his wife, Hena, and their child, Rahul.

At this time the political climate of West Bengal became vitiated by the Naxalite movement that sought to change an inequitable society by violent revolution that was inspired by Maoism and looked to the Chinese Communists for guidance. Though we were not really politically involved, I did feel that there must be some genuine grievance behind the movement since so many brilliant young men and women had joined it.

Because the law and order situation deteriorated to a great extent in West Bengal, and the college localities in particular were in violent turmoil, we sent Apala to Delhi after she completed her school-leaving examinations. When Apala left to study in Delhi, there were no more children at home, all had left Calcutta. She joined Miranda House and studied economics for her BA degree. Apala's special interests were sports and mathematics. She shared Kasturi's aptitude for sports and was outstanding at rowing. Her drawings were beautiful. Apala spent the next few years studying in Delhi. She was a good student, like her siblings. She is independent and courageous. She obtained an MBA degree from the University of Illinois at Urbana-Champaign, and worked as a financial analyst for an American company. She is married to Jack Egan, and they have two children. For the last ten years she has taught economics and business part-time, at colleges in the San Jose area while bringing up her children. She is now retired and spends her time on volunteer work as well as on translating the writings of her grandmother, Jyotirmoyee Devi, into English.

Apala is the only one of our children to settle abroad, though later, many of my grandchildren were to do so. Kunta's daughters, Srirupa and Nilanjana, were educated at Smith College and live and work in the United States; Srirupa runs her own business while Nilanjana received a PhD in Psychology from Yale University and is a Professor of Psychology at the University of Massachusetts. Srirupa married Pablo, of Argentinian descent, and has a son, Robi, my first great grandson, who was born in 2004.

Somewhere in the middle of 1969, there was an important meeting of the Central Social Welfare Board. The Social Welfare Board had been set up by a parliamentary resolution and all its activities were subject to review by Parliament. We felt that if it were converted to a statutory body, similar to bodies like the Khadi Commission, then it would be much more stable, it would also have much more independent authority, such as budgeting, allotment of funds, and so on. At present, it was no more than a loose coordinating body. As senior members we wanted the Board to be reconstituted as a statutory body, whereas the government wanted to set it up as a registered society, or under the Company's Act. There was a massive argument and clash of opinion on this matter. Being set up as a registered body would put the board on the same level as hundreds of other such bodies, how would it coordinate the activities of other organizations? Similarly, we did not agree with the Company's Act proposal, since we were not a Company, and did not work like one. Some members took the government's side and supported the latter proposal. But many of us felt that this would simply make the Board ineffective. It would lose all its powers, its standing and the respect that it commanded now. Besides, its policies had been formulated back in 1955-56, when we first began coordinating with organizations like the Ramakrishna Mission, Mother Teresa's Missionaries of Charity and several large national agencies. If we became a company, we would simply be meeting once a year, in order to discuss profits and losses, something which had never been part of our agenda. I resigned from the Social Welfare Board when it became a registered company.

The new committee was constituted along the lines of the Company's Act, with a salaried Chairman, and it met once or twice a year. What a difference from our days! We all worked as honorary officials. The Central Board gave no allowance and no quarters to its members. In the Bengal Board we worked on a totally honorary basis, with the use of a government vehicle as our sole 'perk'. The new body had to follow the government's policies absolutely. But I have no regrets about resigning. I know I did the right thing. Even now I feel that registering the Social Welfare Board as a company has not been the right decision. The Board continues to work, its policies remain the same, but it has no powers. All the powers are in the hands of the government. It has to toe the line of the government in power. Therefore, its own policies must change–right or left or centre–according to the views of the government in power. We never faced this situation in my active days. We also worked with organizations like the YWCA, which was a Christian body, or the Ramakrishna Mission, which had their own ideals and principles. Our collaboration worked very well, because we all followed the ideal of service above all else.

In spite of my resignation, for many years, I was a member of the advisory committee of the Bengal Board. I was on the Central Board for ten years–three terms, and then in the state advisory body for three terms–twelve to fourteen years in all. This was possible because at that time, the political leaders, whatever their persuasion, did believe that inviting the older members to discuss and give their opinion on various issues would help to maintain the original trend, the traditions and principles which were indispensable. But by this time, I had realized how limited and constricted the sphere of work had become. There was no longer any pleasure in working for the Social Welfare Board in the state or the Centre.

My work with the AIWC continued as before, I remained a 'constitution' member. I was also nominated on the Board of Viswa-Bharati. Then suddenly, I was offered a position on the Board of Life Insurance Corporation. This came as a surprise to me. Lakshmi Menon had been a member, but she was a very well-known woman, a deputy minister, and an MP. I was indeed surprised to be offered this position. I thought as the sole female member of the Board, I might find an opportunity to serve the cause of women. Even more than today, the discrimination against women was clearly visible in the policies of the LIC. Girls under or over eighteen could not be insured. Mothers wishing to insure their daughters, married or unmarried, had to pay special sums as a cover against the hazards of childbirth. I found this shocking. Boys who dashed around on their scooters were not perceived as prone to accident-risk, whereas, girls were seen as being at risk for what was the most primary natural function, childbirth. I fought long and hard with the other members over this issue. At every monthly meeting, there would be heated discussions on the matter. I actually had to write papers to prove my point. I showed that men were more at risk than women, since they went out of the home to work. However, women faced the same problems of aging and illness as men, so where was the ground for discrimination in policies? Finally, I was able to convince my colleagues and the discriminatory rules were changed. I count this as a very significant victory. I was on the State Board of the LIC for three years, and on the National Board for another three years.

In 1971-72, I became involved with yet another organization. One day, I met Lakshmi Menon at the airport and she said, 'You're on the LIC Board, I hear. But you're no longer on the Social Welfare Board. I want you to devote some time to social welfare in the rural area.' I replied that I would be happy to do so. She said I must join the Kasturba Trust. As mentioned earlier, I had been familiar with the Kasturba Trust and had worked with it, for a long time. Back in 1946, during the riots, the volunteers of the Kasturba Trust had come to help us in our relief work at Noakhali. Later on, when I was in the Central Social Welfare Board, I had been able to extend a lot of help to them, by way of funds, helping them to build a hospital, providing land for buildings, and so on. The Kasturba Trust provided training for the gram sevikas whom we appointed for welfare work all over the country and who did a wonderful job of it. We only appointed girls trained by them, because not only were they trained to do their job efficiently, they were imbued with certain ideals and principles. They truly understood the Gandhian ideals of rural development. It was also because of this association that I was very close to the members of the Kasturba Trust, who were in fact, all associates of Gandhiji: Thakkar Bapa, Vinoba Bhave and Jayaprakash Narayan. Therefore, I accepted Lakshmi Menon's proposal and attended a Board meeting in Bombay.

The main meeting was held at the residence of Lady Thakersay, the smaller meetings at SNDT Women's University. What a galaxy of personalities! J. R. D. Tata, Gulzarilal Nanda, Jahangir Patel, Sushila Nayar, Maniben Patel and many other Gandhians and original Trustees, it was very inspiring to be on the same board with them. These trustees were the original life-members from Gandhiji's time, and were only replaced on death or if anyone left his or her post. There were five or six Trustees from Maharashtra and Gujarat and one at least from every state. Jamuna Ghosh, the sister of Prafulla Ghosh, the first chief minister of West Bengal, had been the trustee from Bengal. She was an excellent social worker, and had been in charge of the Trust's training programmes. She was retiring due to ill health and I took her place.

The meeting was instructive and entertaining. We discussed all our problems and viewpoints. Lunch was a wonderful experience. Wooden seats had been laid out in rows on the floor. Many items were served, from pickles and sweets to vegetables and curries to dal and rice. But the quantities were so small that I began to wonder whether my hunger would be assuaged. But there were so many items on the menu that I need not have worried. The strange thing about a Gujarati meal is that it begins with the sweet and ends with dal and rice. Just like the people of Noakhali, who would serve a complete meal of rice, dal, vegetables, fish, sweets, then again bring round the dal and rice and ask, 'Won't you have dal?'

I attended two meetings of the Kasturba Trust annually and had to tour their state centres. Apart from that, it did not involve any more work. But I had to go once a month to Bombay for the LIC meeting and to Shantiniketan for the meeting of the executive council, the Karma Samiti, of Viswa-Bharati. So I had to plan the dates carefully, as I was travelling regularly. But I had few responsibilities at home now.

Thirty-Four

Bangladesh: War of Liberation

Then came the Bangladesh War in 1971 that affected us like few other events. Those of us who had left our homes behind in former East Pakistan began to hope that at last we might go back to a place that we still thought of as our country. Of course, that did not happen, but I think the very fact that people from both sides could unite on grounds of language was seen as something very encouraging. With the war once again there was that familiar phenomenon—a stream of refugees. Our house overflowed with shelter-seekers. A fact-finding committee was set up in our house. This was the Bangladesh Anushandhan Committee, of which my husband was the Secretary, my brother-in-law, Major General Anil Kumar Gupta, was the Treasurer and Romesh Chandra Majumdar, the historian, was the Chairman. I used to do some of the work but the real burden was borne by my husband. At that time, Mahasweta Devi, Dilip Chakravarty, Sagarika Ghosh, all members of the Committee, would meet at our house and try and chalk out plans for the future. The Committee was in constant contact with the new refugees, offering shelter, trying to help in as many ways as possible. They had a questionnaire on a postcard that refugees filled up and that provided a data base.

We witnessed what seemed to be the final phase of refugee influx: lakhs and lakhs of people poured in. There was chaos in the areas around the airport, at Barasat, and other places in the vicinity. People faced great hardship. At this time, both governmental and voluntary organizations worked together to bring the situation under control. I have rarely seen such wonderful work. The work of the Anushandhan Committee was occasionally vexing and frustrating and full of tension, but we did it. What made us all truly happy was that in the east, the Partition was revoked and Bangladesh emerged as an independent nation.

When Bangladesh was born in 1971, many refugees had high

hopes that perhaps some of their erstwhile property could be recovered. A few took the relevant documents and records and files and went to Bangladesh. They found that all their property had been appropriated, forcibly occupied. Not only that, when the refugees from here took their original documents for identification, they found their houses had now been handed over to new owners. There had been no processing of evacuee property in East Pakistan. Sometimes family members who had stayed back had been forced to sign documents giving up their lands, houses and property. Sometimes signatures had been forged. About 70 percent of the land and houses had changed hands in this way whether in Dacca or Chittagong or in small villages. Even where misappropriation had not occurred, perhaps in 10 percent of the cases, the houses had been occupied, and if the second generation of the refugee family were to go looking for their erstwhile property, they would find no place to stay. Nobody would remember them or know them. Even the names of the villages had been changed. There were many such instances. Subodh Sengupta, the former professor of English at Presidency College, Calcutta, has written about the changing of names in his autobiography *Te He No Divasa Gata.* For instance, a village named Palang had been renamed Shariatpur. Trying to identify where the old village was had become very difficult. Rivers changed courses or became dry and a new village may have been formed that had a different name, and the old name would have been forgotten. Madhupur might have become Iqbalpur. Re-naming is something that people do all the time when they settle down somewhere new. In America, the British named one colony after another with names they were familiar with, and as other settlers came in they gave names from their old countries and now America contains names from all of Europe. This is common, for people want to cling to their own history. In Calcutta, we have a Dacca Colony and a Comilla colony, people from East Bengal have even used the names of their old villages. This is a sort of nostalgia.

Most of the people across the border believe that Bangladesh now belongs only to the majority community, that the Hindus have no rights over there. Even if they do have some rights, they are no better than second-class citizens, they are definitely not first-class citizens. Many Hindus of Bangladesh say that they remain because they love the land, but they feel uncertain of the future. In India, after the terrible Gujarat riots—perhaps Bengal is an exception— it is possible that minorities feel insecure too, and as someone who has fought against communalism all her life, I feel this is a shameful tragedy.

Thirty-Five

The Status of Women

After independence there was a considerable amount of legislation aiming to improve the lives of women and children. One of these was the Juvenile Justice Act, 1986. This aimed to protect children below 18, to provide accommodation in state-run homes and other help. Juveniles were taken out of the ordinary courts and special Juvenile courts were set up to handle their cases. Bengal adopted it in 1988 and there was an amendment in 2002. The new system was certainly an improvement on the old one where children had been lumped with adult offenders and also exposed to them. Another piece of social reform was the Medical Termination of Pregnancy Act, 1971, which was later amended in 2001. Before the original act was passed, it had generated a lot of debate. On the one hand, many people were worried that this would result in an increase in the number of abortions; that once women were given the legal right to do so, they would opt, perhaps casually, for abortion. On the other hand, there were women who were for some reason unable to bring up the child or found themselves pregnant and did not want the child. All the various aspects of the question were discussed, the question of health, medical and moral grounds, psychological grounds, even social factors, such as if the child's mother was a widow or an unmarried woman. Many other social workers, including Masuma Begum and Mrs. John Mathai, were present during an open discussion. Many ordinary women and girls were asked about their opinion on this matter. Men's views were solicited since pregnancy involves both the sexes. We found that most men were very much against the Act. But women actually wanted it. I believe that since women bear the children and carry the burden and the responsibility, they must be allowed to take the decision whether or not to proceed with the pregnancy. Finally, this Act was passed after three years of consultation in 1971. I believe it was very important for our country, given our social and economic realities. When the Act was passed there was no awareness of the possibility of its misuse, that it could be used to abort female foetuses. Women have little decision making powers and the demand for a male child means that the family often forces her to get an abortion. This is an example of the social injustice leading to the misuse of legislation that was framed to help women.

A major victory was the setting up during the International Year of Women, 1975, of the Women's Commission. Many people felt that there was need for a commission similar to the Scheduled Castes and Tribes Commission, by which women would get special recognition. The government initiated discussions, and all the major organizations and voluntary agencies, including the AIWC, were invited to share their opinions. I was interviewed too. I argued that women must receive adequate education and training so that they could earn. This would improve their status at home and would also make their opinions count in decision making. They must have freedom of movement outside the home and be given the right to work outside the home. After a round of discussion, a Status of Women's Commission Report was circulated. The Report recommended that there should be no discrimination against women, that men and women should have the same rights legally and socially, that women should have the same rights regarding education and work, and that there should be no discrimination on grounds of religion. In other words, we were talking about a common civil code. This was the five-pronged recommendation of the Status of Women's Commission Report, which actually led to the Medical Termination of Pregnancy Act.

The Women's Commission was set up, but it lacks the powers of the Scheduled Castes' and Tribes' Commission. The powers of the latter were much more wide-ranging. The Women's Commission has the power to carry out independent investigation and make suggestions, also to provide counselling. At the same time, the Commission cannot exercise its powers on its own, but it has gradually begun to increase its sphere of influence. Side by side, other commissions have also come up, such as the Human Rights Commission.

I believe the main question before women is of rights. Thus the Women's Commission is not quite on par with the Scheduled Castes and Scheduled Tribes Commission, for that is concerned with reservation. Where women are concerned, it is not sim ply a question of reservation because of backwardness or any other social factor, but because across all classes and castes and communities women are discriminated against because they are women. In the case of the SC and ST Commission, there is the need to rectify the imbalances caused to a community by hitherto socially enforced backwardness. But the matter becomes more com plex when we think of women of the Scheduled Castes and Scheduled Tribes who are doubly handicapped because of being so-called lower castes and because of being women. Men must accept that women are equal members of the human race. This is what would bring about meaningful change. I doubt whether men have acquired this awareness as yet.

The years 1977 to 1984-85 were stirring times. The Emergency of 1977 brought its own results, one of which was the setting up of the Civil Rights Commission. Then began the struggle of Jai prakash Narayan and Morarji Desai, and though they were jailed, ultimately Emergency was repealed and a new government was installed. The strange thing was that though this Janata government had come in on a wave of protest against the Emergency, it was not at all progressive. It did nothing at all for the women's movement, did not allow women to take the posts of ministers. I was on the constitution board of the AIWC and I know that we really had to fight for the smallest gains at this time. A major movement was for a common civil code for women since matters of marriage, divorce, custody of children and inheritance are covered by the diverse personal laws of the different communities and male domination has seen to it that women are discriminated against. Far from being protected by the personal laws, women have been oppressed and the way to gender justice lies in an equitable civil code that is applicable to all men and women. It is unfortunate that the Hindu Right has hijacked the cause of the uniform civil code but the women's movement can surely claim it back and work towards a code that persuades the minorities that this is not being forced on them by the majority but is based on justice and applicable to all women. I strongly urge that there should be one civil law for all the citizens of the country: Hindus, Muslims, Christians; men, women, children; people of various castes and tribes. Since personal laws are still extant, these have been a great drawback to certain communities. The Hindu women have won some measure of equal rights thanks to the Hindu Code. But Muslims and Parsis and even Christians are lagging behind in this regard.

I also believe that the policy of reservation is not beneficial. This too brings no real benefit to the community it is meant to be in support of. At least, after independence, perhaps some amount of reservation was necessary for backward communities, now I regard the system as completely without value. There should be a greater debate on reservation. Talent and ability exist everywhere in society and should in theory be separated from caste. This is not to deny that severe discrimination has pushed the backward castes down and must be fought against. To some extent reservation has created a creamy layer that then moves into the mainstream middle class, while the rest remain as they are. Those who have benefited do little for those at the bottom of the heap. The other thing is that the government can no longer provide the number of jobs required to keep reservation going. The demand to extend reservation to the private sector has not succeeded as yet, and it should be borne in mind that the private sector is a very small sector.

I have, however, been a fighter for reservation where women are concerned. Gradually I came to realize that men would not give up their rights to women voluntarily. And so women too needed reservation. On the occasion of the fiftieth anniversary of our independence, Renuka Ray said during an interview, that though women had been granted all civil rights by the Constitution of India, the same was not true socially. We had thought that such rights would come automatically to women, after all, why should men hold back from granting them the rights they themselves enjoyed? In the Parliament, there should be a 50 percent representation of women, but how do women get to the Parliament without getting tickets from the political parties to stand for elections? And show me one political party which has more than 10 percent of women on its rolls! This is true of all parties—leftist or rightist. Men are very loath to give up their rights. When women are given portfolios, these are ones like Health or Social Welfare, as if women are not capable of managing any other kind of portfolio. So I have come to the conclusion that the battle of rights between men and women will not be amicably settled, as men are most reluctant to see women as equal partners. We should have won the battle in the last century, but that did not happen. We have a long fight ahead of us.

Thirty-Six

The All India Women's Conference

After so many years of association with the All India Women's Conference, I still wonder at its achievement in reaching the remotest part of India, touching the hearts of women who were within the four walls of their homes, separated from each other by locale and custom. I think back to the letters of the writer Anindita Devi who wrote under the pseudonym 'Banganari' (a Bengali woman) on the rights of women from her sick bed in Puri to my mother, Jyotirmoyee Devi, a young widow living in purdah in the princely state of Jaipur. They sought a glimpse of the world through the AIWC, exchanging their views on how the organization should react to the proposed social legislation on reforming the Hindu customs of marriage and inheritance, the Sarda Act or the Age of Consent. They condemned or supported many of the moves and resolutions passed by the AIWC in the annual and half-yearly sessions in the 1920s. I believe that the two writers influenced me and made me more aware about the status of women. My generation gained tremendously from the women pioneers who thought about and fought for the rights of women.

I became a member of the AIWC in 1936 in Calcutta at the time of the Hindu Code Bill hearings where my mother gave evidence. Later, as I have recalled in the earlier chapters, I became an active member in Dacca, at Jessore, Krishnanagore, Bankura—the years of the Bengal Famine of 1943—and Chittagong, which led to my work at Noakhali under the inspiring guidance of Gandhiji, one of my life's most cherished experiences. I was a member of the Standing Committee of the AIWC Central Body from 1943 to today. One of the things I am proud of is that I was able to arrange the setting up of the Youth Wing of the AIWC as Member-in-charge in 1970-74.

In 1986, I was elected the President of the All India Women's Conference. I remember that my cousin, Deepali Sen Gupta, my Baromama's second daughter, was the Secretary in 1983, and she was very enthusiastic that I should stand for election to the post of President. I had indeed already stood for election in 1983. From 1970 to 1980, Lakshmi Raghuramaiah had held the post of the President, an anomaly that was not allowed by the AIWC's constitution, according to which a new member must be inducted every two years. This is what had made the AIWC a progressive organization. It had brought in fresh talent and new ideas. But these rules were suspended under Lakshmi Raghuramaiah. It was probably acquiesced in because she was working for the 'Master Plan', the acquisition of the land and the building of our head office in Delhi.

There are some who do not like to give up the position of power, but what was strange was that the members accepted it! However, in 1980, after the Master Plan was completed, Sarojini Varadappan contested and won the seat. After three years, when her term was over, she put her name forward for re-election. At that time, I challenged her, receiving the support of Deepali and others. I was a member of the Constitutional Committee of the AIWC. I lost the election by one solitary vote. I later told Deepali, who, as mentioned earlier, was then the Secretary of the AIWC, that had certain rules not been flouted, I would have won the election by fourteen votes. I stood again in the next elections and this time I won by a large margin and became President during the Hyderabad Session of the AIWC in 1986.

The AIWC had initially had a system of rotating the main posts, and not letting a President continue for more than one term, thus permitting space of equal importance for delegates from all parts of the country. Unfortunately under Lakshmi Raghuramaiah, there was an imbalance and at that time, and in the six years following her tenure, most of the officials were from South India. This meant that the workers from the north, from the east–Bengal, Assam, Orissa–from the west–Gujarat and Rajasthan–were not getting proper support or recognition at the national level. Yet it was northern India which had endured the travails of Partition and had worked for rehabilitation. By comparison, South India had faced relatively few problems during these years, and their work was limited to the eradication of age-old practices like the devdasi system, great social evils that had oppressed women down the ages but not cataclysmic like the Partition. When I became President, there was a chance of correcting this imbalance to some extent, though the Secretary, Padma Seth was a Tamilian who was married to a Punjabi. However, I had no difficulty working with my cosmopolitan team.

By this time, our new building had come up in Delhi. It was a very smart structure, with an excellent design.It was known as the Sarojini House, named after Sarojini Naidu. There was a girls' hostel which could accommodate about 250 girls in single rooms and dormitories. There was also a guest house. Office-bearers, old and present, were allowed to stay in the rooms upon some charge. Each wing of the building was named after a past president of the AIWC, such as the Kamladevi Wing, Lakshmi Menon Wing, and so on. The hostel was known as the AIWC Working Women's Hostel and is now named after Lakshmi Raghuramaiah.

We had a major problem on our hands regarding the hostel. There were many girls who occupied the rooms beyond their proper duration of stay, and refused to leave. We, of course, had certain criteria for admitting girls to the hostel: only women who were employed and earned a certain salary were eligible. We needed a certificate from their employer, and a guarantee that they would leave after three years. However, when I took over, I found that many of the women had continued to live for ten, even fifteen years. This was certainly not wise, because how would a new group of working women find a place to stay? I had to tackle the problem with a firm hand. I created some new posts, such as Hostel-in-charge, Member-in-charge, and so on, to bring some regularity to the administration. Finding solutions to the problems of working women was not a new thing for us. It went back to right after Partition, when we were working for refugee rehabilitation. In Delhi and its surrounding areas, many women had been given jobs and homes had to be found for them. Many refugee girls found shelter in old derelict buildings. That was when a working women's hostel was proposed by the Central Social Welfare Board and the Ministry of Rehabilitation. There was also the question of the safety of the women. However in the hostels started under the Social Welfare Board, we often could not fix rules for safety. Some girls claimed they worked with the airlines, or as nurses and had odd duty-hours. We could not be sure whether they were within a secure environment. That was why the AIWC hostel had very strict rules.

There was a unit, named 'Bapnu Ghar' which I think was unique, and had received the support of Meeraben Jhabwala, a former President. This was a place where women who had faced violence could find shelter. The inception of this unit was our long-standing belief that women who were on the receiving end of domestic violence were really the worst-off. They had nowhere to stay, and no shelter at all. They could stay at Bapnu Ghar, spend some time to recover from their trauma and also receive counselling. It was like a short-stay home, and the AIWC had played a pioneering role in setting up such a shelter. It has also been a revelation to find out what sort of cruelty takes place within the domestic sphere and how helpless women are. I also tackled the problem of the old while I was President. We started an Old Age Home in Vrindavan for the aged Vaishnav pilgrims who, at the end of their lives wanted to die at the 'feet of Radha Rani in Vrindavan Temple town', followed by the setting up of an infirmary. Both are running well.

The AIWC building was a hive of activity. There were working women, those who had sought shelter in the Bapnu Ghar, there were rooms for office-bearers like myself, there were various wings where the manifold activities of the organization were carried out. For example, the Accounts Section, the Welfare Section, each had its own space. By this time, the AIWC was indeed a massive organization. It had 5,00,000 members all over the country, and about 5,000 branches. At present, in Calcutta, we have six main branches and about fifty other constituent branches. Each branch is a complete administrative unit in itself. Each unit conducts its own mohalla meetings and has to follow the ten-point rules and regulations. The latter are to do with women's welfare, such as, women have to be regarded as human beings on an equal plane with men and given equal rights. The main focus is on women and child welfare, and particular emphasis is given to creating awareness for the need for change in social legislation and improvement in the status of women.. The task of coordinating the activities of the branch cells through the main cells is the primary and most important function of the AIWC. Three members from the main branches across the country must attend the general meetings in Delhi, which involve about 300 to 400 members in all.

The AIWC had been founded in 1926 and the first conference was held in Pune in 1927, and when I was president, we began preparing for the celebration of the Diamond Jubilee. We visited every branch to review its work. Our sessions at Pondicherry, Puri, Trivandrum and Gwalior were very successful. At that time, we were entrusted with the task of evaluating the role of the Central Social Board and its socioeconomic projects. Since we were a non-official, non-profit-making organization, we were asked by them to evaluate their economic programmes for women. We were also to advise them on whether stress should be laid on the economic, educational or political rights of women, for economic programmes to succeed. In those days, every President wanted to take up a unique project that would be her special contribution to the AIWC. My special project was to publish an evaluation of the work of the AIWC, a sort of historical perspective of its achievements. The AIWC had taken up a formidable amount of work in its sixty years of existence. Therefore in the Diamond jubilee year, we published the book *Women's Struggle*, which has now gone into its second edition. Dr. Aparna Basu and Dr. Bharati Roy worked on the historical research for the book. All angles were tackled–political, social, economic, even family matters. Many ordinary women and girls have recorded their views for the book. The project was indeed a fitting tribute to the women's movement, pioneered by the AIWC.

In my speech during the first Annual Meeting of my tenure, I said that women needed all kinds of rights, economic, social, political and legal as well. I also argued in favour of a common civil code, which was opposed by many, who argued that Muslims women already had the Shariat, which offered them some rights at birth, which had not been the case in other communities, and why should they place themselves before any other system of law? Neither were Hindu women eager to understand the benefits of a common code. In the end, Hindu women gained a measure of equality through the Hindu Code but this has eluded Muslim women (see Chapter 35). Hazrat Muhammad himself was a humane and farsighted human being. According to the Shariat, as mentioned earlier, women did have some rights, though not on par with men. It must be pointed out that these rights were denied to Hindu women. Muhammad had recognized the rights of wives and daughters to inherit one-third of the husband's or father's property. However, the system of purdah has been the undoing of the Muslim community. Even with property rights which did not exist in other communities, they could not progress. Where women have been confined behind the purdah, how would they come to know about their rights? Most of them only know that they can stay in the house of their husband. They also have rights to property, but if they are not handed the property, they do not know about their rights or how to set about asserting their rights. For this reason, to remove the restrictions that exist on women's rights, specially in the Muslim, Parsi and Christian communities, the AIWC has fought for a common civil code.

Another issue that we took up, as far back as 1937 when no one else was talking about it, was population control. We believed that controlling the population was essential considered from many angles: for the prosperity of society, small families were desirable; birth control was of great im portance for maintaining the health of mothers; and from the social point of view, unless women had the awareness of the benefits of family planning and the control over their own bodies for reproduction, they would remain under the control of men. They would be no more than breeding machines.

When the Constituent Assembly met for the first time, it had sixteen women members, mostly from the AIWC. At that time, they had said they did not want reservation for women along the same lines as reservation for Scheduled Castes and Scheduled Tribes on the grounds that women were gradually coming close to men thanks to education and work-experience. Since equal rights would surely be given to them, there was no need for reservation. However, as Renuka Ray—a member of the Constituent Assembly—has said our dreams have not been fulfilled. In spite of education and advances made in various fields, women have still not been given equal treatment in our country. In my time, Margaret Alva spearheaded a movement of many political and non-political parties that there should be at last 50 percent reservation for women in Parliament and political seats of power. We were never in favour of this policy: we had discarded it at the time of the Constituent Assembly itself, thinking that we would win our share on our own merit. But now things proved to be different. In our system of party-based democracy, candidates have to be given tickets by the parties, and we found that women were being discriminated against. We realized men would never give up their rights of their own volition. At that time, panchayet elections were round the corner, and we made a great issue of getting 33 percent reservation for women in panchayets and the local bodies. Even I felt that we were justified in doing so. Margaret Alva said to me, 'Let's get this through, then we can think of reservation for seats in the Parliament.' When the bill was passed in the Parliament, we were elated. Next, the battle began for reservation of seats in Parliament. But every time the bill is tabled, it is returned to the Select Committee without being passed. So we find that gender injustice still prevails. Women just do not have the strength to overcome their psychological and social barriers and take what is rightfully theirs. This is because men do not want to share their powers with women and react with hostility to women's assertion of their rights.

The end of the struggle is still not in sight. As I had said in my Presidential speech many years ago, women occupy an ambiguous position in society even today. We have been given rights but we are not able to enjoy them, because as yet, we have not been able to establish our right upon gender justice. The government and the legal system have given us rights, but our very own menfolk do not allow us to enjoy those rights. Society has changed many times over, girls are educated, they join the government, they take up careers such as flying planes, joining the armed forces and even fight wars—but always, as if by default, never by open choice. They take up career options the men do not choose or want. Just as in our society, girls' marriages are arranged, they do not marry of their own free will. This is just what my niece had told me, 'See, Mamima, we are married off, we don't marry by ourselves.' Girls cannot choose their own life-partners, they cannot move ahead on their own, they suffer from a sense of inferiority. They do not join politics, or enter Parliament, or take half the seats in the panchayet, all for the same reason. This is why we have come around to accepting reservation for women. We did not want it, but it has been thrust upon us like the seats reserved for women in buses.

Just one instance is enough to prove the true situation of women in this country—the existence of immoral traffic in women and children. There is a market for women. And this exploitation is common to all communities. And till such time as this exploitation continues, we will have to fight for gender equality.

Thirty-Seven

More about the Family

After his Dandakaranya experience, my husband said he was no longer interested in working for the government. He maintained he would be happy with his library, his research, the Federation Hall, the Archives, and being involved with Rabindra Bhavan, Calcutta, which carried out research on Rabindranath Tagore's work. He was also a member of the Karma Samiti of Viswa-Bharati. He wrote a good deal, for exam ple, on the incident at the Rabindra Sarovar Stadium, when women were harassed, about the Bangladesh War and the Emergency. When the government decided to remove English from the school syllabi in Bengal for junior classes, he partici pated in the protest movements against such an unwise policy. He was thus kept very busy, and I too was involved with my own work that required quite a bit of travelling.

Both my husband and I enjoyed working with Viswa-Bharati and I continued to be involved until 1975 when Surajit Sinha was the Vice-Chancellor. Moreover I continued my association even after I had formally retired from the Board. I loved the work because it was rural development. Such a wonderful module had been created by Rabindranath Tagore at Sriniketan that it was adopted as a model for the whole country by the Ford Foundation programme of 1957.

No one has evolved a better one, I believe. At Sriniketan Tagore combined raising awareness with the means of livelihood and economic stability. Thus social progress would go hand in hand with economic progress. In fact, uplift of the masses was a time-honoured ideal in our country. It had been strongly voiced by Vivekananda and of course Gandhiji was its ardent supporter. The Sarvodaya movement took up the same slogan. But the pathfinder was undoubtedly Rabindranath Tagore. He had even worked out the details for village and community development including crafts and banks. I too echo the belief of all these visionaries, and maintain that we will be destroyed if we ape the consumerist West. At the same time, I feel that the moral decay we see all around us in the cities has not yet affected the villages to such a great degree. The simple people of the villages are still untouched by the greed for possession and the self-centred attitude that promises to spoil our urban community. Villagers still care about their community and help each other out to a much greater degree than we city people do. The old motto of my husband's family: 'You cannot have fulfilment without sacrifice', is meaningful even today in the rural situation.

A situation fraught with tension now developed at home. My elder sister-in-law, Bidyutlata, was ill, so her sons and daughters-in-law were coming home quite frequently, also the grandsons, even the daughters. We were all very worried about her health. I was going out of Calcutta fairly often, but this was not a problem, as I was still in good health and could manage everything quite easily. One or two invitations to go abroad did come my way, but I was not quite enthusiastic. I could only have gone if someone offered to sponsor my visit. Our financial state was anything but affluent. In those days, pensions were so meagre that the amount of money my husband received was hardly adequate, and we had to support Apala's studies in Delhi. Then in 1975, she went abroad, on a one-year Rotary Foundation. After that, she chose to pursue further studies in the U.S.A. and we had to help her out financially because there were few scholarships and schemes for educational assistance then as compared to now. It was a very complicated procedure and we had a trying time.

In 1974 Kasturi married S. N. Menon, IAS, also known as Palti, whom she had met in the IAS Academy in Mussoorie. After the training period was over, he was posted in Manipur and used to come over to our house to meet Kasturi whenever he was in Calcutta. However, I did not know that they meant to marry till Lakshmi Menon, who was his distant relative, told me about it. The wedding took place in Calcutta, and a group of Palti's relatives came as the bridegroom's party to attend the marriage festivities. Thanks to Narayani's guidance, we were able to organize the rituals in the way Palti's family wanted and everything went off well. Some of their customs were totally different from ours. For example, we had to give rice filled in 'elephant-foot' containers and also keep some coconut flowers! This was an added experience for my cosmopolitan family!

The late 1960s and 1970s saw the birth of our grandchildren. My first granddaughter, Srirupa, was born in 1965, the elder daughter of Kunta and Kajal. Her sister, Nilanjana, was born in 1969. Both went to Smith College as undergraduates and live and work in the USA. When Srirupa was a child, she used to spend a lot of time in my house, and my mother was very fond of her. She has married a handsome young man of Argentine origin called Pablo. They were married in Calcutta according to Hindu traditions! Nilanjana teaches psychology at the University of Massachusetts. Partha and Narayani's son, Himadri, our eldest grandson, was born in 1973, and their daughter, Niharika, was born in 1978. After studying physics at IIT Kanpur, Himadri went on to do a PhD at Rutgers University and now works at the Max Planck Institute in Berlin. Niharika went to Oxford on a Rhodes scholarship and has returned to work as a freelance editor. Kasturi and Palti's son, Raghuvir, qualified as a lawyer from the National Law School of India University, Bangalore, with a first class and a gold medal and is working with a law firm in London. Apala and Jack have an eighteen-year-old son called John and a younger son, Conrad, who is thirteen. They came to India a year after their wedding and try and make regular visits to this country.

Our family is spread out in many directions now, and has become even more cosmopolitan, with the inclusion of an American son-in-law, Jack, and an Argentinian-American grandson-in-law, Pablo. Being true to the open-minded system of my family, I welcome this turn of events. It does not really matter that five of my grandchildren are abroad. What I wish for them is to be good human beings, not narrow-minded or self-centred in any way. And these are universal values, values I imbibed in my childhood, values that were present also in my in-laws' household. I feel my children have all successfully imbibed these principles and have been able to impart them to their children as well. All my children have a great love for Bangla literature and language. Partha helped me to edit some of my mother's works. Apala, the one who left Calcutta at the age of sixteen, has maintained her interest in Bangla and is translating some of my mother's stories. I find that nowadays, she performs many traditional rites and rituals as well! When she learnt of the death of Gopalbhai, the servant who used to look after her as a child, she made it a point to find out the whereabouts of his wife and children so that she could give them some money. She keeps up that gesture even now. It is strange how one's upbringing suddenly finds expression. As for patriotism, while it was the cardinal principle in our lives, and I continue to regard it as very important, I do not believe in the kind of patriotism that makes one narrow-minded. Let the members of the young generation love the country they live in, while also cherishing their Indian roots. I believe this must be the path for the present age, and I think my grandchildren will be able to follow it successfully.

Thirty-Eight

Reflections

From the 1990s, the nature of my work has changed. Now I work more as a committee member involved in policy making and consultation rather than as a very active field worker. My special interests now are the adult literacy programme, my school and old-age home, and the S.O.S. Children's Homes. Children's rights is an area that I take a special interest in. Networking with adoption agencies in India and abroad and finding homes for orphans or abandoned children are extremely important for me. There are those who question the credentials of foreign foster parents and believe that Indian children adopted by foreigners are discriminated against and treated badly. But I have found the opposite to be true. I have myself visited the homes of such foster-parents who have adopted Indian, black and white children and are bringing them all up together with perfect equality. I believe we must forego our narrow prejudices and see what is good for the individual. If these orphans get a far better quality of life, much greater opportunities abroad, why should we allow our prejudices to come in their way? Moreover, often a physically or mentally challenged child finds a willing home abroad as fewer Indians in comparison will readily take on such a child. Sometimes it is easier for foreign parents to provide the necessary medical care which is often free or subsidized in their societies. Unfortunately, officialdom does not always regard these things as simply, and so I often have a battle on my hands!

Another issue I am working on, and indeed, have been engaged with for many decades, is the need to delink a child's identity from that of his parents if the latter are criminals or offenders in any way. Many NGOs are doing commendable work with the children of women convicts who have spent time in jail with their mothers. Often such children are rescued, but they are still introduced as children of convicts, so that the stigma gets attached to them for a lifetime. Yet what wrong have these innocent children done? I believe passionately that they should not be penalized.

The kind of work I am engaged in can never be complete. Since there is a vast gulf in our society between those who serve and those who are served, since there is tremendous discrimination against women, since poverty and ignorance compound these evils into something far worse, there is always room for personal involvement. I have always believed that to help a single individual makes more sense than to mouth slogans and engage in politics. So my work continues. Unfortunately, our generation has failed to create another generation to take over our commitments. Six decades after independence, the situation in the country is far worse than before, the gap between the rich and the poor seems to have increased and social and economic divides and discrimination have increased rather than decreased. Moreover, where is the commitment, the love for the country that motivated us? Institutions like the AIWC itself are no longer in touch with the grass-roots and have become a shadow of their former selves. Nowadays, people are so self-centred, so intent in the pursuit of their own needs and pleasure that they do not spare a thought for others. Women who spend thousands of rupees on their clothes are unwilling to donate twenty rupees for a worthy cause. Many people remark that I have been a 'selfless' worker. I cannot agree with them. I did not work because I wanted anything! I have followed the dictates of my own 'self' and it is my 'self' which has directed me to the path of work–the path which brought me true satisfaction and freedom. Was I truly happy measuring the rice to be cooked for my family and cutting vegetables for the family's lunch? That work was not fulfilling for me–it was stifling. Yet, when I could help a single stranger, I felt I was somehow doing something important. Why is this feeling missing in today's generation?

Many wonder whether social service is the outcome of a person's individual feelings and psychology, whether it fulfils an individual's need for social interaction. While this is true, I believe that even social service is truly meaningful only when one works in a team, interacting with others. If one can build up a team and work together, not only does the work progress much better, the whole outcome is truly beneficial to society. The team, be it of husband-and-wife, or siblings, or an institution like the AIWC, is really a superior tool of society. I am truly grateful that I formed such a team with my husband, in my domestic life and outside. It was he who gave me exposure into rural life, and taught me the Gandhian ideals that later underwrote my life's work. The year 1962, which we spent in Dandakaranya remains the most wonderful period of my life as a time when the two of us were together in mind and spirit, thinking together, staying together, working together.

I have been extremely fortunate in friends, colleagues and co-workers, persons with whom I have been involved in total teamwork, which has been such an enriching experience. I was fortunate in getting a chance to work with such extraordinary men who dwarfed their contemporaries because of their great gifts and character, such as Dr. B. C. Roy and Dr. Prafulla Ghosh. I recall Ashok Mehta, C. D. Deshmukh and H.N. Kunzru as three outstanding personalities. The latter was also an excellent Scoutsmaster. Others like Gulzarilal Nanda and Mangaldas Pakwasa were eminent personalities I remember with great respect. After my first meeting with Vijaylakshmi Pandit and Kamladevi Chattopadhyay, I kept up a correpondence with them to the end of their lives. Then I had the good fortune to know Sucheta Kripalani, with her dedication, her self-sacrifice and her sincerity, and Renuka Ray whose organizing ability and leadership qualities were simply outstanding. What a great deal I learnt from Mrs. John Mathai whose vision and resourcefulness went into making the Punjab rehabilitation story a success. Durgabai Deshmukh, the wise and far-sighted legislator was the pioneer of the Status of Women Report. Lakshmi Menon, with whom I later became very close was a tireless worker, a great colleague. Past Presidents of the AIWC, Masuma Begum and Mitha Lam, my partners on the visit to Russia, remained friends and colleagues with whom I exchanged views and ideas.

Closer home, two of my closest associates were Romola Sinha and Sneharani Kanjilal, the former a so-called society lady with indefatigable energy and zeal and a selfless mission to rescue distressed girls; the latter, a simple, middle class housewife who answered Gandhiji's call to arms and never again left her chosen path of social work. My dear friend Sushila Singhi, who, in a life full of courage and determination, broke the barriers of orthodox tradition and showed the women of her community a new path—these are but a few of the many who gave a new definition to social service, who by their dedication, tried to make the dream of a new India come true. Many of them are no more today. But a younger band of equally enthusiastic and tireless workers is at my side, ready to lend me support and carry the team forward towards new horizons to the idea of a more equitable world.

The Partition took place over half a century ago. Why do we feel sad even now, at this age? After all, the country is not only an area, a geographical expression, it is an identity, it is land and light, air and water. Tagore said, 'O my country, I reverently lay my head upon thy lap.' D. L. Roy sang, 'This is the land of my birth, may I die here.' But such sentiments are not held widely anymore. Many of us are born in one country but live in another. How can the love of one's country be nurtured under the circumstances where people have perforce to leave and go off elsewhere? Obviously, they do not have the old-fashined patriotism. Battles are being fought over ethnic principles in places like Chechnya, where religious identity becomes of prime importance. Religious differences cause wars, religious affinity threatens to break national boundaries and create fresh communities. It becomes the driving force behind the partition and division of nations. We see this in the case of Egypt and Palestine as well. There is prejudice against the Jews. Nowadays, we face this divide between the communities, between Hindus and Muslims. We cling to our own faiths. We refuse to accept each other's cultures. I feel the only way out is inter-marriage, when some amount of understanding would be reached. Though of course, it would take a long time to achieve that.

What a unique life I have led! So many extraordinary incidents have lent colour to my life! On the one hand, a vast household, on the other, an unending sphere of work. My fate has spurred me into many avenues, to many different corners of my own country, indeed, of the whole world! Always moving ahead, I have often looked back, but not allowed the nostalgia for the past to slow me down. From one situation to the next, from one ideal to the next, from one place to the next, I kept moving, always learning, always experiencing the thrill of creativity. Such great ideals inspired us; icons like Rabindranath Tagore and Gandhiji were our actual gurus. Their vision of rebuilding India incorporating the age-old ideals of harmony and equality, their dream of a progressive village sector, their path of service to the nation and the community has vanished today! I feel, there has been such a change in the outlook of the modern generation; that qualities like generosity and nobility of character have disappeared. That we should all move forward together, that we should share the fruit of our success with all, are alien concepts now. Instead, cheating, lying and stealing and other types of immoral behaviour have become much more common. Thus, the future of the country appears very dark, as if everything is going outside our control and as if a negative energy is all set to destroy us!

A time comes when the present or the future do not appear clear or easily visible. It is then that the past emerges from the shadows, larger than life, bold and direct. The past is then History, a changeless Truth, and the present and future must be judged through this prism. To me, my past is a unique document of History and I gift it to those who wish to understand why the present has acquired this hazy, murky quality.

Index